Public
Communication
Campaigns

Second Edition

Public Communication Campaigns

Second Edition

edited by

Ronald E. Rice
Charles K. Atkin

SAGE PUBLICATIONS
The International Professional Publishers
Newbury Park   London   New Delhi

For information address:

SAGE Publications, Inc.
2111 West Hillcrest Drive
Newbury Park, California 91320

SAGE Publications Ltd.
28 Banner Street
London EC1Y 8QE
England

SAGE Publications India Pvt. Ltd.
M-32 Market
Greater Kailash I
New Delhi 110 048 India

Printed in the United States of America

Library of Congress Cataloging-in-Publication Data

Main entry under title:

Public communication campaigns / edited by Ronald E. Rice and Charles
   K. Atkin. — 2nd ed.
      p. cm.
   Bibliography: p.
   Includes index.
   ISBN 0-8039-3262-6. — ISBN 0-8039-3263-4 (pbk.)
      1. Mass media—Social aspects—United States   2. Government
publicity—United States.   3. Propaganda.   I. Rice, Ronald E.
II. Atkin, Charles K.
HN90.M3P8   1989
302.2'34—dc19   89-4274
                                                                   CIP

THIRD PRINTING, THIS EDITION, 1990

Contents

Preface

Trends in
Communication Campaign Research

Most of us have frequently viewed television public service announcements, heard radio spots, seen posters, read magazine ads, conversed with community volunteers, called hotlines, or received pamphlets about topics such as planning our families, conserving our energy, reducing our alcohol or cigarette consumption, saving our forests, and registering to vote. These are some of the elements of public communication campaigns, which are purposive attempts to inform, persuade, or motivate behavior changes in a relatively well-defined and large audience, generally for noncommercial benefits to the individuals and/or society at large, typically within a given time period, by means of organized communication activities involving mass media and often complemented by interpersonal support (adapted from Rogers & Storey, 1987).

After the early belief in the power of the media to persuade any audience (as a reaction to the extensive propaganda of World War I) faded, communication researchers were generally pessimistic about the probable success of such public communication campaigns. This pessimism was reflected in two journal articles, "Some Reasons Why Information Campaigns Fail" (Hyman & Sheatsley, 1947) and "The Obstinate Audience" (Bauer, 1964). The belief in the minimal effects of the media rested not only on evidence of several famous unsuccessful campaigns such as the Cincinnati campaign to win support for the United Nations (Star & Hughes, 1950), but also on the conceptions that media influenced individuals primarily via a "two-step flow" through opinion leaders (Lazarsfeld, Berelson, & Gaudet, 1948), and that audiences consisted of a homogeneous mass of "know-nothings" who selectively exposed themselves to, perceived, and retained media content that conformed to their previous knowledge and attitudes (Hyman & Sheatsley, 1947).

But the mood of communication researchers gradually changed, as indicated by the title of the journal article "Some Reasons Why Information Campaigns Can Succeed" (Mendelsohn, 1973) and successes of some campaigns in the 1960s and 1970s. Over the years, theoretical developments and evaluations of effective campaigns have shown that the chances of success are increased through research (by assessing needs, identifying relevant audiences, identifying program failures, and evaluating messages and effects continuously), systematic planning (especially developing message strategies and considering external social factors), and use of a complementary mix of the most appropriate mediated and interpersonal channels.

Changes in the Second Edition of
Public Communication Campaigns

With this altered mood and wider body of literature came the need to consolidate the developing understanding and expertise about campaigns. The 1981 edition of *Public Communication Campaigns* brought together the state of the art in public communication campaigns at that time. This second edition continues that tradition, bringing to bear the continual advances—and challenges—in campaign theorizing and research over the past decade.

This volume, however, is not just a spruced-up version of the first edition—it represents a major revision and establishes some new directions in campaign research. We surveyed readers, teachers, researchers, and campaign designers for suggestions for improvements. We dropped a number of chapters that, although worthwhile in their own right, were either too specific or not central to the needs of the readers.

The remaining original chapters have been significantly revised, bringing to bear a fuller body of research and experience. Paisley refines his historical overview of U.S. campaigns with a case study of cancer campaigns. McGuire includes recent developments in persuasion research and suggests how persuasion theories can aid campaign design. Dervin lays out the theoretical justifications for her sense-making approach, and summarizes recent results. Solomon reviews the latest contributions of the social marketing approach. Flora, Maccoby, and Farquhar describe theoretical and implementation aspects, as well as recent results, from the Stanford Heart Disease Prevention Project. Flay and Cook compare how three evaluation models match up with four fundamental problems in communication campaigns. McAlister, Ramirez, Galavotti, and Gallion review results from three antismoking campaigns that applied social learning theory.

We have also added completely new chapters. Perhaps the most exciting addition is a "Campaign Sampler" chapter that briefly sketches 11 notable campaigns or categories of campaigns and their implications, and provides some historical context for the more recent studies. The new chapters include Atkin and Freimuth's tutorial on formative evaluation, Alcalay and Taplin's discussion of community campaigns, with an appendix on media audience data, Rice and Foote's presentation of a systems-based evaluation planning methodology, Meadow's analysis of the conduct of political campaigns, Reardon's suggestions for the use of persuasion in adolescent AIDS prevention campaigns, Hornik's critique of alternative channel effectiveness hypotheses, and Singhal and Rogers's study of a remarkable prosocial television soap opera in India. Wallack's critique of the role of mass media closes the book by challenging some of the basic campaign assumptions about the role of mass media.

The introduction to each part of *Public Communication Campaigns*—Prologue, Theory and Design, Experiences from the Field, and Epilogue—provides abstracts of each of the chapters. Chapters of the book address these (and other) general questions:

(1) What communication strategies have been found to be successful in informing and influencing the public?

(2) What theories of communication process and effect help to account for the success of these strategies?

(3) What new theories or paradigms challenge these more traditional theories?

(4) Which of these strategies may be applicable in fields where they have not yet been employed?

(5) What is the appropriate mix between the use of various media and the use of interpersonal support?

(6) What are some promising designs for planning and testing strategies in field settings in order to evaluate their effectiveness?

(7) What social issues and policy debates are explicitly or implicitly involved in public communication campaigns?

Developments in campaign research, including the chapters in this volume, have led to the following generalizations (extending and adapted from Rogers & Storey, 1987):

(1) While campaigns are typically viewed as merely applied communication research, the most effective campaigns carefully review and apply relevant theories; further, campaign results can be used to extend and improve theories about media effects and social change.

(2) Mass media can be used to improve awareness and knowledge, to stimulate interpersonal communic: .ɔn, and to recruit others to join in, but commercial media may also heip to create or reinforce the initial problems.

(3) Formative evaluation of specific campaign objectives and media messages is crucial to developing effective campaigns; it is also necessary to identify and understand the needs and media habits of the relevant audiences.

(4) Campaign objectives must, in some way, appeal to the values and cost-benefits of individuals rather than abstract collective benefits, a distinction developed in analyzing the management of natural resources, such as a town's common sheep-grazing area (Hardin & Baden, 1977). Depending on your view of humankind, this lesson may be very useful, but it may also be the most philosophically disappointing point of much campaign research.

(5) Long-term prevention objectives seem more difficult to achieve than more immediate campaign benefits; so campaigns aimed at prevention need to link future benefits to present benefits or currently held values.

(6) Characteristics of the message source or medium—such as viability as a social role model, or credibility—influence a campaign's effectiveness; however, this influence may be in the opposite direction than intended or may conflict with other message components.

(7) The campaign message must reach a sufficiently large proportion of the desired audience, but the message must be a product of individuals' needs and must contribute to their own goals.

(8) Campaigns must make their messages available through a variety of communication channels that are accessible and appropriate for the target audience, but the message must also communicate specific information, understandings, and behaviors that are actually accessible, feasible, and culturally acceptable.

(9) Behavioral change is more likely generated and maintained through interpersonal support, especially through preexisting social networks, but for many campaigns this approach may not be cost-effective.

(10) Campaign objectives and criteria for success should be reasonable; not only is it difficult to pass through all the individual's information processing stages and to overcome constraints on resources, beliefs, and behavior, but many public communication campaigns have typically set higher standards for success than the most successful commercial campaigns.

The tension and possible contradictions among some of these guidelines are intentional; several of the chapters challenge deeply held assumptions about public communication campaign theory, design, and effects.

Intended Audiences

Public Communication Campaigns is intended for a wide-ranging audience, including theoreticians, policymakers, planners, implementors, practitioners, and evaluators who have an interest or stake in communication efforts to improve the lives of individuals and the fabric of our society.

(1) *Academic researchers:* The greatest interest will be from scholars in the mass communication, interpersonal communication, and public health fields. There will also be interest among researchers studying telecommunications, public relations, public opinion, and social psychology. A secondary audience will be found among those in advertising, marketing, education, political science, sociology, and behavioral medicine.

(2) *Applied professionals:* Researchers and planners in the following types of organizations will find certain material especially useful: government health agencies, media consulting firms, public opinion polling companies, and public relations firms.

(3) *Educators:* This volume will be a primary text for campaign courses taught at the upper-division undergraduate and graduate levels in several departments: communication, journalism/mass communication, and public health/behavioral medicine. In addition, it is likely to be a supplemental text in other departments in the general communication field (telecommunication, advertising, public relations, speech communication), the social sciences (psychology, sociology, public opinion, political science, social work), marketing, and education.

—*Ronald E. Rice*
New Brunswick, New Jersey

—*Charles K. Atkin*
East Lansing, Michigan

Acknowledgments

The forestry community initiated the first edition of *Public Communication Campaigns*. Although Smokey the Bear is widely known, tremendous natural and human costs continue to arise every year from preventable wildfires. Dr. William Folkman, from the Pacific Southwest Forest and Range Experiment Station in Berkeley, had realized the need to share interdisciplinary insights about campaigns to inform and influence the public, and contacted the Stanford Institute for Communication Research because of its experience in communication campaigns. Ronald Rice and William Paisley were fortunate to become involved with Dr. Folkman and with Dr. James Murphy. The Wildfire Section of the U.S. Forest Service and the Prevention Working Team of the National Wildfire Coordinating Group (comprising agencies of the U.S. Department of Agriculture, the U.S. Department of the Interior, and the National Association of State Foresters) sponsored a national conference on Communication Strategies for Wildfire Prevention, held at Asilomar, California, in October 1980. The first edition was just one of the results of that conference.

We thank Sage Publications, especially Sara McCune and Ann West, for taking the risk in publishing the first edition (which persisted through a fifth printing), and for encouraging the present revision.

We thank Jean Campbell at the University of Southern California for her help in keeping track of the year-long flurry of letters, telephone calls, manuscripts, diskettes, and express mail packages generated by multiple revisions of each of the contributions. We thank Carolyn Spicer, Cecilia Pastriana, and their assistants for providing bibliographic support, and we thank Rich Cook for producing the artwork. And we thank all the authors for their contributions and for their tolerance of our editorial intrusiveness.

Part I

Prologue

William Paisley provides a historical as well as a political context for communication campaigns in the United States. Communication campaigns are only one means of influencing public knowledge, attitudes, and behavior. However, the limited authority of American governments, both colonial and national, created an early reliance on communication campaigns as instruments of social change. Over three centuries of American communication campaigns, there are more similarities than differences in the objectives and methods of campaigners and in public response to different types of campaigns. Paisley surveys the development of American public communication campaigns in terms of four categories of stakeholders (associations, government agencies, mass media, and social scientists); the social contract; the agenda; American belief in reform through collective action; the successive eras of the associations, mass media, government, and social science; definition of campaigns via objectives or methods; the "three Es" of education, engineering, and enforcement; individual and collective benefits of campaigns; the concepts of first-party and second-party entitlement; systematic planning; and process-based evaluation. He illustrates many of these topics through a case study of the interactions among the four stakeholders in the development of the National Cancer Institute and its Office of Cancer Communications.

1

Public Communication Campaigns: The American Experience

WILLIAM PAISLEY

The social science chronology of public communication campaigns begins with key studies in the 1940s that are cited repeatedly in this volume. Important as these studies are, we should recognize that social scientists are only the latest group of stakeholders to be involved in public communication campaigns. Prior to World War II, the principal stakeholders were *voluntary associations*, the *mass media*, and the *federal government*. These stakeholders are as active and as interdependent as ever. Voluntary associations possess the "entitlement" to advocate certain issues, the mass media provide access to the public, and the government funds campaigns on behalf of its information and outreach programs.

Social scientists' main contribution to campaigns is their theory-grounded approach to planning, conducting, and evaluating campaigns. This approach sometimes clashes with the beliefs of other stakeholders, but social scientists are also the catalysts of a new era of cooperation in campaigns, because their research confirms the roles played by other stakeholders.

This chapter is largely devoted to campaigners who came before these social scientists. Over three centuries of American communication campaigns, there are more similarities than differences in the objectives and methods of campaigners and in public response to different types of campaigns. The chapter begins with an identification of some key ways to characterize communication campaigns, along with the implications of these distinctions. The subsequent section summarizes major reform movements and stakeholders of pre-World

War II campaigns. The final section presents a modern case study involving all four stakeholders.

Public Communication Campaigns: Defining Characteristics and Implications

Two Defining Characteristics of Campaigns

Two quite different but complementary definitions of public communication campaigns are found in the literature. Definition in terms of *objectives* focuses on one group's intention to influence other groups' beliefs or behavior, using communicated appeals. This definition comes to the fore when the intentions are controversial, such as campaigns about abortion or AIDS.

Public communication campaigns can also be defined in terms of the *methods* they employ, such as "promotional messages in the public interest disseminated through mass media channels to target audiences" (Atkin, 1981b, p. 265). This definition comes to the fore when campaigns employ innovative or controversial methods, such as "guerrilla theater" in the Vietnam era or the confrontational tactics of antiabortion groups today. It is also the common focus of discussions to improve campaigns, if only because most campaigns have mandated objectives that are less amenable to change.

Reform is a unifying principle of public communication campaigns, whether the structure of society itself is affected (e.g., change in the status of minority groups) or only the life-styles of individuals (e.g., behavior changes to reduce the risk of disease; also see Wallack, chap. 16, this volume). This principle invokes reform in its generic sense. Reform is any action that makes society better or makes the lives of individuals better. *Better* is defined by emerging values in a society during each period in its history, such as today's attempts to reform our unhealthy life-styles, undemocratic practices, abuse of the environment, and ineffective public systems such as education and health care.

Thus the definition of public communication campaigns can be approached via *objectives*—are they *strategies of social control* insofar as one group intends to affect the beliefs or behavior of another group?—or via *methods*—are they a *genre of communication* that might be called noncommercial advertising?

Implications of
the Social Control Definition

If campaigns are defined as strategies of social control, then their relationship to other social control strategies is thought-provoking. One government agency, the U.S. Forest Service, has developed a paradigm of the "three Es" to protect the forests from public misuse: *education, engineering, and enforcement.* Public communication campaigns concerned with wildfires, vandalism, pollution, and so on constitute the education part of this triad. Foresters also try to make the forest "people proof" without limiting access: They engineer campsites that are fire-safe and install fixtures, such as steel trail signs, that are hard to vandalize. If the public persists in damaging the forests, then enforcement takes over: The foresters can limit access, require fire permits, prosecute vandals, and so on.

Each society in each era of its development has an ideology of change that guides its use of education, engineering, and enforcement to promote change at the societal or individual level. In the United States, if engineering promises a quick solution, as it often did from 1850 to 1950, then the education and enforcement strategies will not be employed until engineering has had its chance. The first hope in solving a health problem is that a "miracle drug" or its equivalent in other sectors will be developed. Education is often the second strategy to be employed, unless delays in public response are too dangerous or costly. Only if an issue is well bounded by laws, which in itself implies that the engineering and education strategies are ineffective, is the enforcement strategy fully employed.

Enforcement ranks higher in authoritarian societies where public opponents cannot take the government to court, a step that frequently follows the American government's efforts to enforce controversial laws. Education ranks higher in societies where citizens are still "united by firm and lasting ties," to paraphrase de Tocqueville. The more that values and perceptions of self-interest are shared in a population, the more effective an education campaign can be.

The social control definition of public communication campaigns helps us to see, from the policymaker's perspective, how investment in communication is part of an overall plan that may involve the engineering and enforcement strategies as well. Campaign planning should always take account of the contributions and limitations of the other two strategies.

However, the social control perspective has two limitations. First, many campaigns are not plausibly defined as social control. For example, a campaign to reduce the risk of heart disease is more related to *individual benefits* than to the *collective benefits* that abortion opponents or adherents would claim for their position. Second, engineering and enforcement are not strong alternatives to education in many cases. Looking at Table 1.1, a sort of "magazine barometer" of attention to issues on the public agenda, we see a mixture of issues for which all three strategies seem to be viable (e.g., drug abuse, acid rain, energy conservation), but also issues for which enforcement strategies are judged inappropriate, while engineering strategies are not yet effective (e.g., AIDS, nutrition).

The early 1960s were marked by an eager faith in engineering solutions. Buoyed by successes in medicine (e.g., polio vaccine), which were linked metaphorically to social "ills," John Kennedy's and Lyndon Johnson's social engineers drafted programs to combat poverty, illiteracy, inequality, and so on. Some of the programs benefited some people, but it was obvious by 1970 that social engineering was more alchemy than science.

The favored solution of the 1970s was enforcement. Harmful or wasteful conditions were targeted for regulation. Richard Nixon signed a bill banning cigarette advertising on television and radio. With the blessing of the Supreme Court, the Federal Trade Commission expanded its antitrust powers to ban deceptive advertising. The Occupational Safety and Health Administration, the Equal Employment Opportunity Commission, and even the laid-back Federal Communications Commission took their turns as "enforcers" in the 1970s.

Dissatisfaction with both the engineering and enforcement strategies became evident in the 1980s. The engineering strategy fails because of a faulty analysis of the problem, its constraints, incentives for change, and so on. The enforcement strategy fails because it emphasizes the negative aspects of noncompliance rather than the positive aspects of adaptive behaviors.

Implications of the Process Definition

When education is the only strategy that can be pursued or is worth pursuing, attention shifts to the process of communicating. Modern campaigns draw upon the techniques of journalists, media producers, educators, small group specialists, and others. Campaign planners synthesize these techniques into a variety of different approaches designed for different target audiences, because each target audience lives in its own communication environment, which filters the messages that reach it, and responds in its own way to appeals based on altruism, self-interest, fear, and so on (see Dervin, chap. 3, this volume).

The process-based discipline of planning campaigns in terms of objectives, messages, contexts, and audiences leads to conceptual frameworks for understanding what a campaign should accomplish, clarifying the roles of the campaign's stakeholders, adapting approaches to audience differences, sequencing and coordinating campaign activities, monitoring the campaign's possible failure points, improving the campaign on the basis of field trials, and transferring the successes of one campaign in one setting to other campaigns in other settings.

The Essential Concepts of "Agenda" and "Entitlement"

In the busy "marketplace of issues" in which campaigns vie for "consumers," careful attention to process has become the key to a successful campaign, but it does not ensure success in itself. The success of a campaign also depends upon public perception that the campaign's issue is an important one, as reflected by its position on the public *agenda* of issues (see Table 1.1), and that the group supporting or opposing the issue has an *entitlement* to advocate that view.

The concepts of agenda and entitlement originate in a society's *social contract*. Early acceptance of the American social contract probably owed less to the arguments of Hobbes, Locke, Rousseau, or even Jefferson than to the imperatives of life at the frontier. The first "negotiated settlements" in America were just that: places where people agreed to live together. They adapted their compact of rights and obligations to the immediate circumstances and their reasons for being there. Agreement and disagreement had a novel geographical dimension. If dissenters could move on to the next valley, then those who stayed were agreeing to build a community.

Laws set minimum standards for the social contract, but public behavior usually conforms to higher standards that must be explained in terms of what people believe is the "right thing" to do, not just what is required of them by the laws. In American society, which has been pluralistic from the first years, when settlers from many European

TABLE 1.1 Rise and Fall of Issues on the National Agenda, as Reflected by Coverage in All Types of Magazines: 1960-69, 1970-79, 1980-84, and 1985-88[a]

Issues	1960-69	1970-79	1980-84	1985-88
Issues That Rose				
AIDS	0.0	0.0	2.9	33.1
Apartheid	2.9	2.6	2.2	20.3
Nutrition	7.3	15.5	18.4	19.6
Abortion	4.3	9.5	11.4	9.5
Drug abuse	1.1	5.0	5.6	9.5
Heart disease	2.3	3.7	5.5	7.9
Whales	3.0	6.4	7.0	7.1
Illiteracy	3.0	2.6	4.9	7.0
Pornography	1.4	3.1	3.5	6.1
Acid rain	0.0	0.8	4.9	5.6
Child care	0.3	1.3	1.6	5.4
Prolife activities	0.0	0.4	1.3	4.3
Affirmative action	0.0	4.5	3.2	4.2
Women's rights	0.0	2.4	4.0	4.2
Child abuse	0.7	3.5	3.2	4.0
Famine	1.4	1.9	1.3	3.5
Drunk driving	0.5	0.6	2.4	2.6
Prochoice activities	0.0	0.1	0.2	2.4
Teenage pregnancy	0.0	0.9	0.8	2.0
Greenpeace	0.0	0.2	0.3	1.4
Issues That Fell				
Vietnam	164.8	28.8	16.5	21.0
Communism	84.2	17.4	16.8	19.5
Desegregation	31.9	5.0	3.9	4.0
Polio	2.9	0.3	0.4	0.8
Issues That Peaked and Fell				
Civil rights	21.9	20.5	30.2	19.8
Nuclear power	16.5	25.9	21.3	15.0
Disarmament	17.7	14.9	27.6	12.4
Energy conservation	0.7	18.5	16.2	5.1
Solar power	0.6	15.0	9.7	2.7
Waste recycling	0.0	3.8	2.2	1.4
Busing	0.4	4.0	1.3	0.4
Nuclear freeze	0.0	0.0	2.0	0.4

(*continued*)

TABLE 1.1 Continued

Issues	1960-69	1970-79	1980-84	1985-88
Issues That Stayed About the Same				
Pollution	20.6	26.9	23.0	23.0
Smoking	7.0	5.0	5.6	9.5
School prayer	1.8	0.5	1.7	0.6
Voting rights	0.9	0.5	1.4	0.5
"Control Issues"				
Death	29.8	40.8	55.0	62.3
Taxes	9.6	9.5	10.1	10.3
Cancer Issues (see case study)				
Cancer, all references	18.0	22.9	25.0	28.6
Cancer treatment	0.4	3.0	4.2	5.2
Cancer prevention	0.6	1.3	2.3	4.0
Breast cancer	0.5	2.9	2.3	3.9
Diet and cancer	0.1	0.6	1.6	1.6
Colorectal cancer	0.1	0.2	0.5	1.3
Skin cancer	0.4	0.3	0.7	1.3

SOURCE: *Magazine Index* online (May 1988).
a. Number of articles on each topic per 10,000 articles on all topics.

countries encountered the Indians and each other, it is often hard to know what is the right thing to do.

The possibilities of believing or acting in different ways are not forced upon the American public by agitators or reformers; these possibilities are manifest in the beliefs and behaviors of neighbors. The marketplace of issues is overstocked. More possibilities must be rejected than can be accepted. Hence the importance of the twin tests: agenda and entitlement.

The public agenda, when measured by pollsters, always contains some universal "gut issues" such as disease and "pocketbook issues" such as inflation. However, few issues are truly universal, and many issues that are now high on the public agenda were once special-interest issues that have risen in importance because the problem has grown worse (e.g., drug abuse), because changes in life-styles or demography have made the problem relevant to more people (e.g., heart disease), or because public "consciousness" has caught up with the problem (e.g., apartheid).

The American agenda is also divided between issues representing public *obligations* and other issues representing public *opportunities*. Therefore, some campaigns call for action motivated by altruism, while other campaigns call for action motivated by self-interest. These two motives seem quite different, but altruism is said to arise in what de Tocqueville (1835/1961) called "the principle of [self-]interest rightly understood," which "produces no great acts of self-sacrifice, but suggests daily small acts of self-denial" (p. 147). A single campaign may appeal to altruism in one group and self-interest in another. Measures to redistribute benefits, from national health insurance to school desegregation, rely on the combined strength of these motives.

We come to the question of *entitlement* to be the advocate of an issue. Is entitlement mainly a question of law, public policy, or public acceptance? Because of the courts' broad interpretation of First Amendment rights, constitutional entitlement is a given in the United States. As recently as 1915, however, Margaret Sanger was indicted for sending birth-control tracts through the mail, and abolitionist literature was routinely confiscated by southern postmasters prior to the Civil War. Authorities and citizens still harass unpopular campaigns, but the courts reliably affirm the First Amendment right of the campaign to proceed.

Public policy affects entitlement when there is a jurisdictional or "ownership" dispute over issues. A new stakeholder may seem to encroach on the entitlement of older stakeholders. For example, a recently formed agency may have a more activist charter or more funds for public outreach than an established agency. Cooperation, when it is achieved, usually involves "dividing the territory" to use each agency's entitlement effectively (see the case study presented later in this chapter).

Public acceptance is the final test of entitlement. The public is ready with the American comeback, "None of your business," unless the communicator is clearly a stakeholder in the issue. Aggrieved groups have *first-party* entitlement to communicate in their own interest. *Second-party* involvement is more suspect; the public wonders why a group is involved if it is not directly affected by an issue.

Some issues have no first-party group to claim entitlement. Whales, seal pups, and future generations of children have been among the first parties of campaigns, but they are not their own advocates. In such cases, second-party groups identify themselves symbolically with first-party groups in order to serve as their advocates. For such campaigns to be successful, the public must be willing to transfer some entitlement to second-party groups.

Second-party groups can increase their involvement and hence their entitlement by "putting themselves on the line" as surrogate first parties. For example, the dramatic interventions of the "save the whales" and "save the seals" groups in the late 1970s increased their entitlement because the public could see them risking personal harm on the ocean and on the ice floes. A similar transfer of entitlement is available to second-party groups, at the same cost, even when first-party groups are their own advocates. Such groups as white civil rights workers in the South during the 1960s, Vietnam draft protesters who were beyond draft age, and men who advocate feminist causes earned their entitlement "on the line."

Entitlement based on *expertise* is subject to public acceptance as well. Expert entitlement is a limited license that can be used up if the expert publicizes too many issues or issues outside the area of expertise. In the late 1980s, Surgeon General C. Everett Koop has been perhaps the most effective expert communicator in America. He has shown great skill in spending his entitlement on only the major issues of smoking and AIDS prevention, resisting the temptation to use his "bully pulpit" on behalf of all the other health issues.

Two Centuries of American Public Communication Campaigns

Communication and Reform in the United States

The history of the United States is interwoven with communication campaigns from the colonial era to the present day. Communication campaigns are only one means of influencing public knowledge, attitudes, and behavior. However, the limited authority of American governments, both colonial and national, created an early reliance on communication campaigns as instruments of social change.

The French writer Alexis de Tocqueville was one of the first to describe how communication informs and mobilizes public action in America. In his notes on traveling throughout the United States (translated as *Democracy in America*, 1835/1961), he described "the skill with which the inhabitants of the United States succeed in proposing a common object to the exertions of a great many men, and in getting them voluntarily to pursue it" (p. 129).

Reform was accomplished differently in America than in England or France, according to de Tocqueville: "Wherever, at the head of some new undertaking, you see the Government in France or a man of rank in England, in the United States you will be sure to find an association. . . . If it be proposed to advance some truth or foster some feeling by the encouragement of a great example, [Americans] form a society" (pp. 128-129).

In his American travels, de Tocqueville witnessed the flowering of the abolition, temperance, and women's rights movements as well as the ferment of Jacksonian democracy and westward expansion. The public agenda was crowded with other issues as well: treatment of the insane, reform of prisons, education of children, education and other opportunities for the deaf and the blind, better housing for workers and particularly the "mill girls" of New England, control of gambling and prostitution in the cities, construction of libraries, and always the latest news of utopian communities and their experiments with property, labor, marriage, child rearing, nutrition, and so on.

Individual Reformers in the Eighteenth Century

Prior to 1800, American public communication "campaigns" were often conducted by strong-willed individuals who reached the public through the pulpit or the printing press. One of the earliest and best examples in the colonial era was Reverend Cotton Mather's campaign to promote inoculation during Boston's smallpox epidemic of 1721-22. Mather was able to show that death from smallpox was nine times more prevalent among the uninoculated than among the inoculated. Mather's pamphlets and personal appeals were opposed by the city's physicians and the *New England Courant*, published by James and Benjamin Franklin. In November 1721, at the height of the controversy, a bomb was thrown into Mather's home.

For a time, Philadelphia was the headquarters of many types of campaigns. In 1775 the first abolition society in America, the Society for the Relief of Free Negroes Unlawfully Held in Bondage, was founded there by Benjamin Franklin and Benjamin Rush. In the same year in Philadelphia, Thomas Paine published the first American defense of women's rights in his *Pennsylvania Magazine*. In 1776 Thomas Paine's *Common Sense* sold 100,000 copies in less than three months. Since the population of the 13 colonies at that time was about 1% of today's national population, a comparable best-seller today would sell 10 million copies.

In 1784 the first important temperance tract, *Inquiry into the Effects of Spiritous Liquors on the Human Body and Mind,* was written by Benjamin Rush. In 1787 Rush wrote *Thoughts on Female Education,* which argued that the education of women was necessary to ensure that children would be properly instructed in citizenship. Thus the three intertwined issues of American social reform in the nineteenth century—abolition, women's rights, and temperance—were all brushed by the eighteenth-century quill of the Philadelphia physician, Benjamin Rush. In 1812, one year before his death, Rush also published *Medical Inquiries and Observations upon the Diseases of the Mind.* However, actual reform in the treatment of the mentally ill did not begin until Dorothea Dix's crusade in the 1840s.

Associations and Reform
in the Nineteenth Century

One crusader, or even a Philadelphia circle of crusaders, cannot achieve reform until large numbers of citizens agree that action is necessary. Even then, if the issue is entrenched in law or custom, decades of campaigning, lobbying, and confronting the opposition may lie ahead of them. The numeric strength and continuity of associations have proved to be essential in achieving reform over the long term.

Abolition associations were the first to adopt the modern form of local chapters coordinated by a headquarters office. The American Anti-Slavery Society was founded in 1833. Its membership grew with each act of violence against the movement, such as the mob beating of abolitionist publisher William Lloyd Garrison in Boston in 1835 and the murder of another abolitionist publisher, Elijah Lovejoy, in Alton, Illinois, in 1837. Mobs had demolished the printing press at Lovejoy's *Alton Observer* three times during 1836 and 1837. He was killed defending the fourth press. By 1838 the American Anti-Slavery Society had 1,350 chapters and 250,000 members. Adjusted for population growth, an association of comparable size today would have more than 4 million members.

The organizing experience of the abolition movement was soon transferred to another principal movement in nineteenth-century America: women's suffrage. When Lucretia Mott and Elizabeth Cady Stanton were rebuffed as delegates to the World Anti-Slavery Conference held in London in 1840, they realized that their loyalties were divided between Negro rights and women's rights. Several years of increasingly public protest led to the Seneca Falls (New York) Convention on Women's Rights in 1848, where 68 women and 32 men signed a Declaration of Principles for women's suffrage. Frederick Douglass, the Black abolitionist and publisher of *The North Star* in Rochester, spoke in support of the Declaration.

The intertwined character of these nineteenth-century reform movements is evident also in the lifelong temperance campaigning of feminists. Mott, Stanton, Lucy Stone, Susan B. Anthony, and Frances Willard (chief organizer of the Women's Christian Temperance Union) spoke on suffrage one day and on temperance the next. The "evil" of alcohol was not primarily a moral issue for the feminists, but an economic issue. Not until legislatures began to pass property reform laws, led by Vermont in 1847, could married women retain title even to real estate they had owned prior to marriage. Nor were women guaranteed a share even of their own earnings. A drunkard husband was an economic threat to the household.

The Women's Christian Temperance Union (WCTU) was founded in 1874. By 1878, after Frances Willard took over from more conservative leadership, it was sponsoring "Home Protection Drives" to petition state legislatures for local option on the manufacture and sale of alcoholic beverages. Although well-funded countercampaigns by the "liquor lobby" often blocked these petition drives, the WCTU worked effectively on other issues related to the welfare of women, such as hygiene, prisons, kindergartens, physical invalids, prostitution, and, of course, women's suffrage.

Susan B. Anthony learned her formidable skills of organizing and communicating in the temperance movement. She founded the Daughters of Temperance not only as a protest to the exclusion of women from national temperance societies but also as a solution to the problem of how women could work together as temperance campaigners.

The strong coalition against women's suffrage drew its oratory from southern politicians and its funds from the liquor lobby. The politicians were determined to deny the vote to Black women, while the liquor manufacturers were determined to keep protemperance women away from the polls in states with local prohibition referenda (Flexner, 1975, p. 307).

The suffragists' communication strategy was multifaceted. Anthony's New York campaign of 1854 was the first to use county "captains" to gather petition signatures. In the same New York campaign, Stanton testified before the state legislature. Such testimony was a favored strategy of the suffragists both because it brought publicity and because there was a chance that sympathetic legislators would introduce bills on suffrage or property rights.

Mass communication was another strategy of the suffragists. Several suffrage newspapers were published after the Civil War, notably Anthony's *The Revolution,* the masthead of which proclaimed, "Men, their rights and nothing more; women, their rights and nothing less." There was also, inevitably, a newspaper that embarrassed the suffragists: *Woodhull and Claflin's Weekly,* edited by the sisters Victoria Woodhull and Tennessee Claflin. Their newspaper advocated not only women's suffrage but also free love. Woodhull's colorful reputation was a problem for the movement.

In addition to *grass-roots organizing, legislative testimony,* and *mass communication,* a fourth strategy of the suffragists was *confrontation,* which brought publicity in newspapers that ignored their peaceful efforts. In the general election of 1872, Anthony led a party of 16 women to the polls in Rochester, New York, where they registered and voted illegally. The Grant administration chose to make an example of Anthony, and she was tried and convicted in 1873.

Anthony's other famous confrontation with authority was literally a once-in-a-century opportunity to steal headlines. The time was July 4, 1876; the event was the Centennial Celebration at Independence Hall, Philadelphia. At a peak moment of the celebration, Anthony and four other women strode to the platform and presented a Declaration of Rights for Women to the chairman. The startled chairman accepted the document and bowed to the women, who then walked out of the hall, distributing printed copies of their declaration to the audience.

Confrontation was a strategy of other nineteenth-century movements as well. The abolitionists did not need to seek confrontation, which awaited them in many northern cities; neither did they avoid confrontations by meeting only in safe settings such as churches. Although the temperance movement did not have an official confrontation policy, Carry Nation made headlines in Kansas and New York. Her hatchet was a newspaper cartoonist's delight, but saloon keepers dreaded the sight of the her 6-foot, 175-pound frame at the door. She was repeatedly beaten by saloon patrons, and she was arrested at least 30 times.

Mass Media and Reform
in the Twentieth Century

The role that mass media would play in America's increasingly pluralistic society was anticipated by de Tocqueville's (1835/1961) observation:

> When men are no longer united amongst themselves by firm and lasting ties, it is impossible to obtain the concurrence of any great number of them, unless you can persuade every man whose concurrence you require that his private interest obliges him voluntarily to unite his exertions to the exertions of all the rest. This can only be habitually and conveniently effected by means of a newspaper; nothing but a newspaper can drop the same thought into a thousand minds at the same moment. (p. 134)

At the end of the nineteenth century, the initiative for reforming many social problems shifted from associations to the mass media. Many of the problems, by their very nature, were not the rallying causes of organized activity. The muckrakers writing for *McClure's, Cosmopolitan, Collier's, Hampton's, Pearson's, Everybody's,* and other magazines first had to convince the public that impure food, monopoly price-fixing, employment of young children, and unavailable health care for the poor were social evils. They then had to document where these evils were found.

Newspapers and magazines had been preparing for their new role since the 1870s. To sustain the rapid growth in their circulation (one daily newspaper for every five households in 1850, one for three in 1870, two for three in 1890, and better than one for one in 1910), writers, editors, and cartoonists went beyond covering the news to creating news on causes of their own choosing. The circulation wars of the closing years of the nineteenth century required each successful newspaper and magazine to differentiate itself from its competitors. The worst of yellow journalism and the best of muckraking were both tactics of differentiation. Muckrakers such as Lincoln Steffens, Ida Tarbell, Upton Sinclair, David Graham Phillips, Ray Stannard Baker, and Samuel Hopkins Adams made new enemies with each story. The publications faced legal and economic sanctions; their strategy for survival was to build readerships so large that advertisers could not afford to boycott them.

The muckrakers' issues comprise a new century's agenda of social reform. The main issues of nineteenth-century reform—slavery, women's suffrage, and temperance—were recognizable as evils by the light of America's original social contract. The issues of twentieth-century reform required a new interpretation of social *responsibility*: Food producers should not adulterate their products; corporations should not conspire to fix prices; children should be in schools, not in factories; and so on.

Another important difference between the nineteenth- and twentieth-century reform agendas is apparent now as we reluctantly acknowledge that many reforms begun in the early years of the twentieth century cannot be completed by its end. The nineteenth-century reformers believed that an issue was resolved when legislative or judicial action was taken. The abolitionists' record of accomplishment consisted of the Thirteenth, Fourteenth, and Fifteenth Amendments. The suffragists first achieved reform in state property laws, then secured suffrage in a few western states and capped their struggle with the Nineteenth Amendment. Temperance advocates won local prohibition referenda, then swept the country with the Eighteenth Amendment. Many of the abolitionists, suffragists, and temperance advocates "retired" when their amendments were ratified. The freed slave, the enfranchised woman, and the family of the drunkard could now work out their own fortunes.

For better or worse, twentieth-century reforms focus on *outcomes* rather than on *processes*. Laws and judicial decisions enable twentieth-century reforms but do not ensure them. The twentieth-century reformer has learned to claim victory not when a law has been passed but when a particular quality of change has occurred in people's lives.

The muckrakers were the first twentieth-century reformers to know the ambiguity of a "solution." First, the solution might not be substantively implemented for months or years after it was decided upon. Second, the opposition's legal staff would find loopholes; compliance would be token and evasive. Third, the solution to one problem could generate another problem.

The muckrakers savored few victories. Many of the issues they raised are still unresolved. There was a limit to how far the muckrakers could carry their reforms. They were journalists, not administrators. They could conceive a reform and even attend its birth, but they could not rear it. Ironically, they were investigators of government corruption and ineptitude, yet their writings played a major role in building today's bureaucracy. Inadequate health care required a board of health, impure food required a pure food agency, and so on. Most of the reforms conceived by the muckrakers had to be reared by government officials. Thus twentieth-century reform passed into the hands of the civil service.

The Federal Government: Always a Problematic Stakeholder

At the turn of the century, the laws that the federal government passed as expedient solutions to reform pressure from the associations and muckrakers drew it into causes that were further and further removed from its original charter. After passage of the Interstate Commerce Act in 1887, the government's right to regulate interstate commerce became the slim thread for tying the 1906 Pure Food and Drug Act, the 1910 "White Slave Traffic Act," the 1916 Child Labor Act, and many other social reform laws to the Constitution. The Supreme Court struck down some of these laws, such as the Child Labor Act, but sustained others.

The two other watersheds of reform legislation in this century, during the early years of Franklin Roosevelt's New Deal and Lyndon Johnson's Great Society administrations, completed the pattern of federal involvement in almost all of the issues that had formerly occupied the associations and mass media. To a greater extent than Congress may have understood or intended at any time, the government became a permanent stakeholder in social reform.

Coordination between the associations and the mass media had been relatively uncomplicated. When the associations sought coverage, they supplied information to the media and staged events that served as news pegs for their information to be published. When the media needed sources and facts for investigative features, the associations were happy to help them.

Inevitably, the federal government's communication programs overlapped with both the associations and the media. Associations found that their programs, built up over decades with the help of volunteers and contributions, could be overshadowed by federal programs with large budgets and urgent mandates from Congress.

As federal agencies developed their own public information arms, their ability to scoop the media with "breakthroughs" discouraged the essential but slower process of investigative reporting. Communication roles were reversed, on occasion, when government experts exaggerated the extent of progress in their areas of responsibility. Reporters without privileged access to the evidence then had to evaluate the government's claims in order to cover the stories either as presented or with input from other sources.

From the associations' perspective, the greatest problem with federal agencies as allies in public communication campaigns is their unpredictability. As administrations change and election years come and go, federal agencies may be extensively involved in campaigns or they may be largely silent. Adversarial issues especially bring out this chameleon trait in agencies. For example, federal attention to civil rights fluctuates more than its attention to cancer treatment.

The Four Stakeholders Working Together: A Brief Case Study

The following case study illustrates many of the principles discussed above. The communication program of the National Cancer Institute (NCI) is just one example from many that could have been chosen. It happens to be more positive than negative, more cooperative than antagonistic, more long term than short term in its planning perspective, more multifaceted than singular in its strategies, and more research guided than most programs.

War on Cancer

The National Cancer Act of 1971 was promoted by the Nixon administration as a declaration of war on cancer. The act thrust the otherwise research-oriented National Cancer Institute into a spotlight of media coverage and communication responsibilities (NCI's coverage in magazines and newspapers outstrips other national institutes by more than two to one, according to the *Magazine Index* and *Newspaper Index*).

The National Cancer Institute was founded by the National Cancer Act of 1937. It had no strong communication mandate in its charter of "conducting research, investigations, experiments, and studies relating to the cause, diagnosis, and treatment of cancer" (National Cancer Act, 1937). However, after the extraordinary growth in biomedical research funding during the Eisenhower and Kennedy administrations—from $60 million to $880 million—some of NCI's most influential friends were impatient with its focus on basic research only. In 1966, President

Lyndon Johnson said that "too much energy was being spent on basic research and not enough on translating laboratory findings into tangible benefits for the American people" (Greenberg, 1986, p. 53). After the 1971 National Cancer Act was passed, the NCI Office of Cancer Communications (NCI-OCC, 1975a) echoed Johnson: "One significant area of national concern is NCI communications and information services so findings can be widely and effectively used" (p. 1).

However, cancer public communication was already spoken for. NCI is only a youngster in comparison with the American Cancer Society, which was founded as the American Society for the Control of Cancer in 1913 under the private philanthropy of John D. Rockefeller, Jr. The ASCC, which changed its name to the American Cancer Society in 1944, originated many innovative forms of public communication, beginning with *Campaign Notes* for ASCC volunteers. ASCC declared a "Cancer Week" in 1920; it became "Cancer Month" by presidential proclamation in 1938. The famous *Danger Signals* pamphlet was first widely distributed in 1922. Augmenting its general campaign with site-specific campaigns (e.g., lung and uterine cancer), ASCC founded the Women's Field Army in 1935 as a means of communicating the facts of breast and uterine cancer to women.

ACS's national campaigns understate the amount of activity that the association directs, because its local chapters are governed by independent boards and determine many of their own priorities for campaigns. There is a national competition for the most effective local programs, and descriptions of the winning programs are shared with other chapters as suggestions for campaign planning.

The sudden increase in NCI funding in the early 1970s changed the balance of public communication activity between ACS and NCI. The growing regional network of federally assisted Comprehensive Cancer Centers brought NCI into the community for the first time—into the center of ACS strength and the source of its funding.

There was generally an ACS program in place for every community program that NCI wanted to launch through the Cancer Centers. There was not only potential duplication of effort but also disagreement over guidelines—for example, with respect to mammography for women of different ages. Nor was ACS reassured by NCI plans to launch larger programs, with stronger research components, and using health professionals rather than volunteers.

Similarly, at the national level, the ACS media office was well known to medical reporters who were working the "cancer beat" and television producers who wanted guidance in treating cancer themes in their programs. ACS could claim credit for many documentary and dramatic presentations on cancer in the media.

However, from the public's perspective, cancer communication was not markedly better than other types of health communication. Public understanding of cancer causes and treatments was still limited, and cancer prevention behaviors were far short of the ACS or NCI goals. The ACS record of public communication was good, but many problems remained to be solved.

NCI's Office of Cancer Communications thus had a role to play if it could define that role to the satisfaction of the federal chain of command as well as to the satisfaction of the American Cancer Society, whose ill will it could not afford.

Differences between the well-funded federal agency and the well-connected private association became the cornerstones of NCI-OCC's program to fill the identifiable gaps. These included (1) the budget and the justification to operate a national "hotline" for cancer information, (2) a requirement to use research in program planning and evaluation, (3) a different agenda of issues to claim media attention, and (4) a need to serve as a "communications wholesaler" for "public access groups" such as "the American Cancer Society, labor unions, churches, health care institutions, etc." (NCI-OCC, 1975b, pp. 2-3).

The Hotline: 1-800-4-CANCER

One of the country's best-known toll-free numbers is operated by the Cancer Information Service (CIS), a network of 21 regional offices at the Cancer Centers and a national office in Maryland. The trained hotline staff do not dispense medical advice; they answer questions, mail out pamphlets covering frequently requested topics of information, and refer requests for medical advice to NCI's list of cancer-treating physicians in the caller's area. In recent years the CIS has responded to nearly 1,000 calls daily. A third of the calls come from cancer patients or their relatives and friends. About half the calls come from individuals seeking general information about cancer, and almost one-fourth come from health professionals. The staff also respond to nearly 500 written information requests daily. The hotline becomes even busier when national cancer news, such as Nancy Reagan's breast cancer, reaches the public.

Thus the hotline fills a gap by ensuring that callers receive reliable information and by connecting them with local resources, including ACS. Symbolically, the hotline reassures callers that information about cancer prevention, diagnosis, and treatment is being shared nationally through a network of cancer knowledge.

Research-Based Campaigns

The theme of this volume is that campaigns succeed or fail on the strength of their planning, implementation, and evaluation, as well as prior research on similar campaigns. However, some of the most effective messages come from writers and graphic artists who trust their experience to tell them when the work is good and when it needs improvement; this is the only basis on which many creative people can function. Unfortunately, researchers' results often tell a different story ("Respondents admired the booklet but could not recall its five key facts and three recommended actions"). Furthermore, even if one booklet or film works well in the field, the principles of its success may be locked in the head of its creator, who cannot personally produce all the messages that are needed; nor can he or she score a success every time.

The American Cancer Society is skilled in leveraging the efforts of other organizations, such as advertising agencies, to develop communication campaigns (often in concert with the Advertising Council; see Rice in chap. 9, this volume). ACS directors understand the value of research and conduct surveys on a regular basis, but they often do not believe that it would be wise to insist on a field evaluation of a campaign created pro bono at a cost of hundreds of thousands of dollars.

Most of the circumstances and considerations at the National Cancer Institute are exactly the opposite. NCI-OCC pays for its campaign development, and developers are expected to test materials in the field as they are created (formative evaluation; see Atkin & Freimuth, chap. 6, this volume). When the full campaign has been launched, measurement of effects (summative evaluation; see Flay & Cook, chap. 8, this volume) will probably continue for the life of the campaign. Nor could NCI eliminate the research steps if it wanted to. Federal overseers of NCI programs rely on research findings, among other inputs, to choose which programs to expand, which to hold steady, and which to discontinue.

A typical NCI-OCC campaign and its evaluation are described in *Progress Against Breast Cancer* (NCI-OCC, 1980). This campaign was launched in the late 1970s because of NCI's beliefs and concerns that (1) breast cancer had finally become a discussable topic, partly because of the publicity surrounding the illnesses of Betty Ford and Happy

Rockefeller, (2) the safety of mammography was being questioned, and women were avoiding this examination without turning to alternatives such as physicians' exams and breast self-examination, and (3) advances in breast cancer treatment and rehabilitation were new reasons for early detection. Furthermore, the opportunity arose to design the campaign to reach women at their places of work and to implement it in collaboration with a major employer, AT&T.

A substantial kit of materials was developed for stand-alone use in workplaces: booklets, slide-tape presentation, reprints of articles, poster, presenter's guide, and book of additional resources. As the materials were developed, they were pretested with members of two cooperating organizations, the National Council of Catholic Women and the American Federation of Teachers.

AT&T participants were surveyed on three occasions—before the program and one month and five months after the program. The knowledge, attitude, and behavior responses showed that the program had achieved many of its objectives while missing some others. For example, participants gained knowledge about most symptoms of breast cancer but mistakenly chose one incorrect symptom more often than before. Most important, participants knew more about detection and treatment procedures, and they not only understood the procedure of breast self-examination better but also reported performing it more often.

Following this generally successful trial, NCI-OCC was able to enlist the cooperation of several other corporations such as Pillsbury and Xerox, religious and service organizations such as B'nai B'rith and the Florida Farm Bureau Federation, and government agencies.

However, the most innovative NCI-OCC contribution to cancer public communication is probably the Health Message Testing Service, sponsored by NCI but largely designed and administered by the Porter-Novelli research and public relations firm. The HMTS is not only based on current social science knowledge but also adds to it, since the experience of pretesting hundreds of messages has created a unique data base of findings.

The HMTS is based on OCC's six "Stages in Health Communication": (1) planning and strategy selection, (2) concept development, (3) message execution, (4) implementation, (5) assessing in-market effectiveness, and (6) feedback to Stage 1—testing and redesign of messages continue throughout the course of a campaign (see Atkin & Freimuth, chap. 6, this volume).

To assist campaign developers in conducting their own pretests, HMTS also provides a "cook book" on pretesting methods, ranging from readability testing to individual in-depth interviews. The book contains many examples of materials that seemed excellent prior to pretesting but missed their mark with target audiences. Of course, the most useful role of pretesting is to explain why messages fail, and the HMTS methods emphasize explanation as well as prediction.

Both Good Guys and Bad Guys to the Media

The main difference between ACS and NCI with respect to media relations is that ACS is generally praised in the media while NCI spends part of each year in hot water. *Fortune* magazine's recent description of ACS in an article titled "America's Best-Run Charities" (Kinkead, 1987) is typical. The author notes that ACS spent $152 million on education and research in 1986 and is moving its head-quarters from New York City to Atlanta to reduce overhead. Relatively rare criticisms of ACS (e.g., Moss, 1980) focus on its friends in high places and its industry connections rather than on its programs.

In contrast, NCI has become the national lightning rod for fears and frustrations about cancer. Its federal obligation is to report the bad news along with the good news about cancer as new studies and statistical compilations are released. One recurring case of mixed news is the *Atlas of U.S. Cancer Mortality among Whites* (1987). The *Atlas* is needed as a research tool by epidemiologists, but it is subject to misinterpretation by readers who do not understand its methodology. Inevitably, cancer rates rise in some areas while falling in others. Members of Congress want to know what NCI intends to do about the increased rates in their districts. Local chambers of commerce are upset with NCI for publishing the rates at all.

When the *Atlas* was rereleased in 1987, NCI-OCC decided to be proactive rather than reactive in presenting and defending it to the media. A "backgrounder" was prepared on the important research that was made possible by previous editions of the *Atlas*. Epidemiology is often medical detective work focusing on unexpected causes, and the "backgrounder" is quite interesting to read. Additional press releases and a press briefing were part of NCI-OCC's preparation for the release of the *Atlas* on June 9, 1987. (See Alcalay & Taplin, chap. 5, this volume, for a discussion of the relation of public relations and public affairs to communication campaigns.) As a result, the media generally described the new edition of the *Atlas* as a research tool and mentioned the caveats in interpreting cancer rates.

A final incident shows how beneficial NCI's media connections can be. In May 1985, Dr. Frank Field broadcast four brief segments on WCBS (New York), dealing with the possible relationships between diet and cancer. He held up and described the NCI booklet *Diet, Nutrition and Cancer Prevention: A Guide to Food Choices*. He said that the 52-page booklet of guidelines and recipes could be obtained by calling 1-800-4-CANCER or by writing to NCI. The response was immediate and unprecedented for an on-air "plug"—75,000 requests were received, 12,000 by phone and the balance by mail. Fortunately, NCI had printed a large quantity of the booklets and was able to fulfill the requests. Over time, a million copies of the booklet have been distributed.

Campaigning from the Rear Lines

The 1970s taught Washington that no communication program can reach the entire country without the committed involvement of "intermediaries"—whether individuals or organizations—that have access to target audiences. NCI-OCC learned this lesson along with other federal agencies. Several metaphors have developed around this relationship, including "front lines/rear lines," "wholesaler/retailer," and "upstream/downstream."

NCI-OCC has had two long-standing intermediaries, the American Cancer Society and the network of Cancer Centers. It is constantly cultivating others, ranging from corporations to nonprofit organizations. The NCI-OCC Partners in Prevention program was created to provide recognition and an official status for these liaisons. According to one report, the cancer communication partnership formed in a typical state consists of the regional Cancer Center, ACS, Blue Cross/Blue Shield, State Health Department, Cooperative Extension Service (rural development), and community hospitals (NCI-OCC, 1986). All of the partners have their own communication media of some type; they agree to cover particular cancer topics at particular times to capture public attention.

Summary of the NCI Case

While this case study has attempted to cover only a limited number of years and events in public communication campaigns about cancer, it should be clear that all four stakeholders—a private association, a

government agency, mass media, and social scientists—have worked
out constructive roles for their joint effort, which is more or less
keeping pace with the growing national concern about cancer and
particularly cancer prevention and treatment (see the "Cancer Issues"
section of Table 1.1).

Conclusion

Public communication campaigners may wish that the world in
which they work could be as simple as it was a century ago in the
heyday of Susan B. Anthony's campaigns. Or they may wish that the
charisma of a William Lloyd Garrison or the appalling disclosures of
an Upton Sinclair could be as effective now as in the past. The world
of AIDS, drug abuse, cancer, and the like has moved beyond these
appealing simplicities.

However, the world of modern campaigns contains solutions as well
as problems. Campaigns learn from the successes and failures of other
campaigns and thereby grow in sophistication. Thanks to the detached
perspective of social scientists, campaigns are entities that are separate
from the subjective experiences of campaigners. Campaigns are documented, compared, and reassessed for the new concepts and techniques
they may suggest. As a result, there has been more progress in designing and conducting campaigns in the past 20 years than in the 125 years
separating the Philadelphia circle of 1775 from the muckrakers of
1900.

As we end the century, the great figures of past campaigns will not
reappear, and future campaigns will be less exciting for their absence,
but the science of public communication campaigns now comes to the
fore and generates its own excitement. As the agenda of social issues
changes, campaigns will continue to change in increasingly adaptive
ways to meet the new challenges.

Part II

Theory and Design

There is no simple separation of theory, design, and application in communication campaigns. Different theoretical approaches and perspectives—such as models of persuasion, rejection of linear models of communication, social marketing approaches, community orientations, formative evaluation, systems perspectives toward planning evaluations, and summative evaluation designs—suggest different ways to design, conduct, and analyze campaign efforts. This section discusses some of the paradigmatic foundations of campaigns, as well as different approaches that can contribute to improved campaigns. It moves from theoretical considerations of persuasion strategies and audiences, to conceptualizations of campaigns as social marketing and community efforts, to frameworks for formative, process, and summative evaluation. It also identifies problems and obstacles that campaigns must attempt to overcome.

William J. McGuire is one of the foremost authorities on persuasion theory, and his comprehensive overview of concepts, processes, and theoretical mechanisms provides a solid foundation for understanding communication campaigns. He describes how basic directive and dynamic theories from social psychology can be applied in designing effective campaigns to influence audiences. After outlining the popular input-output matrix of communication and persuasion variables, McGuire draws insightful implications for avoiding common fallacies in developing campaign strategies. His chapter features a new assessment of recent variants of this matrix model, including alternative routes through the output steps, activation of self-persuasion processes, and reordering of the output sequence. Sixteen families of theories about the dynamic aspects of the person are briefly sketched to help identify key forces that motivate individual response to persuasive messages. In closing, McGuire offers a useful seven-step checklist for designers to keep in mind as they plan and implement campaigns.

Brenda Dervin challenges some of the most fundamental concepts in communication campaign design and research. Dervin argues that an information-as-construction model is more appropriate in communication situations than an information-as-description model. The former model assumes that information is created by human observers, is inherently a product of human self-interest, and can never be separated from the observers who created it. Switching from conceptualizing information as a description of reality also changes the concept of communication from an act of transmission to a process of dialogue. This shift has consequences for how we think about audiences, the practice of communicating, and the nature of society. Dervin describes her own approach to this changed conceptualization of the audience: the sense-making approach. It combines ethnographic, qualitative, quantitative, and systematic procedures. The core construct of sense-making is the idea of the gap—how people define and bridge gaps in their everyday lives. The sense-making approach, along with results and implications for designing interventions, is illustrated with examples from a library desiring more Hispanic patrons, a blood center desiring repeat donors, and a cancer clinic wanting to handle anxious patients better.

A much different perspective on communication campaigns, drawn from the field of marketing, is introduced by academic turned market researcher Douglas Solomon. He demonstrates how the philosophy, concepts, and techniques of commercial marketing can be adapted to public sector programs through the "social marketing" approach. Solomon emphasizes several key ideas for improving traditional public communication campaigns, such as responsively meeting the needs and wants of the audience, broadly considering product, price, place, and positioning elements as well as promotion, precisely segmenting and understanding submarkets, and carefully assessing the competition. He presents numerous illustrations of the ways that social campaigners can achieve greater effectiveness by applying the principles used so successfully in the private sector.

Researchers and policymakers have not paid sufficient attention to the particular challenges and needs of community communication campaigns, with respect to both appropriate theories and the need for useful, informed guidelines. Rina Alcalay and Shahnaz Taplin point out that because "community" involves a context, a process of interaction, and a problem, campaign designers need to understand power distributions and need to use available media effectively within limited budgets. Their chapter outlines advantages of conducting community campaigns, identifies principles from prior campaign research that can guide community campaigns (such as the "spiral of silence," cultivation effects, agenda-setting, and knowledge gaps), and describes a planning process for community health campaigns. They argue that part of the process should consider how best to place messages in various media, both from a commercial advertising perspective and from a public relations and public affairs perspective. The chapter includes a short but explicit appendix that explains basic media placement and research terms (such as ratings, reach, frequency, and gross rating points) and summarizes sources of placement research for broadcast and print media. Community campaigns on tight budgets cannot afford to ignore the considerable insights of media placement research and practice.

One of the primary reasons mass media health campaigns have achieved only limited success is the lack of sophisticated formative evaluation research in the development of campaign strategies. Charles K. Atkin and Vicki Freimuth discuss the role of preproduction research and message pretests in identifying target audiences and target behavioral outcomes, specifying critical intermediate response variables, ascertaining channel exposure patterns, determining receptivity to potential message components, and testing preliminary versions of messages. At each stage, information is obtained from audience samples using empirical data-gathering techniques such as survey questionnaires, focus group discussions, in-depth interviews, and scaled ratings of messages. These authors go beyond simple description of methods to provide a conceptual framework for approaching the evaluation task. The formative research process is illustrated with a detailed case study of drunk driving campaign planning and selected examples of other health campaign applications. Atkin and Freimuth argue that the collection of precampaign evaluation evidence enables strategists and producers to design more effective public communication efforts.

Using campaigns in Honduras and The Gambia promoting oral rehydration therapy as a response to infant mortality and morbidity caused by diarrheal disease as examples, Ronald E. Rice and Dennis Foote present a systems-theoretic evaluation planning framework for identifying relevant environment, system, and component variables as well as stages and phases. Stages described include specification of objectives, inputs and outputs, prior state, constraints, individual-level processes, short- and long-term poststates, and implications for measurement and design. Some implications from this approach include identifying sources of program versus theory failure, guiding the selection of variables and units of analysis that match the target pre- and poststate conditions, allowing for nontraditional causal links among interpersonal and mass media communication and outcomes, and identifying social and economic constraints that are generally underemphasized in development campaigns.

Brian R. Flay and Thomas D. Cook focus on assessing the effects of prevention campaigns that have a substantial media component. Their chapter serves two major purposes. First, after summarizing six basic questions that summative evaluations attempt to answer, they explicate what is special about evaluation in the context of prevention campaigns. Their thesis is that such campaigns are characterized by diffuse target audiences, with few persons at risk for the health problem being targeted, campaign messages that are of low salience to most of the target audience, complex but underspecified theories of the underlying process relating interventions to effects and impacts, and small sample sizes of the aggregated units exposed to the campaign. The traditional suggestion for dealing with the first three of these problems is to conduct large-sample research. But the fourth issue precludes precisely this possibility, presenting us with the conundrum that undergirds most of the discussion in this chapter. Flay and Cook's second purpose is to illustrate how these four sets of problems have been dealt with in three different models of campaign evaluations: the advertising model, the monitoring model, and the experimental model.

2

Theoretical Foundations of Campaigns

WILLIAM J. MCGUIRE

This chapter describes how basic theories about the structure and motivation of the person can be used to design public communication campaigns that are effective in persuading people to change their beliefs, feelings, and behaviors. While theory and practice are sometimes regarded as polar opposites, the astute practitioner of the art and craft of persuasion will appreciate Lewin's dictum that there is nothing so practical as a good theory. The first section discusses the nature and functions of theories, so clarifying the organization of the remaining sections.

The Nature and Functions of Theories

Theory differs from informal everyday knowledge by being more explicit, formally organized, and abstract. Its broad abstractness magnifies both advantages and limitations of ordinary knowledge: its broadness provides guidance for coping with a wide spectrum of reality, but its abstractness increases its remoteness from reality represented, aggravating the oversimplifications, unwarranted extrapolations, and distortion inherent in all knowledge. The art of effective theorizing is to use any theory in the very limited contexts and perspectives in which it is relatively adequate, and to discard it in favor of alternative theories when the reality is being viewed from other perspectives (McGuire, 1983, 1986).

Theories that reduce reality to simplified categories and relationships are needed for processing not only the world in itself, but also the results of research on that world, especially in an area as heavily studied as persuasive communication. About 5% of the 25,000 books and articles summarized in *Psychological Abstracts* each year deal directly with communication effects on attitudes and actions, and much of the related bibliographic information is retrievable by computer (Reed & Baxter, 1983).

The categories of theories discussed below provide the public communicator with conceptual frameworks for analyzing this large amount of social influence research, storing its implications in memory, constructing new public communication campaigns, and providing checklists for analyzing and improving the effectiveness of existing campaigns. Some persuasion theories deal with directive, channeling aspects of the person (how he or she processes the persuasive information); others deal with dynamic, energizing aspects (why he or she processes it). The section that follows will describe directive theories, including the most popular input/output, communication/persuasion model, followed by a section noting some alternatives to it. The subsequent section describes dynamic theories, including sixteen views of the motivational forces that drive the person onward in persuasion situations. A final section outlines a seven-step procedure for designing a public communication campaign.

Directive Theories
of the Persuasion Process:
The Communication/Persuasion Matrix

The most popular theory of how persuasive communication operates is sketched in the input/output matrix displayed in Figure 2.1. The inputs (the column labels) include the various components out of which one can construct the communication to change attitudes and actions; the output steps (the rows) consist of the successive information-processing behavioral substeps that the communication must evoke in the target person for the persuasive impact to occur. This communication/persuasion matrix will be discussed as regards first the input factors, then the output factors, and then its implication for avoiding commonly made errors in public communication campaigns.

The Input (Communication) Variables

The input factors in a public communication campaign are the independent variables and persuasive message options that can be manipu-

INPUT: Independent (Communication) Variables / OUTPUT: Dependent Variables (Response Steps Mediating Persuasion)	SOURCE				MESSAGE					CHANNEL			RECEIVER				DEST-INATION		
	number	unanimity	demographics	attractiveness credibility ••	type appeal	type information	inclusion/omission	organization	repetitiveness ••	modality	directness	context ••	demographics	ability	personality	life style ••	immediacy/delay	prevention/cessation	direct/immunization ••
1. Exposure to the communication																			
2. Attending to it																			
3. Liking, becoming interested in it																			
4. Comprehending it (learning what)																			
5. Skill acquisition (learning how)																			
6. Yielding to it (attitude change)																			
7. Memory storage of content and /or agreement																			
8. Information search and retrieval																			
9. Deciding on basis of retrieval																			
10. Behaving in accord with decision																			
11. Reinforcement of desired acts																			
12. Post-behavioral consolidating																			

Figure 2.1. The Communication/Persuasion Model as an Input/Output Matrix

lated, the components for constructing the persuasive communication. A commonly used analysis starts with Lasswell's (1948) interrogative formulation of communication as a matter of who says what, via what medium, to whom, directed at what kind of target; in information-theory jargon these same input categories are termed source, message, channel, receiver, and destination, each of which can be further sub-divided as sketched in Figure 2.1.

Source factors. Source variables in persuasive communications refer to characteristics of the perceived communicator to whom the message is attributed (e.g., in the case of a forest fire prevention message, the secretary of agriculture, the friendly forest ranger, or Smokey Bear), not of the person in the Ad Council, Forest Service, or creative department who actually produced the message. Much research has been done on how persuasive impact is affected by source demographics such as age, socioeconomic status, gender, and ethnicity, on such issues as whether a given message has more impact when presented by a male or a female source (Eagly, 1983). McGuire (1985) and Petty and Cacioppo (1986) provide detailed reviews of how such source factors as perceived credibility, attractiveness, and power affect persuasive impact.

An illustrative source issue is how persuasive impact is affected by whether or not the audience is aware of the source's persuasive intent. This awareness reduces persuasive impact by lowering the source's perceived trustworthiness, but enhances persuasion by clarifying the point of the message or by anticipatory belief change to maintain self-esteem (Cialdini & Petty, 1981; McGuire & Millman, 1965), opposed tendencies that have yielded a rich set of findings.

Message factors. The message category provides the richest sublist of input variables for persuasive communications, including delivery style, types of appeals, inclusions and omissions, organization of the material included, and quantitative aspects such as length and repetition. Each of these sets of variables is rich in subcategories; for instance, delivery style includes input variables such as humorousness, literal versus figurative language, speed of speech, and vividness, with considerable research on how each affects persuasive impact (Mc-Guire, 1985; Petty & Cacioppo, 1986; Zanna, Olson, & Herman, 1987). For example, research on a style variable, speed of delivery, corrects the cliché that the fast-talking used-car salesperson loses persuasiveness by sounding untrustworthy. Miller, Maruyama, Beaber, and Valone (1976) show that faster-talking sources not only produce more attitude change but also are perceived as more knowledgeable and even as more trustworthy. This is especially good news for communicators who have to buy television or radio time, because technology makes possible the compression of auditory (and even visual) messages by up to 25% without noticeable distortion and without loss of liking or recall (LaBarbera, 1980), suggesting that they can pay less to get more.

Channel factors. Media (channels, sensory modalities) through which persuasive messages are transmitted include variables such as audio versus visual versus both, written versus spoken words, verbal versus nonverbal messages, vocalic versus visual nonverbal cues, immediate versus mediated, in various contexts (alone versus with others, with or without background clutter, pleasant versus unpleasant atmosphere). Too often public persuaders choose the channel solely on the basis of the number of people it reaches, as when television ads are placed according to Nielsen ratings without consideration of differences in perceived credibility, likability, and comprehensibility. Findings reveal interactions or intricacies that are usable once recognized, such as that when the message is fairly complex, more comprehension and persuasion are produced via print than via electronic media, but electronic media are more persuasive with simple messages (Chaiken & Eagly, 1976), though perhaps not to an extent that justifies the added production and time costs of televised ads. It is important to recognize that the message is being communicated not only via verbal channels but also via nonverbal channels such as posture, facial expression, gestures, and vocalic quality of speech.

Receiver factors. Campaigns should be designed with regard for audience characteristics, including capacity variables such as age, education, and intelligence; demographic variables such as gender and ethnicity; and personality, life-style, and psychographics variables (Eagly, 1981; McGuire, 1985; Wells, 1975). Even campaigns that must be directed at the wide public may focus especially on special subpopulations, such as forest users, people at high risk for some health hazard, or parents of preschoolers, all of whom have distinctive demographic profiles, media consumption patterns, values, and so on that should be taken into consideration. Receivers' age is a variable of special concern to the FCC and FTC because of worries about advertising on Saturday morning television shows directed at children, who are assumed to be particularly gullible. However, research indicates that age is nonmonotonically related to influenceability, with maximum suggestibility occurring in middle childhood, at about age 9, with lesser susceptibility in younger children, who are protected by their lesser tendency to attend to and comprehend the persuasive message, as well as in older children, who are protected by their more critical attitude toward communications (McGuire, 1985).

Destination factors. This fifth and final input category includes variables having to do with the type of target behavior at which the communication is aimed, such as immediate versus long-term change, change on a specific issue versus across a whole ideological system, or change in an existing belief versus conferring resistance against subsequent attacks. Studies on persistence of persuasion effects show that inputs that produce greater immediate effects may be less effective in the long run (Cook, Gruder, Hennigan, & Flay, 1979; Evans, Rozelle, Lasater, Dembroski, & Allen, 1970), that persuasive impact may continue even after the initially persuading material is no longer remembered (Watts & McGuire, 1964), that the message has impact on remotely related issues not mentioned in the message as well as on the explicit issue (McGuire, 1981), and that mentioning rather than ignoring counterarguments against the audience's position enhances their resistance to subsequent attacks (McGuire, 1964).

Output Factors
in the Communication/Persuasion Matrix

Figure 2.1 shows a twelve-step analysis of the output side of the persuasion process, the successive response substeps required if the communication is to be effective; for example, the public must be exposed to the message and, having been exposed to it, must attend to it, like it, learn what and how, agree, store and retrieve, and decide on the basis of it, down to behaving on the basis of that decision (Step 10), getting reinforced for so behaving, and engaging in postcompliance activity (such as proselytizing others or reorganizing one's related beliefs) that consolidates the new position induced by the communication.

These dozen substeps constitute a useful checklist for constructing and evaluating a communication campaign. To decide, say, whether it would be more persuasive to use a male or female source, to use literal or metaphorical expressions, to show a talking head or a visual scene to accompany the sound track, or whatever, one should take into account each alternative's relative power to evoke each step in this long output chain. And to evaluate an existing campaign, one should analyze the input factors' potential for evoking each of the dozen output steps and, where they seem deficient for evoking one or more steps, the communication should be beefed up by adding input factors that will elicit the neglected response steps.

Using the Matrix Model
to Avoid Common Communication Errors

Both input and output sides of the communication/persuasion matrix are quite straightforward, yet they serve to avoid common fallacies in persuasion campaigns, six of which will be described below.

The attenuated-effects fallacy. The probability that the communication will evoke each of the twelve output steps is conditional upon the occurrence of all preceding steps; for instance, Step 2 (attending to the message) occurs with a limited probability, given the probabilistic occurrence of Step 1 (exposure to the communication). If the probability of each of the steps up to the desired behavioral Step 10 (behaving as urged in the communication) were .50 (an unrealistically high estimate), then the probability of the message evoking the behavior would be only .50 raised to the tenth power, or .001. Hence a first implication of the communication/persuasion matrix is that one should guard against exaggerated expectations regarding the likely size of one's persuasive impact.

The distant-measure fallacy. All too often the campaign or its component parts are evaluated in terms of a response step early in the chain, quite distant from the behavioral Step 10 that is actually the payoff output (see Flay & Cook, chap. 8, this volume). Advertisers buy billions of dollars' worth of time and space each year on the Step 1 (exposure) criterion of Nielsen ratings or circulation figures, as if it sufficed simply to reach the public. More sophisticated advertisers select copy in terms of its Step 2 (attention) efficacy (when ad recognition tests are used) or by a Step 4 (comprehension) criterion (when readability or aided-recall tests are used), but these are still remote from behavioral-payoff Step 10 and leave the strong possibility that an ad alternative chosen because it scores higher in liking or recall may bomb on later steps and so be inferior in evoking Step 10.

The neglected-mediator fallacy. Campaign designers often select inputs on the basis of their promise for evoking just one or two momentarily salient output steps among the dozen, as when they add music or humor in order to enhance Steps 2 and 3, attention and liking, without considering possible negative effects of these distracters on Steps 4 and 6, comprehension and agreement. The communication/persuasion matrix helps in the assessment of the net efficacy of adding a given input by drawing attention to each of the possible effects, thus revealing possible negative side effects via some steps in the chain that may outweigh its benefits.

The compensatory principle. I have already mentioned a number of input variables (amount of arguments, humor, and so on) that affect ultimate behavioral compliance (Step 10) in opposite directions via different mediating steps, a quite common situation (McGuire, 1968b). Recipients' education (or intelligence) level is typically expected to reduce persuadability by lowering their likelihood of yielding (Step 6); but this overlooks their raising persuadability by enhancing attention and comprehension (Steps 2 and 4). Hence the educated public may be more vulnerable to persuasion, as in the World War II studies of the U.S. Army's indoctrination program that found that the soldiers' educational level enhanced rather than reduced their susceptibility to the propaganda (Hovland, Lumsdaine, & Sheffield, 1949).

The golden mean principle. It is common for a communication input to affect an ultimate persuasive impact in opposite directions via different mediating steps, leading to an inverted-U relationship between input and impact (McGuire, 1968b). For example, if length of message (or level of fear arousal or of recipient's intelligence or whatever) affects ultimate compliance behavior (Step 10) positively via some mediating steps and negatively via others, then the overall relationship between the communication input and the ultimate impact will have this inverted-U nonmonotonic shape. Keeping this in mind guards against a "more is better" style of thinking such as deciding that if a little bit of anxiety arousal slightly enhances persuasive impact, then a great deal of anxiety arousal should add still more; rather, intermediate levels on input variables tend to be golden (McGuire, 1968b).

The situational-weighting principle. The advice to set communication variables at an intermediate level is vague until we specify where the optimum lies in the broad middle range. The communication/persuasion matrix helps resolve the ambiguity. First, one checks off which output steps the input variable (such as anxiety arousal) enhances versus which steps it inhibits (e.g., anxiety arousal would enhance Step 6, agreeing with the arguments comprehended, but reduce Step 4, comprehending the arguments). One then analyzes the situation regarding the amount of variance in persuasion likely to be contributed by the enhanced and reduced steps to deduce the optimal level at which to set the input variable (e.g., the simpler the message, the higher the optimal level of anxiety).

Summary. The basic theoretical communication/persuasion matrix model is sufficiently straightforward to help one keep up with the research literature, design new campaigns, and evaluate and improve existing campaigns, and provides campaign-constructing warnings and guidelines that might otherwise be overlooked.

Variants of and Alternatives to
the Communication/Persuasion Matrix

In addition, there are several more adventurous departures from the commonsense aspects of this input/output model. This section first describes variants of this matrix theory that take into account alternative routes through the output steps. A second, more radical, variant analyzes persuasion, not in the usual way as brought about by an outside source's communicating new information, but by making information already within the person's cognitive system more salient. A third variant depicts the persuasion sequence not in the usual way, as inducing attitude change so that behavioral change will follow, but instead as compelling behavioral change so that attitudinal change will follow.

Alternative-routes variants of the input/output model. Output analyses of the persuasion process like the twelve-step sequence in Figure 2.1 attempt an exhaustive listing of successive behavioral responses that must be elicited if the communication is to have the intended persuasive impact. This long output list is paradoxically both obvious, as regards its individual steps, and implausible in toto; each of the dozen steps seems obviously needed and yet the composite set seems too demanding to be performed even by an unusually cooperative audience on an issue of great import. Audiences are likely to take shortcuts that shorten or even reverse this long list of steps (McGuire, 1969, 1985), accomplishing their adaptive end with less cognitive work. Krugman (1965, 1977) has suggested simplified processing of noninvolving messages, and Petty and Cacioppo (1986) have developed their "elaboration likelihood" model of central versus peripheral routes to persuasion whose different mediating paths may alter the relationship of a given input variable to output impact, depending on the audience's need for correctness.

More radical departures from the commonsense dozen-step path shown in Figure 2.1 reverse the commonsense ordering of the output steps, as in the "selective exposure" tendency (Sweeney & Gruber, 1984), such that whether the audience already agrees or disagrees with the persuasive material (Step 6) determines whether they seek out or avoid exposure to it (Step 1). Also, the affective response (Step 3) may

after all this time we cannot say anything from this

precede as well as follow comprehending what the message says (Step 4), as when audiences may like or dislike the contents of a communication before they are aware of what it says (Lazarus, 1984; Zajonc, 1984). In the "perceptual distortion" reversal of Steps 4 and 6, what the audience believes determines what they perceive the message to be (Sherif & Hovland, 1961). Work on multiple paths to persuasion, including some that reverse the commonsense ordering of the output processes, has been developed on the basis of both theoretical (Ray, 1973) and empirical (Bagozzi, 1982) analyses. Another provocative way of modifying the output side of the Figure 2.1 matrix is to refine some of the steps further, as when Marascuilo and Zwick (1983) divide Step 6 (attitude change) into separate shift and certainty components, Zanna and Fazio (1983) subdivide Step 8 (retrieval), and Irle and Katz (1982) subdivide Step 9 (decision making).

Persuasion from within. The classical matrix model sketched in Figure 2.1 assumes that persuasion involves communicating new information from an outside source. A radically different conceptualization is that persuasion involves activating information already within the person's cognitive repertory, increasing the salience of supportive information that the target person already accepts. I have long advocated this self-persuasion position in opposition to the Yale/Hovland theory that persuasion involves absorption of (generally new) information communicated by an outside source. This self-persuasion alternative model underlies the work my colleagues and I have done on inducing resistance to persuasion by prior exposure to threatening material that stimulates the person to develop arguments against impending attacks (McGuire, 1964) and on inducing anticipatory belief change as a forewarning of impending attack (McGuire & Millman, 1965), and especially our probabilogical theory research (McGuire, 1960, 1989).

A rich illustration of this self-persuasion theory is our Socratic method that manipulates the person's belief on a core issue by asking questions about related issues, thus heightening their salience, with the result that the person's belief on the unmentioned core belief is changed into line with the related beliefs made salient by the questioning. Since first used (McGuire, 1960), this method's efficacy has proven to be robust (Henninger & Wyer, 1976; O'Malley & Thistlethwaite, 1980). Variants include Rokeach's (1979) value-confrontation procedure and Tesser's (1978) mere-thinking procedure. More generally illustrative of this alternative theory of persuasion as a self-induced process is the work of the Ohio State "cognitive responses" group (Greenwald,

Brock, & Ostrom, 1968; Petty, Ostrom, & Brock, 1981), which suggests that compliance with a persuasive communication may be predicted less well from how many of the message arguments are recalled than from how many new arguments (not explicit in the message) are evoked in the audience by the message (Calder, Insko, & Yandell, 1974).

Attitude change as the consequence of behavioral change. Another radical departure from the fashionable information-processing theory of persuasion sketched in Figure 2.1 is the theory that behavioral change produces attitude change, rather than the reverse, so that to change people's attitudes one should not present new information on the issue but rather should compel the public's behavioral change; attitudes will then be adjusted to fit the new behavior. This theory of persuasion has had considerable political significance ever since the nineteenth century, when controversies arose regarding the relationship between religion and economics (e.g., Marx, 1859/1913; Weber, 1903/1930). American presidents since World War II can be found on both sides. Eisenhower doubted that the courts could effectively legislate school integration until the public's attitudes were changed to accept it; but Lyndon Johnson, in response to the contention that military action against the Viet Cong would not succeed until the enemy's hearts and minds were won, argued that if one grabbed one's opponents by the necktie and yanked (actually, Johnson suggested an alternative gripping place), then their hearts and minds would follow.

This alternative view of persuasion, that change in attitude is the consequence rather than cause of behavioral change, receives more support in laboratory than in natural-world research. Much basic research stemming from dissonance theory (Wicklund & Brehm, 1976) supports the notion that if the person is maneuvered into behaving in a new way, then his or her attitude will change to justify the behavior, particularly to the extent that the person perceives his or her behavior to have been volitional, to have serious consequences, and so on. Freudian theorists also contend that forced overt compliance will result in internalized belief change. However, in naturalistic research on legislating morality, only slight changes in attitudes regarding the morality of the behavior have resulted from vast changes in behavior brought about by legalization of homosexual behavior (Berkowitz & Walker, 1967; Walker & Argyle, 1964), prescribing school integration (Rodgers & Bullock, 1972; Wirt, 1970), or proscribing school prayer (Birkby, 1969; Muir, 1967). My own view is that these two opposite theories of persuasion are not mutually exclusive but supplementary. As in most theoretical controversies about the persuasion process, it is

INITIATION OF ACTION / Need — TERMINATION OF ACTION / Provocation / Relationship / State		Stability		Growth	
		Active	Reactive	Active	Reactive
Cognitive	Internal	1. Consistency	2. Categorization	5. Autonomy	6. Problem-solver
	External	3. Noetic	4. Inductional	7. Stimulation	8. Teleological
Affective	Internal	9. Tension-reduction	10. Ego-defensive	13. Assertion	14. Identification
	External	11. Expressive	12. Repetition	15. Empathy	16. Contagion

Figure 2.2. Dynamic Theories: Partial Views of the Motivational Aspects of Human Nature That Lie Behind Communication/Persuasion Research

best to use all of the alternative theories creatively but to have modest expectations about the magnitude of any predicted relationship.

Theories About the Dynamic Aspects of Persuasion

Theories described in the preceding sections deal with the directive aspects of the person, how he or she processes the social influence exerted by a public communication campaign. We turn now to theories dealing with the dynamic aspects of the person, the forces that energize or drive the person to do this processing.

The typical dynamic theory is a partial view of the person, focusing on one aspect of human motivation as it provides insight into how communication campaigns can be made more effective. In earlier work, I have described the assumptions underlying these diverse motivational theories and shown that they differ on four bipolar dimensions, each dimension made up of contrasting ways of looking at some characteristic of human motivation (McGuire, 1974, 1985). The first two dimensions (shown as the column headings in Figure 2.2) deal with forces that initiate human action, while the third and fourth dimensions (the row headings in Figure 2.2) have to do with end states that terminate action. The first dimension distinguishes between stability and growth (being versus becoming) theories, depicting the person as striving to maintain the current homeostasis versus striving to develop to higher levels of complexity. The second, active versus reactive, initiating dimension distinguishes between theories depicting the person as actively initiating behavior in response to internal needs and those depicting him or her as reacting to forces in the external environment.

The other two dimensions, shown as the row titles in Figure 2.2, distinguish dynamic theories on the basis of the end states they depict as terminating action. The third dimension distinguishes between cognitive and affective theories, depicting the person as tending toward ideological end states versus toward feeling states, respectively. The fourth dimension distinguishes between internal and external theories, those that depict action as terminating when a satisfying internal relationship is attained among components within the personality versus when a satisfying external relationship is attained between the person and the outside environment. Arraying these 4 dichotomous dimensions orthogonally produces 2 raised to the fourth power, or 16 cells, in each of which falls a family of theories about the dynamic force that drives the person in persuasion situations.

The Cognitive Stability Theories

The four families of dynamic theories shown in the upper-left quadrant of Figure 2.2 are all cognitive stability formulations, depicting the person as acting to maintain his or her present equilibrium (rather than to grow) and as tending toward a cognitive (thought) rather than affective (feeling) stability.

Consistency theories. The 1960's persuasion research was dominated by the upper-left cell consistency notions under such terms as balance theory, dissonance theory, probabilogic, congruity theory, symmetry theory, graph theory, and psycho-logic, reviewed by McGuire (1966). They depict the person's beliefs, feelings, and actions as being highly interconnected, and the person as striving to maintain high internal coherence among them by avoiding or reducing any discrepancy among these components by such modes as selective avoidance of belief-discrepant communications and internalized attitude change to justify overt compliant behavior. These theories predict that persuasive communications will induce changes on remote issues to keep them consis-

tent with the direct attitude change induced on the explicit issue, and
suggest the Socratic method of changing opinions and behavior
through using questions that sensitize the person to internal inconsistencies (McGuire, 1960, 1981).

Categorization theories. This second family of theories depicts the
person as a filing clerk, coping with stimulus overload by sorting the
incoming information among existing cognitive categories. This concept of the person was particularly popular in the 1930s, when Sherif,
Luchins, and Asch used it to investigate the importance of first impressions as providing a frame of reference to which subsequent events
were assimilated. Woelfel, Cody, Gillham, and Holmes (1980) present
a more recent variant. These theories suggest that persuasion involves
not so much changing one's attitude or behavior toward a situation as
changing one's perception of the situation to which one is responding
(Asch & Zukier, 1984). For example, regarding wildfire prevention,
these theories suggest that one should design communications not to
change people's behavior in the wild as they perceive it, but to change
the way they perceive the wild in such a way that the new perception
evokes the fire-preventing behaviors.

Noetic theories. During the 1970s the field was dominated by attribution and other noetic theories that depict the person as a meaning-
giver who is bothered by unexpected or unexplained experiences until
he or she can construct an explanation that accounts for it. Eagly and
Chaiken (1984) provide an analysis of persuasion from attributional
(and other cognitive) viewpoints. These theories call attention to the
importance of designing persuasive communications to establish a
context within which its recommendations make sense; for example,
wildfire-preventing communications can describe destructive fire occurrences with details that evoke an appropriate attribution of respon-
sibility·for the undesirable behavior.

Inductional theories. These Cell 4 theories are similar to noetic
theories in stressing the person's need to explain experience, but assert
that this explaining need arises only in reaction to outside pressures to
account for what is happening rather than from an internal need to
know. Then the person interprets what is transpiring by observing his
or her own behavior (as in the "radical behavioralism" of Bem, 1972)
or by comparing that behavior with that of others as in Festinger's
social comparison theory (Suls & Miller, 1977). Symbolic inter-
actionists like Mead and Blumer stress this aspect of the person. These
theories depict ideology as deriving from action, so that a campaign
should first arrange the situation to induce the desired behavior in

target persons (perhaps by instruction, modeling, social pressure, or elimination of alternatives); then the persons would be asked to express an attitude regarding the situation, which they will formulate by observing how they have been behaving; and they will subsequently adhere to this self-defining pattern of behavior.

The Cognitive Growth Theories

The four theories in the upper-right quadrant of Figure 2.2 agree with the previous four in depicting the person as motivated to attain a cognitive end state, but differ by postulating a need for cognitive growth rather than for maintaining cognitive equilibrium. These growth formulations are usually advocated by humanistic theorists, while the previous equilibrium tetrad tend to derive from mechanistic orientations.

Autonomy theories. Partial views of human nature stressing the person's need for freedom (or at least for the illusion of control) over his or her own destiny and environment are periodically popular within social psychology, such as during the 1980s, and previously in the early 1950s by theorists such as Erikson and Maslow. Brehm's reactance theory (Wicklund, 1974), Lazarus's work on anxiety, Steiner's on the illusion of control, and Levinson's (1978) on "becoming one's own man" all stress the person's need for autonomy. It implies that persuasion campaigns should guard against the danger that compliance will be perceived as entailing a loss of personal freedom (e.g., that complying would mean giving up one's right to behave in a way that might start wildfires); rather, the campaign should communicate that complying would expand one's freedom (e.g., that prevention of wildfires would expand one's recreational options by preserving the forests).

Problem-solver theories. This sixth family of dynamic theories stresses the partial view of the person as a coper, oriented to solving problems in a way that maximizes his or her goal attainment, and as obtaining gratification from enhancing and exercising skills. The purposive theories of Lewin and Tolman represent creative use of this type of dynamic theorizing at midcentury, and currently it is represented by the various expectancy × values theories (Ajzen & Fishbein, 1980). The persuader can utilize this partial view of the person by consulting national norms on the public's values (e.g., Rokeach, 1973) and composing persuasive communications that show how the behavior being urged would realize the highly ranked values.

Stimulation theories. These theories depict the person as stimulus hungry, an exploratory seeker after novelty, play, and excitement, driven by curiosity to obtain varied experience. Both animal researchers such as Hebb, Kendler, Harlow, and Dember and human personality researchers such Zuckerman (1974), Berlyne, Bieri, and Maddi have stressed the person's need for excitement and stimulation. These curiosity theories suggest that unexpectedness and novelty should characterize the style and content of persuasive messages. More subtle two-factor versions of the theory (Berlyne, 1967) imply a non-monotonic, inverted-U relationship such that people would be most attracted to messages of intermediate novelty, unexpected enough to stretch their preexisting categories but not so novel as to evade them entirely. The communication should depict compliance as allowing exciting participation in the prevention campaign rather than as eliminating experience of the dangerous behavior.

Teleological theories. These theories depict the person as a pattern matcher who carries a representation of a preferred state, and manipulates the self and the environment in order to bring the situation as perceived into accord with this internal representation. Such theorizing was shunned as theological in the first half of this century but has gained popularity in recent decades because it can use imagery and metaphors derived from computer flowcharts or guided-missile homing devices (Powers, 1978). These theorists use concepts such as plans that structure behavior (Miller, Galanter, & Pribrum, 1960) or scripts that people impose on ambiguous situations to provide templates that guide their behavior. This theorizing suggests that the persuasive communication should provide a vivid image of the desired end state and an appropriate plan or script of a sequence of behaviors to that end, preferably a script already in people's cognitive repertory.

The Affective Stability Theories

The eight partial views of human nature just considered depict humans as motivated to attain one or another type of cognitive (thought) end state; the next eight depict the person as tending toward affective (feeling) end states, either toward affective stability (the four in the lower-left quadrant of Figure 2.2) or toward affective growth (the four in the lower-right).

Tension-reduction theories. This family of theories stresses the person as striving for a state of nirvana, so that any reduction of excitation level is rewarding, and the behavioristic postulate (Miller & Dollard,

1941) that drive reduction is the basic positive reinforcement. On persuasion topics like public health that are intrinsically arousing, the audience will try to reduce arousal by either coping with the problem or putting it out of mind (Lazarus & Monat, 1977; Leventhal, Meyer, & Nerenz, 1980). Persuasive communications should be designed to channel response into coping via prevention; for example, Smokey the Bear ads should communicate not the horror of forest fires, but their preventability.

Ego-defensive theories. These theories focus on the human tendency to maintain self-esteem through selective attention, distorted perception, fantasy, and so on, as in psychoanalytic ego-school theorizing about defense mechanisms. Applied to persuasion (Adorno, Frenkel-Brunswick, Levinson, & Sanford, 1950; Katz, 1960), the person's attitudes and actions toward some object are seen as deriving not from cognitions about that object, but from a need to maintain self-image. To persuade the ego-defensive arsonist, the communication should depict environment-preserving behavior as a sign of personal strength rather than of weakness.

Expressive theories. These conceptualizations stress the acting-out aspects of human personality, deriving gratification from physical exertion in strenuous sports, from risk taking, and from fantasy play. Such cathartic views of human motivation appear as early as Aristotle's theory that tragedy provides the spectator with relief through vicarious expression of pity and fear, a theory still proposed, although without much direct empirical support (Geen & Quanty, 1977), to justify televised violence as a fantasy outlet for aggression that might otherwise have been expressed in action. Campaigns against risky car driving or drug taking by teenage males should recognize that these activities may be attractive not in spite of their dangerousness but rather *because* of their dangerousness. Those persuading against dangerous behaviors should consider separately the seriousness and the probability of the negative outcome and the likelihood that moderate risk may have positive appeal. Also, arguments against risky activities should avoid seeming to limit active outlets and instead point out how compliance will actually expand outlets.

Repetition theories. These theories are most prominently associated with Freud, behaviorists, and some other biologically oriented theorists who argue that past performance of a response enhances a person's tendency to perform it again in the present, particularly if past performances were in similar situations and were rewarded (though a minor congruity-theory variant argues that repetition alone, even without reinforcement, suffices). Such theorizing by Hullians and Skinnerians dominated the 1940s and 1950s. Both basic researchers (Hovland, Janis, & Kelley, 1953; Sawyer, 1981; Staats, 1975) and advertising researchers (Stewart, 1964) have studied how repetition (at least for three to five repeats) can enhance the impact of public communication campaigns. Such theorizing also indicates the importance of presenting the persuasive message in a context that induces a positive mood in the audience, by choice of presentation circumstances, or by making the message intrinsically entertaining (Janis, Kaye, & Kirschner, 1965).

The Affective Growth Theories

The final tetrad of dynamic theories, shown in the lower-right quadrant of Figure 2.2, stress human needs for emotional growth, rather than for maintaining or reducing emotional level, as emphasized by the preceding four.

Assertion theories. These "hard hat" views of human nature, associated with social philosophers such as Hobbes and Nietzsche and popularized in current self-help books on assertiveness and power, stress egotistical, power-oriented aspects of the person as achievement-oriented, longing for success and eager to leave a mark on the world. They often posit an additional interpersonal need to attain superiority over and control of other people. McClelland (1975) and Weiner (1974) have summarized psychological work on assertion needs. This view suggests that persuasion appeals should describe how compliance with the recommended behavior would enhance personal achievement, attainment of power, status, and the like. Continuing the example of a fire prevention campaign, messages could show that a creative way of leaving one's mark and asserting oneself is to take actions that preserve rather than destroy the wilderness.

Identification theories. These formulations stress identity-accruing, role-playing drives in human nature, the need to create and expand identity by adopting distinctive thoughts, feelings, and actions, as advocated by role theorists such as Linton, Newcomb, and Sarbin, reference group theorists such as Hyman and Sherif, and self-presentation theorists such as Goffman. E. Erikson, in extending psychoanalytic developmental theory into adolescence, stressed the drive toward identity creation in teenage males, a demographic group contributing disproportionately to disturbing sociopathic behavior, at which public persuasion campaigns are often aimed. The campaigns

could turn these developmental trends to advantage by depicting youthful identity creation via prosocial rather than antisocial behavior.

Empathy theories. This family of theories concentrates on the human
need for affection, most primitively manifested in the drive to be close
to other humans physically (as in the gregarious need stressed by
Giddings and McDougal), which develop to include a need to be liked
(Berscheid & Walster, 1978). For instance, antismoking campaigns
aimed at teenagers might more effectively stress smoking's cosmetic
damage to teeth, skin, and breath than its life-threatening harm to heart,
lungs, and so on.

The need to be loved can evolve further into the need to love, as in
the altruism research by Berkowitz, Latane, and Darley, reviewed by
Staub (1979). Even when persuading the current "me" generation, the
efficacy of altruistic appeals should not be overlooked: Women may be
more willing and able to stop smoking in order to save their unborn
fetuses than to save themselves; men may be more willing to get
physical checkups to protect their families' economic well-being than
to protect their own health.

Contagion theories. These social facilitation (modeling, imitation,
social learning) theories stress the person's imitativeness, his or her
readiness to adopt the thoughts, share the feelings, and match the
behaviors of observed models. Earlier social facilitation theorists such
as Le Bon, Binet, and Charcot regarded this imitativeness as innate,
while recent modeling theorists describe how these matching
proclivities grow out of past reinforcement for imitating others (Bandura, 1977b; Gambrill, 1977; Hilgard, 1971; Miller & Dollard, 1941).
This aspect of the person suggests the "bandwagon" approach to persuasion—showing that other people are already complying—and suggests the importance of going beyond just advocating a behavior to
modeling exactly how it is performed.

Summary. Each of these sixteen families of theories has numerous
variants whose supporters argue with proponents of other variants in
the same or other families of theories, but these theories should be
recognized as supplementing one another rather than mutually exclusive. The person is in part a consistency maximizer, a meaning-
giver, a tension reducer, an ego-defender, and so on. Each need can
drive the person to action and each theory has creative potential in
suggesting persuasive appeals. The campaign designer should be ready
to make use of any one theory and then to switch to exploring others;
the creative trick is to love one's preferred theory wisely but not too well.

A Seven-Step Procedure for
Constructing Public Communication Campaigns

The theories of directive and dynamic aspects of human personality so far discussed provide guidance for designing public communication campaigns, suggesting both input options and criteria for choosing among these options. This final section summarizes a seven-step process that uses these theories to design public persuasion campaigns. Each of the seven steps is discussed here as regards what is to be achieved and what techniques are available for achieving it (see also McGuire, 1980, and other chapters in this volume).

 Review the Realities

This first step is to identify high-priority persuasive goals that meet three criteria: seriousness of the problem, effectiveness of the solution, and suitability of mass persuasion as a way of achieving the solution. To use public health campaigns as illustrations, a target problem such as vitamin deficiencies in the U.S. diet might fail to meet the first criterion in that such dietary problems are not widespread; a target such as urging people to avoid Alzheimer's disease might fail to meet the second criterion in that at present preventive measures are not known; a target such as getting heroin addicts to break their addictions might fail to meet the third criterion in that escaping heroin addiction is possible (if at all) only through one-on-one treatment and support systems that mass persuasion campaigns do not provide. Failure to meet one of these three criteria can usually be solved by simply modifying the goal rather than dropping the campaign—for instance, by converting the Alzheimer campaign from a prevention to a family-coping aim, or by altering the heroin campaign from providing treatment to informing addicts about where treatment can be found.

 Examine the Ethics

Public communication campaigns are designed to manipulate people to do something other than what they are initially inclined to do, an interference that raises moral issues however much the campaigner feels that the change would be for the public good. One should be hypersensitive to any initial moral uneasiness about goals or means of a campaign before one becomes heavily committed and can withdraw only at heavy cost to the campaign and oneself. When a moral problem arises it is usually possible to resolve it, especially when it is detected early, by modifying rather than abandoning the campaign. Ethical examination is here listed as an early step and discussed primarily in terms of campaign goals, but it should also be a continuing process and should focus on means to attain those ends as they develop. One must consider the intended and unintended effects of the campaign, both its proximate and distal impacts, in order to arrive at a cost-benefits judgment of the relative acceptability of alternate campaign goals.

Survey the Sociocultural Situation

This third step reveals situational circumstances that instigate and maintain the undesirable target behavior (teenagers' taking up smoking, drunken driving, or whatever) or that sustain the desired target behavior (donating blood, intergroup tolerance, or the like). One obtains such information by using anthropology and sociology procedures such as participant observation, open-ended interviews, questionnaire surveys, and interviews with informed observers to identify circumstances that initiate and maintain the target behaviors and the types of people and situations in which they are most likely to occur.

Map the Mental Matrix

In this fourth step one wears cognitive and personality psychologist hats, identifying the thoughts, feelings, and actions associated with the target behavior—for example, those that distinguish between parents who have their preschoolers immunized and those who do not. One can use clinical techniques (such as critical-incident analysis, free association, and projective techniques) or more structured mental mapping procedures to identify mental states of the person that channel behavior in the target area.

Tease Out the Target Themes

Here one uses the information gained from the third and fourth steps about the situational and personal variables affecting the target behavior to tease out the most promising themes to emphasize in the persuasion campaign, typically employing a least-effort criterion. For example, persuasion campaigns can more effectively supply information than change values; hence, if in a campaign to induce teenagers to adopt better dental hygiene practices the information collected in the third and fourth steps reveals both informational and value deficits (both ignorance of the immediate cosmetic dangers of dental neglect and awareness of, but indifference to, the remote health dangers), the campaign should economically be focused on the former deficit because it is easier to provide the information than correct the indifference. Quite often persuasion campaigns waste effort urging some value on the public when what is really needed is instruction on how to comply with the value (Leventhal et al., 1980); Smokey the Bear may spend too much time exhorting against starting forest fires to the neglect of providing more information about how to avoid starting them.

 Construct the Communications

This step involves using source, message, and channel inputs as outlined in Figure 2.1 to construct a communication that will evoke the dozen Figure 2.1 output steps to induce the campaign's target behavior, a task that falls most obviously within the special competence of the social-influence communication professional, and so we have concentrated on this sixth step in the other sections in this chapter. While this is the one most important step, campaign planners should not continue the common neglect of the other six steps when designing a campaign.

 Evaluate the Effectiveness

Any undertaking as important and expensive as a public persuasion campaign should have evaluations built into it. I list this step last because there should be postcampaign evaluations to measure immediate and delayed impacts (see Flay & Cook, chap. 8, and Rice & Foote, chap. 7, this volume). However, additional evaluations should be built into the campaign from the outset as ongoing tests of one's decisions in each of the preceding six steps to obtain feedback for improving one's choices. Some ongoing tests will be informal, as when in the second step one checks one's own ethical evaluations of the means and ends of the campaign by asking for outside opinions by moralists who can take a perspective different from one's own or by an ethics committee set up inside or outside one's institutions to provide such guidance. Other tests involve cross-checking the agreement among the yields of alternative procedures, as in the fourth step, where one uses several different methods to map the mental matrix. Formal tests (such as copy testing) will also be used, as in the sixth step, to determine how one or another of the twelve output steps are affected by variants of the inputs.

Conclusion

This chapter is intended neither to praise nor to bury theories but to urge their creative use. Any one theory views the phenomenon from only one perspective, but does provide a selective insight that can provide needed direction and confidence. The person beginning to design a public communication campaign is like a person lost somewhere in a dense forest of possibilities. He or she can find a way out by following old scout training to keep calm and keep moving in one direction, and sooner or later will reach the clearing; the only real dangers are freezing in place or losing all sense of direction and wandering around in circles. Even when the chosen theory is not optimal for the situation (in that an alternative direction would have led us out more easily), it suffices to lead us out to terra cognita with deliberate speed.

3

Audience as Listener and Learner, Teacher and Confidante: The Sense-Making Approach

BRENDA DERVIN

The most widely accepted rationale for the idea of public communication campaigns is embedded in a social engineering philosophy.
It assumes that social engineers have noble purposes: the prevention of
individual and collective disasters; the protection of the citizenry, their
abodes and environment; and the preservation of democracy. These
purposes translate into responsibilities to the public that require that
institutions designated as "protectors" use communication campaigns
to educate, inform, and entice members of the public concerning the
acceptance and execution of these responsibilities (see Paisley, chap. 1,
this volume).

Working within the framework of this rationale, researchers and
campaign planners can point to a number of successes, as some of the
chapters in this volume illustrate. However, practitioners and academ-
ics alike acknowledge that public communication campaigns are effective only at great cost and within very definite constraints.

Author's Note: I am grateful to the following individuals whose writings strongly inform
this chapter: Carter, for his rich conceptual developments; Rakow, for one of the first
extensive critical assessments of the idea of campaigns; Murdock, for a critical assessment of the idea of audience; Freire and Habermas, both of whom move us toward the
idea of communication-based democratic structures; Slack, whose history of the concept
of communication need assists in breaking us out of the transmission mentality; and
Sandman and colleagues, whose applications to risk communication practice begin to
provide us with a model of communication planning based on dialogue principles. I also
owe thanks to Kathleen Clark, Frank Nevius, and Vickie Shields, graduate students at the
Ohio State University Department of Communication, who assisted with literature review
and bibliography development. A longer version of this chapter with extended notes and
references is available from the author.

When all is said and done, the effectiveness of most campaigns is far less accounted for by campaign design than by the brute force of the public's experiences, direct or vicarious. Somehow, and usually quite independent of any campaign planner's efforts, members of the public become cognitively involved with the subject that a public communication campaign addresses.[1]

Sometimes these experiences are direct—six cars pile up on the way to work and only people wearing seat belts survive; a daughter comes home after her health education class and begs her father to stop smoking. Sometimes these experiences are vicarious but made real by repeated personalized involvements with media personalities—Betty Ford faces her problem with drugs; Nancy Reagan is diagnosed as having breast cancer after a routine examination. Occasionally the magnitude of a crisis is sufficiently large that media coverage allows more members of the audience than usual to connect in their minds with groups of strangers—the blacks of South Africa, or the citizens of earthquaked Mexico. Through these experiences, individual members of the amorphous public potentially act in new ways: A mother insists that her children buckle up; a father tries to stop smoking.

At least two factors operate here. The first factor is that whatever the action the campaign calls for, campaign messages will be attended to only if the dangers and/or benefits associated with those actions have taken on some kind of personal reality or usefulness for the individual. The individual must choose to attend to and ascribe reality and significance to the message. The second factor is that at whatever point this happens, a connection between the individual and the campaign will be made only if campaign messages are around to be attended to or have in some way become part of the individual's stored understandings of the world.

When one examines the set of strategies that have become commonplace in the design of public communication campaigns, one finds an acknowledgment of these factors. Two universally accepted campaign strategies are these: Find ways to make the campaign's prescribed actions real to the individual, and buy as much redundancy as you can afford. Three corollary strategies also exist: Reach the captive-audience young through the school system (so that the young, in turn, will carry the message home), get the media gatekeepers on the campaign's side to get the boost of media hype, and incorporate networking and community-based programs as part of a campaign.

Even when reality, actual or vicarious, is entirely cooperative, any given campaign measures its success in small degrees of change. Further, some campaign goals seem unachievable beyond a certain point. At best, it is agreed, the business of launching public communication campaigns is difficult, chancy, and costly. The question raised here is this: Is this the limit—the best we can do? The answer this chapter presents is no. But going beyond this limit requires a fundamental reconceptualization of both the *nature of audiences* and the *nature of campaigns.*

Audiencing and Being Audienced

The conventional concept of public communication campaigns is based on a very stable set of assumptions about the nature of audiences and the nature of campaign messages. Campaign messages are assumed to be truths, usually discovered by scientific research, that must be diffused to the populace. Because many issues demand attention in society, campaign messages must compete in the marketplace of ideas. Audiences are conceptualized as people to whom these truths must be transmitted—audiences, like messages, are treated as commodities. Since audiences are known to be evasive at best and recalcitrant at worst, every effort is made to communicate artfully and well. While communication is conceptualized as a one-way flow, efforts are directed at targeting messages for different audience segments and promoting audience involvement wherever possible.

In this scenario, the populace is *audienced*—they are objectified by the campaign planners, who define the relationship as follows: me, source; you, audience. In the context of recent advances in communication scholarship, we can identify several related difficulties with this conceptualization. These will be examined below in terms of both the inappropriateness of the models on which the conceptualization is based and the impact of the conceptualization on our thinking about audiences, the practice of communicating, and the constitution of society.

Models of Information

The model of *information* that provides the foundation for public communication campaigns assumes that information has truth value, that it is objective, and that when one acts on information the resulting actions must lead to better ends. Many theoretical and ideological arguments currently circulate in the communication field about the construct information.[2] The most fundamental of these arguments has to do with the nature of the reality described by information. Stated in polarized extremes, one view says the world is "out there" to be described and the problem is human inability to observe accurately; the other says no world exists outside the human act of creation.

For the purposes of this chapter, both views are accepted. First, it is assumed that a world out there exists apart from the human act of creation. For example, a geological formation that we humans have put into a class of objects we call mountains and have given a specific name—"Mt. St. Helens"—did erupt at a time we have agreed to call May 1980, spewing forth a great deal of a substance we call volcanic dust on a place we call western Washington State.

However, it is assumed that in actuality only a small portion of human existence involves this kind of "natural" event, that "natural events" are in part discontinuous, that most of human reality exists in acts of human creation, and that all "observations" of "reality" are human creations. Further, it is assumed that the observations that human beings create of "reality" are both constrained and illusive. Constrained because they are limited to a particular time and space and to whatever capacities humans have for observing generally and a particular human has for observing specifically. Illusive because, given that no direct, immutable observation exists, all "observations" are created by some unknown combination of the human ability to observe what is out there and the inherent, ever-present reality-creating powers of the species.

This means that whatever one group of individuals calls "information" or "knowledge" at any given point in time is applicable only to that time and space and to the self-interests and observing capacities of the "observers." Untangling which factors account for the "observation" is impossible, and even when observation is prescribed by a set of rules (as in scientific observation), most scholars agree that even the most "brute" of those observations—the so-called empirical facts—are subject to the same limitations.

In this context, what decides whose "observations" get preference when observations disagree? Power decides. Certain "knowledges"— the knowledges created by those in power—get preferential status. Other knowledges are "subjugated," reduced in availability to "alternative" outlets or diminished by lack of media space or resources.[3] History provides us with numerous examples of the difficulty that innovative views and the views of the oppressed have in finding a place. Recent emphases in social science scholarship document how knowledges are tied to power structures and how knowledges serve to reify and maintain those structures.

These points are important in understanding the need for a change in how we conceptualize audiences and campaigns. To illustrate, let us take one campaign directive—one that is so emotionally charged that it will serve our purposes well: *Women should have breast cancer check-ups.* From the perspective of the conventional Western medical system (allopathic medicine), this statement is a conclusion based on a series of assumed facts: Women get a disease that is called breast cancer, the rate of this disease goes up as women get older, early detection means early treatment, early treatment means longer life.

Yet, a number of competing perspectives exist. Some come from alternative or "countercultural" institutions, such as practitioners of naturally oriented medical approaches who challenge the very defini-tion of cancer as disease and the value of allopathic treatment, or environmentally and/or feminist-oriented groups who see the demand that women have breast cancer checkups as focusing the problem in the wrong place—on women instead of on corporations who pollute food and environment with harmful chemicals. The challenges also come from individuals based on their experiences, such as women who refuse to submit themselves to what they see as the emotionally demeaning and/or physically devastating medical regimes endured by their friends while undergoing allopathic diagnosis and/or treatment.[4]

The arenas of breast cancer and women's health serve as particularly good examples for looking at models of information because, despite the very factual tone of communication campaigns, there is evidence of informational "contests" on many fronts. Popular women's magazines often feature first-person stories of how women disagree with the ways in which they are objectified and defined by medicine. Well publicized is how many nonessential surgeries are recommended for women "for the good of their health" by male doctors. Many women experience an a priori climate of mistrust between themselves and the medical estab-lishment. Many aspects of alternative medical treatments for prevent-ing cancer rejected as recently as 15-20 years ago now are being supported by allopathic medical research. And the way in which con-ventional medicine treats breast cancer has itself changed, making what was "fact" as recently as the 1970s (e.g., that women with breast cancer required radical mastectomies) no longer "fact" in the 1980s.

The above serves to portray the arena of "breast cancer treatment" as one charged with informational contests. Within this arena, those in the allopathic medical establishment have a preponderance of power to name and define the reality that gets prime attention and space. In such a contest, most people's reality is defined within the dominant frame. But some do contest, and those who do so must try to make space for their viewpoints, working against the overwhelming access to resources, time, and space given the dominant pictures.

The irony is that, from a communication standpoint, this power to create dominant pictures of reality has its limits. This power can produce the accepted definings and orderings of reality. It can try to demand that women have breast cancer checkups. It can severely restrain the individual's capacity to create or have access to alternative orderings. But such power *cannot* make women attend to messages or force them to the doctor's office. And, once women are at the doctor's office, such power cannot command compliance.[5]

While the informational arenas of some campaigns are not as contested as in the example provided above, all are in some way contested. It is because of this pervasive contesting that this chapter assumes that an *information-as-construction* model is more appropriate in communication situations than an *information-as-description* model. The information-as-description model assumes that information has truth value, has a known, testable descriptive relationship with reality, and can be separated from observers. The information-as-construction model assumes that information is created by human observers, is inherently a product of human self-interest, and can never be separated from the observers who created it.

From a communication standpoint, the information-as-description model implies a transmission model of the communicative relationship. A source, assumed to be privy to specialized observations, is charged with the responsibility of transmitting that information to people who need it. The receiver is pictured as an empty bucket into which these informational gems may be deposited.

No matter which way one looks at the difficulties of this model, the conclusion is that it is inappropriate communicatively. The inherent discontinuities of reality, the marked differences in human experience, and the variable ways humans deal with discontinuity mean that informational descriptions of reality are inherently contestable.[6] Communication cannot be conceptualized as *transmission*. Rather, it must be conceptualized in terms of both parties involved in creating meanings, by means of *dialogue*. The sense people make of the media messages is never limited to what sources intend and is always enriched by the realities people bring to bear.

Deleterious Consequences

It is important to review some of the consequences of using the information-as-description and communication-as-transmission models because they provide a context within which to place our understandings of the limitations of the current perspectives used in communication campaigns and to define the possible goals for an alternative conceptualization.

CONSEQUENCES FOR THINKING ABOUT AUDIENCES

The most obvious impact of these models is casting the audience as "bad guys" who are hard to reach, obstinate, and recalcitrant. Audience members get most of their information from friends and neighbors even though expert advice is available. They like entertainment more than information. They watch too much television. Some subsegments of the population are simply unreachable. These conceptions about audiences are pervasive in society. The context of communication campaigns merely crystallizes the use of these conceptions as explanation for the failure of messages to reach targeted audiences. Yet, the application of the alternative information-as-construction and communication-as-dialogue models directs us to ask if it is our systems and messages that are inaccessible and irrelevant.

CONSEQUENCES FOR THE PRACTICE OF COMMUNICATING

Our conceptions of the audience lead directly to our conceptions of how we involve ourselves in communicating. The impacts can be seen in every realm of communicative activity.

When *interpersonal communication* occurs in professional contexts, the interaction between professionals (e.g., librarians) and lay persons (e.g., library users) is oriented toward categorizing lay persons in system terms. Patrons are asked in the library "reference" interview to describe needs, not on their own terms, but in terms of how they fit within a series of dichotomous cuts of the collection: Do you want a or b? If a, do you want a1 or a2?[7] In *small group* and *organizational* settings, a common set of procedures applied to group processes is parliamentary procedure. By focusing discussion on the presentation of motions and arguments for and against motions, the procedures constrain discourse that focuses on getting unconfused, exploring, and brainstorming. Further, use of these procedures both inhibits contributions by those not seasoned in their use and facilitates manipulative control by those who are practiced.[8]

In *mass communication* settings, news programs rely heavily on the use of the single authoritative voice, spot news, and personality journalism. Each of these communicating strategies assumes that "information" can be "observed" by any single trained observer and moved from place to place without damage. In the context of such a view, the "personality" of the deliverer becomes one of the few remaining marketable commodities.[9] In *community participation* programs, community input is relegated to reacting rather than acting. Even when citizen participation is mandated, frequently citizens are involved only at the very end of decision-making processes.[10] In *international* arenas, non-Western journalists call for attention to communication issues such as whether Third World countries get a chance to describe themselves on their own terms in the media.[11]

"Audience" research conducted in all these communication settings is both a product and a reification of the communication-as-transmission model. The typical audience research project defines as respondents all members of the "targeted audience," with little regard for how these targeted individuals define themselves. Respondents are typically asked to respond to predefined options. Does the respondent believe a or b or c?

A conception of communication-as-dialogue requires an open-endedness in the institution's approach to the audience. At a minimum, the institution and the audience should be conceptualized as equal partners. More fundamentally, the institution—particularly when mandated as an institution that serves the public—should be conceptualized as responsive to that public (see Dervin & Clark, 1987; Dervin & Nilan, 1986; Rakow, 1989). The public would then become empowered with voice, and communication strategies would constitute a repertoire.[12]

CONSEQUENCES FOR THE NATURE OF SOCIETY

The difficulties outlined above lead to larger negative consequences for society. Some scholars suggest that the communication-as-transmission model creates a communication context within which the rich get communicatively richer while the poor get communicatively poorer.[13] Further evidence suggests that as various new communication technologies are introduced, the gaps between the managed and the managers grow larger and those who wish to move in the communication "fast lane" have to sacrifice their uniqueness and cultural diversity to do so.

To assume that the "information poor" are only society's least educated peoples would be a mistake. One excellent instance of well-educated people remaining information poor is the case of the large data-base system designed to speed the process by which the findings of social science research are introduced into the practice of teaching in the nation's classrooms. In actuality, the nation's teachers rarely use the system. Filled with "information" from researchers, the data base is most used *by* researchers.[14]

The difficulty may be conceptualized generally as our communication systems reifying and legitimizing only one set of "knowledges" about the nature of reality. This robs society in several senses. Institutions mandated to serve the public often fail. The professionals who work for those institutions burn out. Society is denied the process of bringing different understandings together, comparing, deliberating, negotiating, and constructing a shared reality. Those left out of the process are isolated from the messages of our systems and, more important, do not contribute to the construction of those messages.[15]

More subtle is the impact on our collective understandings of "reality." A fuller comprehension can be realized only by the sharing and confronting of many perspectives, differing in small ways and in large, contestable, unresolvable ways. By comparing and trying to understand why and how perspectives differ, humans anchor themselves in an informed sense of their own time-place and become able to take individual and collective actions.

Without this kind of sense, a woman cannot decide to have a breast cancer screening, or choose a mode of treatment should she be diagnosed as having cancer. Nor can she accept with any degree of equanimity the consequences if a mode of treatment is imposed on her by others. From such points of non-sense, evidence emerges about how seldom patients follow doctors' orders, or how often they are angry after having done so because their actions have not arisen from an informed personal sense, but rather from submission to professional directive.

Audience Research as Dialogue

The remainder of this chapter uses audience research as an exemplar of the utility of adopting a communication-as-dialogue approach.

Several points need to be made before proceeding. The problem is not only to conceptualize communication-as-dialogue, but also to practice it as dialogue.[16] One major reason that we have not developed a dialogue-based communication practice is that until very recently demands to do so were not compelling, and even when humans have attempted and achieved communication-as-dialogue, they have not built up a systematic practice. Second, adopting a communication-as-dialogue approach to audience research yields a fundamental change in the conception of the audience and the campaign. In one sense neither term is any longer applicable. The terms will be retained in this chapter with the assumption that the "audience" involved is both the public and the institution, both willingly audienced and audiencing, and that the campaign involved is one consented to and dealt with in shared and interactive consent.[17]

Finally, the findings from research based on the communication-as-dialogue approach inherently mandate responsive system design—that is, that the perspectives of those defined as "respondents" will be not only heard but acted upon. Further, appropriate "audiences" in campaign designs based on dialogue principles will involve not only the public but the planner and other institutional actors as well.

The Purpose of Sense-Making:
A New Way of Listening

Audience research, conceptualized within the framework of a communication-as-dialogue perspective, is a new way of listening to the public. In recent years, communication scholars from a wide variety of perspectives have called for new approaches to audience research.[18] While these scholars differ on important details, all agree that the new approach ought to focus on finding effective ways to hear how members of the audience make sense of their everyday lives and how their personal actions are linked to both the messages they attend to and the social structures they live in.

For the purposes of this chapter, one particular approach is used as an exemplar—the sense-making approach. Developed through a programmatic series of studies since 1972,[19] the approach is simultaneously *ethnographic* because it allows respondents to define and anchor themselves in their own realities, *qualitative* because it is built on open-ended interviewing and reports findings primarily in qualitative terms, *quantitative* because procedures for quantitative analysis have been developed, and *systematic* because a general theory guides the approach to listening—a theory that is applicable to all situations but allows specificity in any situation.

The term *sense-making* is used both to designate the approach (called the sense-making approach) and the focus of the approach (how people make sense of their worlds). Sense-making as an approach is primarily a methodology, providing a conceptual framework within which to specify what aspects of situations ought to be attended to and how. Sense-making attempts to provide a systematic approach to listening to the audience—how they see their situations, past, present, and future—and how they move to construct sense and make meaning of these situations.

Sense-making rests on the discontinuity premise.[20] It assumes that, given discontinuities in natural reality and in human observations of reality, the useful research focus is how humans make sense of discontinuity. The core construct of sense-making is the idea of the gap—how people define and bridge gaps in their everyday lives. Discontinuities (gaps) are faced everywhere—when attending to messages, when relating to others, when attempting to pursue tasks or reach goals, even when attempting to stand still. Gaps are always cognitive (i.e., constructed in the head) and sometimes are overbearingly physical as well (i.e., coping with illness).

The sense-making methodology is built on the metaphor pictured in Figure 3.1. The human moves cognitively through time-space using whatever sense he or she has already constructed based on personal as well as vicarious experiences. Given that life is inherently discontinuous, sense frequently runs out. A gap is identified. The human must build a bridge across the gap. In doing so, the human will answer questions, create ideas, and/or obtain resources. The situation that leads to the gap, the gap itself, the bridge, and even what the human does after crossing the bridge, are all best understood as constructions.

In all sense-making methods, the listener (i.e., the researcher) is mandated to listen to the respondent tell of how he or she moved through time-space. In particular, for each step of the journey, the researcher is mandated to attend to what is called the *sense-making triangle*: how the *respondent* sees the situation, what gaps the respondent sees self as facing and/or bridging, and what ways the respondent saw self as helped by the bridge he or she built.

The core method of sense-making is the time-line interview. The researcher asks the respondent to recollect what happened in a situation as a series of steps—what happened first, second, and so on. This does not impose a linear time order on the respondent's recollection—the

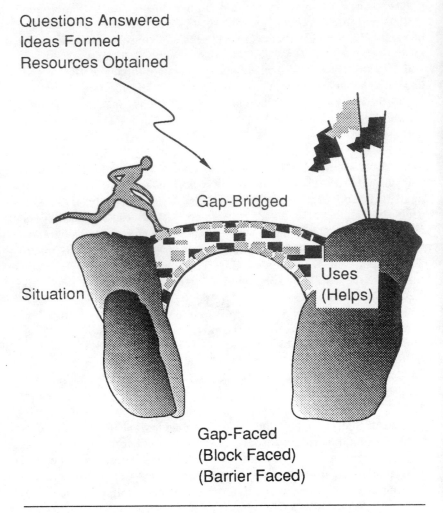

Questions Answered
Ideas Formed
Resources Obtained

Gap-Bridged

Uses
(Helps)

Situation

Gap-Faced
(Block Faced)
(Barrier Faced)

Figure 3.1. Metaphorical Portrayal of the Sense-Making Approach

respondent may recollect things in whatever order is relevant to him or
her at the telling. Further, the time frame may be extended to include
historical moments as well as anticipated future moments. Finally, for
each step in the time-line, the researcher explores with the respondent
how the respondent saw and defined that situation, its gaps, its gap-

bridging, its helps, and so on. Sense-making also incorporates a number of alternative methods, all derived from the core time-line interview. Some are encapsulated and abbreviated versions of the time-line. Others zero in on particular aspects of the gap or the gap-bridging.

Sense-making has been used to address a variety of questions potentially useful to those planning public communication efforts, including the following: What ideas or images have people created about a particular topic, institution, or program? How useful have people found the efforts of a particular institution? What sense-making needs do people have that if bridged would allow them to inform themselves more usefully in a particular arena? What barriers do people see as standing between them and their efforts to make sense?

An important aspect of sense-making methods is that they are all situated in real moments in time-space. Sense-making posits no hypothetical questions to respondents, nor does it present elaborate lists of options as defined by institutions to which respondents must reply. While sense-making occasionally uses closed-ended interviewing approaches, these uses are all defined within the framework of understanding how respondents see themselves stopped in their movement through time-space and with how they make sense of discontinuity.

Example Studies and
Their Implications for Action

Since 1972, some 40 studies have used the sense-making approach.[21] They have focused on a wide variety of topics, including cancer communication, family planning, public opinion, library use, media use, blood donating, coping with a toxic waste site, and coping with university life. They have involved a wide variety of "publics": general population adults, minorities, teenagers, children, patients, students, peasant women, recent refugees. They have been conducted in a number of countries.

Many of the studies have focused on general methodological issues in the continuing attempt to develop and perfect systematic ways of listening to people on their own terms. The result has been the development of a set of listening methods for conducting audience research as well as for conducting in-person one-on-one interviews with people (e.g., patients, patrons, clients) who have come to professionals with needs.[22]

General Conclusions
from Sense-Making Studies to Date

The sense-making studies to date have provided confirmation for many of the general assumptions that led to the creation of the sense-making approach. The research has shown that people inform themselves primarily at moments of need. Given needs, people rely first on their own cognitive resources. If these are not sufficient, they reach out first to sources closest to them or those contacted on their habit paths. When they find useful information, they judge it not on its expertise or credibility, but rather in terms of how it helped them. They find it useful because they can put it to use. Only when it does not help do they focus on credibility and expertise of a source or message as explanations of why what was offered did not help.

People seem inherently interested in contested views. They deal with competing information claims well when these claims are anchored and explained in terms of what it is about the observers and/or time-places of the observings that made a difference. In study after study, people have indicated that they want to learn about motives and reasons and the causes of events. These "why" questions have been asked frequently, ranked as important, and judged as least addressed by information systems.

Results have also suggested that people treat the use of information (and of information and communication systems) as means to ends and not ends in themselves. Their seeking and use of information is best predicted based on how they see their situations, the constraints they face, the gaps they need to bridge, and the kind of bridges they would like to build across their gaps. Except for those information-seeking and -using behaviors such as habitual channel use, most information-seeking and -using behaviors are not predicted well based on across time-space attributes of people such as personality and demographic characteristics.

The following sections briefly describe three sense-making projects selected because they illustrate different conceptual conclusions pertaining to the use of a communication-as-dialogue approach to audience research.

Goal: A Library Wants More Hispanic Patrons

A public library with a large number of Hispanic citizens on its mandated patron roster searched for ways to entice the Hispanics into the library (see Dervin & Clark, 1987, pp. 211-230; Dervin & Nilan, 1986). Previously, a number of study approaches were tried and met with hostility. The traditional methods of publicity had failed. The sense-making research project focused on users of the library's audiovisual services and serendipitously provided a breakthrough for serving the Hispanic community. One study asked 30 randomly selected recent users what happened that brought them to the library, what they got while there, and how they were helped. A second study asked 64 randomly selected borrowers of library videotapes how the specific videotapes helped them.

The librarians reported that for the first time they had conducted interviews with Hispanic patrons and were not met with hostility. They learned that their videotape checkout service was providing these patrons with enormous numbers of important helps. Further, the videotapes were an important link for these patrons with other library services—literacy training, juvenile books, and how-to books, for example. One librarian summed it up: "It helped us see patrons from a different point of view, to understand them better, and to be better able to tolerate the crowds around the audio-visual desk." The library staff voted to move funds from other services to video services.

Goal: A Blood Center Wants Donors to Donate Again

A city blood center commissioned research because staff were convinced that they lost some donors because the donors left unhappy or confused about the donating experience (see Dervin, Jacobson, & Nilan, 1982; Dervin, Nilan, & Jacobson, 1981). A recent study had specifically suggested that they lost some repeat donors because the potential donors were not aware of eligibility requirements for repeat donating.

One study involved in-depth time-line interviews asking "what happened during your most recent donating experience" of 80 randomly selected frequent and new donors. For each event respondents reported as happening, they were asked what gaps they faced, what questions they had, whether they got answers to their questions, and how they were helped or hindered. Results showed that while demography did not predict donor information needs and seeking, where respondents were in the process did. Each step in the donating time-line was associated with its own characteristic set of questions. Eligibility questions, for example, were more likely to be in donors' minds when they checked in to donate, whereas blood center personnel had been trying to convey eligibility information when donors were recovering and leaving.

A second study compared 105 new, dropout, and frequent female blood donors in terms of their recollections of what facilitated and what stood in the way of donating. Results showed that the primary difference between dropout and frequent female donors was the ease of access to donating.

The two studies provided directions for communication planning. They showed that a public communication campaign to convince women to repeat their donating would be ineffective. Attention was redirected to improving access. Second, a plan was established to provide a user-friendly computerized question-answering system at five different points during the donating process. Typical questions at each point were to be displayed on the screen of a terminal. Donors would simply touch the question of interest to them. Answers would be available from a variety of sources—center personnel as well as other donors.

Goal: A Cancer Clinic Staff
Wants to Handle Anxious Patients Better

A cancer detection and treatment clinic staff felt that patient confusions and resentments were contributing as much to the daily stress of their jobs as the seriousness of cancer as a disease.[23] A sense-making study of 30 randomly selected patients asked them to detail the events of their contacts with the clinic, the ways in which they felt impeded, the types of confusions they had, and the ways in which they wanted to be helped as well as the ways in which they were actually helped.

Results showed that patients wanted more chances to explore and discuss their confusions and concerns with others who were sympathetic; they wanted acknowledgment of the contested nature of the information circulating about cancer and its treatment; they wanted help getting more information, particularly from other cancer patients; they wanted social support; and they wanted staff to see them as human beings and not walking tumors.

Clinic staff responded by designing group support sessions for patients in which concerns were openly discussed and disagreements openly admitted. They also instituted a "mass communications" wall of information sheets, each of which addressed a common patient question. "Answers" to the questions implemented the idea of contested information. Answers were provided by different doctors and nurses and by patients. Each answerer was asked to interpret what he or she thought accounted for how his or her answers differed from that of the others. In addition, clinic intake personnel began using sense-making approaches when they talked with patients. Questions asked were those defined in the sense-making metaphor (see Figure 3.1): What brings you here today? What confusions or problems are you facing? How do you hope we can help you today?

Sense-making interviews were also conducted with clinic staff—nurses, technicians, and doctors. Results indicated that staff needed their own support groups and needed to connect with their patients outside their "cancerness." They also indicated that staff needed a more rational way of handling the inherently contestable nature of the medical services they were providing. These results led to regular staff support groups and to staff volunteering to rotate their own attendance at patient support groups in order to be able to see patients as people. In addition, staff decided to take whatever steps were needed to empower each patient or each patient's family to make their own decisions.

Results of these actions to date have been favorable. Staff report, for example, feeling more hopeful about their relationships with patients and their capacities to be genuinely helpful. They also report a significant reduction in clinic stress levels and greatly reduced time spent with upset patients.

Conclusion

In each of these examples the audience is no longer conceptualized as an amorphous mass. Rather than being portrayed as a sample of people of whom x% agreed with this and y% wanted that, the respondents become situated in real circumstances for which the logic of what the respondents have to say is validated by and anchored in that experience.

Each of the three example studies provides results that inform the institution about the experiential realities of the respondents. In each case, institutional representatives learned something they did not know, and even had their expectations changed. The librarians had thought they had had few successes with Hispanic patrons; they identified an open door of acceptance. The blood center staff was planning to spend money advertising for woman donors by emphasizing eligibility requirements; they learned they had to emphasize access and provide actual means of access. The cancer clinic staff felt they had to protect patients from the uncertainties of cancer treatment information; yet most of the patients wanted the full picture no matter how uncertain.

In each case, too, results of these studies provided professionals with explicit avenues for possible negotiated interactions. The librarians, for example, transferred more funds to their video collection and at the same time planned activities to tie the video collection to the book collection and literacy services. They also found a potential hunger for public service advertisements to the community. At the same time, they gained respect for an aspect of their own service that previously they had undervalued.

The same kind of give-and-take potential is illustrated in the blood center and cancer clinic data. Blood donors indicated, for example, that there was a lot they wanted to learn about donating, but only when the learning was pertinent for them. The staff began to think about the use of a flexible computerized question-answering system. Cancer clinic staff reported that once patients understood that their questions would be taken seriously, they became remarkably more willing to consider alternative points of view.

One parsimonious way to think of these studies is to suggest that each told the institution how it could change *itself* rather than how it could change the audience. In doing so, the results laid out for the institution explicit possibilities for dialogue.

Also of importance is the fact that the results focused on what "audience" members need rather than on "campaigns" and possible "message" elements. Because of this the results lend themselves to a number of different avenues of communication design. Mass communication is not artificially separated from interpersonal communication; communication is not artificially separated from action; the "campaign" is not artificially removed from its consequences. The librarians, for example, uncovered keys for both program design and public service advertising messages; cancer clinic staff ended up creating their own mass communication messages (information sheets answering typical questions) as well as changing how they greeted patients; blood center staff planned ways to increase access for women donors and to use a computerized information system to allow donors access to information at the moment of need.

Of particular importance is the way in which these studies provide findings that directly informed communication practice. By focusing on real situations in which members of the audience are relating to real experiential circumstances, the point of focus moves from people, conceptualized as static entities, to circumstances and to actions that can be taken with people in those circumstances. While past sense-making studies have confirmed the greater predictive power of situational conceptions, the important utility of the situational approach is in practice. In essence, findings from these studies provide practitioners with some insights about how to be both *efficient* and *effective* in their communicating efforts.

Traditionally, communication efficiency and effectiveness have been conceptualized as opposing trade-offs. Efficiency requires members of the audience to be treated amorphously and to bend to the institution. Effectiveness requires that individuals be helped on their own terms. Traditional communication approaches have argued that the only way to communicate systematically is to ignore individuality. In contrast, these sense-making studies suggest that individuality has been conceptualized inappropriately. In sense-making, individuality based on across time space characterizations of people is replaced with a concept of individuality based on situatedness.

A public communication campaign conceived within a communication-as-dialogue perspective is, by definition, a campaign pointing in at least two directions: one to the public, the other to the institution. The communication dilemma for the institution is that if it expects its communicative efforts to be used and useful, it must treat communication as dialogue and it must find ways to empower publics. Recent testimony from the arena of the practice of risk communication confirms the point again and again. Even in this highly technologized arena, people are willing to involve themselves, to listen, to be reasonable, and to act, but only if empowered and heard.

Institutions in our society have a long tradition of top-down, information-as description, and communication-as-transmission practices. Habits are hard to break, but developing new ways of listening is of prime importance. The research approaches exemplified in this chapter illustrate that alternatives are possible.

Notes

1. Dewey emphasized the point as early as 1938. Dupuy (1980) made a recent strong restatement.

2. The conceptualization of information and communication rests heavily on Carter's (1974, 1980) explication of the discontinuity condition, as well as on Foucault (1980), Freire (1983), and Habermas (1984).

3. The term is Foucault's (1980). See also Wallack (chap. 16, this volume).

4. For examples of feminist versions of information contests, see Ehrenreich and English (1979) and Ferguson (1984). The stories reported here come from interviews with women patients of naturally oriented clinics in Seattle.

5. Patient "compliance" rates may be only 50% (Dervin & Harlock, 1976; Ley, 1982).

6. Giddens (1989) emphasizes the point that there is something inherently contestable about being human and that social scientists must incorporate this in both their theorizings and their observings.

7. See, for the medical context, Pendleton (1985), and for the library context, Dervin and Dewdney (1986).

8. For discussion of the constraining and defining impacts of communicating procedures in group and organizational contexts, see Conrad (1985) and Putnam (1982).

9. Many authors discuss the potentially inhibiting and biasing impacts on society of prevalent journalist news practices (Bennett & Edelman, 1985; Gitlin, 1980; Tuchman, 1978).

10. The arena within which citizen participation is receiving its sternest test and greatest challenge is risk communication (such as the siting of toxic waste dumps) (Sandman, 1987; Sandman, Weinstein, & Klotz, 1987).

11. For a review of the controversy regarding the UNESCO mass media declaration, see *Journal of Communication*, Vol. 34, No. 4.

12. *Repertoire* in this context means a set of alternative communicating behaviors arranged in some kind of coherent, theoretically organized pattern that allows for choice based on understanding of need and expectation.

13. See Gandy (1987) and Rice (1980); for related references, contact the author.

14. DeMartini and Whitbeck (1986) and Ward and Reed (1983) discuss the underutilization of the social science literature by public school teachers.

15. Baudrillard (1983) makes this point.

16. This chapter rests heavily on Carter's (1982) conceptualization of communicating behaviors as the tools by which members of collectivities may arrive at shared ideas, and the need to develop new tools continually.

17. In no sense does this chapter mean to suggest that communication-as-dialogue processes alone will solve the problem of the gaps between institutions and people; appropriate communication models are necessary but not sufficient (see Dervin, 1980).

18. The call for the development of approaches to studying human behavior that are dependent on contests and full of individualized meanings are not new. See, for instance, Dworkin (1986), Jensen (1987), Liebes (1988), Murdock (1989), and Rakow (1989).

19. See the Reference section of this volume for works by Atwood, Dewdney, Dervin, Dworkin, Grunig, and Nilan.

20. The sense-making use of this premise rests heavily on the work of Carter (1974, 1980) and Carter, Ruggels, Jackson, and Heffner (1972).

21. A comprehensive overview (Dervin, 1983) may be obtained from the author.

22. A technique for interacting with clients, patients, users, and patrons called "neutral questioning" is based on sense-making assumptions and is termed "neutral" only in the sense that it allows the "listener" to ask only sense-making questions (about moving and facing discontinuous situations, and not about content in the usual sense of the word). Closed-ended or dichotomous queries are not permitted (see Dervin & Dewdney, 1986; Dewdney, 1986).

23. This reimbursed project is unpublished by agreement with clinic staff. The purpose of the study was to make full use of an offered and tough setting for the application of sense-making principles. See, however, Dervin, Harlock, Atwood, and Garzona (1980).

24. The unpublished results are available from the author.

4

A Social Marketing Perspective on Communication Campaigns

Douglas S. Solomon

The field of social marketing was probably born in 1952, when Wiebe raised the question, "Why can't you sell brotherhood like you sell soap?" Wiebe examined four social campaigns and found that they were successful to the extent that they were similar to marketing programs, with their emphasis on typical marketing variables such as product design, distribution, and cost.

Not much was made of this innovative thinking until the late 1960s, when several marketing scholars began to write about a new phase in the evolution of marketing, that of the generic conceptualization of marketing. According to this analysis (Kotler, 1972; Kotler & Zaltman, 1971), there exists a generic concept of marketing that is the study of an exchange process that goes far beyond applicability in solely commercial transaction situations. This emphasis on utilizing many of the concepts, philosophies, and techniques of marketing has become a specialized area of study within marketing itself. Social or public sector marketing has been defined as

> the design, implementation, and control of programs seeking to increase the acceptability of a social idea or practice in a target group(s). It utilizes concepts of market segmentation, consumer research, idea configuration, communication, facilitation, incentives, and exchange theory to maximize target group response. (Kotler, 1975)

The field of marketing itself has gone through tremendous changes during the past 50 years, moving from a Ptolomaic view, with the product and producer at the center of the universe, to a Copernican view, with the consumer at the focal point. This same sort of change

87

process has been occurring in the field of communication campaigns, perhaps in part due to the increased acceptance of social marketing.

The goal of this chapter is to discuss briefly 11 important concepts of social marketing that have a great deal of applicability to the design and implementation of social campaigns: (1) the marketing philosophy, (2) "profit" orientation, (3) the four Ps of marketing, (4) hierarchies of communication effects, (5) audience segmentation, (6) understanding all the relevant markets, (7) information and rapid feedback systems, (8) interpersonal and mass communication interactions, (9) utilization of commercial resources, (10) understanding the competition, and (11) expectations of success.

The purpose here is to whet the reader's appetite for the value of marketing concepts and stimulate some thinking, rather than to provide an exhaustive textbook approach to the field. Several useful books provide a more complete marketing overview, of which social marketing campaigns are a part (Frederiksen, Solomon & Brehony, 1984; Kotler, 1975; Manoff, 1985; see also the Appendix to this volume). A secondary purpose is to share some of the insights and excitement that marketing may hold in store for social communicators and decision makers, citing examples from the Stanford Heart Disease Prevention Program Five City Project (SHDPP) (Farquhar, Maccoby, & Solomon, 1984; Flora, Maccoby, & Farquhar, chap. 10, this volume).

Distinctions in Social Marketing

First, it should be noted that social marketing is a much broader concept than social advertising. Social advertising is simply the use of advertising media for a social purpose. Virtually all of the campaigns one sees on public service television spots are social advertising, because they deal only with the promotion variable of marketing. Social marketing, on the other hand, deals with all four of the marketing variables discussed below: product, price, place, and promotion. Social advertising is often effective in providing information on a simple concept or product; it can even increase motivation. However, it will fail with multifaceted, complex concepts, when a needed product or service is not locally available, or when the target audience must learn new skills to change in some way.

Second, it should be noted that Wiebe was wrong; you cannot sell brotherhood like you sell soap. Over the past few years it has been consistently found that marketing concepts cannot be adopted wholesale by public sector programs. For example, private programs can easily ignore marketing to less profitable segments of the population, while public sector programs are often specifically designed to reach these hardest-to-reach segments. This is particularly the case in efforts to narrow knowledge gaps, so that those with initially higher knowledge levels about some social good do not achieve proportionately even higher levels than those with initially lower levels (Rogers, 1983). Many other differences between for-profit and social marketing have also been brought to light (see Bloom & Novelli, 1981; Lamb, 1987; Lefebvre & Flora, in press). Webster (1975) provides a brief summary of the ways in which social marketing differs from commercial marketing, including the following:

(1) Clients are not always asked to pay in dollar terms for products and services.

(2) A political dimension is usually present because social marketing programs require broad public support and may run counter to vested interests (see Wallack, chap. 16, this volume).

(3) Product/service use is often not desired or seen as valuable by potential clients.

(4) Marketing efforts must be directed at both clients and funding sources (which are often not the same) and the needs of these groups may be mutually exclusive, for example, marketing to meet consumer needs may require segmenting the market and treating various segments in different ways, and funding agencies usually frown on this practice.

(5) Increased demand for services and products is not always desirable because sufficient resources may not always be available.

The major difference is a broader and more far-reaching one: Marketing is accepted in the commercial world as a method for facilitating the transaction between buyers and sellers. This basic assumption is not always accepted in the public sector world. From this basic issue most of the other issues are ultimately derived.

The Marketing Philosophy

According to Kotler (1972), marketing should be looked at as an exchange process whereby something of value is exchanged among two or more parties because they themselves feel this exchange will best meet their individual needs. This entity of value can be a product with a corresponding physical reality, or an idea or practice. Two main implications follow from this perspective. First, the marketing philosophy says that the goal of an organization (though not always met in reality) should be to meet consumer needs and wants. Therefore, the consumer should be at the top of the organizational pyramid, directing the plans and products of the organization. Second, the notion of an exchange process is critical, since in order to accomplish an exchange the parties must interact roughly as equals, each with something to offer the other and each in a position to benefit from the exchange.

There are many examples of where the marketing philosophy obviously has been overlooked in the public sector. Health care systems that serve the health practitioner rather than the patient, libraries oriented toward keeping the books neatly on the shelves and not in people's hands, and public utilities that are not responsive to consumer needs are only a few examples of what has been called "marketing myopia" (Levitt, 1960). There are many examples of commercial companies, such as the U.S. automobile industry, that have lost sight of their core activities and of the consumer. The computer industry has also witnessed a major struggle over the past several years between these competing views of the marketplace: the mainframe-centric view, with the powerful mainframe computer at the center of the computing universe, versus the user-centric view, with the individual and personal computer at the center of the universe, accessing information from all sources and communicating with all others as peers. Not all marketing experts agree, however, with Kotler. Ries and Trout (1986, p. 7) liken marketing to warfare, with the battlefield inside the mind of target individuals and audiences.

It is clearly a great challenge for public- and socially-oriented organizations to try to think in marketing philosophy terms and examine whether they are best meeting needs from a consumer's point of view or whether the procedures, products, and practices being promoted are designed from the organization's point of view.

A "Profit" Orientation

Profit is most simply defined as what is left over after the expenses are deducted from the revenues for the sale of products or services. Profit is usually the ultimate, or "bottom line," measure of the success of an operation. This simple concept is fairly foreign to social program planners. But profit need not exist only in monetary terms; it can also be measured in social terms such as increased job satisfaction, happiness, or decrease in mortality. Indeed, even many bottom-line businesses evaluate the profits of a campaign in terms of goodwill and/or the potential impact on subsequent sales.

In one sense, meeting or exceeding a social program's objectives (assuming the objectives when originally set specified a benefit exceeding the program's and society's costs) can be considered as profit. The important point is that campaigns should have measurable profit objectives, and actions and outcomes should be constantly weighed against some profit criteria. When this is done, expenses (the typical measure of a non-marketing-oriented operation) become much less important when compared to a cost/profit analysis. If profitability were the evaluation system used, many social programs would simply not exist, because their contribution to society (i.e., profit) is simply not greater than their cost.

However, the measurement of cost versus benefits is often exceedingly difficult. An extensive literature exists on the evaluation of social programs and the determination of their cost/benefit ratios (see Flay & Cook, chap. 8, and Hornik, chap. 14, this volume). In the health field, for example, a standard measurement of social profit from a family planning campaign has been derived from comparing the calculated births averted to the cost of caring for those infants who might have otherwise been born.

The Four Ps of Marketing

A very useful set of marketing concepts of wide applicability in social campaigns is the four Ps: product, price, place, and promotion.

A *product* is defined as the focus of the transaction between the marketer and the target market. A product can have a physical component or consist only of ideas, practices, or services. Sometimes, in fact, it is advantageous for an organization promoting ideas to link them with some physical product, to make the ideas more tangible and attractive to the target group. For example, you do not need any physical product to stop smoking. However, a physical product such as a book or set of special cigarette filters may make the idea more concrete and may also enhance the probability for a successful attempt at self-behavior change.

Organizations generally define both a core generic product (for example, a major copying machine manufacturer defines its core product as information handling) and specific physical products (such as the copying machines themselves). By defining products in these terms, the organization will not easily lose sight of its primary consumer need-satisfying mission and get lost in a product focus rather than a consumer-satisfaction focus. Social marketers, and those who do not yet define themselves as such, often find a useful challenge in trying to define what their core and physical products are. This can lead to an interesting and useful process of evaluating each product from the point of view of the target markets of the organization.

The concept of a "product line" flows logically from a customer-based view of products and how they might interact with buyer wants and needs. Most commercial organizations have found that a number of related products (i.e., a product family or product line) can increase sales over simply having a one-size-fits-all product strategy. Imagine how health campaigns could be transformed if they provided a product line ranging from, in the case of physical exercise campaigns, for example, low-cost information-only products, to one-shot activities, to higher-cost life-style changes or ongoing daily participation programs. This concept of product differentiation has a great deal of applicability to social campaigns.

The *price* of a product or service consists of far more than just the monetary cost. Other factors to be considered are time costs (how much time it takes to obtain a product or service) and opportunity costs (which benefits or other opportunities will be missed because of taking part in obtaining a given product or service). For example, many health services in developing countries have been quite surprised that their free health clinics are underutilized. People shun these services due to nonmonetary costs, including difficult travel conditions, long waits, cultural costs in accepting Western medicine, and psychological costs concerning the sometimes degrading treatment received from the higher-status clinic staff.

It should also be remembered that price sometimes carries with it the notion of value. In some countries it has been found that it is easier to sell contraceptives for a small fee (not too high, so the product is not priced out of the reach of the target audience) than to give them away for free (Sinha, 1973). Price sensitivity or elasticity (i.e., how strongly related changes in price are to changes in purchase of a product or service) is another of the many other price-related factors relating to promoting products or services. The critical point here is that it is not always obvious how consumers will perceive the price of a product or service, how sensitive they are to caring about and/or even perceiving differences among various price levels, and how much weight they even put on the price of a product or service in the decision-making process.

Place refers to the distribution channels used to make the product, service, or idea available to the target group. Many social campaigns have failed because they did not have an adequate distribution system for their messages and products. No commercial company would consider promoting a product that is not available on the shelves of the local store, yet many social campaigns have simply said, "Contact your local [agency] office," without giving specific telephone numbers or addresses, without having adequate staff on hand to answer requests, and without supplying adequate printed materials.

The channel in a distribution sense serves a similar purpose to the channel in a communication sense; however, the distribution channel is generally an organization and/or individuals who actually physically transport the product or service. After selecting channels that are appropriate to the target group(s) for the campaign, the channel must be designed or trained to handle and support the products. Representatives must understand what the product/service is, who should or would want it, how to promote it (i.e., psychological and other "selling strategies"), and how to support and service the product/service over time.

The distribution channel must also be constantly motivated to sell a product or service. This involves maintaining attention (commonly called "mindshare") and providing incentives for promotion of the product or service. Maintaining distribution is costly. Many organizations have found that having a smaller distribution channel that it can more easily support and motivate is better in the end than having the largest possible number of distribution points but at a lower quality. There is a lesson here for public sector organizations that try to obtain the greatest number of outlets rather than focusing on the cost/benefits of distribution.

Promotion is an extremely broad area that includes the publicity about a campaign, the mass media campaign message design and dissemination, and the campaign monitoring and modification. Ultimately, promotion involves making consumers aware of the product or service with which the public sector organization is involved, and converting this awareness to positive attitudes, knowledge, intention, and finally to behavior. Promotion is far more than simply and superficially placing advertisements. It is actively reaching out to the right people with the right message at the right time in order to obtain the right effects. And this is not easy to achieve, especially with the large number of competing messages and media. Just as there is a world of difference between the sophistication level, analytical process, and planning of a classified advertisement for a garage sale and one for McDonald's hamburgers, so there is a world of difference between a TV spot done by a local quit-smoking clinic and those developed by an agency such as the National Cancer Institute (1982) (see Paisley, chap. 1, this volume) or the SHDPP.

In summary, these four elements (product, place, price, and promotion) are essential to the design and implementation of each social campaign (see Solomon, 1984, for more detailed examples). None of these factors can be overlooked without jeopardizing the outcome of the entire campaign. The *marketing mix* is the resulting campaign or marketing program, which allocates resources and emphasis on each of these four elements of the planned efforts. This concept of a mix is critical, because it reinforces the notion of the interrelationships among the four Ps and reminds planners of the importance of making conscious decisions on resource allocations. This usually involves the creation of a hypothetical model of the marketplace and how these four factors can influence "buyer" behavior.

There is also a fifth P that provides another marketing concept useful to social planners: the concept of *positioning*. Positioning involves the psychological location of a given product or service in relationship to others that target market individuals contain in their perceptual set of like products or services. For example, a classic positioning strategy was for Avis Rent-a-Car to position itself as the number-two car rental agency. Avis determined that the size of agency was a primary decision factor in consumer choice and therefore dedicated their marketing program to encouraging consumers to consider them as next to the biggest company (Ries & Trout, 1980).

Positioning can also involve defining what a product or service is in the mind of the consumer. For example, the SHDPP successfully positioned physical activity as a form of relaxation rather than as a terrible ordeal. Another strategy is to reposition the competition rather than to change one's own product's position. For example, a major telephone company is attempting to reposition the competition as having inferior quality products and service, and, ultimately, to maintain their position as having the best quality product. Often, research is done to determine a product's positioning versus the competition and this is represented in the form of a perceptual map. The map (which may be multidimensional) usually shows the major organizing criteria that are in the minds of the target audience and then positions the competitive products on

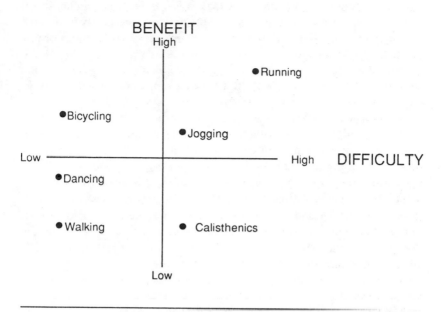

Figure 4.1. Hypothetical Perceptual Map of Competing Physical Activities

these dimensions. Figure 4.1 provides a hypothetical map of some competing exercise programs. Simply knowing what these criteria are is a major step for understanding how to position or reposition and promote a product or service.

Hierarchies of Communication Effects

Originally derived from communication research, the hierarchy of communication effects model is a hypothetical process that an individual moves through from a state of unawareness of the message being promoted, through awareness and attitude change, to behavior change and maintenance of that behavior. McGuire (chap. 2, this volume) reviews this useful framework, and Ray (1973) presents a version from a marketing point of view. There are many such formulations that are often complementary; there is no single correct hierarchy of communication effects that operates across all topics and situations. The key is to choose a hierarchy that makes sense for a particular social campaign and use it to analyze where the audience currently is situated and how they are likely to proceed from one stage in the hierarchy to another.

Bem (1970), McGuire, and Ray all remind us that people do not always move from awareness to attitude change to behavior change. This is particularly true when people are forced to enact some behavior (such as when they are prisoners of war, or even the victims of social pressure), but it also occurs when people make choices among similar objects (usually inexpensive commercial products) that are relatively unimportant to them (i.e., toilet soaps). This possibility of a nonlinear or stalled progression forces us to ask questions about the order in which knowledge, attitude change, and behavior might occur in a specific situation, and the current processing stage of the members of the target audience. This kind of analysis can help an agency to avoid wasting money trying to change people in ways they have already changed or trying to have them move directly from one stage to another without passing through appropriate intervening stages.

For example, formative research in the SHDPP demonstrated early on in the campaign that most smokers were already aware of the importance and need to quit smoking. Indeed, a large proportion of them had tried unsuccessfully to quit many times (see McAlister, Ramirez, Galavotti, & Gallion, chap. 13, this volume). Therefore, in a departure from the vast majority of quit-smoking campaigns that dealt with information or knowledge, the SHDPP moved directly into communications designed to influence skills learning, self-efficacy, and maintenance behavior. Again, while this may seem obvious to a skilled communication researcher, it had not previously been done by a large number of campaigns, which had simply assumed that knowledge enhancement was the needed communication effect.

Audience Segmentation

Audience segmentation is the process of breaking down the mass audience into a small number of subgroups that are internally as homogeneous as possible and as different from each other group as possible (Fine, 1981; Frank, Massy, & Wind, 1972). This enables the campaign planner to allocate particular elements of a campaign to meet the needs of each particular group. For example, the messages and program delivery channels of a nutrition education program aimed at pregnant women should be very different from those for school-age children or middle-age single men. Any single campaign attempting to change all of these groups with the same messages or channels will probably fail miserably.

There are many bases for audience segmentation, including demographics, life-style, audience needs, benefits derived, mass media targetability, attitudes, purchase process used, geographic dispersion, distribution channel availability, and language (Murphy, 1984). The key is to consider and learn about each key segment and plan a campaign to reach each segment efficiently and effectively. A wide variety of research techniques are available to assist in the segmentation process. Quantitative methods include factor analysis, cluster analysis, regression analysis, and multidimensional scaling. Alcalay and Taplin (chap. 5, this volume) consider the use of broadcast ratings and print circulation as ways to segment an audience. There are also many qualitative methods that can be used to derive insights into segmentation. Dervin (chap. 3, this volume) discusses new ways to conceive of and thus segment audiences that can lead to specific campaign messages and methods. Within the United States there are quite a few commercial suppliers of demographic- and life-style-based segmentation analyses (such as SRI and Yankelovich), along with publicly available sources such as the census, that might provide relevant information and are available to public sector campaign planners and managers.

The SHDPP used a wide variety of segmentation methods, including language segmentation (reaching Spanish-speaking adults on Spanish-language radio stations), attitudinal segmentation (designing and aiming messages specifically at those with a particular predisposition to change), and distribution channel segmentation (targeting subelements of the campaign at those who frequent certain channels, such as barber shops, grocery stores, and libraries).

Understanding All the Relevant Markets

A common concern of marketers and, to a lesser extent, of social campaigners is the multiple markets that are important for the success of a given program. Kotler (1973) calls these "multiple publics" (what Paisley, chap. 1, this volume, calls "stakeholders") and defines them as a distinct group of people and/or organizations that have an actual or potential interest in and/or impact on an organization (p. 17). He provides as an example a university, which has internal publics (i.e., faculty and staff), groups supporting the university (alumni, foundations), groups consuming the organization's offerings (students), and groups regulating the organization (government agencies). Any university-oriented campaign would need the support of all of these markets to succeed.

In the area of social campaigns, the concept of multiple markets has often been overlooked. For example, in the initial stage of one of the earliest social marketing campaigns in Ghana, the planners forgot to gain the support of political and religious leaders and directed all of their efforts to the consuming public alone. The campaign was abruptly halted after a very short time due to the objections of these neglected markets (Obetsebi-Lamptey, 1973). The awareness, understanding, and involvement of secondary but influential target markets that might not be the ultimate consumers of a campaign are quite critical to its success.

For example, the SHDPP took great pains to involve the medical community in each of the five cities, by keeping them informed of the design and progress of the program and using them on advisory panels. By enlisting their support, the SHDPP avoided possible reduction of the campaign's effectiveness through counter or negative messages to their patients.

Information and Rapid Feedback Systems

Social marketers have learned from commercial marketers the importance of rapid information and feedback for use in planning programs and monitoring and modifying their progress and effectiveness over time (see Atkin & Freimuth, chap. 6, and Flay & Cook, chap. 8, this volume). The typical social campaign has an evaluation component tacked on at the end of the proposal, designed to answer a very narrow question: Did the campaign work?

Although social marketers are interested in the answer to this question, they consider it of lesser importance than the broader question: Why did it work or not work? Outstanding campaigns plan research to provide an answer to this question, by setting up a model of the hypothetical process of change and monitoring guideposts in that process over time. In this way there is still time to modify the campaign if the milestones are not being reached. For example, a simple model for a fire prevention program could be as follows: Students in elementary schools are presented a series of filmed messages about fire prevention, they are given brochures to take home to their parents for discussion, and they are taught a special Smokey the Bear song to sing to remind their parents the next time they visit a forest or wildlife preserve. Based on this simple model, a series of guideposts could be set up to monitor the process. Simple research techniques can be used to monitor whether the booklets are passed out, whether they ever reach the home, whether children understand the message and have the relevant skills to talk to their parents, whether they learn the Smokey the Bear song, whether they sing the song upon visiting the forest, and so on. If a campaign monitored in this way fails, it will be fairly easy to understand the reasons for failure and make corrections in subsequent efforts (see Rice & Foote, chap. 7, this volume).

Commercial firms use their ongoing management information systems to make information readily accessible to decision makers, often electronically, on such factors as unit sales, sales dollars, sales measures versus a planned amount at a given point in time, sales broken down by various internal divisions such as geographic ones and by segments of the market, profitability, and backlog in shipping products or performing services.

The SHDPP created many such process models for its physical activity and nutrition behavior change programs. Through the use of very inexpensive small random sample telephone surveys (called "snoops") and simple short questionnaires administered at community events (such as classes and fun runs) designed to understand how people came to be aware of and to participate in a given program, it was relatively easy to diagnose how well various campaign processes were proceeding.

Interpersonal and Mass Communication Interactions

A rather complex area to which we cannot do justice in a brief overview is that of the interactions that occur between mass and interpersonal communication (see Hornik, chap. 14, this volume). Meyer, Maccoby, and Farquhar (1977) have demonstrated that mass media-stimulated interpersonal communication can be effective in a campaign for disease prevention in a community setting. The combination of mass and interpersonal communication through the use of organized listening groups in Tanzania's health campaigns (Hall & Dodds, 1977) and in India's and Canada's radio farm forums (Rogers, 1983) have been quite successful.

Marketers are highly sensitized to the need for effective interpersonal communication (this is commonly called "personal selling" in sales parlance, and is considered to be the standard of effectiveness to which all nonpersonal but less expensive means are compared), and social marketers should also think about this as a resource to be used in campaigns. It should not be assumed that all mass media effects will be direct ones on the individuals exposed to a campaign. It should also be remembered that mass and interpersonal communication may serve different functions in a campaign. There is a common assumption in the communication literature that mass media may be better in achieving awareness of a campaign's message and knowledge, while interpersonal communication may be more effective in motivating actual behavior change (see Hornik, chap. 14, and McGuire, chap. 2, this volume). A California grocery chain's campaign theme is "Tell a Friend"; this is a good example of the purposive stimulation of interpersonal communication through the use of mass media—it need not be left to chance.

The SHDPP found that through the use of mass mailings of "refrigerator tip sheets" with magnets to hold these mini-poster/newsletters on refrigerator doors, there was preliminary evidence of increased discussions of nutrition information topics.

Utilization of Commercial Resources

In virtually every corner of the world there are commercial resources such as advertising agencies, marketing research companies, and distribution companies that can be extremely useful in social campaigns (Alcalay & Taplin, chap. 5, this volume; Manoff, 1985). In the early family planning area, where the majority of social marketing programs were initially conducted, there have been more than 30 social marketing-oriented programs that utilized commercial resources (McMillan, 1973). For example, in the Ghana family planning program (Obetsebi-Lamptey, 1973), the use of the existing retail outlets of the Ghana National Trading Corporation provided, virtually overnight, 200 shops throughout the entire country that could distribute contraceptive products at minimal cost. This distribution system could not have been duplicated in many years by the family planning program working on its own.

One example of an area of potential influence of commercial resources is in planning trade-offs between campaign message reach and
frequency (see Alcalay & Taplin, chap. 5, this volume). *Reach* refers to
the number of individuals in the target audience who are exposed to at
least one campaign message. *Frequency* is the number of times the
average person reached is exposed to a message. There is clearly a
trade-off in terms of cost between these two campaign variables, and
also a need to match campaign goals to these two different processes.
While there is no single best answer to this trade-off, nor is there a
quantitative method for making these decisions short of market-based
tests, the single best source for rules of thumb on reach and frequency
in planning a campaign is a campaign planner within an advertising
agency.

Some examples of commercial resources include advertising agencies, market research suppliers, demographic and life-style information
providers, marketing and communication consultants, media owners
(who may have proprietary data on their audiences), media production
houses, commercial/corporate libraries, specialized industry consultants and analysts (i.e., consultants on consumer product developments
and marketing), commercial distribution channels, public relations
agencies, and financial analysts.

In the SHDPP, commercial resources used included the commercial
mass media (radio, TV, and print) as well as commercial magazine
distributors for the dissemination of campaign brochures through existing point-of-sale outlets such as grocery stores and bookstores.

Understanding the Competition

A very simple lesson from the marketing literature and experience is
to look at the competition for insights into a given product, idea, or
service. However, the competition for social campaigns is rarely given
a second thought, perhaps because it is not usually obvious precisely
what the competition is for social campaigns. However, there is usually
something competing for any given target audience. The competition
may be for dollars, time, "shelf space" (i.e., room to add a new product
to the distribution system), or even "mindshare." For example, in the
heart disease prevention area one is faced with a wide range of competition, including not only commercial concerns promoting unhealthy
products but also competing social climates, competing activities for a
person's time, and so on (see Wallack, chap. 16, this volume). Often a

social campaign may wish to create a new product or service that competes with existing activities. For example, a social work agency may wish to create a place where kids who frequently get into trouble can go to act out their aggressions in an innocuous or even useful way. A side effect of thinking about the competition is that it forces a campaigner to design his or her product as something that can effectively compete in the real world—a product that is attractive, desirable, and accessible.

A key term often used in business is *competitive advantage*. This is some sustainable and recognizable advantage of a given product or service in comparison to the competition as perceived by the marketplace. Competitive advantages may be based on the product (such as a better smelling perfume), the distribution channel (such as having a product available in every grocery store), service and support availability (such as the advantage Sears has in providing nationwide service for its TV sets over the limited service areas of unknown brands), and image (such as Apple Computer's well-recognized friendly image). Thus public sector organizations must think about their advantage, how they can derive it, and how they can sustain it over time.

For example, in the SHDPP, exercise programs attained competitive advantage by providing social contact and support to participants. This was an important factor that strongly influenced the target audience to participate in exercise rather than in competing activities. The programs achieved further advantage by being based in the workplace, providing proximity and ease of access over competing sedentary activities, such as eating long lunches. Other social marketing-oriented campaigns achieve competitive advantage through creating an image of caring (such as through the use of an attractive television personality), through low-cost provision of services, or through confidentiality (i.e., by going to a teen clinic for family planning versus seeing a family physician).

Expectations of Success

A final note concerns what one can reasonably expect in terms of success from a social campaign. Marketing experience tells us that expectations should be modest. For example, a well-promoted commercial television show might reach 20% of the available television households, and this simply represents exposure to a message rather than any passage further through a "hierarchy of effects"; or a commercial marketer can be satisfied with 1% of a large market. However, social campaigners generally set objectives that are quite ambitious, such as teaching everyone about some new idea or changing the behavior of 90% of all citizens. Clearly, some middle ground must be reached, but there is no clear answer concerning how to reach it.

One approach to estimating the success potential of a campaign goes back to the hierarchy of effects model (discussed in greater detail by McGuire, chap. 2, this volume). If one assigns probabilities to each of the steps in the model, one can easily see the probability of reaching the ultimate endpoint. For example, if the model has three stages— exposure to the messages, attitude change, and behavior change—and the probability of each step is (an improbably high) 50%, then the maximum chance of getting an individual to change all three stages is .5 × .5 × .5, or 12.5%. Of course, this simplistic example assumes that each step is equally important, equally probable, sequential, and dependent. Greater complexity is probably more likely than greater simplicity. By using some variation of this approach that best fits a given campaign, one can come up with reasonable estimates of the potential outcomes of the campaign under different assumptions of audience size and changeability.

Conclusion

While borrowing from the concepts and techniques of marketing, social marketing is quite unique in many ways. For example, while commercial marketers typically deal with the most lucrative target audience groups, social marketers typically direct efforts toward the hardest-to-reach and least affluent groups. While commercial marketers are typically trying to encourage people to do something, social marketers are often in the position of discouraging behaviors (smoking, overeating, child abuse), some of which are especially attractive or intractable. The point is that marketing concepts cannot be applied wholesale to social campaigns without a great deal of thought and sensitivity.

Considering the negative image that commercial marketing has in many people's minds, a social campaign designer might best avoid using the term *marketing* at all, and simply apply what he or she has learned from that field. While there is a great deal of interest in social marketing developing in the health and nutrition fields, with many programs currently in process, the field that has had the most experience with social marketing is that of family planning, perhaps because it has physical products associated with it, such as condoms, foam, and pills, that are naturals for a marketing system (Atkin & Meischke, in chap. 9, this volume).

The aim of this chapter has been to provide a new perspective on the design and implementation of social campaigns. This social marketing perspective draws together from the fields of marketing and communication some key concepts that have a great deal of potential for improving social campaigns. None of these concepts provides concrete frameworks that must be adhered to. Rather, they provide a new way of looking at the problem of designing and carrying out a communication campaign that may make the campaign more focused on its "customers" and more powerful in its effects. The addition of this perspective alone will be a great step forward from the design of most previous social campaigns.

5

Community Health Campaigns: From Theory to Action

RINA ALCALAY

SHAHNAZ TAPLIN

This chapter presents a communication framework and a set of strategies and tools to maximize the impact of health education in the community. While health educators have traditionally relied primarily on interpersonal and small group communication, it is increasingly important that they also be trained to use mass communications resources to reach large audiences effectively and to involve communities in health promotion activities.

The historic 1978 United Nations conference at Alma-Ata in the Soviet Union established the goal of "health for all by the Year 2000" (World Health Organization, 1978). The Declaration of Alma-Ata also emphasized the role of the community in the planning and implementation of health education programs and rejected the vertical, paternalistic programs designed unilaterally by authorities and handed down to communities (Manoff, 1985). Positive results from AIDS education programs among the gay community in San Francisco constitute just one example of the power of community-based health education (Shilts, 1987).

While the threat of AIDS draws current attention, deaths due to heart disease, stroke, cancer, and accidents still account for 80% of deaths in the United States. And because many of these deaths are traceable to high-risk behavior, increased and more effective health education is essential. Health educators with a solid background in communication can serve as community leaders and resources in the planning, implementation, and dissemination of health communication campaigns at the community level. In designing community health campaigns,

health educators can use the media for advertising, public relations, and
the discussion of public affairs issues.

Community Health Campaigns

Because primary health care requires that community members
make major changes in their behavior, community participation in
intervention decisions and other activities is essential for both a
project's effectiveness during implementation and its ultimate impact
(Djukanovic & Mach, 1975; Goldsmith, Pillsbury, & Nicholas, 1985).

Community has been defined as a context, as a process of interaction, and as a problem (Cox, 1979). As a context, community includes place, people, shared values, and a social system. By defining
community as a process of interaction, the health care practitioner
examines the distribution of power within the community and thus
assesses the channels through which various practical objectives may
be realized. And by seeing the community as a problem, the practitioner
approaches health education with a clear agenda of community health
issues in need of solution or amelioration.

Because cultural, economic, demographic, and health priorities vary
from one community to another, there is no single best way to design a
community campaign. Thus community-based interventions for health
education and health promotion offer advantages and challenges not
found in general mass media campaigns.

In terms of project planning, by working with local resources, health
care practitioners involved in an intervention can translate general
health education project goals into locally meaningful ones and project
activities into culturally acceptable and affordable ones (Goldsmith
et al., 1985).

In terms of project implementation, some advantages of a community-based approach include (1) the ability to gain the support and
participation of key members of the local power structure, such as local
media opinion leaders, community leaders from target populations, and
health leaders; (2) the prospect of decreasing dependency on limited
external resources and thus increasing the likelihood that project goals
will be maintained once intervention is over; (3) the ability to develop
a more accurate assessment of community needs and, therefore, an
intervention better tailored to those specific needs as weil as to local
characteristics, knowledge, and resources; and (4) the potential to
recruit the active participation of community members in the project's

specific health education and health promotion activities as well as to achieve behavioral changes in the individual members of the community (Brown, 1984; Goldsmith et al., 1985).

Although community-based campaigns are tailored to the needs of individual communities, the theoretical framework and the communication skills required to design, implement, and maximize the impact of these campaigns are based on principles from the communication field in general and are thus not unique to community interventions. The following sections summarize these principles and present three main strategic components of media-based community health campaigns: the planning process, advertising and media placement, and public relations.

Campaign Principles

Historically, the assessment of the effects of mass communication can be divided into three distinct eras: (1) a direct or "hypodermic needle" era, in which media were thought to have immediate, universal, and causal effects on people, derived from the stimulus-response school in social psychology; (2) a "minimal effects" era, in which media were considered close to useless and incapable of affecting people except as reinforcers of previously held beliefs; and (3) the current era of "contingent effects," in which media are considered useful in influencing people, but indirectly (working through mediating variables) and cumulatively (effects occur not after just one incident of media exposure but as a result of continuous exposure to certain kinds of messages) (Katz, 1980; Maccoby & Roberts, 1985).

Mass media can have powerful effects on setting "healthy" or "unhealthy" agendas (McCombs & Shaw, 1972-1973) for communities by emphasizing certain behaviors, for example, nonsmoking or smoking. In this capacity, media can either increase the "spiral of silence" (Noelle-Neumann, 1974) regarding a given health issue or serve as positive behavioral examples. If, for example, the media counteract smoking advertisements by showing that the majority of adolescents do not smoke and emphasizing the reasons for not smoking, teenagers may feel more support to be outspoken in their opposition to smoking, thus breaking the "spiral of silence."

Media can also have powerful effects by "cultivating certain beliefs" regarding health behaviors and models (Gerbner & Gross, 1976). Through a cumulative portrayal of certain health behaviors among characters seen in prime-time television, for example, media can present distorted images of illness and of health professionals that do not represent reality.

Finally, media can exert powerful effects by widening or closing the knowledge gaps among different groups of people, usually of different socioeconomic backgrounds (Manoff, 1985; Tichenor, Donohue, & Olien, 1971). According to Manoff, there are several kinds of communication gaps that weaken public health education. One advantage of community interventions is that the health educator has a better chance to design a campaign specifically tailored to reach the more disadvantaged groups and to monitor more closely whether the campaign is reaching those at higher risk, thus reducing the knowledge gap effect within a given community.

The aforementioned principles illustrate ways in which the media can influence communities in their health knowledge, attitudes, and behaviors. Media can be effective if they are used as part of a carefully planned campaign process, as the following sections summarize.

Media Planning Process
for Health Campaigns

The media planning process is common to both advertising (paid or public service) and public relations campaigns, locally and nationally. The following planning process results in the development of a media plan such as that summarized in Table 5.1.

Plan the Campaign

The campaign planning process starts with an analysis of the health problem to be addressed in the advertising or public relations campaign. This analysis should discuss statistics and research findings, risk factors associated with the health problem, detection methods, and prevention treatment and costs. It should also identify the extent of the health problem, the difference in incidence rates between men and women and among different age, income, education, and ethnic groups. The public's awareness and perception of the particular health issue and its response to that issue should also be assessed. At this stage, the

TABLE 5.1 Sample Media Campaign Plan

Goals	to increase awareness among teens about the use of contraceptives
Objective	to reach 10% of teens in San Francisco Bay area
Target	demographic: black, white, Hispanic teenagers geographic: Northern California
Media timing	January and June

Media used	For advertising: For public relations:
	   radio press kit
	   television press conference
	   print talk shows
	   outdoor
	   transit

practitioner must also consider what factors might motivate people to take some action regarding the health problem to be addressed (U.S. Department of Health and Human Services, 1983b).

The planning process should then define the goals, objectives, targets, and budgets for the media campaign. While goals may be stated generally (e.g., "to decrease level of smoking among Hispanics"), objectives should be realistic, clear, and measurable (see, for example, Table 5.1).

The next step is to identify the "target audiences" or the population groups that need to be reached, in order of priority, that is, primary or secondary. Target audiences should be defined as narrowly as possible by demographic and psychological characteristics—sex, age, income, education, marital status, and geographical area. In recent years, the Stanford Research Institute has developed a Values and Lifestyles (VALS) grid, which is based on a variety of characteristics called psychographics (Riche, 1982; Wells, 1975). These include personality (e.g., introvert versus extrovert), life-style (e.g., heavy drinker versus light drinker), health care usage patterns, and other characteristics. The point of segmenting target audiences is to make possible a better understanding of the special needs of each target group and thus the formulation of messages tailored to address those needs (U.S. Department of Health and Human Services, 1983b). Dervin (chap. 3, this volume) suggests yet more qualitative ways of understanding both the audience's and the sponsoring agency's needs and understandings.

Developing a year-long media calendar will facilitate the planning of media campaigns promoting a particular health agency or addressing a given health issue (see Figure 5.1). The year-long calendar is based on the premise that message retention among consumers lasts only 6-8 weeks and that reinforcement and maintenance of the message through phased repetition is thus essential. A high campaign profile can be maintained by combining advertising (paid or nonpaid), public relations, community relations, and public affairs programming, depending on the campaign's media budget.

(2) Select a Media Strategy

The strategy selection process consists of formulating short statements that define the communication strategy, selecting the media, deciding on the timing of the media campaigns, and setting the media goals for both advertising and public relations campaigns. The defining statements should support the overall campaign objectives, be tailored to each of the designated target audiences of the campaign, and address the reasons people should change their attitudes or behaviors (e.g., to reduce infant mortality or to live longer). The media selections are determined by the budget, the cost-effectiveness of each medium in communicating the message to the target audience, and the particular strengths of each medium (see Table 5.2). The timing of the campaign is of the utmost importance and generally is designed to coincide with the natural peaks and valleys of high-risk behavior among the population, the problem, and available community resources (see Rice & Foote, chap. 7, this volume). Media goals for advertising campaigns are generally set in gross ratings points for radio and TV, and gross line rates for newspapers (see the section on advertising and media placement, below).

(3) Develop and Produce Messages

For both the advertising and public relations campaigns, strategy statements can be developed into key messages for the media. Messages are designed based on analysis of the knowledge, ignorance, or misconceptions of the audience about a health issue (see Atkin & Freimuth, chap. 6, this volume). For example, campaigns that promote the use of the pill as a birth control method among low-income Hispanic women should include messages about the need for daily use of the pills. Many Hispanic women believe that they should take the

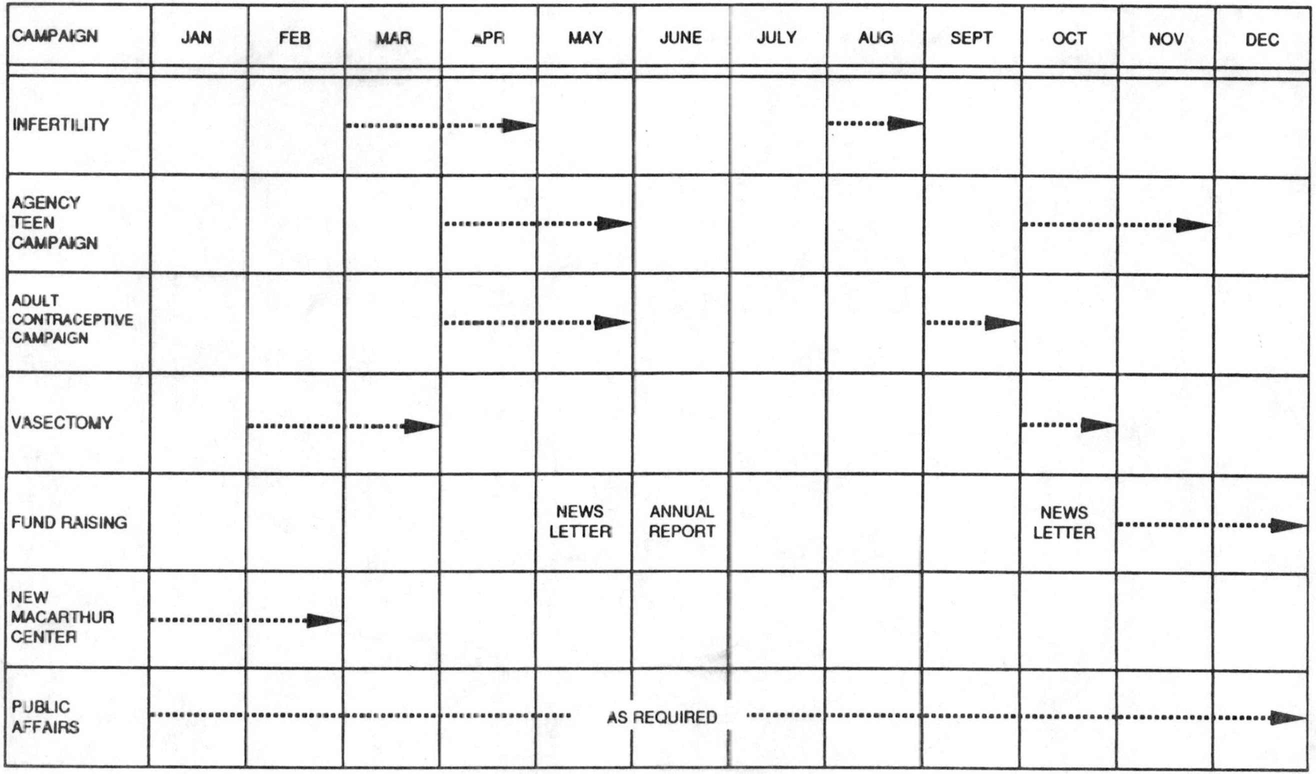

CAMPAIGN	JAN	FEB	MAR	APR	MAY	JUNE	JULY	AUG	SEPT	OCT	NOV	DEC
INFERTILITY			••••	••••►								
AGENCY TEEN CAMPAIGN				••••	••••►						••••►	
ADULT CONTRACEPTIVE CAMPAIGN				••••	••••►				••••►			
VASECTOMY		••••	••••►							••••►		
FUND RAISING					NEWS LETTER	ANNUAL REPORT				NEWS LETTER		••••►
NEW MACARTHUR CENTER	••••	••••►										
PUBLIC AFFAIRS	••••				••••► AS REQUIRED		••••					••••►

Figure 5.1. Sample Media Planning Calendar

111

TABLE 5.2 Primary Sources of Media Ratings, Circulation, or Exposure Information, with Summary Campaign Attributes, for Various Media

Medium	Source	Attributes
Television	Nielson or Arbitron ratings	high credibility, good mass penetration, limited effectiveness on complicated issues, cost-prohibitive for nonprofit organizations
Radio	Arbitron ratings	broad frequency, small but loyal audience, allows for narrowly targeted campaigns
Newspapers	SRDS Reports (newspaper)	excellent in communicating complex problems, high credibility in newspapers of record
Magazines	SRDS Reports (consumer magazines), Simmons Market Research Bureau	wide latitude in selecting audiences, can reach more affluent consumer, offers prestige to advertisers, allows pass-along readership
Billboards	SRDS Reports (outdoor)	can select geographical market, high repetitive value, low cost, good color reproduction, reinforcement medium, large physical presence and attention
Transit cards		reinforcement medium, captive audience, can be placed on specific routes, good for localized campaigns, messages must be short

pill only when their partners are around, which may be at interrupted intervals, especially when partners are migrant workers, resulting in unwanted pregnancies.

 Implement and Place Messages in Media

The advertising campaign is implemented by the placement of ads in various mass media, as well as in community brochures, posters, slide shows, and so on, supplemented by interpersonal communication (described in the section on media placement below).

Evaluate the Campaign

The need for evaluation—even if budgets are slim—cannot be overemphasized, and is considered in detail in other chapters in this volume. Yet our experience in community-based interventions shows that evaluation is often underemphasized. A key reason for evaluating campaigns is to find out which of the communication strategies worked. This knowledge is essential to the implementors of future campaigns.

Advertising and Media Placement

Commercial Advertising
and Social Issues Advertising

Advertising is the communication of a message to a defined target through paid broadcast time, print, or outdoor space. The capability of the mass media to provide advertising is overwhelming; the average viewing time per TV home per day is over 7 hours (TV Bureau of Advertising, 1986); radio listening averages more than 3 hours per day (Ziegler & Howard, 1978) (see also Wallack, chap. 16, this volume). Advertising's greatest strength is that it gives the advertiser virtually total control over the message, the placement (size, shape, and time) of the ad, and specific information on the audience reached. The prohibitive part of advertising for nonprofit social services agencies is that it usually requires significant budgets.

The social cause advertising approach outlined in this section is based on the work of Public Media Center (PMC), a San Francisco-based public interest advertising agency. PMC's philosophy of advertising, which focuses on community participation and empowerment of people to be advocates for social change, is described because of its fundamental compatibility with the goals of health education. Established in 1974, PMC has an impressive list of liberal cause clients that includes, among others, local and national Planned Parenthood, the National Campaign Against Toxic Hazards, Chinese for Affirmative Action, and Medical Aid for El Salvador. PMC's community-based strategy is aimed at social change by imparting new knowledge, creating new attitudes, and empowering people to change their behavior and become advocates for social change.

Social cause advertising is akin to controversy advertising, which includes any kind of public communication or message from an identified source and in a conventional medium of public advertising that presents information or a point of view bearing on an issue publicly recognized as controversial. For example, an issue such as contraception and the availability of birth control for teenagers is disputed by several adversarial groups for larger economic and social reasons than simply product efficiency.

Groups taking part in public controversy want maximum control over the message delivered and the environment in which it is delivered. This is why paid advertisement is often preferred as a communication strategy by community organizations. However, few social issues campaigns can afford to be genuine mass media campaigns. Herb Chao Gunther, PMC's executive director, equates a good public interest advertising campaign with a good political campaign in that the real focus of the campaign is not 100% of the target audience, but the 2-3% of that audience who are opinion leaders and change agents, the influential and attentive public. For the most part, such people are conscientious readers of print ads who are motivated by a sense of idealism and social values. Eventually, these individuals and those they influence add up to a significant aggregate whole (Frankel, 1986).

For the past three years, PMC has developed multimedia campaigns dealing with abortion, teen pregnancy, and international family planning for Planned Parenthood. While all three campaigns included education and advocacy, a strong grass-roots campaign was activated by having readers of the print ads send newspaper coupons from the ads to members of Congress and even to the president.

In defining an effective social issue advertising campaign, Gunther stresses that PMC strives to define an issue in a strikingly different way by creating "breakthrough campaigns" that strategically place an issue on the community's agenda or in the popular mind. An example of this was the teen sexuality campaign for Planned Parenthood. This campaign shifted the blame away from the teen victim and challenged the three major TV networks' ban on contraceptive advertising, which was inconsistent with their portrayal of rampant sexuality on the air (see Wallack, chap. 16, this volume, for other examples of this contradiction).

The $600,000 teen pregnancy campaign, aimed at teens and their parents nationally, consisted of 22 hard-hitting ads for print media and 8 for radio and television. The goal was to combat the epidemic of teen pregnancy by urging birth control education. Encouraging a discussion of sex education, one spot asked, "What would you do if your 15-year-old daughter asked you about birth control?" Another directed at sober talk about sex was headlined: "He said if I didn't do it, he wouldn't love me anymore." Some print ads aimed at upscale, educated men were placed in the *New Republic* and, interestingly, in *Playboy*. Basing some messages on the effects principle of the "cultivation of beliefs" (Gerbner & Gross, 1976), PMC communicated the need to promote contraceptive use among teenagers through television by exposing the constant sexuality and the lack of regard for the consequences of sexual behavior typical of commercial TV. "They did it 9,000 times on TV last year. How come nobody got pregnant?" was the headline in their print ad. This generated news stories in the *New York Times* and *Washington Post*, which, according to Gunther, added a news component—an invaluable bonus for any ad campaign. The campaign successfully focused public attention on the networks and their role in the teen pregnancy epidemic and ultimately resulted in the networks' accepting ads for contraceptives on a limited basis.

Media Placement and Media Research

Given the tight budget constraints under which most community health campaigns must operate, the careful placement of messages is crucial. The keys to effective ad placement or media buying are audience research and an understanding of the principle of cost-efficiencies.

Determining cost-efficiencies is the process by which the health agency or media buyer/planner determines how much it costs to reach each person with a message on a specific medium (e.g., TV or newspaper) at a specific time or in a specific space on a certain day. The cost per person (CPP) is computed by dividing the cost of placing the ad (excluding production or creative costs) by the number of viewers, listeners, or readers exposed to it. For example, if a 30-second spot costs $2,000 and there are 16,000 adult viewers age 25-54 in the audience during a prime-time commercial break, it costs the advertiser approximately 12 cents to reach each person. To compute cost per thousand (CPM), the more commonly used measure of media effectiveness, multiply the CPP by 1,000. In deciding which television program or newspaper to buy, one must analyze the cost-effectiveness of a spot on one TV program versus a competitive program in the same time slot or versus a weekly newspaper or other medium.

While cost-efficiency is the dominant factor in buying time and space, credibility for the issue and overall image are also important considerations. For example, if a campaign is targeted to upscale, highly educated people and opinion leaders, the media planner/buyer, for increased credibility, might choose to place an ad on a program such as *60 Minutes* or in the *New York Times*, even if it is less cost-effective than another placement might be. For a concise analysis of media placement research pertaining to television, radio, and print media, see the Appendix to this chapter.

Public Relations

For health educators, public relations provides greater access than does advertising. This section provides an introduction to public relations and public affairs, and discusses the health educator's role in public relations and the tools required for news, PSA, and editorial campaigns, referring to discussions by Newsom and Scott (1985).

Opportunities and Challenges
of Public Relations

Public relations is news (as opposed to paid-for advertising) about an issue, service, client, or product. It consists of publicity about an issue that cannot be guaranteed to appear in the press but is likely to appear if the activities are newsworthy enough.

The major advantages of public relations are that it is largely free and it has a high degree of "third-party" credibility, because it is attributed to a nonbiased "news" source. Another advantage is visibility, which is a tremendous asset for the agency's external image, for client and donor recruitment, and for public policy work. However, the ability to reach significant numbers of people through the media with public relations is often offset by distortions, misquotes, and lack of control regarding content, timing, and point of view in news stories. Another disadvantage is that it is more difficult to measure the effectiveness of public relations than of advertising, because it is harder to determine the use and impact of the public relations materials that are sent to the media.

In discussing the role and importance of public relations, PMC's Gunther advises allocating 15-30% of advertising campaign resources to public relations. He explains that health campaigns have an advantage in that many of their issues—such as smoking, drugs, and alcohol—are of inherent interest to the press. However, the challenge is to develop new angles, spins, and twists about the issue to draw new rounds of press attention.

Planning Public Relations Campaigns

MANAGING THE ISSUES

In planning and developing a public relations campaign for a health issue, the challenges include making the issue newsworthy, positioning the agency's stance, and promoting the key messages, all of which culminate in creating an "image."

Based on a conceptual knowledge of the nature and type of mass media effects, a health educator must set the agenda on a certain health issue, provide ammunition to the public for fighting against a "spiral of silence" regarding controversial issues, promote favorable beliefs or fight against negative beliefs regarding the agency's health issue, and ensure that the health messages will reach those who need them most, helping to close the information gap regarding the health issue.

For example, recognizing that all the information disseminated through the media sets a certain agenda, a health educator must determine the key issues on which the health agency wishes to be visible (proactive) and the issues on which the agency wishes to maintain a low profile (reactive). Planned Parenthood (PP) of San Francisco, in its annual media planning process, chose to focus on birth control for teens and adults, infertility, and advocacy issues. Based on the premise that the public perceived PP as an "abortion mill" (a perception that was later also identified through focus group research), management decided not to initiate abortion campaigns. Rather, PP responded articulately, promptly, and substantively to reporters covering the abortion issue. Working with the press, either by initiating stories through press releases, materials, and interviews or by responding to reporters on any particular issue, PP consistently presented its full range of family planning and educational services to the public, thus eventually altering the public's perception of PP as an abortion agency. By achieving increased press exposure about these services and about their availability at low cost, PP has been able to reach underinformed, high-risk groups such as minorities and teens.

Issues that deserve special emphasis when presented to the press include new trends and research studies in the field; local angles, local statistics, and local experts on national stories; new legislative developments and their potential impact on a particular social service agency and its clientele; and identification of people who can be effective spokespersons either from a personal perspective or from a public policy perspective.

MEDIA STRATEGY AND THE MEDIA PLANNING CALENDAR

The management team should plan strategy annually regarding the services and issues the health agency will actively promote through the media in the upcoming year. In an ideal world, the nonprofit agency would have conducted some research to determine its image among its clients, volunteers, and donors. In the absence of any research data, the management staff should rely on informal feedback from their staff and clients and on their own observations.

Once the agency's composite "image" has been determined, management can proceed to set priorities concerning the services and issues that need to be highlighted, especially the larger issues that easily get lost in day-to-day management. Discussing the larger issues should enable management to ascertain areas in which the agency should be proactive and areas with which the public is sufficiently familiar that they allow for a low-profile, responsive media strategy.

We have noted that the main differences between advertising and public relations campaigns are that advertising is more controlled and more easily measurable, while public relations is much less controlled with regard to the timing, content, and point of view of news articles. The similarity between advertising and public relations exists in the process of media selection, which in both cases is based primarily on audience research and cost-effectiveness data. Public relations campaigns use audience research as a guide to select the most suitable media for a certain target population, but because time is not actually bought, these campaigns must develop a series of tools to maximize the probability of getting exposure in these most appropriate media and times.

MEDIA TOOLS

Public relations campaigns use certain basic tools—press releases, press kits, press conferences, public service announcements (PSAs), and calendar items—in order to attract media coverage through hard news, soft news (features), and editorials.

Hard news is a story that contains most of the following ingredients: timeliness, proximity, significance, and prominence. *Soft news*, unlike hard news, is not necessarily tied to an immediate specific event. Editorial commentary, while difficult to obtain for commercial products, is certainly within the purview of the nonprofit sector and enjoys high credibility and a substantial audience.

Most hard news is obtained through *press releases*, interviews, press conferences (and briefings), and coverage of events. Most soft news is obtained through press releases and kits leading to interviews, which then result in feature articles, or through on-air interviews on talk shows (taped or live; sometimes live interviews include call-in segments). PSAs also fall under the soft news category because they carry general messages of value to society and may be placed at a station's convenience.

There are three reasons for issuing press releases: to announce an upcoming event and invite the press to cover it (this is called a press advisory), to issue a statement or take a stand on a news development or issue, or to provide background information for or to supplement late-breaking news. The content of the press release is expressed through the journalist's five Ws—who, what, where, when, and why. The lead paragraph should provide the "hook" and should include as many of the Ws as possible. Each press release should have a carefully worded headline that capsulizes the essence of the release and a standard closing paragraph stating the overall goals and services of the agency or health campaign. Follow-up phone calls to the important media are an essential part of public relations campaigns.

Press kits provide substantive briefing on an issue; each should include a press statement articulating key points, biographic information, positive editorials from newspapers of record, statistics, program information, an annual report, a recent newsletter, and a service brochure.

Press conferences should be used only if the vital information about an issue cannot be communicated adequately by a press release. A press conference should be convened by a knowledgeable and experienced moderator, and the key messages presented by press conference participants should be rehearsed and coordinated. Physicians, patients, experts, and organizational leaders are effective spokespersons (but there should be no more than three spokespersons at a single press conference).

In preparing for *an interview*, for print or electronic media, one should prepare by taking the following steps: Determine three key points that best describe the health issue that is being addressed, and be sure to articulate these in the interview; anticipate questions that might be asked beforehand, and rehearse the answers; research the reporter's style (e.g., Is the reporter interested in substantive issues, or is his or her approach inflammatory?) or the talk-show host's past performance (Is he or she well informed? Combative in style?).

Public service announcements are radio or TV messages of varying lengths (usually 10, 15, 20, 30, or 60 seconds) that promote programs, services, events, or issues of community interest sponsored by nonprofit agencies. The broadcast time for PSAs is donated to certified nonprofit agencies by the electronic media, but competition for public service time is intense.

Research shows that the public sees PSAs as important and reliable sources of health and medical information. A 1979 survey conducted by Louis Harris and Associates for the National High Blood Pressure Education Program found that, next to the doctor or clinic where treatment is received, television PSAs are seen as the most important source of health information (U.S. Department of Health and Human Services, 1983b). However, PSAs are limited in their impact. PSAs alone are not likely to cause behavior changes, especially with such ingrained and complex behaviors as smoking, sedentary life-style, or inappropriate diet. For this reason, communications programs that are designed to affect behavior use PSAs as only one component of programs that also include an array of mass media and interpersonal communication activities. (For more information on PSAs, see Atkin & Freimuth, chap. 6, this volume.)

While each media market is somewhat different, San Francisco television stations usually run well-produced PSAs for one year, rotating them through dayparts (daytime television programming segments), with a few prime-time placements. The TV stations that are willing to produce PSAs for nonprofit agencies tend to run them frequently. A television station's community affairs director is the key gatekeeper for agencies to contact.

Editorials, both in print and broadcast over electronic media, are an excellent means of reaching the general public and particularly opinion leaders. Op-ed pieces and letters to the editor are other editorial options. Editorials are written by the editorial board of a media outlet. Mailing recent and relevant studies on health care, analysis of legislation, and information about pilot programs that are of value to the community are important ways of maintaining contact with editorial boards.

On an annual basis, an agency should identify a significant health issue worthy of editorial comment and schedule a meeting with editorial boards around a milestone date or event, such as the Great American Smoke-Out Day or the anniversary of the introduction of the polio vaccine. The agency should identify a small delegation of spokespersons, develop key points to highlight the issue, and prepare a press kit for the meeting.

Many radio and TV stations broadcast 30- or 60-second editorials, which can be powerful. It is useful for agencies trying to generate editorial coverage for a health issue to send a press kit on the issue to editorial directors at radio and TV stations. If stations do not or cannot broadcast editorials, they usually allow for community representatives to tape unedited free speech messages or public opinion messages stating their particular points of view. Agencies should identify effective spokespersons to represent them on the air.

In writing an op-ed piece for a particular newspaper, one should determine the length of the piece (650-850 words) and the particular angle from which it should approach the issue (e.g., whether it should be strictly medical or should deal with the social welfare aspects of the issue). Op-ed pieces can be written in support of or in opposition to an editorial, or on timely topics not covered in the editorial column.

Research shows that the letters to the editor section is one of the most widely read sections of any newspaper. To heighten visibility for the health campaign that is being addressed, an agency can call constituents in support of the issues and request that they send original, well-written, succinct letters.

In sum, to assure maximum exposure for health issues in the media, those in charge of public communication campaigns should position the health agency as an advocate and resource to the media on the issue (see Paisley, chap. 1, this volume), respond effectively to the specific needs of reporters, develop long-term relationships with the media, and continually inform and educate the press through effective mailings.

Public Affairs

Public affairs involves lobbying and working on regulatory or legislative issues with administrators and legislators. Electoral politics (i.e., working for or against candidates running for political office) is usually included within the purview of public affairs, but it is tightly regulated, and involvement in electoral politics varies for government agencies, tax-exempt nonprofit organizations, and private corporations.

Public affairs enables health and welfare agencies to advocate for themselves effectively in the public policy arena. Through advocacy, health care programs can gain legislative visibility, apprising and educating legislators about important health care issues in their communities that directly affect the legislators' constituents. While health and social service agencies are imparting vital information about their programs and clients to legislators, they are simultaneously privy to public funding trends, budget information, and other legislative developments pertaining to health care from their legislators.

Two specific results that ensue from the communication process with legislators is that a relationship is established with them before a crisis hits (related to new bills, antagonistic legislation, or funding), and the social service agency can anticipate funding trends and the broader health care picture.

While many nonprofit agencies and social service programs lack significant dollar resources, a public affairs strategy can be implemented easily by inviting legislators to events and to appear as keynote speakers; by presenting exceptional legislators with awards; by mailing health agency or campaign newsletters, news stories, editorials, recent studies in the field, and cost-effectiveness data; by visiting them in the district, in state capitols, and in Washington; by developing personal contacts with legislative aides; and by hosting candidate forums in clinics and community centers.

Conclusion

This chapter has presented a set of strategies available to the health communicator for maximizing the impact of health education and promotion efforts in the community. Current communication literature shows that mass media can have powerful effects on some people under certain circumstances. At the start of the chapter we discussed briefly the nature of these effects, such as the agenda-setting effect of the media and their effect on the spiral of silence, on the cultivation of beliefs, and on the knowledge gap. By understanding these concepts, health communicators can develop effective media campaigns to increase the presence of positive health information and to counteract negative health messages promoted by the media via commercial advertising and programming.

In order to promote health education in the community, a health communicator can use a variety of approaches depending on the availability of resources and on the nature of the health issue. These strategies include social advertising, public relations, and public affairs. In most community campaigns, the use of social advertising is often limited by the lack of sufficient financial resources. Furthermore, the use of advertising exclusively is not always the best choice in health campaigns given their complex goals, which often focus on changing attitudes and behaviors and are not restricted simply to the dissemination of knowledge.

Public relations and public affairs are essential components of community campaigns and are generally cost-effective and appropriate strategies for health education. They allow an ongoing presence in a wide variety of media and community organizations and events, access to free time and space in media otherwise out of reach for most community health campaigns, and the possibility of affecting policy on the relevant health issues through effective public affairs.

Although these tools are available to the health educator, he or she must nonetheless confront powerful obstacles, including the interests of companies that invest heavily in commercial advertising promoting unhealthy life-styles, such as smoking and the consumption of alcohol and junk food, and well-organized adversarial groups, such as Right to Life, that oppose sex education strategies for teenagers needed to counteract the "sex without consequences" messages presented by the media.

It is in this less-than-favorable environment in which the health educator must operate. By discussing some of the ways in which the media can be used to influence people's knowledge, attitudes, and behaviors and by providing some specific tools for the design of community campaigns, this chapter attempts to make this worthy task more effective.

Appendix:
Audience Research Relating to
Broadcast and Print Media

This Appendix defines some sources, terms, and applications of ratings-based audience research as it relates to broadcast and print media (see Table 5.2). Excellent discussions and examples of ratings data, ratings applications, and media planning are provided by Belville (1988), Surmanek (1986), and Wimmer and Dominick (1987).

Television

The primary research source for TV audiences is the Nielsen rating book. TV ratings data are published from overnight to annually, depending on the complexity of the information and the size of the market, termed *designated market area* (DMA) by Nielsen or *area of dominant influence* (ADI) by Arbitron.

In order to understand TV buying, one needs to become familiar with the following terms and definitions (from Belville, 1988): "A rating is the estimated percent of all television households, or of all people within a demographic group in the survey area sample who view a specific program or station" (p. 310). *"Households using television* (HUT) is the percent of all television households in the area surveyed with one or more sets in use. It is the sum of all program ratings for each time period" (p. 310). (Similar variables can be computed for specific demographic groups, such as women 18 years and older, to obtain measures related to *people using television.*) "A *share* is the percent of households using television (HUT) tuned to a particular program or station for a specific time period" (p. 310). The shares of all stations at any one time sum to 100%, unless two or more programs are viewed simultaneously on multiple sets in the household. *"Cumulative ratings* (cumes) reports the number of different households or persons who tune to a particular program or station or combination of either over a specified time period" (p. 313); thus cumes represent the relevant net unduplicated audience.

In buying TV and radio time, advertising media planners frequently rely on *gross ratings points* (GRPs) to determine an optimum schedule and specific stations to buy. The GRP is "the sum of all rating points achieved (or sought) in a given market area for a particular time span" (p. 312). For example, if a spot aired on KPIX TV in San Francisco Monday through Friday, 6:00-6:30 p.m., during the evening news, received a rating of 10, and the spot airs five times, its GRP would be 50. The GRP represents a percentage of the cumulative universe (i.e., TV households) that tuned in to that station during that time period. The GRP is the product of the reach (number of distinct households) times the average frequency (the average number of times each distinct household is exposed to the message). The figure 50 GRPs does not translate to 50% of all TV households being tuned in every evening from 6:00 to 6:30 p.m., but rather means that the spot was seen by, for example, 50% of all households once, or 10% of all households five times. Finally, a *gross impression* (GI) "is the sum of the average audience (households or persons) for all commercial placements" for an advertiser's schedule (p. 314).

One rating point is equivalent to one percentage of the population in a given DMA presented in the Nielsen rating book or ADI in the Arbitron book. Therefore, if a particular media market has a population of 500,000, one rating point in that market would translate to 5,000 viewers. To determine exactly how many people are watching a particular program in the ADI, multiply the rating by 1% of the population in the market.

One other key principle of TV buying is *dispersion*, which is the accumulation of different adult viewers. High dispersion means exposing as many different viewers to as many different programs as possible (e.g., increasing reach while probably reducing frequency). If there are two advertisers buying 100 women GRPs per month, but one advertiser buys spots on two programs while the other buys spots on four different programs, the advertiser using four different programs will probably expose more unduplicated viewers (i.e., achieve greater dispersion).

Nonprofit agencies and health campaigns precluded from paid TV and radio advertising have access to public service air time, as discussed in the Public Relations section of this chapter.

Radio

Audience research on radio is provided primarily by Arbitron ratings. Typically, radio is bought on the basis of reach and frequency. Media buyers determine reach and frequency from a given GRP level or determine GRPs needed to achieve a "reach" goal. In buying radio time or planning a PSA schedule, it is important to target audiences narrowly, combining dayparts (6:00 a.m.-10:00 a.m., 10:00 a.m.-3:00 p.m., 7:00 p.m.-midnight) and a sufficient number of stations to achieve, for example, an overall 60% reach goal and share of radio listeners in the particular target audience. Radio is often bought on a 12x, 24x, or 36x spot schedule on a weekly basis adding up to the GRP goal or the "reach" goal.

While rating and audience information is largely the same for radio and TV, there are some noteworthy differences. While the geographical

TABLE 5.3 Example Four-Week Reach and Frequency for Different Daypart and Demographic Packages

Monthly Gross Rating Points	Drivetime Package		Adult Females Midday Package		Teenagers Afternoon-Evening Package	
	Reach	*Frequency*	*Reach*	*Frequency*	*Reach*	*Frequency*
200	55	3.6	35	5.7	56	3.6
300	66	4.5	46	6.5	64	4.7
400	74	5.4	48	8.3	73	5.5
500	76	6.6	52	9.6	84	10.0

SOURCE: Barban et al. (1981)
NOTE: Based on stations per market needed to achieve at least 60% share of market's radio audience (combined/daypart).

area for TV is defined as DMA, for radio it is referred to as the *total survey area* (TSA). The TSA includes the metro area and those counties where at least two home market stations provide substantial strength. *Shares* are the percentage of listeners belonging to a given station during an average quarter hour. For example, a station may command 19.0% of the females 18-24 listening between 6:00 and 10:00 a.m. *Cume listening* is the unduplicated audience measure. It is the estimated number of *different* persons who will listen to the station for at least six minutes of, say, a given quarter hour within a specific daypart over a specific period of time. For example, while a station may average 300 young male listeners 18-24 per quarter hour (6:00-10:00 a.m., Monday-Friday), on a cume basis (or at the end of one week), a considerably larger number of *different* men in that age group may hear the station for at least one quarter hour sometime between 6:00 and 10:00 a.m. during the week.

By looking at Arbitron ratings, the planner for a radio buy or PSA placement can reach narrowly defined target populations. For PSA campaigns, even though the planner has no control over the rotation of the spots and the time of broadcast, this information at least tells the planner that a certain station is important for this target; the planner might devise creative ways to promote the campaign by working closely with the station's public affairs director. Radio, like TV, is also bought on the basis of gross ratings points or a "reach" goal. Table 5.3 shows a sample 4-week reach and frequency schedule. To achieve 200 teenager GRPs or a 56% reach goal with a 3.6 frequency in an afternoon-evening package, it is necessary to purchase a certain number of spots on at least three, if not four, of the top stations in the market.

Newspaper

The primary sources for newspaper audience information are the Standard Rate and Data Service (SRDS) for Daily Newspapers and the Simmons Market Research Bureau guide. For planning purposes, advertisers today look at more than circulation numbers. Measures that show degrees of coverage or household penetration are also important.

Metro area coverage reflects the federal government's standard metropolitan statistical area (SMSA) borders. The coverage is computed by dividing each paper's circulation (theoretically, one copy sold = one household) by the total households in the metro area. *Gross metro coverage* is the sum total of each market's newspaper coverage (e.g., New York's newspaper coverage is 56%, which is the sum of the three dailies, or 33 + 12 + 11). There is a degree of duplication (homes receiving more than one daily newspaper), but the newspapers do not provide the overlap factor or the net circulation for households. *Gross line rate* is the cost of one line of advertising in the number of daily newspapers listed in any market and of course varies by edition, size, color, and placement. *Cost per rating point* is calculated in the same way as broadcast estimates (i.e., cost of advertising placement is divided by audience coverage or gross rating point) (Simmons Market Research Bureau, 1985).

Magazine

The common practice in magazine buying is to use space in several magazines concurrently. This requires the planner to determine the unduplicated readers from magazine combinations. The two main measurement sources for magazine audiences are the Standard Rate and Data Service (SRDS) for Consumer Magazines and the Simmons Market Research Bureau (SMRB) guide.

> Magazines handle custom-area (i.e., regional edition) space costs on the basis of per-thousand-circulation used per insertion. First, the advertiser determines what areas are needed. Then the circulations for each area are added together to find the total-issue circulation. Next, the magazine's rate card is checked to find the appropriate per thousand factor. CPM factors can involve color, size of advertisement, the number of insertions . . . the range of circulation, the presence of color, the number of issues involved [and various combinations]. Once the factor is identified it is multiplied by the number of thousands of circulation to learn the per insertion rate. (Barban et al., 1981)

The SMRB provides readership research by product use levels. This means that the reading habits of individuals are matched by what products they buy and the degree to which those products are consumed. SMRB provides readership and circulation numbers for single magazines, but also publishes figures on two-magazine combinations. For more than two magazines, mathematical projection models need to be used to determine net or unduplicated audiences.

The key is to determine whether the target audience is a better-than-average, average, or lower-than-average prospect as a user of a particular product, in the context of other campaign goals. For example, for headache remedies and pain relievers (nonprescription) consumed by adult users, the 1985 SMRB reports show that while *Time* magazine has over 5 million adults who are classified as medium users of these medications, only 13% of all consumers of these medications read a typical issue of *Time*. Credibility, image, and status are important issues in magazine ad placement. For example, *TV Guide* has a circulation of over 39 million, while *Time* magazine has a circulation of 23 million (Simmons Market Research Bureau, 1985). Yet, a health campaign might benefit more from an ad in *Time* than in *TV Guide* because of status and credibility. So while *Time* magazine, from a cost-effectiveness perspective, may not be an advisable placement for a print ad, it might be worth considering from the perspective of image, credibility, and status.

Public service space is offered by some magazines to nonprofits on a limited basis.

6

Formative Evaluation Research in Campaign Design

Charles K. Atkin
Vicki Freimuth

Over the past two decades, the mass media have presented an increasing array of health campaigns intended to combat heart disease, cancer, smoking, drug and alcohol abuse, and unsafe driving. Researchers have concluded that these education and persuasion campaigns achieved only limited success, and have identified a key reason: Most are underdeveloped at the preparation, production, and dissemination phases of implementation due to poor conceptualization and inadequate formative evaluation research inputs (Atkin, 1979, 1981a, 1981b; Blane & Hewitt, 1980; Flay, 1981; Novelli, 1982; O'Keefe, 1985; Palmer, 1981; Solomon, 1984; Wallack, 1981). This situation is in distinct contrast to commercial advertising campaigns, where strategies for influencing the audience are based on extensive precampaign research activities, such as market segmentation analysis, consumer opinion surveys, focus group interviews, and message pretesting.

Evaluation research seeks to answer questions about the target audience for a project, program, or campaign, including collection of background information about audience orientations before initiating a campaign, and assessment of the implementation and effectiveness during and after a campaign (Flay & Best, 1982; Flay & Cook, chap. 8, this volume). According to Palmer (1981), *formative research* provides data and perspectives to improve messages during the course of creation. He divides this type of evaluation into two phases. The first involves *preproduction research,* "in which data are accumulated on audience characteristics that relate importantly to the medium, the message, and the situation within which the desired behavior will occur" (p. 227). The second type of formative research is *production testing,* also known as pretesting, or copy testing, in which prototype or pilot messages are pretested to obtain audience reactions prior to final production. There has been significant progress toward standardizing and implementing production testing methods in health campaigns, with the creation of the Health Message Testing Service program (Bratic, Greenberg, & Peterson, 1980) and the preparation of the handbook *Pretesting in Health Communications* (U.S. Department of Health and Human Services, 1984b). The principles, guidelines, and pragmatics of message pretesting are described in the latter half of this chapter.

However, health educators have not typically used systematic approaches at the preproduction stage, as mass media campaign efforts often proceed in the absence of a research foundation. Instead, messages tend to be produced in a haphazard fashion based on creative inspiration of copywriters and artists, patterned after the normative standards of the health campaign genre. Only minimal background information about the audience is utilized in devising message appeals and presentation styles, in selecting source spokespersons and channels, and in identifying specialized subgroups to be reached. Furthermore, the formulation of basic campaign goals and specific objectives is seldom based on research identifying priority areas of concentration and critical stages of the communication process that must be addressed.

This chapter seeks to show why formative evaluation research is a valuable resource in developing more effective health campaigns, to describe the two phases of formative research, and to illustrate the preproduction process in the case of drunk driving prevention.

Conceptual Framework for Campaign Persuasion

The conventional approach to designing persuasion strategies involves dissecting the communication process into source, message, channel, and receiver variables as inputs and a series of information-processing and response variables as outcomes. One widely used model is McGuire's (chap. 2, this volume) input-output matrix, which includes the four variables mentioned above along with destination factors on the input side of the matrix.

The source, channel, and message components are manipulable by the campaign designer. The *source* is generally the visible presenter (rather than the ultimate sponsor or person who constructs the message) whom the audience perceives as delivering the message, characterized in terms of demographics (age, sex, socioeconomic status), credibility (expertise, trustworthiness), and attractiveness. Each *message* can feature a variety of content dimensions (themes, appeals, claims, evidence, and recommendations) using various formats of organization and styles of packaging; the overall series of messages in a campaign can vary in volume, repetition, prominence of placement, and scheduling. The *channel* variables comprise both the medium of transmission (television, radio, newspapers, magazines, booklets) and the particular media vehicle (e.g., specific radio station or magazine title).

Although *receiver* factors are not subject to manipulation, sensitivity to the background attributes, abilities, and predispositions of individuals enhances the effectiveness of campaign stimuli. Finally, the *destination* encompasses the array of impacts that the campaign aims to produce, such as immediate versus long-term change, prevention versus cessation, direct versus two-step flow of influence, and intermediate responses versus ultimate behavioral outcomes.

The output variables have been conceptualized in a number of ways, typically beginning with exposure and processing, followed by the hierarchy of cognitive, affective, and behavioral consequences of the campaign inputs. McGuire lists twelve successive response steps, while Flay (1981) separates the responses into four intermediate processes and seven dependent variable outcomes. Other models adapted for health persuasion, such as Rogers's (1983) innovation adoption sequence (knowledge, persuasion, decision, and confirmation) are reviewed by Albert (1981) and Atkin (1981a).

Combining elements from various models, this chapter proposes that receivers move through five basic stages, each with several substeps. The first is exposure, which includes encountering the stimulus and paying attention to it. The next stage is information processing, including comprehension of the content, selective perception of source and appeals, and evaluative reactions such as liking, agreeing, and counterarguing. The third stage is cognitive learning, which involves knowledge gain and skills acquisition. Fourth, the yielding stage encompasses the formation or change of affective orientations such as beliefs, saliences, values, attitudes, and behavioral intentions. Finally, a utilization stage includes retrieval and proximate motivation, the action itself, postbehavioral consolidation, and long-run continuation and maintenance of the practice.

Considering the dynamic forces that explain how campaign inputs and individual predispositions move the audience through the output stages, several social psychological theories are relevant to mediated campaigns on topics such as health. The instrumental learning perspective of Hovland, Janis, and Kelley (1953) focuses attention on factors such as source credibility, the incentives in the message appeal, and repetition. The social learning or imitation approach articulated by Bandura (1977b) emphasizes the importance of the characteristics of source role models, the explicit demonstration of target behaviors, and the depiction of vicarious positive and negative reinforcements. The cognitive response perspective focuses on the thoughts that the receiver generates while processing messages (Petty & Cacioppo, 1981); the individual actively relates content to prior knowledge and experience and forms new connections or arguments.

Most pertinent are expectancy-value formulations, particularly the Ajzen and Fishbein (1980) theory of reasoned action. Their model stresses the role of beliefs concerning the likelihood that performance of a behavior leads to certain consequences, which, when combined with evaluations of the outcomes, determine the attitude. Another feature of their model is the influence of subjective norms, based on beliefs about the orientations of particular referent groups or persons toward the behavior. For a more elaborate extension of the approaches introduced by Bandura and Fishbein, see Flay's (1981) integrative model of attitude and behavior change. Also relevant to micro-level processes in health persuasion are concepts from the health belief model (Maiman & Becker, 1974), protection motivation theory (Kleinot & Rogers, 1982; Rogers, 1975), and self-efficacy theory (Bandura, 1977a). This brief overview of the campaign influence variables suggests some types of information that should be obtained to facilitate campaign planning.

Preproduction Research

In preproduction formative evaluation research, the strategist attempts to learn as much as possible about the intended audience before specifying goals and devising strategies. The campaign designer needs to identify target audiences and target behaviors, specify critical intermediate response variables, ascertain channel exposure patterns, and determine receptivity to potential message components.

To collect these kinds of information, two research techniques are most commonly employed at the preproduction stage. *Focus group* sessions are conducted by a moderator who stimulates extensive open-ended discussions of selected issues in a small group setting (see the Pretesting section of this chapter for a detailed description of this method). More quantitative data are provided by formal sample *surveys* of audience members, using standardized questionnaires or interview schedules to measure a broad array of variables systematically. LaRose (1980) and Mielke and Chen (1983) discuss a wide variety of other methods also available to the formative researcher.

The preproduction stage of the formative research process will be illustrated with selected findings from a series of surveys and supplemental focus group interviews carried out as part of a drunk driving prevention project (Atkin, Garramone, & Anderson, 1986). Since drunk driving poses one of the most serious health problems in the United States, numerous campaigns to combat it have been mounted over the past several decades. Although certain campaign messages have exhibited clever creativity and featured manifestly convincing arguments, the overall campaign efforts appear to be poorly designed and executed due in part to insufficient preproduction research information (U.S. Department of Transportation, 1985). Thus the U.S. Department of Transportation sponsored a project to conduct a social marketing analysis of the drunk driving topic; the preproduction phase included seven telephone, mail, and classroom surveys of samples of 500-800 respondents representing key target audiences (teenagers, parents, college students, party hosts, and the general adult public).

Identifying the Target Audiences

Effective campaigns seldom aim at a broad cross-section of the public; instead, they focus on specialized segments of the overall audience. Formative research is useful in identifying the high-priority target subgroups by providing data regarding which categories of individuals are at risk, which are most receptive to media persuasion on the topic, and which are in a position to influence high-risk persons interpersonally.

Survey measures with representative samples are typically used to segment the audience along a number of dimensions defined in terms of demographic and psychographic characteristics, social role position, behavioral risk profile, predispositions, future behavioral intentions, and media exposure patterns.

In the case of drunk driving, the surveys show that 16-24-year-old males who drink heavily at weekend parties are far more likely than other groups to drive while intoxicated or ride with a drunk driver; this high-risk segment constitutes less than 5% of the population. The research also indicates that several other target audiences display promising potential for attempting interpersonal intervention to prevent drunk driving: parents of high school students (who can prohibit their teenagers from attending unsupervised drinking parties), adult party hosts (who can discourage excessive drinking by guests, or arrange alternative transportation for intoxicated drivers), and female passengers riding with heavy-drinking dates or mates (who can warn their drivers not to overconsume, or take over the driving role on the ride home). In terms of receptivity, parents are an example of a favorably predisposed segment; the data show that most disapprove of teenage drinking, believe that teenage drunk driving is a serious problem, and desire to know techniques to prevent their sons or daughters from becoming involved in drunk driving incidents.

Specifying the Target Behavior

The ultimate goal of a campaign is typically behavioral change, such as reduction in the incidence of drunk driving. However, most practices are a product of various component behaviors (e.g., drunk driving may be reduced if the driver abstains from alcohol, drinks limited quantities, or allows a sober person to drive home), which in turn are determined by social and environmental factors (e.g., availability of attractive nonalcoholic drinks, or suggestions by companions to limit consumption). Formative research is helpful in specifying which particular behaviors and external factors are most influential in altering the focal practices and which are most amenable to change via campaign messages; these variables are then incorporated as concrete objectives in the campaign plan.

In the case of social intervention to prevent drunk driving, survey research reveals two examples of priority target behaviors. One potentially effective tactic is to encourage the female passenger to drive the car back from a drinking occasion, because the data show that women tend to become less intoxicated than their male drivers, and yet most allow the male to drive. Findings also indicate that half of young adults planning to ride back with a driver hesitate to put pressure on that person to stay sober enough to drive safely, while most drivers say they would respond cooperatively to such dissuasion by cutting back on consumption; thus an important target behavior is more frequent influence attempts by companions to prevent their driver from exceeding the safe drinking limit.

Regarding target audience receptiveness to behavioral recommendations, the survey of party hosts asked the sample to rate 22 potential hosting techniques in terms of acceptability (how comfortable they would feel in using each strategy, and how offensive they believed each strategy would be regarded by guests). Results indicated that a number of effective techniques are rated as highly acceptable (e.g., actively offering food to drinkers, arranging for another guest to drive an intoxicated person home, expressing concern that a driver is drinking too much), while other actions are disdained (e.g., having guests check in their car keys upon arrival, warning drinking drivers about accident risks, stopping service of alcohol two hours before the party's end). Such formative evaluation data enable designers to narrow the list to the most promising techniques, and to isolate which less acceptable but critically important behaviors would require extra persuasive emphasis in order to be changed.

Elaborating Intermediate Responses

As a means to attaining the behavioral objectives, campaign messages must first have an impact on preliminary or intermediate target variables along the response chain, ranging from exposure and processing to learning and yielding to actual utilization. In particular, campaign designers face certain barriers that must be overcome; these individual resistance points often involve misconceptions, dysfunctional attitudes, and behavioral inhibitions. Isolation of the most crucial response stages is facilitated by an understanding of the characteristics and predispositions of the target audience. Focus groups and sample surveys are both valuable tools providing topic-specific background information for mapping the domains discussed below.

Knowledge and lexicon. Research illuminates the target audience's entry-level awareness and information holding about the subject of the campaign, identifying what is already known, what gaps exist, what confusions must be clarified, and what misinformation must be corrected (see Dervin, chap. 3, this volume); the level of familiarity with and comprehension of topic-related vocabulary and terminology can also be ascertained. For example, only one-fourth of the surveyed drinkers knew the legal blood alcohol level (.1%) that would result in arrest for driving under the influence, just half realized that eating food before drinking substantially reduces intoxication, and one-fifth incorrectly thought that drinking coffee helps to sober up a driver. The surveys show that people have diverse meanings for key terms such as *social drinker* and *moderation*, diverse labels for the state of intoxication, and limited understanding of concepts such as intervention and designated driver.

Beliefs and images. Since many campaign message strategies seek to alter subjective conceptions such as perceived social norms or estimated probability of outcomes associated with the behavioral practice, it is important to measure precisely the preexisting cognitive orientations held by individuals. For example, data show that drinkers underestimate the degree of social disapproval of drunk driving (fully two-fifths believe that others excuse drunk driving, while just 5% of the public is actually tolerant) and overestimate the statistical risks of both crashes and police apprehension (the typical driver perceives that the odds of arrest while driving drunk on a given evening are 1 in 100, while police figures show the chances are 1 in 2,000). This tells a strategist that messages should feature information about social norms, but should not emphasize facts about arrest probability.

Attitudes and values. Affective predispositions are also a significant consideration in message design, particularly evaluations of outcomes associated with practices. Depending on the direction, intensity, and structure of relevant values and attitudes, the campaign may concentrate on creation, conversion, reinforcement, or activation. The last two strategies are appropriate for most drivers, who already hold a negative attitudinal set toward the act of drunk driving and regard the crash and apprehension consequences as undesirable; messages that intensify the negativity of outcomes (e.g., monetary costs of conviction or difficulty of coping without a license) appear to be promising. On the other hand, the research shows that most men dismiss the embarrassment or threat to masculinity resulting from a wife or girlfriend driving them home, indicating that this presumed obstacle need not be addressed in campaign appeals.

Salience priorities. Research also provides guidance concerning which cognitive and affective orientations need to be made more or less salient. Since most drivers already believe that there is a substantial risk of crash involvement, but only one-fourth consciously contemplate this possibility, increasing the salience of this outcome would lead drivers to give it greater weight relative to other factors when setting a limit or deciding whether or not to consume additional drinks. By contrast, the vast majority regards drunk driving as a serious problem facing society, indicating little need for campaigning designed to raise this issue on the public's agenda.

Efficacy and skills. For certain practices, many well-intentioned and highly motivated individuals fail to carry out appropriate acts because they lack confidence in their ability to perform the behaviors competently (see McAlister, Ramirez, Galavotti, & Gallion, chap. 13, and Reardon, chap. 12, this volume). If research shows that this is a barrier, messages can seek to enhance personal efficacy or provide training for specific skills. For example, survey findings demonstrate that while most companions agree that it is important to help drivers limit consumption and to prevent intoxicated friends from driving, many of them wish they knew better techniques for discouraging excessive drinking or handling a drunk friend who insists on driving.

Ascertaining Channel Use

In deciding which channels are most efficient and effective for disseminating campaign messages, strategists need to determine the mass media preferences and interpersonal communication patterns of target audiences. While many basic exposure figures are available from commercial audience measurement services such as Nielsen (see Alcalay & Taplin, chap. 5, this volume), customized surveys provide a much more elaborate and relevant array of data.

At a general level, it is useful to know the following information about the intended receivers: amount of time spent watching television, listening to radio, and reading magazines and newspapers; usage of specific media vehicles (local radio stations, magazine titles); attention to various types of media content (news, public service messages); exposure to secondary channels (movie theater slides, pamphlets, direct mail, billboards, bumper stickers, posters, matchbooks); and interpersonal contact networks.

Topic-specific data are more pertinent to campaign planning: consumption of media content presenting subject matter that complements or competes with campaign messages (product ads, news items, feature stories, entertainment portrayals); interpersonal communication about topic (interactions with opinion leaders, informal conversations, peer pressures); and exposure to prior campaign messages (attention to topical PSAs and posters).

Beyond sheer exposure, formative researchers can obtain credibility ratings for media channels, vehicles, and content categories, and measure audience recall and evaluative reactions to messages disseminated in previous campaigns. For example, the drunk driving surveys found that teenage male drinkers tend to listen to rock music stations, while adult party hosts are heavy readers of local newspapers; that the typical person is exposed each day to a dozen prodrinking portrayals in beer commercials and prime-time television shows and to several depictions of risky driving behavior in crime dramas; that one-fourth of adults have tried to discourage a drunk person verbally from driving; that teenage drivers perceive moderately strong peer pressure to avoid getting drunk if driving; that young adults pay attention to an average of two anti-drunk driving TV PSAs per week, but see almost no promoderation spots; that more than half the public has noticed news stories about local police efforts to catch drunk drivers, and most of these people report being more likely to drink safely or warn companions as a result of the publicity; and that many teenage drinkers discredit safety threats featured in PSAs.

Preliminary Evaluation of Message Components

Before campaign stimuli are drafted, strategic and creative approaches are facilitated by both informal feedback and formal ratings for prospective source presenters, message themes, persuasive arguments, and stylistic devices. In the drunk driving project, focus group discussions explored reactions to altruistic versus fear appeals for motivating intervention attempts and examined the appropriateness of humorous versus serious treatment of the subject. Survey questionnaires presented a listing of several dozen spokespersons, arguments, and claims under consideration for campaign messages; believability and effectiveness scores for each component were measured along a scale from 0 to 10.

Armed with the background information collected in the preproduction phase of campaign design, the strategy and research specialists are in a position to work with creative personnel in formulating potential message ideas (and specific headlines, slogans, copy points, layouts, formats, artwork, music, and special effects), selecting visible source presenter talent to appear in the messages, and determining the most appropriate media for communicating the material (such as the telenovelas or rock music videos discussed by Singhal & Rogers, chap. 15, this volume). As this stimulus construction process progresses, further research inputs are provided in the form of message pretesting.

Pretesting Research

The second basic phase of formative evaluation conducted in developing campaign messages is pretesting, the process of systematically gathering target audience reactions to preliminary versions of messages before they are produced in final form (Bertrand, 1978; U.S. Department of Health and Human Services, 1984b). Pretesting can help determine which of several alternative ideas or draft message executions are most effective, or it can identify strengths and weaknesses in single executions. Pretesting research is used at two stages in message creation: concept development and message execution.

Developing the Concept

Concepts are partially formulated message ideas, consisting of visual sketches and key phrases that convey the main elements to be represented in the finished product. Pretesting at this stage provides direction for eliminating weaker approaches and identifying the most promising concepts. Sometimes entirely new concepts emerge from audience responses, while original ideas are revised and refined. This initial concept testing saves considerable time and money by narrowing down choices before production of complete messages is undertaken.

For instance, in the development of a mass media campaign to increase public awareness of the health risks associated with exposure to asbestos, four message concepts were prepared and pretested (Freimuth & Van Nevel, 1981). These concepts were based on a communication strategy that sought to increase public understanding of the problems of asbestos exposure and also to convey the importance of taking certain actions if exposure has occurred. The message concepts were pretested among panels of older, blue-collar males and females typical of the target audience. To give each message concept a visual dimension, a representative drawing was positioned next to several lines of copy and presented in poster form. Several different characters were used to present the message (e.g., an elderly shipyard worker, a doctor, the family members of a former shipyard worker, and a movie celebrity). Pretesting indicated that the message concept using a doctor as presenter did not fare well with male respondents and was considered the least interesting visually. In the end, the shipyard worker and his family were selected as the most appropriate and effective presenters.

Another advantage to pretesting rough concepts is the generation of words, phrases, and vernacular utilized by the target audience so that appropriate language can be used in formulating complete messages (as noted in the section on knowledge and lexicon, above). For example, pathologists believed that a lay description of the symptoms of melanoma (a form of skin cancer) should be "notched, blue-black, irregular spots." Interviews with members of the target population, however, suggested different adjectives entirely. When shown pictures of the symptoms, respondents' descriptions included "looks like a bad sunburn," "a small rash," "blotchy," or "a bad scrape" (U.S. Department of Health and Human Services, 1984b).

Executing the Test Message

Once the concepts with the most potential have been selected, complete messages can be created in rough form for the next stage of pretesting: message execution. Rough executions of televised PSAs may include animatics, photomatics, or informally shot live-action spots. In the animatic form, motion is simulated by sequentially videotaping or filming artwork, storyboards, or cartoon frames that realistically represent the planned final product. Photomatic spots simulate motion through the sequential videotaping or filming of a minimum of eight still-frame photographs. In the rough live-action spot, an actual "run-through" of the spot is filmed or videotaped using simplified sets, nonprofessional talent, and preliminary audio tracks.

Radio PSAs and print materials also can be prepared for testing in rough form. If music or sound effects will be used in the final audio product, they also should be included in the rough message.

At the message-execution stage, pretesting can be used to predict how effectively a message will move the target audience through the five basic stages of reaction to campaign stimuli discussed earlier. Specifically, pretesting can assess the attention value of a message, measure its comprehensibility, determine its relevance to the target audience, identify strengths and weaknesses, and gauge any sensitive or controversial elements.

Assessing attention. An essential ingredient of messages is their ability to attract the target audience's attention. Since messages are rarely seen or heard in an isolated media environment, they should be tested in the context of other messages. For commercial advertisements and public service announcements, attention is usually measured by an unaided recall item on a paper-and-pencil survey instrument. After exposure to a clutter format of five to seven spot messages placed within an entertainment program, the audience is asked to list all the ads or public service messages they remember seeing. More direct observational methods also have been used to assess attention. Children's Television Workshop has used the distracter method, which measures attention by observing whether children's eyes are focused on the program or on a competing stimulus (LaRose, 1980). The program analyzer technique equips subjects viewing messages with individual digital audience response stations; by moving their dials or pushing appropriate buttons, subjects can continuously record their interest in a message (LaRose, 1980; Mielke & Chen, 1983).

Measuring comprehension. Messages must be understood before they can be accepted. Procedures for measuring comprehension range from highly structured, closed-ended questions to open-ended requests for recall of main ideas. For example, the rough form of a PSA on teenage smoking used "balloons" similar to those found in cartoon strips to represent the characters' thoughts. During pretesting it was discovered that this approach only confused the audience, so the balloons were dropped from the finished spot.

Identifying strong and weak points. Pretesting prior to final production and distribution can help ensure that each element of a message is likely to meet the information needs of the audience. For example, messages promoting long-term compliance with high blood pressure medication regimens have been pretested and found to have some weaknesses. First, there was a question as to whether the most important point in the messages—the need for daily medication—was understood to be about medication for hypertension, or simply to be the need for medication in general, as prescribed for any illness. Second, respondents had trouble understanding the jingle lyrics even after two exposures. As a result, these PSAs were changed by clarifying the specific need for daily antihypertension medication and by rearranging the musical delivery (U.S. Department of Health and Human Services, 1984b).

Determining personal relevance. Target audiences must perceive that a message personally applies to them for the message to be effective. Pretest results for a booklet on high blood pressure revealed several important differences in the responses among hypertensives versus the general public. Hypertensives recalled and understood more specific points related to high blood pressure control than did the general audience group. Further, when asked whom the booklet was for, a higher proportion of hypertensives felt the booklet was "talking to someone like me" (U.S. Department of Health and Human Services, 1984b).

Gauging sensitive or controversial elements. Questions about audience sensitivity to subject matter often arise in developing messages. Pretesting can help in finding out whether messages may alienate or offend target audiences. For example, will a bare-breasted woman who demonstrates breast self-examination on television be an affront to adult viewers? Pretest results for such a campaign indicated that most respondents felt that the message performed a useful public service, although consensus was not as strong in regard to the issue of the message's suitability for a general audience, or for airing at any time of day. Based on pretest data, the decision was made to broadcast the message (U.S. Department of Health and Human Services, 1984b). This example is quite different from another instance in which a major medical institution in Texas produced a similar message. In that case, a physician in charge of the health education program took one look at the bare-breasted demonstration, decreed that it was offensive to the lay public, and killed the project.

Types of Pretesting

The six methods of pretesting discussed in this section have been employed in the development of public service messages; these techniques are presented in the order that they are typically applied in moving from earlier to later states of pretest research. (Wimmer & Dominick, 1987, provide more detail on the strengths and weaknesses of these and other data-collection methods.)

Focus Group Interviews

Focus group interviews are a form of qualitative research adapted by marketing researchers from group therapy (Higginbothan & Cox, 1979). They are conducted with a group of some 8-10 respondents simultaneously. Using a discussion outline, a moderator keeps the session on track while allowing respondents to talk freely and spontaneously. As new topics related to the outline emerge, the moderator probes further to gain useful insights.

Focus group interviews are especially useful as a pretesting tool in the concept-development stage of the communication process. They provide insights into target audience beliefs on an issue, allow program planners to obtain perceptions of message concepts, and help trigger the creative thinking of communication professionals. The group discussion stimulates respondents to talk freely, providing valuable clues for developing materials in the consumers' own language.

As with any qualitative research approach, however, care must be taken not to interpret focus group interview results quantitatively. If, for example, 5 out of 10 respondents in a focus group do not understand portions of the messages, it does not necessarily mean that 50% of the total target population will be confused. Such lack of understanding among the pretest respondents suggests, however, that the message may need revisions to increase comprehension. In sum, focus group testing is indicative, not definitive.

As with all pretesting research, focus group respondents should be typical of the intended target audience. Subgroups within the target audience representing relevant positions on the issues should be included, usually in separate focus groups. For example, in testing message concepts on smoking aimed at a general audience of smokers, a cross-section of individuals—males and females, heavy and light smokers, older and younger—might be recruited for the groups.

Respondents are recruited, typically by field recruiting services, one to three weeks in advance of the focus group sessions, usually by telephone but also by mail. Respondents may be randomly recruited, using the telephone directory, and screened to determine if they qualify for the group, or they may be recruited from a local organization that represents the target population.

An experienced, capable moderator should lead the groups. The moderator must be well informed about the subject and the purpose of the group sessions. A good moderator builds rapport and trust and should probe respondents without reacting to and thereby influencing their opinions. A good moderator keeps the discussion on track while talking as little as possible and makes it clear that he or she is not an expert on the subject under discussion (Higginbothan & Cox, 1979).

 Individual In-Depth Interviews

Individual in-depth interviews are used for pretesting issues that are very sensitive or must be probed very deeply and for respondents who are difficult to recruit for focus group interviews, such as physicians, dentists, and chief executive officers. Such interviews can be quite long, lasting from 30 minutes to an hour, and are used to assess comprehension as well as feelings, emotions, attitudes, and prejudices.

Pretesting through individual in-depth interviews is often applied at the concept-development stage. Like focus group interviews, in-depth interviews yield qualitative rather than quantitative results that must be interpreted carefully. Even though in-depth interviews are very costly and time-consuming, they may be the most appropriate form of pretesting for sensitive subjects (e.g., breast reconstruction) (see Dervin, chap. 3, this volume).

Central-Location Intercept Interview

Central-location intercept interviews involve stationing interviewers at a point frequented by individuals from desired target audiences and asking them to participate in the pretest. One advantage to this type of pretesting is that a high-traffic area can yield a large number of interviews in a reasonably short time. For instance, a Baltimore shopping mall was used to interview 340 men and women about messages on DES (a drug once used to prevent miscarriages) in two days (U.S. Department of Health and Human Services, 1984b). The second advantage is that using a central location for hard-to-reach target audiences can be a cost-effective means of gathering data. For example, in pretesting messages designed for expectant mothers, a prenatal clinic was used.

A typical central-location interview begins with the intercept. Potential respondents are stopped and sometimes are asked screening questions to determine if they belong to the target audience. If they are willing to participate, respondents are taken to the interviewing station, shown the pretest messages, and asked a series of questions to assess their reactions to the message concepts or executions.

This method of pretesting usually involves more respondents than either focus group interviews or in-depth interviews, and the questions are more structured. However, the sampling is not random and the results cannot be generalized to a larger population. A significant disadvantage of this pretesting method is the lack of camouflage; since respondents know they are participating in a test, their responses may be less valid.

Self-Administered Questionnaires

Self-administered questionnaires also can be used to pretest concepts and rough messages. These questionnaires can be mailed to respondents along with pretest materials or distributed at a central location. Each respondent is asked to review the materials, complete the questionnaire, and return it by a certain date.

Although the use of self-administered questionnaires is relatively inexpensive, they do have several disadvantages. First, response rate may be very low. It may be necessary to do several follow-up mailings even to reach a modest 50% response rate. Moreover, there is the additional problem of the differences between respondents and non-respondents. Indeed, only individuals who like the pretest materials may respond, resulting in a systematic bias in the pretest results and possibly in the completed message.

 Theater Testing

Theater testing uses forced exposure to test rough television message executions in controlled settings. Although this technique is generally used with commercial messages, it has been modified to test public service announcements for television. Testing takes place with several hundred respondents representative of the message's target audience.

Respondents are recruited by random-digit telephone calls that invite them to preview and evaluate new television or radio program materials. The television or radio program material is used to camouflage the intent of the testing situation. At each test location, respondents are seated in groups of approximately 25 around large television monitors. To avoid interviewer bias, all questions are prerecorded and administered over TV monitors.

Test commercials and the PSA are embedded in two half-hour television programs. Respondents are exposed to each message twice. The first exposure occurs in a program consisting of four variety acts that are interrupted by a station break in which seven commercials are played back to back. This "clutter" sequence is meant to stimulate an on-air viewing situation, with four test spots separated by three constant control commercials. After respondents answer a series of questions on their opinion of the variety acts, two open-end response items are administered, about 30 minutes following exposure to the test messages. Respondents are asked to recall, on an unaided basis, all the messages they remember by brand name, product type, or public service—the attention measure. They are then asked to write down the central point each message was trying to get across—the main idea communication measure.

Another exposure to the test messages takes place in the context of a pilot situation comedy. In this case, each message is shown individually, separated by about six minutes of program content. After the second exposure, diagnostic questions are administered that probe respondent reactions, including personal relevance and a believability measure (i.e., Is the message convincing?).

Theater testing also provides an opportunity to use electronic devices to record moment-to-moment evaluations of messages. For example, Baggaley (1988) used an electronic system called the Program Evaluation Analysis Computer (PEAC) to pretest AIDS PSAs. These hand-held response units allowed respondents to make push-button responses at two-second intervals on the following scale: good, fairly good, neutral, not very good, poor. A graphic display of these ratings was superimposed on the PSA so that respondents could indicate strengths and weaknesses in specific audio and video portions of the message.

Day-After Recall

A more naturalistic pretesting technique that is used primarily to test televised commercials is day-after recall. It also has been adapted to pretest PSAs. Potential respondents are contacted by telephone and invited to view a program on cable television in their own homes that evening and then participate in a follow-up telephone interview the next day. Test commercials and PSAs are embedded in the program. The interviewer calls back the next day to determine if the viewers remember seeing the commercials or PSAs, and if they recall any details about the test messages. (One variation intended as an alternative to theater testing presents the questions on screen, for immediate telephone interviews.)

Gatekeeper Review

Public communication campaigns often rely on various gatekeepers to disseminate materials (see Alcalay & Taplin, chap. 5, this volume). In the broadcast media, for example, the PSA director or station manager decides if the PSA is ever aired, when, and for how long. Frequently the flow of print messages is controlled by "intermediaries" such as health professionals and organizations. If these gatekeepers do not like the messages, it is unlikely that the target audiences will ever be reached. Thus it may be important to have key gatekeepers review materials in a rough stage of production concurrent with audience pretesting. The asbestos awareness campaign mentioned above, for example, cleared copy for its television spots with all three networks prior to production. Suggestions made by the public service directors were incorporated into the final spots (Freimuth & Van Nevel, 1981).

Cumulative Knowledge
Gained from Pretesting

In addition to the specific feedback that pretesting can provide about individual messages, general guidelines for effective messages can be developed from the cumulative knowledge generated by these pretests. In fact, LaRose (1980) suggests that formative evaluation can offer alternatives to traditional mass communication models.

In 1976, the National Cancer Institute and the National Heart, Lung, and Blood Institute, agencies of the U.S. Department of Health and Human Services, developed a standardized system to pretest radio and television messages. This system, called the Health Message Testing Service (HMTS), was a modification of a commercial copy-testing service that uses the theater testing approach described above (U.S. Department of Health and Human Services, 1984b).

A total of 65 messages were pretested during the operation of HMTS, making it possible to develop norms and compare the scores of each new message along the nine response criteria: attention, main idea recall, made its point, believable, informative, pleasant, convincing, interesting, and well done. For example, a PSA may receive an attention score in the top 25% of all previously tested health messages, indicating to the producer that the final version of this message will do better than average in gaining the attention of viewers.

The results of the HMTS testing also have been used to identify general message attributes associated with high-scoring PSAs, as a guide to improving subsequent productions. Using regression analysis, Freimuth (1985) found that the following characteristics were the best predictors of audience attention, recall, and believability: straightforward presentation of information, statement of social benefits from performing the healthful behavior, moderate or high emotional appeal, demonstration or slice-of-life rather than dramatic vignettes, depiction of only a few actors rather than a large crowd scene, use of an audio slogan, and multiple audio repetition of the subject. While this set of guidelines is useful for message producers, it is oversimplified and may not be applicable in specific cases. Parallel analyses of pretested product commercials and print advertisements also have isolated message attributes that predict consumer response; see listings of generalizations by Belville (1988), Ogilvy and Raphaelson (1982), and McCollum/Spielman and Company (1980).

Conclusion

More extensive use of preproduction research and message pretesting is one of the most promising avenues for increasing the effectiveness of public communication campaigns. Formative evaluation techniques provide campaign strategists and message producers with valuable information for decisions along each step of the design process from identifying target audiences to refining rough executions.

Formative research has played an instrumental role in the success of educational television programming produced by the Children's Television Workshop, including *Sesame Street* (Lesser, 1974), *Feeling Good* (Mielke & Swinehart, 1976), *Latin American Health Minutes* (Palmer, 1981), and the Be Smart, Don't Start campaign (see Atkin, in chap. 9, this volume). Formative evaluation is centrally featured in several major campaign projects described in this volume (see LaRose, in chap. 9; Flora, Maccoby, & Farquhar, chap. 10; McAlister, Ramirez, Galavotti, & Gallion, chap. 13; Singhal & Rogers, chap. 15), and is a mainstay in the commercial campaign sector. However, such research is still the exception rather than the rule in the public service domain; it is rarely conducted during development of mass media campaigns because of insufficient funding, lack of technical expertise, and minimal appreciation for the value of background information and feedback. Until this important form of evaluation is given higher priority by managerial and creative personnel, noncommercial campaigning will continue to be handicapped and only sporadically influential.

7

A Systems-Based
Evaluation Planning Model for
Health Communication Campaigns
in Developing Countries

RONALD E. RICE
DENNIS FOOTE

Systematic evaluation of health and nutrition communication campaigns in less developed countries is of paramount importance, because poor health conditions continue to stifle human and national potential, high levels of governmental and individual resources are involved, and the cumulative knowledge about how to design communication interventions effectively in such settings is inconsistent. This chapter presents a systems-theoretic framework for planning evaluations of health communication campaigns in less developed countries, to identify relevant variables and processes, and to facilitate more effective and focused efforts.

Simply stated, systems theory argues that there are common structures and processes operating in phenomena regardless of the research

Authors' Note: We would like to acknowledge the contributions of the following members of the Stanford project team: Dr. Carl Kendall, Dr. Reynoldo Martorell, Dr. Judith McDivitt, Dr. Barbara Searle, Dr. Leslie Snyder, Dr. Peter Spain, and Ms. Susan Stone. USAID developed the concept of the communication campaigns described herein, in the form of the RFP that led to the contract award. The Academy for Educational Development was the project implementor, under Project Director Bill Smith, while Stanford University and Applied Communication Technology were the project evaluators, under Dr. Foote. Research was funded through the offices of Education and Health of the Bureau of Science and Technology, U.S. Agency for International Development, under project AID/DSPE-C-0028. Assistance was also generously provided by the USAID missions in Honduras and The Gambia, the Ministry of Public Health in Honduras, and the Ministry of Health, Labour and Social Welfare in The Gambia.

discipline applied (Berrien, 1968: Bertalanffy, 1968; Buckley, 1968). These structures include a system (a set of interacting elements, components, or subsystems functioning within a common boundary) and a surrounding environment (a set of inputs and constraints). A system such as a rural community exists in an initial state in an environment (such as the state of high infant morbidity and mortality in a developing country), receives inputs (such as a health campaign), processes them according to goals and constraints (such as improved health, insufficient water, or cultural norms concerning illness and maternal care), and develops outputs (such as lower infant mortality or a reorganized health care delivery system). Campbell, Steenbarger, Smith, and Stucky (1982) have applied this systems perspective in evaluating a community counseling project, concluding that taking a systems perspective leads to a widening of the scope of the original evaluation questions, increasing the range of evaluation tools necessary to understand the system—from a linear, experimental model to a multi-methodological description of interacting subsystems, expanding the kinds of measures and data sources deemed appropriate, and developing some relativistic interpretations of results.

The proposed evaluation planning model (derived to some extent from Suchman's 1967 four-part evaluation model) involves the following stages, although in an ongoing project these stages represent processes that are interrelated and interactive:

(1) specifying the goals and underlying assumptions of the project

(2) specifying the process model at the project level

(3) specifying prior states, system phases, and system constraints

(4) specifying immediate as well as long-term intended poststates

(5) specifying the process model at the individual level

(6) choosing among research approaches appropriate to the system

(7) assessing implications for design

This chapter describes the model in detail, using examples from evaluations carried out on infant health interventions in Honduras and The Gambia. The evaluations, while not perfect implementations of the model, follow a process very close to that described in the following sections.

Specifying the Goals and Related Projects

Assessing Behavior Change
and Causal Processes in Health Campaigns

Development health communication campaigns, and more specifically infant health and nutrition campaigns, have a considerable history (some of which is reviewed and referenced by Hornik, 1985, 1988, and chap. 14, this volume). Early health education interventions perceived their role as information provision, without special emphasis on changing people's behaviors. Over the past two decades, projects have given behavioral outcomes an increasing priority.

One of the earliest mass media-based health education campaigns to evaluate behavioral changes as a measure of success was conducted in Tanzania. In 1973, a major campaign titled *Mtu Ni Afya* (Man Is Health) was carried out, and in 1975, a Food Is Life campaign was conducted (Hall & Dodds, 1977; Mahai et al., 1975). Both campaigns used formative research in the preparation of radio messages, study guides, and the training of indigenous group leaders. The listeners were organized into study groups; a total of more than 1.5 million adults participated in the campaign. Evidence from the Man Is Health campaign showed that behavior change was possible on a large scale at a low cost. The most striking example from the health campaign was the construction of 700,000 latrines, as promoted on the radio broadcast. The Food Is Life campaign created an increased awareness of the need for more food production, the establishment of vegetable gardens and poultry production, improved dietary habits, day-care center creation, and changes in certain food habits.

Other nutrition campaigns have improved their success through a social marketing approach (see Solomon, chap. 4, this volume). Early examples of this approach include projects carried out in the Philippines, Ecuador, and Nicaragua by Manoff International, Inc. (Cooke & Romweber, 1977a, 1977b, 1977c). In the Manoff projects, for example, the contractor prepared and arranged the broadcast of a series of commercial radio spot announcements recommending a particular nutrition behavior. Each series was broadcast several times a day for more than a year. The themes covered depended on local conditions; in Nicaragua, for example, the project encouraged families to combat children's dehydration resulting from diarrhea by relying on a drink mothers could prepare easily at home, a rehydration fluid consisting of sugar, salt, water, and lemon juice.

The principles underlying these approaches have been adopted and refined in many subsequent projects, with the campaigns discussed in this chapter representing the next major step—paying particular attention to preassessments of the intended audience's needs and characteristics; to the social, material, and logistical support needed to reinforce behavioral change; to the quality of the message propagated; and to the causal relationships among components of the intervention. These general classes of improvements in evaluating health campaigns, then, are specifically addressed in the evaluation planning model developed below: identifying behavioral as well as attitudinal and cognitive subsystem elements, understanding the preexisting states of the social and individual contexts, and detailing the processes linking each subsystem.

The Honduran and Gambian Projects

One of the major causes of infant mortality in developing countries is diarrheal disease. It occurs at significant levels in practically every country, made worse by poor nutrition and bad sanitary conditions. The percentage of infant deaths in 1982 attributed to diarrhea ranges from 10% in Indonesia to 50% in Sri Lanka and Laos (World Health Organization, 1981). In 1985, there were more than 5 million diarrhea-related infant deaths worldwide (Rohde & Northrup, 1986). Death is typically caused by dehydration—loss of fluids and electrolytes—before the child's natural defenses can defeat the cause of diarrhea. Less acute consequences—malnutrition and waste of human and material resources—are even more common (CIBA Foundation, 1976). In the 1970s, the infant mortality rate in Honduras reached nearly 1.2 per 1,000, nearly ten times the overall mortality rate, a quarter attributed to, and two-fifths associated with, diarrhea (Ministerio de Salud Publica y Asistencia Social, 1972, 1977, 1978). Figures from The Gambia are less well documented, but in general are probably slightly lower.

Since the 1960s a diverse set of approaches to reducing diarrhea-related infant mortality have been studied, including immunization, improved water availability, disposal of excreta, weaning education, reduction of infection through animals and insects, and oral rehydration therapy (ORT) (Ashworth & Feachem, 1985; Esrey, Feachem, & Hughes, 1985; Feachem, 1986; Feachem, Hogan, & Merson, 1983; Hornik, 1985). ORT is a comprehensive approach that includes breast-feeding, improved nutrition, and sanitary practices. In addition, an inexpensive oral rehydration solution (ORS) that treats the dehydration by replacing fluids and electrolytes has been developed. ORT-oriented campaigns have significantly decreased diarrhea-related infant deaths in Bangladesh, India, Trinidad and Tobago, Haiti, Nicaragua, and Turkey (World Health Organization, 1983: 20), and have improved many aspects of infant health status in these and other countries (Milla, 1985). There are, however, considerable problems associated with ORS, such as dangers from improperly mixed solutions, worsening of diarrhea symptoms, and difficulties in distributing ingredients (Hornik, 1985).

In a joint effort to improve prevention and treatment of diarrheal infant mortality, the U.S. Agency for International Development (USAID) and the Ministries of Public Health of Honduras and The Gambia have collaboratively supported a large-scale project in Mass Media and Health Practices (MMHP). A subsequent USAID-supported project, HEALTHCOM, has expanded the approach to more than 20 countries, and has helped to carry on the effort in Honduras. In Honduras, ORS (comprising sodium, glucose, potassium, and bicarbonate, called Litrosol) was distributed in packets to be mixed with one liter of water. In The Gambia, ORS was mixed at home, with eight bottle caps of sugar, one cap of salt, and three bottles (one liter) of water, partially due to the expense of ORS packets (over a dime, not including internal distribution costs) and partially to avoid production dependencies.

Specifying the System and Its Components

Figure 7.1 presents an overview of the proposed evaluation planning model. Taking a systems perspective, this model shows that before any intervention, there exists a prior state (say, of the people, their family, their community, the environment, the economy, mortality and morbidity rates, sanitary conditions, nutritional levels, and so on) that is the baseline to which ongoing and final evaluation measurements are compared, and constraints existing in the system that affect how the population interacts with the intervention.

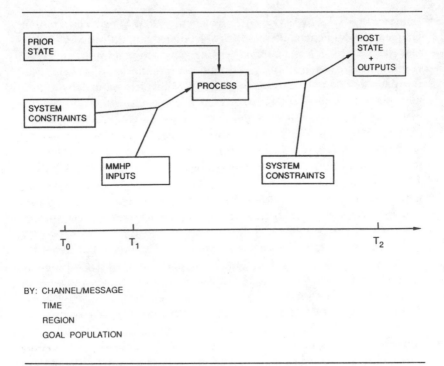

Figure 7.1. Overview of Evaluation Planning Model

The prior state, system constraints, and the intersection of system constraints and intervention inputs interrelate and feed into the process component. For example, perhaps a family learns new approaches to hygiene and wants to perform them, but cannot because personal, cultural, or economic conditions prevent them from buying soap or using sufficiently clean water. Thus system constraints can "block" or transform the progression from process to output.

The subsequent condition of the goal population constitutes a new or poststate. This poststate, which includes outputs from the process components, consists of the information, attitudes, behaviors, and health status of individuals, as well as many of the conditions measured in the prior state component. Many of the values of the variables measured may not have changed; some would not be expected to change. And some new aspects of the system may have been introduced, such as new health communication infrastructures, different administrative procedures, or, in the long run, a rise in population growth, leading to a new set of constraints and conditions. Of course, because such interventions occur over time (for the original intensive interventions in both Honduras and The Gambia, over two years), this whole model may repeat itself in various phases (in the two original interventions, five phases).

Perhaps the most important analytical aspect of an evaluation of a complex campaign is the need to consider, measure, and assess the effect of the major variables that help explain why certain outputs occurred, as well as why certain others did not. These explanations are typically couched in terms of *program* or *theory* failure. Broadly, program failure results when the program is not or cannot be implemented as planned (such as the use of inappropriate messages or language, dependency on an insufficient distribution system, or reliance on unavailable resources). Theory failure, assuming successful program implementation, occurs when one or more of the hypothesized causal links do not occur (such as when people who know what the appropriate behavior is, understand why it might be to their advantage to adopt it, and have access to the necessary resources nevertheless fail to adopt), or have unexpected effects (such as when greater participation in a campaign-related event is associated with decreased learning).

The likelihood of program and theory failure increases as we move along the process components from more immediate outcomes (such as knowledge levels) to longer-term outcomes (such as health status or mortality rates), for three basic reasons. First, we generally hypothesize that the components are causally related and thus those subjects who do not choose to, fail to, or are unable to complete one component become unavailable for the remaining components. Second, the cumulative effect of constraints and intervening variables, over which the implementor has no control, is almost certain to decrease the probability of occurrence of the postulated causal processes. Third, even if each component is accomplished, the relative strength of change is stochastic, so that the final outcome from many successful components may still be hard to detect (see McGuire, chap. 2, this volume, for a summary of this as well as alternate models).

Specifying the Prior State
and System Constraints

Specifying the Prior State

The prior state of the environment can be conceptualized as clusters of variables, identified by theoretical processes and prior empirical results. For the MMHP evaluation, the clusters of variables by content included the following:

(1) *community/population* variables such as anthropological, economic, social, and demographic characteristics of the population; health, communication, government, and kinship infrastructures; and cultural beliefs and behaviors that affect MMHP issues

(2) *household* variables such as enumeration of household occupants, number of young children, SES level or other appropriate measure of wealth and status of household, educational level, and household literacy rate

(3) *communication* variables such as access, exposure, usage, and preference for various media; individual literacy; interpersonal communication channels; community volunteer networks; and fieldworkers and medical practitioners

(4) *sanitation* variables such as water sources, food preparation practices and facilities, cleaning beliefs and practices, and the "goal" concepts and practices as the primary contents of MMHP messages

(5) *information, attitudes, and behaviors* relating to child diarrhea such as causes of diarrhea, response behaviors, relative seriousness of diarrhea, and distinctions among the severity of episodes

(6) *nutrition* variables such as dietary recall, feeding patterns at various ages, and maternal/infant nutritional status

(7) *general health* variables such as health histories, birth and death histories, medicine use, contact with medical/health agents, anthropometric measures, and national decline in health due to economic conditions

(8) *child-care practice* variables such as caretaker responsibilities, exposure to contamination, conceptions of normal infant development, breast-feeding beliefs and practices, and supplemental feeding beliefs and practices

Specifying System Phases

Fundamental to understanding the evaluation process is the fact that the system, and thus the implementation of the treatments, exists and changes over time—perhaps in phases, even through economic and military upheavals. (For example, while the results of the two MMHP projects generally show significant improvements, some measures of health status declined, likely due to the tremendous drop—26%—in per capita income from 1981 to 1987 in the region due to Central American conflicts; Bell, 1987.) Description and analysis of the prior state and system constraints will lead to specification of variables by system phase, identifying when certain interventions should be applied, and for which goal populations.

The MMHP campaigns organized their messages in phases according to temporal fluctuations (the rainy and dry seasons affect the type and amount of diarrhea) and a model of cumulative impact. Activities were phased to train health workers at the beginning, and to follow a sequence of information, enabling behaviors, and reinforcement in messages for the general population. Figure 7.2 shows the relative emphasis on prevention versus treatment, and on media versus interpersonal communication, during the five phases in Honduras. During Phase I, prior to the rainy season, the diarrhea rate was low. This phase focused upon critical enabling messages identified during the preprogram investigation, to establish ORT as standard operating procedure. Training included instruction in ORT. During the rainy season of Phase II, diarrhea rates were high. The central messages here, conveyed by the intensive media intervention, were the purpose, availability, proper mixing, and regimen for ORS. In Phase III, after the rainy season had passed, the intervention messages promoted selected prevention behaviors, as well as maintaining the treatment behaviors. Phase IV was during the next rainy season, with a high rate of diarrhea, so the intervention returned to its treatment focus, with selected prevention messages. In Phase V, after the rainy season had passed, the role of breast-feeding in ORT, and its more general benefits, was emphasized.

Specifying System Constraints

The sociocultural/economic characteristics of the goal audiences play a very important role in communication interventions, due to the

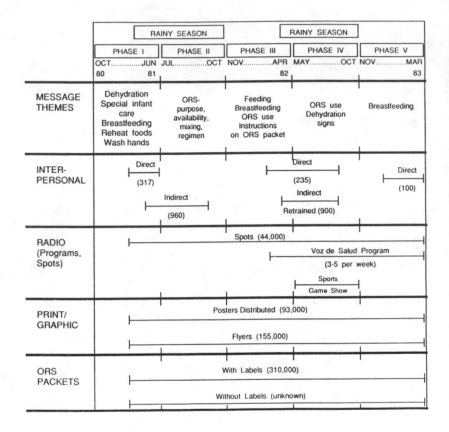

Figure 7.2. Intervention Plan by Phase: Honduras
SOURCE: Applied Communication Technology (1985, p. 13).

difficulty of translating new information into firmly held behaviors. Other more practical constraints operate as well. It is thus necessary to detect and measure system constraints that may block or transform the progression from inputs to outputs. Major categories of constraints include the following:

(1) *resource* constraints such as access to water, heat, soap, medicine, health agents, media, literacy, and ORS packets (for example, in Honduras, mothers most likely to use ORS were in more rural, less educated, and

less wealthy regions, indicating that home ORT filled a need not provided by local health services or resources in poor regions)

(2) *cultural* constraints such as traditional beliefs about causes of diseases, difficulty in distinguishing between bottle- and breast-feeding, and notions of privacy in using hygiene facilities (for example, diarrhea is often seen as a normal way to purge harmful illnesses such as measles, or as unrelated to dehydration; Green, 1986)

(3) *medical community* constraints such as resistance to new treatments, maintenance and extension of training, infrastructure in rural areas, and conflict with traditional rural health actors

(4) *environmental* constraints such as weather, possible epidemics, unintegrated institutional constituencies in various ministries, and discrimination against the rural poor in clinics

(5) *input delivery* constraints such as delays or reductions in broadcasts, insufficient broadcasts, transport difficulties, uneven or restricted ORT materials, legal obstacles to distribution, and insufficient working radios

The pervasiveness of system constraints, even as manifested in how interventions are designed (see below), may well prevent any substantive improvement in the population's health status (Wallack, chap. 16, this volume). Once the linkages between intervention inputs and potential outputs (different system components) are specified theoretically (as in the process component), it becomes crucial to identify distinctions among planned inputs (media, medical practices, ORS packets, and so on), delivery constraints, real inputs, resource and access constraints, and engaged inputs, and final engagement by target individuals (what is perceived as being input by the target audience).

Between the planned intervention inputs and the engagement of such inputs by the goal population lie possible constraints. For example, a series of radio spots with a given frequency of broadcast may be planned inputs, but the broadcasters do not receive the scripts in time or choose not to broadcast all the spots according to schedule; the result is "real inputs," which in turn are greater than the inputs actually "engaged" by the goal population. In The Gambia, 60% of household compounds have at least one working radio receiver; in those compounds 75% of the women listen to Radio Gambia, which delivers the MMHP spots, so only 45% of the women in the general population can potentially directly engage in processing the campaign's radio messages. Compare this "engaged" radio input to the 3% literacy rate by individual women, which would prevent any substantial engagement with print messages. Thus one strategy in the Gambia project was to provide color-coded flyers or wall posters, which were explained and reinforced through radio messages. These "engaged inputs" must be considered the basis for potential measures of exposure, attention, and recall in analyzing change and poststate measurements, and as such still do not represent the final basis upon which to assess theory failure or success. Thus tests of program success should use data on planned and real inputs; tests of theory success should use data on real and engaged inputs.

Media inputs. Each planned media input (such as radio spots) could be coded for goal audience and frequency, region, and station. Specific messages can be coded, by implementation phase, within each specific input. That is, only a few messages in certain media are project inputs in each phase for each subaudience. Therefore, the relative efficacy or recall of those messages, by medium, can be compared to the relative efficacy or recall of different messages, by medium, in later phases (as discussed by Flora, Maccoby, & Farquhar, chap. 10, this volume). For example, in the Gambia project, the color-coded mixing-instruction flyers were the most significant media/print input: Having one at home predicted earlier learning and use of ORS, and less forgetting and lack of adoption (Snyder, 1987; also see Griffiths, Zeitlin, Manoff, & Cook, 1983, who report similar results from an Indonesian campaign). Recall of radio spots, on the other hand, was most influential only as a reinforcement after the respondent had already learned about ORS. In Honduras, 80% reported that they had a radio, and 85% of those (or 67% overall) demonstrated that they had a working radio. Averaged over several waves, from 9 a.m. to 10 a.m., 19% listened to their radios, and 60% of those reported hearing the campaign spot, representing 12% of the population. From noon to 1 p.m., the figures were 35%, 81%, and 28%, respectively. Collecting such data for specific times helps planners and evaluators identify where the greatest engagement may occur.

Resource inputs. The distribution of ORS packets, with associated print material, is considered a planned resource input, which also must be monitored to determine engaged inputs to goal populations. Differential distribution by channel (say, commercial and public health outlets) or by geographical region (closer or farther from roads) may prove to be a factor in explaining why intervention efforts were differentially successful in various regions. Constraints to delivery of ORT packets to goal populations can be monitored through questionnaire data, but might be also monitored through delivery invoices or inventory records.

Audience inputs. Relevant populations other than the goal caretaker/child population—direct contacts such as health workers and physicians, and indirect contacts such as volunteer care workers—can be viewed as additional inputs or constraints. Goal audiences can be asked about these interpersonal diffusion channels that may help to spread or resist mass media inputs (Coleman, Katz, & Menzel, 1966; Flora et al., chap. 10, this volume; Hornik, chap. 14, this volume; McAlister, Ramirez, Galavotti, & Gallion, chap. 13, this volume; Rogers & Kincaid, 1981). For example, local health workers have been shown to be a significant influence in campaigns to teach correct ORS mixing, or to support proper weaning as one approach to reducing diarrhea-related infant deaths (Ashworth & Feachem, 1985; Kumar, Monga, & Jain, 1981).

In order to assess possible degradation or elaboration of input content, throughout the progression from mass media and medical contacts to the goal caretaker/child population, intervening populations could be measured during the poststate component, during their interaction with the goal audience, and in interviews with health care providers and community leaders. For example, in The Gambia, village health volunteers trained by the health workers were identified by red flags outside their compounds. Local mothers could come to these "red flag volunteers" to learn how to mix the ORS correctly; however, the volunteers were not supported throughout the campaign by the health workers, so this indirect interpersonal channel disappeared.

Specifying Immediate and Long-term Project Goals

Measures of success in a health communication project may include a wide variety of outcomes (summarized in Figure 7.3). In the Honduran and Gambian projects, categories of *cognitive* outcomes included attention to—and recognition, recall, and knowledge of—nutritional and preventive behaviors and ORT messages. Categories of *behavior* outcomes included response to diarrheal episode (administration of ORT, taking child to clinics, and the like), infant feeding practices, water purity, and prevention and personal hygiene. Categories of *health* outcomes included nutritional status (weight and height relative to international age norms), morbidity (frequency, severity, and duration of diarrhea), and mortality. Categories of *system* outcomes included the

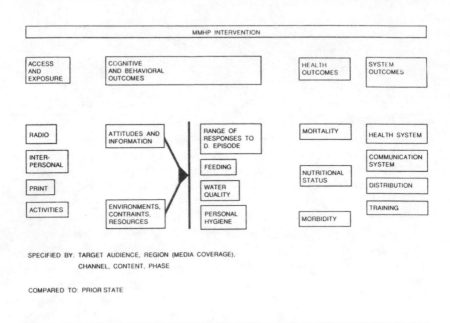

Figure 7.3. Categories and Relationships of MMHP Outcomes

institutionalization of ORT in the health system and the communication system (Are the messages incorporated in the content of other development messages and projects?), distribution of ORT in clinics and through community outlets, and incorporation of ORT in national and local training. Table 7.1 summarizes a few selected results from the Honduras and The Gambia projects under each of these categories of outcomes.

Specifying the Process Model at the Individual Level

The individual-level process model used in the MMHP projects is derived from three theoretical foundations of health communication campaigns:

(1) The public health belief model, which considers whether individuals believe they are susceptible, whether the messages are relevant, and whether the individuals have options: Concepts such as self-efficacy, internal information processing, and attitudes are important components of this model (Fishbein & Ajzen, 1975; Flora et al., chap. 10, this volume).

(2) The social marketing model, which emphasizes the identification of markets and audiences, and how to place and price a product (see Alcalay & Taplin, chap. 5, and Solomon, chap. 4, this volume).

(3) The twelve-step communication/persuasion matrix: McGuire (chap. 2, this volume), in this matrix, shows communication variables as inputs (source, message, channel, receiver, and destination factors) and the "successive response steps that must be elicited in the public if the communication campaign is to be effective" as outputs. McGuire (and others, such as Petty & Cacioppo, 1986) argues forcefully that there are crucial and complex interactions among the inputs and outputs of the matrix process. One input factor that may facilitate an early response step may inhibit a later one. Clearly, a national health communication project will be hard put to evaluate these kinds of microprocesses. The focus, in this process stage, will often be on more easily observable or measurable groupings of the 12 response steps.

Attention (Step 2 in McGuire's matrix) generally can be measured only by the surrogate of recall (Step 8), which really lies after the most crucial steps: exposure, attention, reaction, comprehension, yielding, and storing. Evaluation efforts should gather information on some factors affecting these prior stages, such as cultural constraints against yielding to a particular argument about, say, the amount of liquids a baby can ingest, or against comprehension of the distinction between bottle- and breast-feeding.

Adoption of the advocated message is based on this decision process, but takes form in the behavior stage (Step 10), which can be measured directly via observations, indirectly by a respondent's report of behaviors, or indirectly via system measures such as ORT distribution or clinic patient load. Postbehavioral consolidating (Step 12) would take the form of changed cultural, family, or personal norms and behaviors.

Figure 7.4 shows how the MMHP evaluation attempted to monitor or measure some of these individual processes. Each of these steps is accompanied by measurement or monitoring of intervening variables and system constraints that prevent full linkage to the next step, and of

TABLE 7.1 Selected Results from Evaluations of ORT Campaigns in Honduras and The Gambia (in percentages)

Variables	Pre (1981/82)	Post (1983/84)	Long-Term Post (1987)
Honduras Project			
Access and exposure			
has radio in home	77	73	67
has heard radio spot featuring			
project characters	59	78	69
has seen a poster		47	
has instructional flyer		15	3
Learning			
knows product name	49	71	99
can complete project jingles	50-70	20-83	12-80
can define dehydration	38	39	22
learned about ORS from			
community health workers		29	12
nurse, doctor, or clinic		39	61
ORS packet		49	4
radio		27	6
knows should continue			
breast-feeding during diarrhea		83	82
Behavior			
has tried ORS	0	62	85
percentage of cases treated	9	36	49
continued breast-feeding			
during diarrhea		72	98
gave more liquid than normal			
during diarrhea	65	79	
Health status			
stunting	29	36	
wasting	<1	<1	
percentage of deaths of			
children under 5 that			
involved diarrhea	39	29	
The Gambia Project			
Access and Exposure			
has radio in compound		68	73
has heard radio messages about diarrhea		69	81
has copy of mixing instructions		77	55
has been to clinic in last three months		80	82

(*continued*)

TABLE 7.1 Continued

Variables	Pre (1981/82)	Post (1983/84)	Long-Term Post (1987)
Learning			
aware of ORS	55	89	95
could name ORS ingredients			
and quantities	1	78	41
knows to give ORS at first sign			
of diarrhea	85	73	
knows to make ORS fresh			
every day	32	62	
knows proper amount to give	11	21	
learned about ORS from			
health workers/clinics	95	89	76
posters	0	23	0
radio	2	36	5
Behavior			
has tried ORS	48	85	86
percentage of cases treated			
with ORS	4	62	10
continued breast-feeding			
during diarrhea	88	88	96
stopped other feeding			
during diarrhea	32	3	7
Health status			
stunting	16	17	
wasting	4	14	

unforeseen outputs of a prior step. Table 7.1 provides a few of the measures and values of access and exposure used in the projects.

The application of this evaluation approach has generated several useful outcomes for designers of these and similar interventions. They relate both to diagnosis of problems within a given project (what this model calls *program* failures) and to design principles for this type of project (here subsumed as *theory* failures). Some examples of such outcomes in this case, drawn from the information in Table 7.1 and other sources, include the following:

(1) When emphasis and reinforcement of specific messages are not sustained, initial gains can quickly be lost. For example, in The Gambia the intervention was vastly reduced in intensity after 1984, and case treatment ratios dropped from 62% to 10% within a few years. Even prior

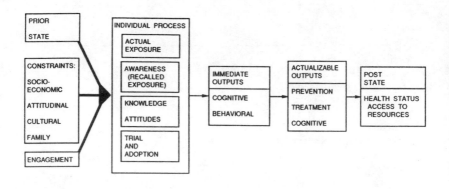

Figure 7.4. Detail of Variables Typically Measured at Stage of Individual Processing, with Classes of Inputs and Outputs

to that, it was clear that mothers were not following a simple pattern of adoption followed by sustained use. Snyder (1987), analyzing seven aggregated waves of The Gambia data, showed that use of ORS was maintained by 70% of the initial adopters after five months, 50% after 13 months, and only 30% after 21 months (also see Table 7.1 for results from the three-year follow-up surveys). Although only 8% started using ORS and then stopped permanently, 57% started, stopped, and started again. Thus behavior maintenance should be a major challenge and goal of future campaigns, rather than just inducing one-time changes in learning, attitudes, or behaviors.

(2) There was considerable difficulty in learning some concepts, such as dehydration, and the benefits of ORS for dehydration rather than for diarrhea. Future interventions will have to consider whether to position such treatments according to the popular views or to teach a scientifically current conception.

(3) Learning through different channels has different adoption and retention characteristics. The presence of mixing flyers that mothers put up in their homes significantly influenced earlier learning about and use of ORS, and later forgetting or disadoption of ORS, whereas the recalling of radio messages led to earlier forgetting and disadoption. One explanation is that putting the flyer up was associated with taking action concerning ORS, while remembering hearing the message was not necessarily associated with immediate action. When hearing was contemporaneous with learning about ORS or adopting it, then respondents learned earlier

and maintained use longer (Snyder, 1987). Campaigns should plan and orchestrate their approaches to take maximum advantage of the differences in impact and timing.

Choosing Among Research Approaches

The MMHP evaluation used six major study groupings that differed markedly from one another in magnitude, study population, and measurement requirements:

(1) a *longitudinal* study (to develop sets of measures and observations, and to detect sequencing and linkage among process components). In The Gambia and Honduras, surveys were conducted monthly. In both projects, about four main instruments were repeated at different intervals on a large panel of women.

(2) a *mortality* study (to detect change in mortality due to infant diarrhea in treatment area). In Honduras, an interrupted time-series analysis was conducted on the proportion of infant and early childhood deaths attributable to diarrhea for two years prior to, and the two years during, the campaign.

(3) an *opinion leader and health professional interview* study (to elicit assessment of project impact and organizational success).

(4) an *ethnographic* study (to provide more anthropological insights into impacts, customs, and beliefs).

(5) an *archival* study (to assess clinical and hospital measures of infant mortality, morbidity, treatment, and so on).

(6) a *cost-effectiveness* study (to aid in understanding relative payoffs for future programs).

Particular project contexts may lead to emphasis or rejection of one or more of these studies. For example, analyzing archival data depends on the existence, validity, and timely availability of relevant data. In Honduras, lack of measurement precision and evidence of marginal returns from changing the media mix or frequency lessened the possibility of a complete cost-effectiveness study. Because of such often unpredictable constraints, along with problems of decreased funding for complete project evaluation, insufficient experimental control, trade-offs between internal and external validity, and the like, triangulation by means of multiple methodologies and data sources is necessary and becoming more prevalent (Heath, Kendzierski, & Borgida, 1982; Schneider, 1982).

Implications for Design

Sampling

Issues of sampling and control groups are crucial to any campaign evaluation (see, for example Cook & Campbell, 1979; Flay & Cook, chap. 8, this volume). Insights from analysis of the prior state and system constraints, given a set of project goals, will help establish proper sampling frames and units of analysis.

For example, because health delivery infrastructure and broadcast media are typically in place before project intervention, these often establish treatment, and thus sampling, boundaries. Because the objectives of the MMHP evaluation included developing a transnational model of health communication evaluation, the primary objective of sampling was to enable generalizations to the full range of conditions (prior states, inputs, and constraints) represented in developing countries rather than to make possible precise statements about aggregate national levels in a given country.

Particular system contexts and constraints will influence the analytical level. For example, noninstitutional infant care is delivered in the "home"; therefore, all individual variables must be linked to a "home unit." But what is a home? In Honduras, a household was defined as a living unit that contains both a place for cooking and a place for sleeping. Thus in Honduras, 750 mothers were randomly selected from 20 stratified villages.

In The Gambia, the "home" is a compound of 10 to 100 people, consisting of physical structures enclosing polygamous multifamily living units. Thus infant care can never be attributed solely to the attitudes and cognitive and behavioral levels of one individual. Thus in The Gambia, 1,029 mothers were sampled from compounds selected randomly from 20 stratified villages.

Control Groups

Because resources for fieldwork are limited, it is crucial to think through carefully the value to evaluation of mounting data-collection efforts in nontreatment areas (see, for example, Cook & Campbell, 1979; Jamison et al., 1975; Suchman, 1967). The Gambia project, which was nationwide from the beginning, was able to have 20 treatment villages receiving multiple measurements and 8 villages measured only once (to test for measurement effects), but no nontreatment controls. In the Honduras project, because the government rapidly expanded from the pilot site to a national campaign to promote the use of ORS, we could not identify a group outside of the treatment area that had not received some kind of treatment, however minor. Furthermore, because the project effort was not a uniform effort within the pilot region, it was not possible to assign households randomly to treatment conditions. Thus neither project involved nontreatment groups, but both projects incorporated nonrepeated measures groups to test for measurement influences.

Comparisons within the treatment area. Five sources of data within the treatment area from the study groupings can be used for within-treatment control purposes, as in the Honduras project:

(1) *Household as its own control:* Local interviewers returned for repeated measurements to households that could then serve as their own controls for many variables.

(2) *Making use of staged implementation:* If, because of phases in system constraints, components of the campaign are introduced in different phases in different regions of the treatment area, the study can compare as-yet untreated segments of the population within the measurement sample to treated segments.

(3) *Natural variations in exposure.* Because of the vagaries that can be expected in mounting a complex intervention, there will be program failure in some components of the campaign. These variations, if inputs are adequately monitored, can be used for comparison purposes.

(4) *Self-determination of exposure:* Some people will select not to expose themselves to a health campaign, because they do not have access to a radio, because they do not choose to talk to health workers, and so on. Although not necessarily comparable, they can be a source of some kinds of information with which to compare exposed respondents.

(5) *Measurement effects:* A smaller sample in both Honduras and The Gambia was interviewed only once or twice across the longitudinal survey to compare to the larger sample, which may have been sensitized by the multiple interviews. The results are, in fact, slightly more positive for those in the repeated waves than for these treatment effects groups, but both were considerably higher than the baseline figures.

Comparisons with nontreated populations. Data about people outside the treatment area can be obtained from several sources. *Archival* data and *ethnographic* studies were mentioned previously. *Other health projects* functioning in many regions can sometimes provide useful baseline information. The MMHP project used similar standardized

SOURCES OF CONTROL	OUTCOMES		
	COGNITIVE	BEHAVIORAL	HEALTH
Within Treatment Area:			
Household as own control	XX	XX	XX
Staged implementation	XX	XX	
Natural variation in exposure	X	X	X
Self-selected exposure			X
Measurement effects	XX	X	
Outside Treatment Area:			
Archival data		X	
Ethnographic studies	XX	X	XX
Data from other studies	X	X	X
One-shot studies	XX	XX	X

Figure 7.5. Usefulness of Control Data Obtained from Within and Outside the Treatment Sample

NOTE: X = source of weak control; XX = source of good control; blank = no control comparison is possible.

data on infant growth and weight available from the National Center for Health Statistics. *Special one-shot studies* may assess the level of a belief or practice in a nontreatment area when results in the treatment area are ambiguous.

The question of controls in a longitudinal study. Figure 7.5 summarizes the usefulness of the sources of control data for variables falling in each of the outcome categories. For example, beliefs, practices, and levels of knowledge can change quickly on exposure to campaign intervention, so repeated measures can capture changes in these outcomes between implementation stages, but probably not levels of health status variables, such as changes in mortality due to dehydration.

In the Honduran and Gambian projects, the focus was on infant feeding and child-care practices in traditional communities, areas where rapid changes are not expected to occur in the absence of external stimuli. Further, with so many regional differences and with other government-supported interventions occurring, it would have been difficult to identify or interpret results from control sites. Thus it seemed that monitoring other information inputs (via the ethnographic and interview studies) into the treatment villages would be a more efficient way to evaluate rival explanations for change than collecting measures on control populations whose comparability is open to some doubt. If mothers begin preparing ORS in the household, this change in behavior can be attributed only to the health education campaign, because it represents the adoption of a new behavior.

A five-year follow-up survey in both countries of women drawn from equivalent samples, as in the original evaluation, enabled analyses of the long-term effects as well as of nationwide historical effects. Table 7.1 provides a few selected results from these surveys.

Conclusion

This chapter has argued that evaluation of purposive communication projects in less developed countries has much to gain from the use of a generic planning model based upon a systems approach. Using the example of ORT projects in two developing countries, the model highlights the need to identify and measure seven evaluation components from a systems perspective. The use of such a planning model could not only help guide the development and execution of evaluation efforts, but, equally important, provide a common framework for use in related projects.

8

Three Models for Summative Evaluation of Prevention Campaigns with a Mass Media Component

BRIAN R. FLAY
THOMAS D. COOK

What Is Summative Evaluation?

There are many definitions of summative evaluation (see Glass & Ellett, 1981; Hennigan, Flay, & Haag, 1979). However, we prefer to describe what evaluators typically do, concentrating on six types of questions they usually try to answer (Cook, Leviton, & Shadish, 1985). One question concerns the *audience* for a program or project. Specific questions about the audience might concern its size, the characteristics of its members, the percentage of special target group members who are in it, and so on. A second type of question concerns *implementation* of the planned program activities. The evaluator asks about the frequency with which different types of people are exposed to activities or media messages, the quality and mix of the services or messages they receive, and any overlapping services they might experience from other program sources or media channels. A unique feature of evaluation is its concern with questions of *effectiveness*, how a program causally affects those who received its services at an acceptable level of quantity and quality, such as how a prevention campaign has influenced knowledge, attitudes, and behaviors. (See Flay, 1986, for further distinctions regarding program efficacy and effectiveness.) A fourth type of question concerns *impacts*, or effects on higher-order aggregates than individuals, as when an intervention influences families, neighborhoods, government agencies, or even other social programs. Impacts are more difficult to obtain than effects; for instance, a smoking prevention campaign's effectiveness depends on its affecting those exposed to it, while its impact depends upon changes in local rates of morbidity and mortality. Evaluation also considers *cost* questions, such as the total dollar cost of a program, the cost per unit per time interval (e.g., the cost per smoker per year of a smoking cessation campaign), the relative cost-efficiency of different methods of achieving a goal such as reduced birthrates, and perhaps even the cost-benefit ratio of a particular project. Finally, a sixth type of question concerns *causal* processes. Though it is useful to know what effects a program has or has not had, it is often even more useful to know why specific effects did or did not come about (Cronbach, 1982; Cronbach et al., 1980; Flay & Best, 1982). Program officials can then enhance strong points of this and related programs, seek to improve weak points, and design novel campaigns.

For any prevention campaign, information about all these six types of questions is desirable. However, it is unrealistic to expect high-quality information on all these issues from a single evaluative study, for a variety of reasons. First, the quality of any one answer usually decreases as the number of questions increases; for example, factors that increase the quality of answers to questions about effectiveness may often reduce the quality of answers to questions about the audience (Cook & Campbell, 1979, chap. 2; Cronbach et al., 1980). Second, answering all the major evaluative questions about a program requires many different disciplinary backgrounds, and few research teams have the funding and experience required to be truly interdisciplinary. Third, and most important, some questions cannot be posed sensitively until answers are available about other questions, especially implementation results. For instance, a sensitive analysis of campaign effects depends on knowing the number, content, and channels of program messages actually transmitted, rather than just those planned, as effects are probably more closely related to activities that actually occur than to those planned (see Rice & Foote, chap. 7, this volume).

There are many potential users of evaluation results, and they place varying emphasis on the six evaluation questions. On the one hand, issues of effectiveness, impact, or cost-benefit are often of interest to federal officials, for their mandate is to see whether or not a program is achieving its intended objectives, though the listed objectives are often vague, unrealistic, or countervailing (Weiss, 1977). On the other hand, the designers and deliverers of services like to assume that what they do is effective, and they usually want to learn how to improve their practices so as to reach more of the target audience, to implement activities more smoothly, or to gain ideas for creating better prevention campaigns elsewhere. Thus questions of implementation, audience, and causal process are of great interest to them, while questions of effectiveness, impact, or relative efficacy can be threatening.

Generic Obstacles to the Sensitive Evaluation of Media-Based Prevention Campaigns

Problem 1: Audiences in Which Some of the Members Are Not at Risk

When evaluating media campaigns, some difficulties arise because of a mismatch between the desirability and feasibility of identifying persons or groups at risk. Our knowledge of who is at risk for a problem is imperfect, and persons at risk usually constitute only a small proportion of the total audience in the coverage area of most media campaigns. Mixing into an evaluation the responses of persons who are not at risk with those who are reduces its sensitivity, because a large number of persons who cannot be influenced by the intervention are treated as though they could have been.

It is therefore desirable to analyze separately those persons who are and are not at risk, but this presupposes a theory of risk that is available and at least partially valid, neither of which is necessarily the case. Thus evaluators often make educated guesses about risk factors, using them as stratification variables or ex post facto blocking factors in the data analysis. Even with useful knowledge of some risk factors, there is an issue of differences in their relevance. Consider smoking: Identifying persons at risk for smoking is not the same as identifying those at risk for the physiological symptoms of smoking; and even if we could predict who smoked and developed symptoms, this would still imperfectly predict which third of all smokers is at risk for dying from smoking. Moreover, predictive data are most often available on gross demographic variables like age, race, sex, and reported household income. Rarely is information available about more proximal and more sensitive indicators of risk, such as the number of cigarettes smoked.

When knowledge of risk factors is not easily available for building into a sampling frame, evaluators have three major choices. First, they can canvas the media catchment area to update and expand the information on risk factors prior to constructing the first sampling design with risk factors used as stratification variables. This is very expensive and time-consuming, and is rarely used. Second, they can stratify by the more easily available, distal predictors of risk, which might mean eventual breakdowns by age, sex, race, or the like. This approach is preferred in most practical circumstances, but it presupposes that extensive prior data analysis has revealed the demographic variables that correlate with the behavior to be prevented. Or, third, they might obtain as large and heterogeneous a sample as resources permit, measuring the risk factors on all respondents. This strategy constitutes a gamble when the incidence of risk is low in the population, for sampling without stratification will then result in only small samples of those who might have benefited most from the media prevention campaign.

Problem 2: Low Treatment Salience

With few exceptions, campaign materials reach inhabitants of a media coverage area in sporadic fashion, if at all. This may be because these subjects have no exposure to the particular channel being used (including pamphlets and signs), or because they fail to attend to the materials when they are presented. Media materials have to compete for attention, and once they have gained it, they still have to compete to hold it. In open social systems, multiple stimuli impinge on humans, who have a limited capacity for dealing with information. Indeed, we suspect that under most conditions individuals are not likely to process materials actively unless their attention is explicitly directed to them or they already have a strong interest in the message or perhaps even in the point of view they anticipate the message will advocate. Although the concept of active processing is very loose, we assume that it facilitates the changing of attitudes and behaviors (Petty & Cacciopo, 1986).

From the perspective of the designers of media campaigns, it would be highly desirable if members of the target audience not only repeatedly noticed the stimulus materials, but also were exposed to them in a variety of different contexts at a host of different times (Flay, 1981). We can increase the probability of prolonged exposure in several ways. First, we might ask (or pay) some persons to pay particular attention to the campaign materials. Second, we might present the stimuli to respondents in their homes, in their cars, or on the street in situations where distractions are fewer and respondents' attention can be better focused. Third, we might present the stimuli in settings, such as workplaces or classrooms, in which it is legitimate to "capture" respondents' attention. Fourth, it is sometimes possible to take advantage of detailed knowledge about audience behavior to maximize the frequency and salience of campaign materials, casting them in ways that stand out from the background and capture attention. And finally, it is advantageous to put out the same message through many different media in many different, heavily frequented locations, at many points in time.

The effectiveness and economic feasibility of the first three methods, based on audience priming, are especially debatable. Moreover, these methods restrict the contexts to which research findings can be generalized, since competition for attention is pervasive in the social world. We would, therefore, like to see this natural competition from other channels reflected in studies, even if only in later studies in a systematic research program. However, when the data from primed and unprimed samples are analyzed together, many inferential advantages result. While primed samples are of high sensitivity for detecting effects, by themselves they cannot guarantee achievement of our goal: the ability to detect small but ecologically valid effects when many persons in the population may hardly have noticed the prevention campaign materials and when these materials consist of persuasion attempts that are often puny compared to the power of the social and physiological forces that lead individuals to acquire and maintain potentially harmful behaviors in the first place (see Wallack, chap. 16, this volume).

The possibility also exists that in open environments, where exposure to media materials cannot be coerced, the persons most in need of information about prevention may be those least likely to receive and learn it, while those who do receive it need it least. When this happens, it is difficult to test whether or not a campaign was effective.

Problem 3: The Length, Complexity, and Questionable Validity of Presumptive Causal Chains

Every campaign designer and evaluator has at least an implicit theory specifying the time-based process (say, attention, processing, belief change) whereby campaign materials should produce such effects as behavior change and such impacts as reductions in morbidity. A crucial part of the evaluator's task is to make explicit all the links in the theorized causal chain. It also involves explicating all competing causal chains (related to other reasonable theories about outcomes).

McGuire's (chap. 2, this volume) theory of attitude change provides an example of each of the probabilistic linkages among causal variables in a campaign. Each of the transitional probabilities from one link to the next is likely to be less than unity, since most cognitions, behaviors, and body states are multiply determined by factors external to the causal chain, thus limiting and modifying processes specified in the causal theory. Slippage in the expected flow of influence also occurs because the underlying theory has to be tested in open and natural systems, which usually involve a restricted number and range of settings and persons (e.g., inhabitants of Gilroy or Watsonville, California, for the Stanford Heart Disease Prevention program). Should there be anything special about these settings that modifies a causal chain, then effects may occur that are not transferable or effects may not appear that would have occurred elsewhere.

Even more important, perhaps, is that many of the postulated theoretical links in a causal chain are likely to be open to sincere doubt. For many reasons we expect reliable knowledge to come from findings that have stubbornly emerged across different operationalizations of constructs and different populations of persons, settings, and times resulting in contingent and specified, but stubborn, causal relationships (Cook, 1985). The underspecified state of most current substantive theory (McGuire, 1985) poses serious methodological problems for the evaluator.

One of these problems is that we must decide where in the causal chain to stop measurement. In a smoking prevention study, should we stop when we learn about the smoking rate, or should we press on to examine physiological indicators, or medical morbidity data, or even mortality data? The later the outcome in the presumed causal chain, the longer the wait for results, the greater the financial expense and attrition of respondents, the lower the likelihood of effects, and the greater the possibility of validity threats such as history, maturation, or mortality, but also the greater the practical payoff for central decision makers (and theorists) if the hoped-for results are obtained. Unfortunately, few decision makers have the political leeway to wait many years. Another problem is that we must decide the relative investment to be put into measurement versus other aspects of research design. Devoting resources to measuring many constructs on several occasions takes resources away from increasing the sample size of respondents and from extending the number of measurement waves, and thus reduces knowledge about causal flow, for any single construct. It is also possible that measurement reactivity will increase, inadvertently sensitizing respondents to the evaluated media materials.

Problem 4: Small Sample Sizes

The picture we have painted thus far is of prevention campaigns designed from uncertain theory and transmitted to audiences who often pay little attention to them and many of whom are not at risk anyway. We could reduce (but not eliminate) these problems by conducting large-sample research that permits and directly measures the extent of presumed personal risk. Respondents could then be stratified so as to allow for separate examination of the data from subgroups at greatest risk. If there were also measures of the quality and quantity of exposure to the campaign materials, we could combine exposure data and risk data in the analysis to assess the effects of the very highest exposure levels on the individuals at greatest risk. The large sample sizes required for such a two-part subanalysis strategy (by risk and exposure levels) will have the added advantage of enhancing the statistical power to detect smaller effects. So large-sample research and extensive measurement of risk and exposure would seem to solve all the problems outlined earlier—but would it?

Alas, there are many compelling reasons that research with many units is often impossible when examining media campaigns. Most mass media have a catchment area in which stimulus materials have the potential to reach all the inhabitants either directly or through interpersonal communication networks stimulated by the media presentations. But where people can communicate with each other about campaign treatments it is not desirable to assign different treatments to different persons because of the probability of treatment contamination (Cook & Campbell, 1979). With some television, newspaper, or billboard campaigns, individual neighborhoods are targeted and it is then possible to have one city neighborhood per treatment group. Sometimes assignment to conditions can even be at the household or individual level, especially with mail studies; and there are even special cases in which different groups of persons enter a catchment area every few weeks (as with some short-term residential training programs). But experience suggests that because media markets are so broad, most treatments are assigned to entire towns or cities, resulting in only a few towns or cities in each study. The loss of statistical power—the ability to detect small differences—due to the resulting small sample size will offset the gain in power due to the higher reliability of aggregated responses of individuals.

The traditional response to this dilemma is to make individuals within each city the unit for statistical analysis even though cities constitute the original unit of assignment and so should also be the unit of analysis. However, it is dangerous as a stand-alone strategy for data analysis because of the excessive number of degrees of freedom it creates and the possibility of correlated errors. Instead, it is advisable to conduct several analyses. One might have low power, making the units of assignment and analysis identical. Another might make individuals the unit of analysis, increasing the statistical power. In such a multiple-analysis strategy based on creating upper and lower bounds in the statistical analysis, more emphasis needs to be placed on the direction of effects than on statistical significance levels.

The Four Problems in Combination: A Generic Low Sensitivity to Effects

The four general questions identified above have implications for the sensitivity of evaluations to detect any true effects that might have occurred in a prevention campaign. If we want sensitive evaluations of community-based prevention campaigns, we have to consider evaluative approaches in addition to the traditional scientific one, and in considering the latter we will have to struggle with trying to improve it at the margin in full cognizance of the four problems outlined above and of their paradoxical interrelationship. In the next section we discuss the advertising, monitoring, and experimental approaches to evaluating mass media campaigns and then briefly consider some of the factors that might help determine when each of them deserves more emphasis in the design of a particular evaluation.

Three Evaluation Models and Strategies for Increasing Sensitivity

The Advertising Model of Evaluation

A brief description. Advertising research takes many forms. Our concern is with those approaches used for evaluating media-based campaigns in the settings where the campaigns take place, relying on audience surveys to (1) determine whether or not the campaign reaches the target audience and, if it does, to measure how often it reaches them (commonly called *exposure*, or, more specifically, *reach* and *frequency*); (2) assess the extent to which members of the exposed audience recognize or recall the campaign messages; (3) assess the degree to which the audience liked the campaign materials; (4) estimate the self-reported intention of audience members to act upon their new knowledge and attitudes; and (5) provide data-based clues about why certain messages reached certain audiences more than others, why certain parts of the message are remembered better than others, and why people do or do not think they will act upon their beliefs. It is advertising surveys with such purposes that are most used in evaluating media campaigns.

When the data have been collected, correlations between exposure and either recall or changes in attitude and behavioral intention are used to determine the campaign's effectiveness. Internal analyses are also conducted to explore reasons for the correlation, usually entailing nothing more sophisticated than subgroup analyses by respondent variables or perhaps the computation of partial correlations. Should there be no relationship worth explaining between exposure and recall or attitude change, exploratory data analyses are conducted to probe why the campaign did not appear to be effective and to suggest likely improvements that might circumvent the difficulties analyzed.

Sensitivity of the advertising model to the four problems. As normally used, the advertising model is generally sensitive to audience issues—especially estimating the audience size and composition. However, there are some special cases in which sensitivity is low. One is when the at-risk population is small, so estimates may be unstable. When a profile of persons at risk is available, evaluators can oversample such persons to improve estimates. But this obvious solution requires a sampling frame containing the individuals or households at risk, and developing this can be difficult and expensive. Most evaluators draw random samples and then stratify ex post facto into those presumed to differ in risk, but this strategy will result in prohibitively small samples of truly needy persons when the population percentages are low.

Evaluators can use data from the advertising approach to describe the salience of a prevention message and to make suggestions for enhancing it. This requires survey questions measuring salience, perhaps asked in several different ways and linked to probes of when, where, and how people become aware of an issue. Interviews, pencil-and-paper questionnaires, and group discussions predominate.

The advertising paradigm is at its most vulnerable when considering causal chains. It focuses on the earliest points in such chains, and so has the potential to detect small effects in exposure, knowledge, and beliefs. In this sense, the advertising model provides the easiest way of making a program look good. But this very sensitivity to effects early in the causal chain can lead to the distal measure fallacy (see McGuire, chap. 2, this volume). Changes in awareness of a campaign do not necessarily entail changes in individual attitudes, changes in attitudes do not necessarily result in changes in behavior, and so on (Flay, 1981). Focusing on immediate effects, typically measures of exposure and possibly recall, runs the risk of lulling consumers of evaluative information into believing that later effects in a presumed causal chain are likely to occur simply because earlier ones did. The psychological false positives that result are all the more dangerous because they complement the statistical false positives likely to arise from the advertising model, placing no emphasis on control groups or other strategies for establishing no-cause baselines.

In the advertising paradigm, the individual is usually the unit of analysis, low statistical power is not an issue, and small effects are usually detectable for the proximal variables typically measured. Moreover, the external validity of audience surveys is usually good, with the target audience usually being sampled randomly from some clearly designated population. However, the population itself may be fairly limited and of interest to few, as when individuals or households are selected within a single city. In theory, the advertising approach is independent of factors that influence the construct validity of causes. In practice, the treatments often have low construct validity because campaigns involve few communities, and local idiosyncrasies in the implementation of the campaign—such as relative isolation of the broadcast media audience—are totally confounded with the theoretical campaign about which we want to make inferences.

Advantages and disadvantages of the advertising model. The advertising model is sensitive to the effects it is designed to detect, primarily because of its focus early in the causal chain and its use of individuals as the unit of analysis. Another advantage of the approach is that it is technically easy to sample from a community at random and to ask respondents questions, often over the phone. The relevant methods are the product of years of practice and are widely accepted by evaluators and other social scientists. The methods are also becoming less expensive and more automated, thanks to computer-assisted telephone interviewing (CATI) and hand-held computer systems. The advertising approach can provide fast feedback inexpensively, such as overnight television ratings from Nielsen or AGB (see Alcalay & Taplin, chap. 5, this volume).

At the local program level, exposure and awareness are valued because they are widely presumed to be precursors of other, more important behavioral effects. With new programs in particular, it is important to know whether or not they are reaching their target audiences and whether or not audience members seem to be attending to the message and comprehending its major points.

However, exposure and awareness measures are not likely to be of high policy relevance when compared to behavioral, health, or economic effects that attract policymakers and legislators. A further disadvantage is that the simple correlations between exposure and learning—the most frequently reported when the advertising model is used—can have mischievous consequences if commentators seek to interpret these correlations as indicating a causal relationship from the campaign to the outcome measured. Though the advertising model is a low-cost, low-risk approach to obtaining evaluative information that may sometimes be important to those who design campaigns or are concerned only with exposure or learning, it will rarely be of much relevance to those who make decisions about preventive practices for broader policies.

Improving the advertising model. Fortunately, the basic advertising model can be improved. The most direct way of doing this is to include measures of outcomes further along the planned causal chain that underlies the model of program design. Evaluators could, with minimal additional cost, include measures of opinions, attitudes, behavioral intentions, and reported behavior in the audience survey in addition to measures of exposure and awareness. However, these are still not measures of actual behavior. When valid indicators of risk are available, the advertising model is more sensitive if high-risk individuals are analyzed separately. Evaluators can also ask carefully worded questions about the recognition of prevention campaign materials so as to probe whether or not those at most risk are least likely to be exposed to the campaign. Such information can also be used to stratify respondents by both risk and exposure levels, for then the likelihood of effectiveness is greatest. Enhancing the internal validity of the basic advertising model is not easy. Some analysts try to describe the differences between individuals who are and are not exposed to campaign materials, using these descriptions to adjust statistically for selection. Is a correlation between exposure and learning due to exposure or to those with higher exposure being better educated? Dealing with selection this way is useful but imperfect, because all relevant antecedent and intervening variables are not measurable.

The Impact-Monitoring Model of Evaluation

A brief description. The impact-monitoring model relies on routinely collected data from a management information system or other archival source (Cook et al., 1985) to monitor more distal effects and impacts that are supposed to occur toward the end of a causal chain. Impact monitoring is possible because most archives were set up to measure the prevalence of a specific problem, whether in economics (with unemployment or inflation statistics), social welfare (health and criminal justice statistics), or the subjective social domain (as with longitudinal survey questions about happiness, satisfaction with government, and so on). Such measures tap into important distal outcomes of great national importance. Agencies that conduct impact-monitoring studies want to learn whether or not the indicators that they rely upon to assess the incidence of a social problem are changing. For them, the indicators have both face and political validity as well as construct validity. The sampling frame is dictated by the need to describe a well-known population, not by the need to answer evaluative questions.

Sensitivity of the impact-monitoring paradigm to the four problems. Impact-monitoring studies are usually not sensitive to what we have called audience and salience issues. This is because archives rarely contain information on characteristics that would allow either the identification of high-risk individuals or estimates of the salience of a particular issue. Impact-monitoring studies are not usually sensitive to the complexity of causal chains, either. They usually focus on the most ultimate of the expected impacts of the campaign. False negative findings are often the result, as McGuire's attenuated effects fallacy suggests they might be. Since there are many causal links prior to the type of distal variable contained in most archives, the probability of influence from the campaign to distal impacts will be much less than unity. Other reasons for the underassessment of effects are also possible, especially insensitive measurement or a treatment's effects being restricted to a subset of all the groups aggregated in the archival data.

Problems commonly associated with archival data also contribute to the insensitivity of monitoring studies. Program and agency records are rarely designed for program evaluation purposes, being more often designed for billing or service monitoring. Also, some measures are not available in the form needed. For instance, detailed cigarette consumption data must be assessed from per capita consumption of tobacco rather than from the number of people who smoke (Warner, 1977, 1981). Further, indicators are often available only at a higher order of aggregation than desired. Information may be available only at the city or county level, even though a program is disseminated to a subset of neighborhoods within the city or county. Moreover, the definition of a variable sometimes changes when a new program is instituted (Cochran, 1978), confounding genuine changes with changes in the recording system. For evaluation purposes, constancy of definition is more important than some marginal increment in validity due to revising a measure.

As commonly practiced, impact-monitoring studies have low internal validity. Rarely are control groups or stable pretest "time series" available; it is more common to compare performance on an indicator for a short period before a campaign with performance afterward. When the study is restricted to sites where a treatment is potentially available to everyone, the major inferential task is to think through how alternative interpretations might be ruled out. The evaluator will have to rely on trying to make unique predictions about effects only the campaign could have caused, and conceptualizing all the plausible alternative interpretations, measuring them directly to see if they occurred and, if they did, conducting a statistical analysis that tries to adjust away the alternative. The first of these strategies is rarely feasible, and the second implies well-developed substantive theory and an expensive data-collection effort that goes far beyond what archives usually contain.

Advantages and disadvantages of impact-monitoring studies. We have seen that impact-monitoring studies are often insensitive to the effects they are meant to detect, primarily because of the use of gross indicator variables that rarely correspond with the expected effects of a campaign, particularly the more proximal ones. If no effects are obtained, it is not clear whether the preceding links in the causal chain were wrong or whether there was simply too little power to detect effects. Even when changes are noted, the inferential task remains of ruling out alternative plausible explanations. The conundrum here is that the number of alternatives will be greater the longer the time period between beginning a campaign and observing changes in an indicator—that is, history effects proliferate over time. Yet, with gross distal indicators, changes are not likely to appear quickly. Moreover, attributing change to a particular intervention normally requires control groups or time series and a close geographic overlap between the population exposed to a campaign and the population on which the archived measures were collected.

Despite these problems, impact studies are potentially of great relevance, especially at the national or state level. The extent to which a campaign solves a problem or meets a social need is usually of great interest to policymakers, and they tend to verify a problem in terms of the archival indicators usually used to assess it.

Another advantage of impact-monitoring studies is their ease and inexpensiveness. This is largely because the data-collection costs have usually been underwritten by the institutions funding the archive for their own purposes. Archival data can also diminish the social and political threats associated with outside evaluation, and it is less obtrusive than when evaluators collect their own data in ongoing social situations.

Improving the impact-monitoring model. To make the impact-monitoring approach more sensitive requires (1) including measures of program effects earlier in the causal chain, and (2) devising ways to rule out, or examine, threats to internal validity, particularly those associated with the influence of historical and cyclical trends. Even using archival data, it is sometimes possible to include measures that are not far along the causal chains usually invoked. For example, if we assessed the effects of a smoking cessation campaign using measures of morbidity and mortality, effects might not show up for many years, if at all. On the other hand, it is possible to examine the records of cigarette companies (providing national-level data) and stores (providing possibly neighborhood-level data) that sell cigarettes in order to test whether or not smoking behavior has decreased.

Another way of marginally increasing sensitivity is by increasing the number of observations and creating an extended time series. When enough preintervention data points are available, a no-cause baseline is achieved. If a number of postintervention time points are also available it is then possible to probe whether or not any initial change occurs and whether or not it is maintained over time. With enough time points, interrupted time-series analysis can be used (see Warner, 1977, 1981, for a smoking example).

Another way of approximating a no-cause baseline is by the use of the nonequivalent dependent variable design (Cook & Campbell, 1979). This involves using archival information on indicators that the campaign should not have affected but that most other plausible causes of major outcome changes should have. For example, for a drug abuse prevention campaign designed to prevent cocaine use by children, the number of child users should decrease, but not the number of adult users; moreover, the number of child alcohol users should not decrease.

The general quality of the impact-monitoring model can be vastly improved by the development and collection, during routine program operations, of program-specific records that tap into potential effects early in the causal sequence (Wholey, 1979). Thus a drug treatment clinic might record not only the number of patients seen, but also the number of relapses, and so on. Receptionists might also report on the number of inquiries made by untreated people each day. Like other records, these would be only partially valid and easily corrupted (Cochran, 1978); nonetheless, it is worthwhile exploring ways to enlarge archival data bases to make routine monitoring more sensitive for evaluation purposes (Cook et al., 1985; Wholey, 1979).

 The Experimental Model of Evaluation

A brief description. The greatest strength of the experimental model is its high level of internal validity. *Internal validity* refers to the ability to infer cause, and depends upon having a credible counterfactual—usually no-cause baseline—against which to compare performance among program recipients and thus refute alternate explanations for the results. Campbell and Stanley (1966) and Cook and Campbell (1979) provide the most comprehensive set of threats to internal validity. The crucial operating assumption behind their work is that evaluations that allow strong causal inference are of greater policy value because costly difficulties arise if decision makers decide to continue supporting a program that seems to work but in actuality does not, or if they decide to reduce the support for a program that does not seem to work but really does. Others have previously advocated the experimental approach to evaluating mass media programs (e.g., Ball, 1976; Haskins, 1970; Towers, Goodman, & Zeisel, 1962). We now consider some features of experimental design that may be useful for evaluating large-scale campaigns.

Random assignment to treatments. The best way to increase internal validity is to have a no-treatment control group that is equivalent to the treatment group. This is usually achieved by randomly assigning units (individuals, households, communities) to experimental conditions before exposing one of the groups to the program. (However, treatment-related attrition can take place during a program, making controls noncomparable by the time postprogram measurement occurs.)

As noted above, with large-scale media campaigns, communities rather than individuals are usually the unit of assignment. Although some media technologies, such as split-cable television, do allow random assignment at the household level (e.g., Robertson et al., 1974; also see Geller, in chap. 9, this volume), it is often not desirable to assign individuals or households to treatments. This is because contamination can occur if individuals see a program and talk about it with others, including members of the control group. Moreover, some media campaigns are explicitly designed to stimulate social support systems or community organizations, and this obviously precludes the random assignment of individuals or households because the same treatment *should* disseminate beyond such units.

The community should be the unit of random assignment for most mass media campaign evaluations, as it was in the Stanford Three Community and Five Community studies (Flora, Maccoby, & Farquhar, chap. 10, this volume), among many others. But random assignment does not ensure equivalence if the number of units being assigned is small. In this situation, a large-sample technique such as random selection cannot achieve the desired comparability, but matching on pretest performance levels is desirable if followed by random assignment.

Nonequivalent control group designs. The small number of communities available for assignment means that evaluators often adopt quasi-experimental designs (Campbell & Stanley, 1966; Cook & Campbell, 1979). The most frequently used are nonequivalent control group designs. These are like randomized experiments in all ways except that the treatment and comparison groups are not made probabilistically equivalent through the random assignment procedure. Instead, treatments are assigned to naturally occurring groups (see Flora et al., chap. 10, this volume).

The major problem with nonequivalent control group designs is that any observed difference between the groups after a media campaign might be due to preexisting differences (i.e., selection) rather than to the campaign. Also, different historical events may happen in each of the intact groups during the course of the study, potentially affecting outcome variables (i.e., there may be a selection × history interaction). Selection biases can occur not only because of self-selection into different treatments, but also because of administrators' decisions about which city (or other unit) should be in a particular treatment group. Designs utilizing control groups obviously cost more than designs without them. Whether the increased internal validity that control groups provide is worth the extra financial cost depends to a large extent on the stage of program development. While control groups may not be necessary for relatively new programs about which little is known, for a summative evaluation of a program that has strong theoretical and experiential underpinnings, an evaluation that permits measurable causal inference seems imperative and well worth the cost.

Internal analysis with partitioning by level of exposure. Control groups create differences in the level of exposure to a campaign. In the basic control group designs, we usually assume that the control group receives none of the treatment and that the treatment group receives all of it. In the real world, the situation is rarely so clear-cut. Some or all of the campaign materials may fail to reach some of the treatment group, or may reach them only intermittently, while some of the same (or similar) materials may come to the attention of members of the control groups, perhaps through explicit treatment diffusion but more likely because the experimental materials are themselves products of a general cultural shift emphasizing prevention (e.g., the use of seat belts or quitting smoking). Partitioning respondents according to the level of treatment they have actually received rather than the level they were supposed to receive usually improves statistical power, particularly when we know that a campaign has failed to reach many in the target audience. However, the resulting test reflects what the campaign achieves when it reaches many people; this represents what the program's potential might be, not the program's actuality.

Partitioning can also improve internal validity by making history a less plausible explanation of any observed effects, since all the persons in a community experience the same events occurring contemporaneously with the treatment. Self-selection is a definite threat, however, because those who selectively attend to a message may be those who would have shown the changes anyway. Consequently, it is very important to develop a selection model to explain whichever pretreatment differences are correlated with the particular outcome under analysis, usually with pretest measures on the same outcome.

The Need for Synthesis in Community-Based Prevention Research

The range of media markets pushes prevention research toward using intact communities as the unit of assignment and analysis, entailing reduced statistical power. The internal analyses we have proposed can serve only as adjuncts to community-level analysis, and by themselves will not be convincing to statisticians. Hence the need is particularly urgent to develop procedures for the synthesis of multiple community-level studies, each of which is itself underpowered statistically.

The current model for such synthesis is meta-analysis (Hedges & Olkin, 1985). Meta-analysis begins with the collection of all studies judged to be similar in the guiding research questions asked. This usually leads to a wide variety of different measures used for the same outcome construct. These are converted to a common standard score metric (effect size) prior to analysis, so different operational representations of the same construct are comparable. Once mean differences are in the same metric for each study, it is relatively easy to compute an average effect size, conduct statistical tests of this average, and probe for any factors that condition the size of the effect (Cooper, 1984). Narrative and comparative meta-analyses of prior studies, such as the wealth of antismoking interventions reviewed by Flay (1987b), can also provide insights and lessons in a less statistical format.

The promise of meta-analysis is considerable. The statistical power problem associated with a small number of communities is attenuated, although there may not be enough community-level studies. The idiosyncrasies associated with any one study (treatment design, site uniqueness, respondent sampling, data collection, and so on) are likely to be made heterogeneous across the studies that enter into the meta-analysis. Moreover, each study is likely to have slightly different populations of settings and persons, which potentially extends external validity. Finally, internal validity can also be enhanced if initial biases are made heterogeneous, as occurs when the treatment group in one small-sample community study tends to be at somewhat greater risk than the controls, while in the next study the direction of difference is reversed.

Of course, there is no guarantee of such countervailing biases; descriptive probes have to be made to partition studies into those where pretest means differ in one direction and those where they differ the opposite way (Cook & Leviton, 1980). If results replicate despite such differences, causal inferences are all the stronger. This is not to say that syntheses, including meta-analysis, are perfect. There is an ever-present danger of a constant source of bias running through all the studies (Cook & Leviton, 1980), and issues have to be resolved of dominance attributable to some studies supplying more effect sizes than others (Glass, McGaw, & Smith, 1981). Also, we never know that all the relevant studies have been found, though procedures do exist for establishing how many null-effect studies would have to be found for an average effect size to be reversed (Rosenthal, 1984). Finally, we must note that, at this time, there are still some research questions for which the number of studies available for statistical synthesis is tiny. Nevertheless, the synthesis, rather than the individual research study, is likely to be the unit of confident progress with media-based community-level studies.

Conclusion:
Choosing Among Alternative Models

We do not advocate any of the above alternative models as being "correct." The three evaluation models we have discussed are not equally relevant to all prevention campaigns, and each campaign must be evaluated on its own merits. Table 8.1 summarizes the comparisons presented in the prior sections. In broad terms, the choice is among the following:

(1) *Advertising-type surveys:* These are inexpensive and focus on the beginning of the causal chain where effects are of lower policy relevance, consequently, there is a danger of "psychological" false positive findings.

(2) *Impact-monitoring studies.* When an archive exists, these are even less expensive than advertising-type surveys, and in concentrating on concepts at the end of a causal chain, their policy relevance is particularly high. But such studies run a great risk of false negative findings.

(3) *Experimental studies:* These are likely to be large-scale, comprehensive, and expensive studies, but they are likely to produce more valid results, and so may be of higher potential policy relevance in the longer term, especially when several different community-level studies are synthesized to provide a global causal conclusion.

The choice among methods depends on several factors, including the resources and time available for the evaluation, the information needs of different groups with an interest in the evaluation findings, and the stage of program development. If the campaign is new, and we have little prior knowledge about it, then we would probably choose the advertising model because of its focus on the early part of the causal chain and on the question of whether or not a campaign is reaching its

TABLE 8.1 Comparisons of Evaluation Problems Across Evaluation Models

	Alternate Evaluation Models		
	Advertising (use surveys to identify exposure, recall, liking, behavior intentions, subgroup differences)	Monitoring (use routinely collected data from systems or archival sources)	Experimental (use research designs to reject alternate explanations, threats to validity)
Major Evaluation Problems			
Diffuse target audiences; hard to identify the small number at risk, thus ex post facto stratification, low effects sensitivity	*strong:* audience size and composition *weak:* difficult to prestratify at-risk sample	*strong:* well-known population *weak:* not sensitive to small audiences, subgroup differences	*strong:* random assignment, especially if prestratified; so more efficient and more sensitive to effects *weak:* attrition
Low salience of, and attention to, message by target audience; high competition by other media messages	*strong:* measuring salience, frequency of exposure	*weak:* not sensitive to message salience	*weak:* problem of self-selection
Complex but unspecified theories of causal processes; contingent conditions obscured by unrepresentative and small samples	*strong:* exposure and awareness are valued effects; difficult to use in making decisions about prevention policies *weak:* focuses on early stages in causal chain, so distal measure fallacy; no control or baseline groups; correlation treated as causality	*strong:* indicators and trends usually policy relevant *weak:* focuses on end of causal chain, so attenuated effects fallacy; low sensitivity to causal complexity or alternate models; possibly unreliable indicators; history effects; no control groups	*strong:* helps policymakers avoid false positives and negatives; can identify causal processes involving various stages of causal chain *weak:* nonequivalent control designs can't control for site effects confounds; expensive and time-consuming

(*continued*)

TABLE 8.1 Continued

Small sample size, especially if unit of analysis is determined by media coverage area; low statistical power	*strong:* individual is unit of analysis, so larger sizes; good sampling strategies; sensitive to valued effects *weak:* confounding with city or region differences, or media influences	*strong:* can extend sample over time *weak:* indicators often not at most usable unit of aggregation	*strong:* provides useful information for meta-analysis *weak:* communities rather than individuals are unit of assignments, so less statistical power

target audience. On the other hand, if a program is well established and there is reason to believe it is reaching a large and relevant audience, then evaluators might want to conduct an impact-monitoring study.

Evaluators probably should reserve expensive, large-scale experiments for two situations (Flay, 1986, 1987a). The first is when some assurance exists that the messages will have an effect if they reach the target audience. Typically, this requires formative evaluation before mounting the campaign proper (see Atkin & Freimuth, chap. 6, this volume). The second situation is when one has some assurance that, in the "real world," the messages actually reach the target audience and are attended to; one may obtain this assurance from prior studies. An alternative approach is a one-shot comprehensive evaluation, in which one attempts to answer all the major evaluation questions in a single study, a more "realistic" time frame. Politicians and program managers may not be able to wait for painstaking programmatic research in order to arrive at answers to questions of effectiveness and impact, and so they will press for the single "giant" study that attempts to answer all the questions at once. Scientists, on the other hand, might prefer to follow the slower and more careful path that does not require so many resources in one project, for they realize full well that the quality of answers to any one question usually decreases as more questions are asked. We do not want to take a stand on the issue, but for each prevention campaign we would like to see the issue tackled head on at the earliest possible time during the development of evaluation plans.

Part III

Experiences from the Field

Campaign Sampler

Over the past three decades, hundreds of major public communication campaigns have been conducted through the mass media to influence the attitudes and behavior of audiences on a wide variety of substantive topics. Chapter 9 presents a sampler of such campaigns, a representative collection of noteworthy case studies from the United States and abroad that have achieved varying degrees of success. Each brief report identifies the important social or health problem addressed in the campaign, describes the communication strategy employed, cites key findings regarding effects, and interprets the implications.

E. Scott Geller examines one of the most notorious campaign failures, the "great seat belt campaign flop" in the early 1970s, and suggests how television can be used more effectively to promote safety belt use. During that same period, the spread of venereal disease posed a major health concern that foreshadowed the more serious AIDS crisis to come; Bradley Greenberg and Walter Gantz report that the classic *VD Blues* TV program was quite effective in educating the public about this problem due to its entertaining format and explicit treatment of the subject. Robert LaRose offers an analysis of the moderately successful 1979 *Freestyle* public television series intended to reduce children's occupational sex-role stereotyping, reinterpreting the findings from the perspective of Fishbein's theory of reasoned action. A high-profile campaign over the past decade has been the "McGruff" public service campaign promoting public involvement in crime prevention activities; Garrett J. O'Keefe and Kathaleen Reid conclude that this multimedia effort produced fairly strong effects under certain conditions.

Two chapters from the first edition of *Public Communication Campaigns* are summarized by Ronald E. Rice. He reviews the famous series of mass campaigns implemented in China during the Mao era, focusing on the intensive mobilization models employed with mixed success in the Communist society. He also examines the long-running Smokey Bear forest fire prevention campaign; while exceptionally high public awareness has been achieved, Rice concludes that there is considerable room for improvement in this well-supported program.

Sandra Ball-Rokeach and Milton Rokeach describe a unique field experiment in which they created and tested the effects of *The Great American Values Test* TV program; they conclude that the self-confrontation induced by this show produced fundamental changes in egalitarian and environmental values and consequent behaviors. The issue of littering is explored by Robert B. Cialdini, who critiques the persuasion strategy employed in the memorable "crying Indian" antipollution television PSA of the 1970s. The recent Be Smart. Don't Start! campaign featuring a music video, TV spots, and support material designed to delay the onset of alcohol experimentation by preteens is profiled by Charles K. Atkin, who identifies a number of strong points in the preparation and implementation of this prevention effort.

Chapter 9 concludes with two important examples from the Third World. Charles K. Atkin and Hendrika W.J. Meischke review mass media family planning campaigns using social marketing approaches to promote birth control in developing countries over the past 20 years. Ronny Adhikarya summarizes the strategies responsible for the highly successful campaigns that motivated Bangladesh farmers to adopt rat control practices in the mid-1980s.

Field Chapters

The Stanford Heart Disease Prevention Project is one of the best-known and most elaborate campaigns ever conducted in this country. Beginning in 1971, the Three Community Study sought to utilize mass media and interpersonal channels to change attitudes and life-style behaviors fundamentally in order to reduce the risk of cardiovascular diseases. June A. Flora, Nathan Maccoby, and John W. Farquhar review the theoretical underpinnings, research design, and final results of this landmark study, and then update the presentation with a progress report on the subsequent Five City Project currently under way. In describing this new phase of the heart campaign, they focus on the role of evaluation research and the implementation of educational interventions in the test communities. Since the Stanford studies are prototypes for the rapidly proliferating programs of comprehensive, long-term, planned social change across multiple levels of the community ranging from individuals to organizations, this chapter merits close attention from campaign strategists.

Robert G. Meadow approaches the topic of political campaigns not from the typical angle of media effects on voting behavior, but by analyzing the design and conduct of political campaigns themselves. Most literature on political campaigns describes the elements of a winning campaign. These treatments are generally atheoretical, failing to place political campaigns within a comprehensive framework of other communication campaigns. Meadow identifies the special characteristics of political campaigns, such as their decisive outcomes, limited evaluation research, incomplete control of campaign communication, and historical and ritualistic dimensions. He views campaigns from the perspective of the campaigner, but recognizes the role of the target audience (voters) in a dynamic relationship. Meadow also discusses the campaign management functions and their relationship to voter communication. He ends by considering implications of new communication technologies for political campaigns.

Perhaps the most challenging and consequential of recent campaign issues is AIDS. The problem of AIDS brings to bear the most difficult aspects of many problems that campaigns hope to solve: Consequences, though devastating, are uncoupled from behavior because they occur so long after exposure to AIDS risks; risky behavior involves activities perceived as pleasurable by the participants (sex and drugs); detection of contagious individuals is socially and technically complex; and moral, economic, and legal issues are raised. For adolescents, these problems are even greater. Kathleen K. Reardon provides some possible persuasion approaches that may be applicable to the difficult campaign goal of AIDS prevention. Based on the proposition that the major obstacle for adolescent prevention programs is the undervaluation of health by children, she suggests five persuasion approaches that may be used to increase the salience of health values that could then activate prevention and education activities: instilling self-efficacy and motivation, involving the person in the persuasion attempt, applying theories of reasoning about one's own as well as others' behavior, using fear appeals in connection with interpersonal question-and-answer sessions, and appealing to strongly held illusions. Each of these approaches is explored for how it may be applied in combined mass media and interpersonal interventions.

Alfred McAlister, Amelie G. Ramirez, Christine Galavotti, and Kipling J. Gallion analyze the evolution of communication strategies designed to influence adults to quit smoking. They emphasize two important aspects of such campaigns. The first notion is that communications aimed at influencing complex and persistent behaviors must perform three functions: informing audiences about those behaviors and their consequences, persuading audiences to cease or avoid those behaviors, and training audiences in skills necessary to translate intent into action. The second notion is the importance of interpersonal support for mediated communications. Although smoking in general is decreasing, it is still increasing for some subaudiences. Additionally, a particularly difficult problem is the maintenance of cessation after the initial attempt. The authors review three studies to describe how antismoking campaigns, guided by social learning theory, were designed to integrate these approaches, and to provide evidence of their success: a pilot study involving sessions of a videotaped expert and a live facilitator, a regional televised program in Finland, and a combined role model and community reinforcement campaign in Houston.

Robert C. Hornik takes issue with the conventional communication campaign belief that when it comes to persuasion to produce behavior change, face-to-face channels are essential—that mass media campaigns must be supplemented by interpersonal channels in order to be effective. Hornik briefly reviews some substantive concerns, including the meaning of homophily, the confusion of the need for social support with the need for change agents, and the legitimacy of the assumption of resistance to innovation. He also notes some methodological concerns, such as using self-reports of message attention, assuming delivery of the message through the medium, and basing conclusions on laboratory studies. The most serious criticism is practical; from the point of view of cost, of feasibility, and of sustainability, organizing an effective face-to-face network is rarely possible. Thus the important question concerns not which channel has greater effects alone or in combination with what other channels, but what the relative effectiveness of various channels is in real situations. Using data from a recent health communication campaign in Swaziland, Hornik tests five alternative models of channel effects, and finds not only that mass media and interpersonal channels have independent effects, but that mass media channels are also more effective.

Prodevelopment soap operas in Third World nations represent a unique combination of entertainment and educational television. Arvind Singhal and Everett M. Rogers describe the effects of *Hum Log*, a prodevelopment soap opera in India that promoted certain socially desirable behaviors that contribute to development. *Hum Log* viewers learned prosocial behaviors from television models, and the television program evoked parasocial interaction between the soap opera characters and the viewers. However, *Hum Log* also led to the commercialization of Indian television, an unanticipated consequence. Prodevelopment soap operas, along with other educational/entertainment messages, offer a promising potential as mass media campaign tools.

9

Campaign Sampler

Using Television
to Promote Safety Belt Use
E. Scott Geller

Motor-vehicle crashes are the leading cause of death of individuals between ages 1 and 34 in the United States (*Injury in America,* 1985, p. 4). It is estimated that 55% of all fatalities and 65% of all injuries from vehicle crashes would be prevented if vehicle shoulder and/or lap belts were used (Federal Register, 1984; Sleet, 1987), yet 75% of adults and 50% of children under 4 years old fail to use a safety belt or child safety seat.

Over the years, numerous communication campaigns have attempted to persuade the public to buckle up, often using a fear approach, warning that any inconvenience or discomfort is minor compared to the disability or disfigurement resulting from a vehicle crash. Perhaps the best-known safety belt campaign is the classic and rigorous field experiment conducted by Robertson et al. (1974). In this campaign, six different safety belt messages were shown during the day and during prime time on one cable of a dual-cable TV system. Homes in Cable System A (6,400 homes) received the safety belt messages 943 times over a nine-month period (for a per-person exposure of two to three times per week), while the control households in Cable System B (7,400 homes) did not receive the messages. In addition, the use of safety belts by vehicle drivers was observed in a systematic rotating schedule from 14 different sites within the community, for one month before and the nine months during the campaign. The vehicle license plate numbers were recorded and later matched with each owner's name and address from the files of the state Department of Motor Vehicles. The TV viewers did not know they were in an experiment, and the field observers could not know the experimental condition of a particular vehicle observation.

Overall mean safety belt use among drivers was 8.4% for males and 11.3% for females for the treatment group, and 8.2% and 10.3% for the control group. The results have been summarized as showing that television campaigns do not have any effect on use of safety belts (Robertson, 1976).

However, before accepting this conclusion, consider that four of the six different TV spots were based on a fear tactic, highlighting the negative consequences of disfigurement and disability. Research suggests that a fear-arousing approach is usually not desirable for safety messages (Leventhal, Shafer, & Panagis, 1983; Winett, 1986; see also Reardon, chap. 12, this volume). The anxiety elicited by the vivid portrayal of the disfiguring consequence of a vehicle crash can interfere with the viewer's attention and retention (Lazarus, 1980), or cause viewers to avoid this unpleasant sight in subsequent TV spots after the first part of the scene is shown. Consequently, many viewers may have missed the end of these spots, which demonstrated the problem's solution (i.e., using safety belts).

Rather than using such fear appeals, communication campaigns to promote safety belt use should adopt the principles of social learning theory (Bandura, 1977b; see McAlister, Ramirez, Galavotti, & Gallion, chap. 13, this volume) and illustrate through behavioral modeling the comfort and convenience of using a safety belt, or how safety belt users would not be hurt in a crash. The most natural way to depict behavioral modeling of safety belt use on TV is not during a public service announcement, but during actual TV programs and movies (McGuire, 1984; Robertson, 1983).

Practically all current TV commercials involving vehicle travel show occupants buckled up. In contrast, most of the entertainment shows on TV do not show safety belt use (less than 1% of drivers or passengers in 1975-1979 prime-time shows; Atkin & Greenberg, 1980). Based on our observations of 5,544 driving scenes from 538 episodes of 21 different prime-time TV shows, the overall rate of safety belt use on TV rose from 8% in 1984 to 17% in 1986, consistent with changes in national belt use statistics.

On *The A-Team*, Mr. T's unusually high rate of safety belt use in 1985 (20% of all driving scenes, up from 1% in 1984) was very noticeable, since he was the only A-Team member to buckle up. During 1986, however, the entire A-Team was more likely to use their safety belts (39% of all driving scenes). The dramatic increase may have been partially due to a nationwide campaign my students and I initiated in 1984 to bring public attention to the inappropriate nonuse of safety belts by TV stars (Geller, 1985). First, we circulated a petition throughout the United States that described the presumed detrimental modeling effects of low safety belt use on TV, and gathered approximately 50,000 signatures. Subsequently, we distributed a list of 30 names and addresses of TV stars, along with instructions to write letters requesting safety belt use by those who did not buckle up and to write "thank you" notes to those who already buckled up on TV. In 1984, Mr. T. received more than 800 "buckle-up" letters from third and fourth graders.

To summarize, the conclusion by Robertson et al. (1974; Robertson, 1976) that TV is ineffective at influencing safety belt use should be refined to indicate that certain kinds of communications are unsuccessful at changing behavior. Social learning theory and much supportive research indicate that showing the convenience, comfort, and reinforcing consequences of using safety belts is likely to affect large-scale increases in actual safety belt use, especially if such demonstrations are frequent, realistic, and viewed by the public. These behavior change criteria are met optimally by the consistent use of safety belts during TV episodes and movies.

Singing the (VD) Blues
Bradley Greenberg and Walter Gantz

For the past few years, media throughout the world have been discussing and reporting the AIDS problem on news programs, talk shows, telethon fund-raisers, PSAs and dramas, newspaper and magazine stories, even novels, often advocating the use of condoms and clean needles, both graphically displayed. What effect is this coverage having on its audiences? Are we more informed or more compassionate? Are we more willing to talk openly with friends, lovers, and other loved ones about the disease and its impact on our own behaviors? Our study on the classic TV show *VD Blues* gives us a good sense of the answers to such questions.

VD Blues achieved notoriety in the early 1970s because it was the first television program to deal candidly with the largely "unmentionable" topic of venereal disease. At that time, the program was too strong for the commercial networks; it aired several times on public television. With a healthy mix of songs and humorous skits and the inclusion of frank words such as *syphilis* and *gonorrhea*, *VD Blues* declared war on the taboo and poked fun at the medical establishment. The fast-paced variety show used a popular talk-show host (Dick Cavett) to lead the proceedings, well-known actors and actresses to portray bumbling doctors, deadly germs, and frightened lovers, and popular singers and rock music groups to drive the messages home. It was, as one reviewer put it, "educational entertainment, a sort of Sesame Street for the sexually active" (Resnik, 1975).

Motivated by the unique approach of the program, a research project was formulated and conducted in 1974. The conceptual framework was that of "taboo topics," issues that people are not comfortable talking about, such as terminal illness, homosexuality, and sexually transmitted diseases. These were messages that Rogers (1972) had referred to as "extremely personal and private in nature" and that Gantz (1975) had defined as "situations in which a behavior should not be performed and/or communicated about." The research question focused on the extent to which public, mediated discussions of taboo topics would stimulate interpersonal conversations. It was our contention that the mass media could intervene effectively, that this television production would increase knowledge, increase the perception of personal knowledgeability, reduce inhibitions that limit talk about VD, and enhance the importance of the topic by increasing its visibility. To examine these hypotheses, we conducted a field survey and a controlled experiment.

Field Survey

The night after the program was aired in the Lansing, Michigan, area, telephone interviews were completed with 923 adults. Of the sample, 15% said they had watched the show the previous evening or in its first local showing several months earlier; this gave us 135 viewers to analyze. Compared to nonviewers, viewers were younger, more educated, and tended to have more prior media-based information about VD, and they tested more highly on the knowledge questions used. Specifically, they were more knowledgeable about relatively complex issues; for example, they could identify more ways in which VD can and cannot be transmitted and they could identify more long-term effects associated with those diseases. Further, their perceptions of being informed were positively correlated with actual information level.

Although viewers did not differ from nonviewers in terms of how much they would be embarrassed if someone wanted to talk to them about VD, there were sharp differences in the number of situations in which these groups thought it would be "okay to talk about VD." Given seven possible contexts (e.g., between marital partners, with parents, with friends, or using different media), 93% of the viewers said that six or seven of these contexts were okay, compared with 77% of the nonviewers.

Finally, a set of exposure variables (seeing the show the previous night or earlier, reading about VD, seeing or hearing other shows) was significantly correlated with the dependent measures of knowledge and tabooness.

Experiment

Subjects were 102 undergraduates; half were shown the program and half were not (26 who had already seen the show were omitted from the analyses). In addition to the survey hypotheses, a new proposition examined the subjects' judgment of the seriousness of the VD problem, an agenda-setting issue. This was confirmed by the results, as 85% of the viewers said that the VD problem was "quite" or "very" serious, compared with 50% of the nonviewers. Viewers scored higher on a summative knowledge index across a variety of knowledge items. Nonviewers scored substantially better on one subindex that asked for symptoms identifying VD. Since the program stressed that people often could not tell if they had VD, viewers may have believed there were fewer clear symptoms associated with it.

There were no discernible differences between viewers and non-viewers for three measures of the perceived communicative tabooness of VD—how comfortable others their age would be discussing VD, how comfortable they themselves would be, and whether or not it was right to broadcast radio and television programs about VD. This non-finding may be attributed to college students' willingness to talk about almost anything.

Implications

This single hour-long show stimulated awareness, knowledge, and concern about a serious problem. Given that three-fourths of the viewers in our survey had seen the show fully three months before they were interviewed, the survey results were a severe test of our propositions and these outcomes.

Results with regard to the alleviation of communicative tabooness were less marked, perhaps because the topic was less taboo to talk about than we had assumed. In the survey sample, less than a majority said they felt uneasy with the issue and, in the college experiment, a ceiling effect limited movement to more openness. There also may have been a methodological problem in that a survey that focuses on such an issue may itself induce less tabooness in talking about the issue. Given that those aware of the show (whether they had seen it or not) may already have been more receptive to talking about VD, it would have been useful to compare this group with those unaware. Even more appropriate would be assessments of the magnitude of topic or issue tabooness prior to broadcast of *VD Blues* as well as after exposure.

Over the years, *VD Blues* has been considered a model for programming efforts designed to promote health issues. Since we did not measure reactions to the show itself (e.g., the perceived appropriateness of the skits and songs), we cannot speak directly about the impact of the straightforward but entertaining manner in which VD information was presented in the program. To our knowledge, however, no data collected since that effort suggest that the persuasive punch delivered by information programs is reduced when the program makes use of attention-grabbing presentation techniques.

With *VD Blues* as a guide, we conclude that a concentrated media presentation focused on particular health issues is likely to result in heightened awareness, knowledge, and salience of health issues such as AIDS as well as increased and more at-ease interpersonal communication about them.

Freestyle, Revisited
Robert LaRose

The *Freestyle* television series was a concerted effort to extend the successful *Sesame Street* model of purposive television for children to the "affective domain" of beliefs, attitudes, and behavior. The goal of the series was to reduce sex-role stereotyping effects on children's preoccupational activities and perceptions of adult work and family roles.

Here we outline one of the many models of persuasion used in the series and recount how selected episodes were in fact "engineered" with it in mind. We then reinterpret the findings of the summative evaluation to assess the merits of this strategy in the context of a mass media campaign, and to account for some of the strongest effects of *Freestyle*.

The theory of reasoned action (Ajzen & Fishbein, 1980; Fishbein & Ajzen, 1975) argues that a person's attitude toward a behavior is conditioned by the perceived consequences of the behavior and the individual's evaluation of those consequences. Perceptions of how significant others may enforce norms pertaining to group-typed behavior can be considered as the social normative component of the model. It is also possible to conceptualize the socially defined standard for the group (i.e., the stereotype) as a special type of perceived social norm (e.g., what "most boys" or "most girls" would do).

The model is also a good story generator. For example, we found through focus groups that one of the salient personal consequences that girls take into account when considering their involvement in traditionally "male" sports is the potential for physical injury. Many girls in the upper elementary grades also seem concerned about how their fathers will react to such "unfeminine" activities. These elements were the ingredients for the "Flag" episode of *Freestyle*: We showed a preteen girl going out for a sex-typed activity (i.e., football) who has to overcome her own fears about injury, win the approval of her peers and parents, and ignore the opposition of the community at large. We showed the heroine taking her lumps on the field, but also took care to point out factual evidence that girls are less likely to be seriously injured than boys in contact sports. We also implied that getting hurt really is not so bad, especially when it leads to the approval of your teammates. In the end, success on the field wins over the doubters in the community, and the parents unite to support the interest of the child in the face of social disapproval.

As the 13-episode series aired on the Public Broadcasting System in 1979, summative evaluation was conducted with nearly 5,000 children in seven treatment groups (two in-home, five in-school) across the United States (Johnston & Ettema, 1982; Johnston, Ettema, & Davidson, 1980). At two sites the treatment condition involved home viewing, in which parents received letters encouraging them to have their children watch the program when it appeared on the local PBS station, followed by weekly reminders to the participating students from their teachers. At three of the five in-school sites, children viewed the series in their classrooms and engaged in classroom discussions with their teachers using the *Freestyle* curriculum guides. At the other two in-school sites, children watched the programs in their classrooms but did not discuss the material afterward. In all cases there was a control group of children in classrooms that were not exposed to *Freestyle*. Measures of beliefs, attitudes, and interests, taken before and after the

series, covered three important curriculum areas: childhood preoccupational activities, childhood behavioral skills, and perceptions of adult
work and family roles.

In the three in-school discussion treatments, *Freestyle* achieved
many of its educational objectives. Boys and girls increased their
acceptance of females performing mechanical activities, boys became
more accepting of girls in athletics, and girls became more willing to
accept boys in helping roles. There were no changes in the perceived
appropriateness of leadership, independence, assertiveness, and risk
taking for girls, but boys did change their attitudes about female leadership and independence in the desired direction. Girls also acquired
more positive attitudes toward female independence. Both beliefs and
attitudes toward adult work and family roles were widely affected,
including perceptions of the sex distribution of persons holding traditionally sex-typed jobs and performing sex-typed activities around the
home. Girls also became more interested in typically male-dominated
"realistic" and "enterprising" jobs and boys more interested in female-
dominated "social" jobs as a result of exposure to the full treatment
condition. However, beliefs and attitudes about whether wives or hus-
bands should support a family were unaffected.

When viewing took place in the two no-discussion school settings,
the magnitudes of the effects were considerably smaller in most cases,
leading the summative evaluators to conclude that mere viewing was
insufficient to achieve the goals of the series. The home viewing
condition was generally ineffective, except among a small segment of
heavy viewers.

It is possible to reconstrue these results within the theory of reasoned action. The measure of "attitude" toward nontraditional activities may be regarded as a type of normative belief about appropriate
behavior for the sexes, while interests in childhood activities may be
regarded as behavioral intentions. Perceived social norms in the form
of beliefs about support from significant others for nontraditional
behavior were not assessed in the *Freestyle* evaluation. However, the
discussion and no-discussion school treatments allow us to address the
central riddle of the summative evaluation study: How could *Freestyle*
be so effective in one condition and so (relatively) ineffective in two
others?

The summative evaluators concluded that when teachers discussed
the programs with the children they may have had a chance to overcome defects in the video materials that restricted their persuasive

impact. If this were so, then the most complex and frequently misunderstood programs—those relating to so-called behavioral skills such as independence and risk taking—should have differed the most between conditions; this was not the case.

A rival explanation comes from the application of the theory of reasoned action. In our formative evaluation studies (Williams, LaRose, & Frost, 1981), we assessed children's perceived social norms relative to various significant others. There was a great degree of uncertainty when it came to norms perceived for the child's teacher; many children said that they did not know what their teacher expected them to do regarding sex-typed behavior. Thus in the no-discussion school condition, this influence was not clear or obvious and so it is no surprise that the series was less effective. Still, the viewing took place in the school environment with the teacher present, which may have implied the tacit approval of the teacher for the *Freestyle* message. In the home viewing condition, there was no definition of the teacher norm and so very limited effects were found, even though parents could have compensated for program defects. The parental norms were already well defined and the related home viewing activities were far less structured than those in the classroom setting, so there probably was no effective activation of normative influence in that condition.

In sum, our retrospective reconceptualization of *Freestyle* allows us to extend some of the claims made for the effectiveness of the series and offers some validation for an approach to solving the problem of stereotyping through the application of expectancy-value theory. It can be argued that the effects of *Freestyle* on the sex-typed behavior of its audience were brought about by the successful manipulation of perceived social norms relating to appropriate behavior for the sexes in the content of the series, and by a manipulation of beliefs about teachers' normative expectations through classroom discussion.

Future campaigns directed against stereotypes could perhaps benefit from a focus on the patterns of normative beliefs that affect group-typed behavior. These include notions about what society expects in terms of behavior for a particular group and what individual significant others expect. A special opportunity arises when the norms of a particular class of significant others are not well defined. Mass media presentations can define such expectations, especially when coupled with discussions that involve the target audience and representative significant others in discussions that lend the impression that the significant others support the behavior in question.

The McGruff Crime Prevention Campaign
GARRETT J. O'KEEFE AND KATHALEEN REID

The Take a Bite Out of Crime campaign was developed in the late 1970s to promote public involvement in crime prevention activities. The campaign was initiated under the sponsorship of the Crime Prevention Coalition, a group of government, private, and not-for-profit agencies, with the major media components of the program produced by the Advertising Council. Major objectives included (1) generating a greater sense of individual responsibility among citizens for reducing crime, (2) encouraging citizens to take collective preventive actions, as well as to work more closely with law enforcement agencies, and (3) enhancing crime prevention programs at local, state, and national levels.

The Ad Council's volunteer agency for the campaign, Dancer Fitzgerald Sample, designed the media materials around an animated trench-coated dog, McGruff, who called on citizens to help "take a bite out of crime" by making their homes more secure, by taking more precautions when outdoors, and by working together with their neighbors in neighborhood/block watch programs. Importantly, the highly publicized national media campaign was supplemented by a full range of locally promoted supplemental activities across the country by law enforcement agencies, community groups, and businesses. The first media messages were disseminated via television, radio, newspapers, magazines, billboards, and posters in late 1979. Hundreds of thousands of supplemental brochures and related materials containing more specific information also were distributed.

Evaluating the McGruff campaign's effectiveness (see O'Keefe, 1985, 1986) presented several noteworthy conceptual and methodological problems, most related to the necessarily scattershot nature of media campaigns reliant upon public service advertising. Because PSAs are disseminated on largely unpredictable schedules convenient to individual media sources, optimal evaluative designs using controlled exposure patterns are virtually impossible. As a "next best" option, a two-phase design was used in which (1) interviews with a national probability sample of 1,200 adults was carried out two years into the campaign, and (2) a panel sample of 426 adults in three representative cities were interviewed just prior to the campaign's onset and again two years later.

The campaign's impact was measured in terms of the extent to which it increased citizens' *competency*, in terms of (1) awareness of preventive techniques, (2) attitudes that they could make a positive difference, (3) sense of personal capability or efficacy in helping prevent crime, (4) concern about crime, and (5) engagement in preventive behaviors.

The campaign had fairly widespread penetration. Over half of the national sample said they seen or heard at least one of the McGruff PSAs by late 1981. Most had seen them on television, and exposure was well distributed across demographic groups and across citizens with widely varying perceptions, attitudes, and behaviors with respect to crime. Substantial selectivity was found in attention patterns, with the more attentive likely to be more generally prevention competent. Respondents indicated a largely favorable response, with the PSAs viewed as effective, likable, and worth mentioning to others. About a quarter of the respondents said that they had learned something new from the PSAs, and nearly half said they had been reminded of things they had forgotten. Almost half reported the ads had made them more confident about protecting themselves and more positive about the effectiveness of citizen prevention efforts. Lesser impact was found for overall concern about crime and sense of individual responsibility. About a quarter reported taking specific actions as a consequence of PSA exposure, mainly in improved household security and cooperating with neighbors, the two main themes of McGruff to that point.

The panel sample confirmed the above findings with respect to information gain and attitude change, and offered particularly strong evidence of behavioral change. The campaign-exposed group reported significantly greater activity in nearly all behaviors specifically advocated by the PSAs, with no such changes found for nonadvocated behaviors. These findings held when potentially confounding variables (e.g., exposure to other crime-related media stimuli and direct victimization experience) were controlled for.

Opportunity for action appeared to be one influence on effects (e.g., women spending more time at home showed more gains in neighborhood cooperation). Importantly, behavioral change at times occurred without corresponding cognitive or attitudinal change, particularly among citizens who already believed themselves more at risk. These results challenge traditional hierarchy-of-effects models (i.e., cognitive effects precede attitudinal ones, which precede behavioral ones) (see McGuire, chap. 2, this volume). On the other hand, those less at risk indicated greater cognitive and attitudinal changes. In some cases, attitudinal change was not uniformly associated with cognitive change.

Recommendations for subsequent campaigns include paying greater attention to community-based prevention efforts and the role of interpersonal communication. Exceptionally careful handling of fear arousal in crime prevention campaigns is also mandated, since the situation is one in which the mere mention of the topic can stimulate concern. More precise audience targeting is also required, not only in terms of demographics but by psychological orientations toward crime and communication-related variables as well. One group with particular needs is the elderly, and subsequent formative research on crime-related and communication habits of aged persons revealed several distinctive campaign strategies for approaching them (O'Keefe & Reid, in press).

Mass Campaigns in the People's Republic of China During the Mao Era
Ronald E. Rice (summary and adaptation of chapter from first edition by Alan P. L. Liu)

From the consolidation of political power in the early 1950s by the Chinese communists under Mao Zedong, until his death in 1976, the People's Republic of China (PRC) conducted more than 74 national mass campaigns (Cell, 1977). Late in this revolutionary and formative period, word began spreading about both the massiveness and the apparent success of such campaigns. The mobilization of an entire nation toward some social conditions, mixed with minimal information about them, lent an air of mystique to the PRC campaigns.

These campaigns typically served one of several purposes: (1) class struggle campaigns designed to introduce a new institution (such as land reform) while simultaneously repudiating the resisting forces, (2) denunciation of purged political figures, (3) support for the study of particular political doctrines, (4) emulation of model workers or institutions, (5) familiarization of the public with new policies, (6) countering inappropriate public opinion, and (7) general information campaigns (such as birth control, antispitting, or snail eradication).

In general, most mass campaigns followed the model Mao used in mobilizing troops during the 1930s and 1940s: Policies, goals, and mechanisms were decided by top leaders, and mass communication and involvement were used to implement and institutionalize them. This approach was accomplished through the pervasive control by the Communist Party and the state bureaucracy of all levels of government as well as mass organizations such as trade unions, women's associations, and youth leagues. A typical campaign involved the following stages (see Liu, 1981, for more detail):

(1) A separate ad hoc organization was established and devoted solely to the campaign, headed by a well-known government figure, in order to accentuate the importance of the campaign, to ensure a high degree of homogeneity in communication, to increase participation of people from various circles, and to overcome the inherent inflexibility and inertia of the bureaucracies.

(2) A special group of "activist" campaign workers was trained, selected primarily on the basis of political reliability and experience in a special line of work. This stage was used to broaden the impact of a policy rapidly.

(3) Several "testing points," a kind of audience survey or formative evaluation, were selected. For example, testing points in the 1956-1958 birth control campaign found that while there was a large demand for birth control information, older people resisted the idea, rural women felt that bearing children was their natural lot, and men and women wanted separate exhibits.

(4) A "key point" application typically followed, which was the methodical execution of the campaign in a region where the target problem or disease was especially common. Once the key point campaign had been refined and appeared successful, and could be used as an administrative and visible model, the full campaign was activated throughout a "plane," such as county, province, or the nation.

(5) During the plane stage, all available communication media were fully brought to bear: "folk" media such as posters, blackboards and bulletin boards, folk plays, and songs, in addition to radio, movies, and newspapers. However, interpersonal communication was emphasized, in the form of group and mass meetings (except where small meetings were more appropriate, such as in the birth control campaign, because public discussion about sex ran counter to Chinese custom). Face-to-face persuasion was especially favored, through processes such as "recollection and comparison" (in which a person is asked to recall "past suffering" and compare that with the "present improvement in living conditions"), "reckoning of accounts" through statistics (e.g., in the birth control campaign, information about birthrates, effects on productivity, extent of child-bearing illness, child expenses, and social welfare

expenses), "airing complaints" (in which hardships that need to be overcome are recounted), and the use of individuals as positive and negative models in support of the campaign and as instances for others to make public their support.

Various social science principles were mirrored in these stages: (1) the human relations principle that communication between hierarchical levels and participation in decision making increases perceived commitment and satisfaction; (2) the two-step flow model, whereby opinion leaders and personal influence diffuse persuasive communications initially delivered through mass media; (3) cognitive dissonance and memory models, which propose that persuasion is more effective if the audience role plays and improvises the message; and (4) conflict-arousal theory, which suggests that addressing conflicts in the mind of the audience may increase the persuasive effect of a communication.

Obstacles were often inherent in many of these campaigns: (1) Because there was only one central government-controlled media delivery channel, resistance by local or regional media gatekeepers could stifle campaign efforts; (2) the basis for much of this campaign approach, the mobilization of the Red Army in the 1940s, may have been an inappropriate foundation for designing communications with the mass public; (3) often the objective reality experienced by the local audiences contradicted the models used in a campaign; (4) the frequent and institutionalized use of group meetings eventually took on a ritualistic and mechanical nature that reduced their novelty and effectiveness; (5) much of rural China was still isolated from the media; and (6) genuine participation and involvement by the masses were often missing. Also, campaign goals often were excessively unrealistic.

Some campaigns were very successful, however, such as the third family planning campaign begun in 1968 and maintained to this day (Aird, 1978; Whyte & Gu, 1987). The desired goal was a two-child family in urban areas and three in rural areas, through the use of contraception, abortion, and sterilization; current policies encourage one-child families in urban areas. The primary persuasive mechanism was to eliminate traditional (Confucian) values such as early marriage, large families, preferences for sons, and privacy in family matters. Rational arguments included a reduced need for large families because of lower mortality rates and state-provided security for old age; sexual emancipation, so that daughters were as valuable as sons; the personal economic benefits of fewer children; and the disruption to the planned economy of high birthrates (Aird, 1978). Concrete economic strategies included incentives and sanctions in the areas of taxes, child allowances, education, and job placement. Although the official position in the early 1970s was that birth control was voluntary, a wide range of coercive activities have been reported, ranging from conversational house visits by leading cadre members through public denunciations to involuntary sterilizations (Aird, 1978; Pear, 1988). This third campaign has been an astounding success: The national birthrate has dropped from 6.1 in 1955 to 2.3 in 1980. Births of a third or more child, as a percentage of all births, dropped from 62% in 1970 to 20% in 1985 (Whyte & Gu, 1987).

In general, however, it appears that the effectiveness of some of even the most famous PRC campaigns disappeared as soon as concentrated government support was removed, or were never successful in the first place—such as the Tachai Brigade, a demonstration farm touted as a successful economic innovation from 1963 through 1978. One of the philosophic insights derived from the failure of these campaigns is that, perhaps unfortunately, emphasizing collective (community or national) benefits at the cost of individual sacrifice cannot be the primary basis of enduring social change.

Smokey Bear
Ronald E. Rice (summary and adaptation of chapter from first edition by Eugene F. McNamara, Troy Kurth, and Donald Hansen)

Each year, nearly 5 million acres of land in the United States are ravaged by wildfires, at a total cost of nearly $1 billion. In central, southern, and eastern regions, 99% of all wildfires are caused by people or by equipment operated by people. This tremendous national problem has been countered with one of the most famous of all campaigns—the Smokey Bear campaign (Morrison, 1976).

This campaign began in 1942, as part of the wartime response to potential wildfires caused by enemy bombing, and to the shortage of firefighter personnel. The newly formed Wartime Advertising Council[1] created a media campaign kit: The first poster's message was "Careless Matches Aid the Axis—Prevent Forest Fires." The idea of using a bear as the symbol of forest fire prevention was conceived by representatives of the Foote, Cone and Belding advertising agency and the

Forest Service. The 1944 Smokey Bear poster was produced by Walt Disney; the 1945 poster had Smokey in dungarees and a ranger's hat, pouring water on a campfire, with the message, "Smokey Says—Care Will Prevent 9 out of 10 Forest Fires." The slogan "Remember, Only You Can Prevent Forest Fires" was developed by Foote, Cone and Belding in 1947. Smokey became a living symbol in 1950 when a black bear cub, badly burned, was rescued from a forest fire in New Mexico and housed in the National Zoo until his death in 1977. The symbol of Smokey Bear became so well known that it was legally protected by Congress in 1952, and it provides yearly royalties for the Smokey Bear campaign. A Smokey Bear Junior Forest Ranger Program, begun in 1953, mails an official fire prevention materials kit to the over 6 million kids who write to Smokey Bear Headquarters; it had to get its own zip code in 1966 to handle the hundreds of cards and letters received each day.

The Ad Council and its supporters continue to work in cooperation with the Forest Service and the Association of State Foresters on the Smokey Bear campaign. During the 1970s, about $50 million was allocated annually to the Smokey Bear campaign. In 1979 alone, over $1 million worth of materials were produced and distributed, involving mailings to thousands of television and radio stations (representing 4 billion electronic media impressions), and messages placed for free (estimated at a total commercial value of over $55 million) in thousands of newspapers and magazines, along with numerous billboards. Smokey also appears on a Rose Parade float, as a Macy's Thanksgiving Day Parade balloon, and at other festivals and fairs.

There has been no comprehensive evaluation of the Smokey campaign, and it would be difficult to pinpoint specific effects of a nationwide campaign over such a long period. However, we can point to some suggestive evidence, as well as some areas for improvement.

Acreage lost through wildfires has dropped substantially from the 30 million per year before the program began in 1942 to less than 5 million. Gross cost-benefit figures for the Smokey Bear campaign are encouraging: The estimated resource savings over the first 30 years of the Smokey Bear campaign amount to $17 billion, yet the annual program budget is half a million dollars, not including Ad Council donations. A public awareness survey conducted in 1976 showed a near-universal 98% aided recall awareness of Smokey Bear (AHF Marketing Research, 1976).

What are some of the reasons for this high visibility and potential success? Clearly, Smokey Bear is both an engaging and a fairly credible source used consistently as a symbol of the fire prevention concept. The extremely large exposure through multiple media outlets, made possible by the Ad Council's continuing support, has provided far greater coverage for a longer period of time than for any other PSA-based campaign. The original slogan—"Only You Can Prevent Forest Fires"—attempts to involve the audience member personally, especially relevant because of the large percentage of fires caused by humans (often out of carelessness or ignorance, but all too frequently intentionally). Other strategies in some of the Smokey Bear campaign materials include emotional appeals (showing burned animals) and personal values (such as maintaining recreational opportunities and natural environments). Smokey Bear is also generally present at school fire prevention programs as well as fairs, generating both excitement and campaign identity among children and adults alike, supplementing the media campaign with interpersonal communication.

The challenge, however, is to continue to increase the allocation of resources to wildfire prevention, educate the public, and change behavior under complex conditions with little maintenance. Some current efforts include Forest Service personnel contact with campers and tourists entering forest areas, discussions with small groups of students in fire prevention school programs, local media coverage of wildfire conditions, and displays and exhibits at fairs and forest entry sites.

As suburbanites expand their residential areas into the countryside, and as more people visit forest areas every year, they bring with them urban habits and minimal knowledge about forest conditions that contribute to the large number of preventable wildfires. The very longevity of Smokey Bear may also work against its effectiveness: The current theme of "Only You Can Prevent Forest Fires" assumes the campaign is well known enough that specific knowledge and behaviors will be activated by these words. Yet every year brings new children into our schools and new visitors into forest areas who have never been exposed to specific information or behavioral models about fire prevention. Thus, when prompted, they are highly aware of Smokey; but they seldom recall Smokey or know what to do to prevent wildfires during their annual vacations or weekend walks in the woods. Indeed, the study cited above found a very low unaided awareness of Smokey Bear in the general population—only 7% (AHF Marketing Research, 1976). So, in spite of the tremendous contributions of the media community and the very real successes of the Smokey Bear campaign, there is much work to be done in the area of forest fire prevention.

Note

1. At the end of World War II, the word *wartime* was dropped from the name of the Advertising Council, and it has continued to be supported by the business and advertising communities. The Council currently receives 300-400 requests per year, and implements approximately three dozen major campaigns representing $800 million in advertising time and space (Mandese, 1987; "Top Events Run Gamut," 1986). Smokey Bear and Savings Bonds are the two oldest. Once the Council approves a campaign, it requests an ad agency from the American Association of Advertising Agencies to handle the campaign by contributing creative talent and message production.

The Great American Values Test
Sandra Ball-Rokeach and Milton Rokeach

The Great American Values Test was a unique field experiment using television to change fundamental values of the mass public. We created a 30-minute television program hosted by well-known TV personalities (Ed Asner and Sandy Hill) that aired on all three commercial channels at the same time (7:30 p.m.) in an experimental city, but not in a comparable control city, cities generally representative of the American population. It was designed not only to appeal to the natural curiosity people have about their own and others' values, but also to heighten the importance that they place upon egalitarian values (equality and freedom) and an environmental value (a world of beauty) so as to effect enduring changes in related attitudes and behavior—antiracist, antisexist, and proenvironmental.

The research entailed a unique blend of two theories, media system dependency theory (Ball-Rokeach, 1974, 1985; Ball-Rokeach & De-Fleur, 1976; Ball-Rokeach, Rokeach, & Grube, 1984) and belief system theory (Rokeach, 1973, 1979; Ball-Rokeach et al., 1984). Media system dependency is defined as the extent to which attainment of personal goals is contingent upon scarce information resources controlled by the media system. We designed and advertised our show to appeal to viewers with strong social understanding and self-understanding dependency relations with television. As such, we sought to control the selective exposure process to serve the research purposes. People with preestablished TV dependency relations for purposes of social and self-understanding, particularly those who also held the expectation that our program would serve these dependencies, should be more likely to process information in a way (greater attention and arousal of feelings) that would lead them to engage in the self-examination process that we wished to generate, and thus should be more likely to be affected by our program.

We also tested a basic thesis of belief system theory—that people can be induced to change their values, attitudes, and ultimately their behavior when given relevant information and prodded by a "Socratic" question to confront themselves about possible contradictions that they discover in their value-attitude systems. This self-confrontation method is free of the ego-defensive or avoidance reactions generated by many accusatory or informational messages. Prodded by carefully phrased self-confrontation messages designed to ask if their beliefs and behaviors regarding egalitarianism and environmentalism are consistent with their conceptions of themselves as moral and competent people, viewers finding themselves inconsistent would experience a state of self-dissatisfaction. In this case, viewers' egalitarian and environmental values and related attitudes (e.g., toward blacks, women, and the environmental movement) were hypothesized to become more important or positively regarded as a result of uninterrupted exposure to our TV program; changes in these deep-seated beliefs were hypothesized to then lead to long-term changes in behavior.

Our research design (see Table 9.1) overcomes typical weaknesses in validity found in most mass media campaign studies. A key feature is that it affords maximal external validity by preserving the "natural media exposure situation," in which research participants (1) are unaware that they are being observed and exposed to an experimental treatment, (2) select themselves into the audience as they would for any other program, (3) control the conditions and duration of exposure, and (4) experience natural forces of interruption (e.g., the telephone or the children). We gathered data in such a way that no connection was made by the participants between the TV show and (1) mail surveys employed to ascertain their values, attitudes, media dependencies, and demographic characteristics, (2) a viewer identification phone survey of the experimental city pretest and posttest samples, and (3) three solicitations mailed from actual preexisting organizations—one antiracist, one antisexist, and one proenvironmental.

The results provide strong evidence for our central hypothesis. Uninterrupted viewers (the 14% who watched without interruption) evidenced significantly more egalitarian and proenvironmental values (such as equality and a world of beauty) and attitudes (such as antiracism and proenvironmental) four weeks after exposure, compared to interrupted viewers (the 12% predisposed to watch, but due to events beyond their control did not see the whole program) and nonviewers

TABLE 9.1 Separate Sample Pretest/Postest Control Group Research Design

Activity	Pretest	Ad Campaign	TV Show Airs	Phone Survey	Postests 1	2	3	4
Week	0	6	7	7	11	15	17	20
Measurement purpose	values/ attitudes	selective exposure	treat- ment	identify viewers	values attitudes	counterbalanced behavioral measures		
Experimental city	X n = 500	X	X	X n = 1,699	X n = 1,199	X n = 1,699	X n = 1,699	X n = 1,699
Control city	X n = 378	0	0	0	X n = 377	X n = 755	X n = 755	X n = 755
Data- collection method	four-wave mail			nonreactive phone	four-wave mail	three mail solicitations from real groups		

NOTE: Preselected random samples were drawn from the telephone books of the experimental and control cities and randomly assigned to either the pretest or the postest. The average response rate was 65% for the mail survey and 82% for the phone survey.

(the remaining 74% in the experimental city, and the sample in the nonviewing control city). Further, these changes in belief led to long-term changes in behavior (such as positive response to the program and contributions of money) more than three months after exposure. Also an important finding is that high dependency upon television significantly increased the effectiveness of the program. For example, among uninterrupted viewers, the average monetary contribution to the egalitarian or proenvironmental behavioral solicitations was 50% higher for those exhibiting high as opposed to low television dependency (64 cents versus 43 cents).

Two implications of these findings for public communication campaigns are that (1) the self-confrontation method can be adopted as a general media intervention strategy for long-term change of socially and personally important beliefs and behaviors, and (2) there is an "effects payoff" in making an effort to control selective exposure such that persons with certain kinds of media dependency relations are drawn into the audience. The understanding dependencies were particularly important given the theory and aims of our research. But other dependencies or other media channels might be more germane for certain kinds of interventions. For example, if the intervention goal is to orient a particular demographic group to act or interact in a certain way, then researchers should first identify the medium with which that group has the strongest orientation dependency relations (see also Alcalay & Taplin, chap. 5, this volume). The emphasis, therefore, is upon the quality of people's relationships with different media, rather than the quantity of their exposure.

Littering: When Every Litter Bit Hurts
ROBERT B. CIALDINI

The classic public service announcement against littering begins with a shot of a majestic-looking American Indian paddling his canoe up a river that carries the scum and trash of various forms of industrial and individual pollution. After coming ashore near the littered side of a highway, the Indian watches as a bag of garbage is thrown, splattering and spreading along the road, from the window of a passing car. The camera pans up from the refuse at his feet to the Indian's face, where a tear is running down his cheek, and the slogan appears: "People Start

Pollution, People Can Stop It." According to the Keep America Beautiful organization, this PSA is the single most memorable and effective message ever sent to the American public against litter and pollution; everyone they talk to about littering recalls the ad.

Despite the fame and recognition value of this spot, it may contain aspects that may be less than optimal and perhaps even counterproductive in their impact upon viewers' littering behavior. In addition to the laudable (and conceivably effective) recommendation in the ad urging viewers to stop littering, there is an underlying theme, as well, that a lot of people do litter: Debris floats on the river and lies at the roadside, trash is tossed from automobiles, and we are told that "people start pollution."

Thus the creators of the spot may well have pitted two kinds of norms against each other: *prescriptive* norms (involving perceptions of which behaviors are societally approved) and *popular* norms (involving perceptions of which behaviors are typically performed). A long-standing research tradition in social psychology indicates that both kinds of norms motivate human action (Deutsch & Gerard, 1955). In the process of communicating that littering is contrary to prescriptive norms, then, the PSA also may have communicated the undercutting message that littering is consistent with popular norms. Theoretically, it would have been preferable to have presented the message in a way that allowed the two types of norms to work in concert.

One such possibility is suggested by some as-yet unreported research conducted by my students and me. We knew from previous research (e.g., Krauss, Freedman, & Whitcup, 1978) that people littered less into a clean area than into a dirty one. We reasoned that a subject who saw someone litter would become focused on the issue of whether people normally litter in the situation; consequently, the subject would examine the state of the environment more intently than usual to determine what people normally did there. Finding a littered area, the subject would be more likely than ever to litter; but finding a clean area, he or she would be less likely than ever to litter.

We conducted a study in which individuals found handbills placed on their windshields when they returned to their cars in a parking garage. Before getting to their cars, however, they witnessed someone else (an experimental confederate) who either dropped one of the fliers on the ground while walking by or who simply walked by, carrying no such flier. Beforehand, we had either littered the parking area with fliers, paper cups, candy wrappers, and the like or had removed all litter from it. We then watched from a hidden vantage point to see what subjects did with the fliers they found on their cars. The results confirmed our expectations in two respects. First, in the no-littering condition, a clean environment received less litter than a dirty one (7 out of 50 subjects versus 11 out of 34, $p < .05$). Second, in the littering condition, this difference was substantially enhanced (2 out of 31 versus 13 out of 24, $p < .001$). We think that these results occurred because witnessing someone else littering focused our subjects on the issue of what other people do in the situation.

It is this latter finding that would appear to have the greater applied value. Take, for example, its implications for the antilittering spot. The creators of the ad described above seem to have been correct in their decision to show an instance of someone (the passing motorist) actively littering into the environment, but they may have been mistaken in their decision to use an already-littered environment, as that combination of conditions produced the greatest littering in our study.

Were we to advise the Keep America Beautiful organization on how to revise the PSA, then, it would be to make the procedurally small but theoretically meaningful modification of changing the depicted environment from trashed to clean. Of course, it would be unwarranted to assume from our data that this ad has been negative in its overall impact on the public's littering actions. Because it is so moving and memorable a piece, it has likely been a strong positive force. Nonetheless, our data suggest that (1) even classic PSAs may contain unintended elements that could undermine optimal effectiveness, and (2) formative research should be conducted before expensive PSA production to detect and help eliminate such unfavorable elements.

Beyond this particular high-profile PSA, the larger antilittering campaign of the 1970s presented a number of other messages in various channels. Based on 30-50% decreases in the amount of observed litter in numerous locales around the country over this period, the Keep America Beautiful organization's campaign appears to have been notably successful overall. Due to a combination of prominently placed messages and a receptive audience willing to invest the small extra effort to dispose of litter properly, this campaign rates as one of the most effective in recent history.

Be Smart. Don't Start!
Charles K. Atkin

Alcohol is the most widely abused substance among America's youth, and drinking is the primary gateway behavior leading to use of illicit drugs such as marijuana and cocaine. Initial experimentation with alcohol is occurring at increasingly early ages, with the typical child starting at 13 or 14 years old (Johnston, O'Malley, & Bachman, 1987). Millions of teenagers experience serious alcohol-related problems, including drunk driving and other accidents, delinquency and crime, suicide, cirrhosis and other illnesses, and impaired social and emotional development.

In the mid-1980s, the Reagan administration set a high priority on prevention of substance abuse among youth. The National Institute on Alcohol Abuse and Alcoholism initiated a major campaign to prevent alcohol use by reaching children before they face intense peer and societal influences to drink. Thus the campaign was targeted to 8- to 12-year-olds and to adults who shape the attitudes and behaviors of children, particularly parents and teachers.

After several months of consultations with a panel of research experts specializing in child development, alcohol education, and mass communication, Macro Systems (a social marketing firm) and Children's Television Workshop (a research and production house responsible for successful educational TV series aimed at the preteen audience, such as *Electric Company*) planned the campaign objectives and strategies.

For the youth target audience, the campaign sought to increase awareness of the risks of early alcohol use, to demonstrate skills for resisting prodrinking pressures, and to establish nonuse as the accepted social norm. Additional objectives included educating parents to act as appropriate role models and to discourage alcohol use by their children, and activating community groups to implement prevention efforts.

Research indicated that the campaign needed to overcome several barriers that would undermine the potential for impact. First, there is strong peer pressure to drink; some youth fear the rejection or isolation that is perceived to result from noncompliance. Second, drinking is projected as an acceptable and glamorous practice in contemporary society, particularly as portrayed in television advertising and entertainment that is popular with young viewers (see Wallack, chap. 16, this volume). Third, there is easy access to alcohol in many homes and communities, and youthful experimentation is condoned by some adults.

On the other hand, the target audience is readily receptive and accessible in certain respects. Preteens tend to dislike the taste of alcohol, and they display widespread concern for alcohol's harmful effects on the brain. Further, this age group is heavily exposed to Saturday-morning television, and most attend schools that have substance abuse units, providing efficient channels of communication.

The strategic planners developed a variety of substantive guidelines for message development: Provide accurate information showing the effects of alcohol on the body and mind, depict the positive consequences of staying alcohol free, illustrate peer support for and positive role models of alcohol-free behavior, demonstrate peer resistance and refusal skills, teach how to evaluate alcohol promotional materials critically, and show alternative ways to assert independence and take risks. Stylistic guidelines stressed the importance of sophisticated technical production quality in the creation of a diverse array of print and videotaped materials featuring entertaining plots, engaging devices, and popular or intriguing characters; a music video format was recommended as the campaign centerpiece.

Preproduction focus group research was conducted with several hundred children in three locales across the country. After pretesting 14 possible slogans, "Be Smart. Don't Start!" was selected because it conveyed a positive theme emphasizing a valued quality and was highly rated by preteens. Because children identified the brain as the body part most adversely affected by alcohol, this consequence was given priority in campaign messages. Formative evaluation also provided information about comprehensible lexicon; for example, the jargony term *alcohol free* was abandoned because many children literally interpreted it to mean free alcohol.

The Children's Television Workshop producers built the campaign around a music video featuring the Jets, a performing group popular with teenagers and preteens (the youthful members of the Jets do not smoke, drink, or use drugs, and thus could serve as positive role models for the target audience). The basic five-minute video portrays a 13-year-old boy skateboarding on his way to a rock concert when he runs into some bad characters who offer him a bottle of beer. In a fantasy scene, his brain cells debate the response, focusing on negative out-comes such as brain cells dying. The boy answers, "No thanks! I've got better things to do!" and proceeds to the concert, where he enjoys the Jets singing the "Be Smart" song.

Two PSAs were cut from the video, and the script was drawn in comic book format for an activity book distributed to elementary school students. This book also contained games, puzzles, and stories relating to alcohol issues. The campaign slogan and logo were also featured on a Jets poster, stickers, and bookmarks. A teacher's guidebook suggested ways that these materials could be integrated into the curriculum.

In addition, a parent's booklet provided suggestions for discussing the drinking topic with children, and kits were prepared for community groups, government agencies, corporations, and the press. Regional workshops were held for campaign coordinators from each state and for local representatives of 35 major voluntary and professional organiza-tions, including the Parent-Teacher Association, American Academy of Pediatrics, American Federation of Teachers, and Mothers Against Drunk Driving. These contacts were important because the campaign was designed to be coordinated with other localized prevention efforts in a comprehensive, integrated approach.

Cooperation was secured with the CBS television network, which agreed to air the PSAs in early prime time and on Saturday mornings for several months. In addition, CBS developed eight spots featuring youthful role models from their own series, showed the music video, and included Be Smart themes in Saturday-morning programming. More than $5 million in air time was donated during 1987, primarily during periods of heavy preteen viewing. Many schools also presented the videotaped and printed materials to upper elementary students.

Unfortunately, no systematic summative evaluation was conducted to measure the impact of the Be Smart campaign formally. Testing of the video scenario showed that children rated it as believable, under-standable, and interesting. According to teachers, the video, particular-ly the brain cell segment, was well received by students. At a conference to review the project, generally positive reactions were expressed and the decision was made to continue the effort with a subsequent "Stay Smart. Don't Start!" campaign to expand upon the original theme.

Family Planning Communication Campaigns in Developing Countries
CHARLES K. ATKIN AND HENDRIKA W.J. MEISCHKE

National family planning programs were initiated in the 1950s and spread rapidly in the 1960s and 1970s, when concern for accelerating population growth stimulated political commitment to these programs in many developing countries. The objectives of most family planning programs are to prevent unwanted births, to encourage the spacing of children, to reduce the number of children couples desire, and to assist couples with infertility problems (Rogers, 1973).

Over this period, family planning strategies have moved from a clinic-based approach to an outreach approach. Until the mid-1960s, the emphasis was on expanding clinics, but the target population did not—or could not—come to these clinics for family planning services.

The outreach era was characterized by the implementation of community-based distribution programs designed to extend family planning services to the most remote areas of a country (Population Information Program, 1980). This approach relied on both interpersonal communication between the outreach (field) workers and the target population and increasing attention to mass media information campaigns. In the 1970s, there was a greater emphasis on motivational messages to influence audiences (Population Information Program, 1977; Rogers, 1973).

Social marketing was introduced in the field of family planning during the 1970s as a comprehensive framework for promoting public health (Manoff, 1985; Solomon, chap. 4, this volume). Most social marketing projects are designed to promote the concept of birth control and to sell contraceptives at subsidized prices through preexisting networks. While commercial marketers compete with one another for market share, social marketing emphasizes market expansion and often complements rather than competes with private sector and government programs to make the project more available (Manoff, 1985).

The implications of social marketing for communication strategies are twofold. At the interpersonal level, salespersons not only sell a contraceptive product but also promote and explain its uses and possible side effects. At the mediated level, social marketing features informational and motivational messages designed and produced by commercial research firms and advertising agencies, in contrast to the traditional campaign efforts of health professionals from various ministries of health.

In Bangladesh, social marketing strategies resulted in condom sales rising from 10 million in 1976 to 82 million in 1983 (Schellstede & Ciszewski, 1984). Raja, the main condom brand, has been promoted through both mass media (radio, newspapers, billboards, and posters) and interpersonal sales channels. In India, a massive advertising campaign succeeded in popularizing Nirodh, the socially marketed condom brand. Nirodh sales rose almost 400% from 1969 to 1973, while the government's free distribution of condoms over that period rose only 50% (Population Information Program, 1984). By 1984, Nirodh condom sales had almost doubled again, to 200 million per year (Population Information Program, 1985).

In Iran, the Esfahan multimedia campaign produced a 54% increase in pill acceptors and a 65% increase in total contraceptive use over a six-month period in the early 1970s. This motivational campaign used media channels intensively (radio, pamphlets, posters, leaflets, mass mailing, film spots, loudspeaker trucks, and newspaper and magazine inserts) (Taplin, 1981).

Although social marketing relies heavily on mass communication, an interpersonal aspect and field support are of great importance for a successful campaign. In Peru, where a recent social marketing campaign for family planning relied solely on mass media communication without field support, there was no apparent effect on contraceptive use (HealthCom, 1984-1985). For a review of social marketing programs in other countries and for a cross-country comparison of programs, see Population Information Program (1984) and Boone, Farley, and Samuel (1985).

Social marketing also stresses the role of formative research, especially audience analysis and pretesting of messages (Atkin & Freimuth, chap. 6, this volume). Audience analysis seeks to determine predispositions of the population in regard to contraception. For example, pretesting research in Bangladesh showed that messages emphasizing welfare of children and family economics played a greater role in motivating couples to inquire about family planning than appeals emphasizing the health and beauty of the woman (Harvey, 1984).

Precampaign analysis also identifies "resistance points" that can be addressed in the messages. Another Bangladesh campaign was targeted primarily at men instead of women after research showed that males are dominant and tend to be the decision makers even in such matters as use of contraception (Manoff, 1985).

The social marketing approach includes product design and delivery as well as promotion (Manoff, 1985). For instance, in Haiti a great deal of money was wasted on the dissemination of colored condoms before consumer studies revealed that the preference among the target audience was for the clear type instead of the colored type (Manoff, 1985).

In addition to promotional campaigns and social marketing of birth control devices, other recent approaches have employed the entertainment media to disseminate family planning messages to far broader audiences than conventional channels can reach. Singhal and Rogers (chap. 15, this volume) describe the use of televised soap operas to address family planning and other development goals.

The Young People Project sponsored by the Johns Hopkins University/Population Communication Services (1986) was an ambitious attempt to promote sexual responsibility among adolescents in eleven Latin American countries using entertainment-oriented messages (see Singhal & Rogers, chap. 15, this volume). For example, two Spanish songs dealing with sexual responsibility were performed by popular young singers Tatiana and Johnny. Research examining comprehension of the songs' meanings showed that adolescents interpreted the messages in the way intended. In a sample of Mexican teenagers, 64% said that the underlying message of the song "Detente" was to postpone sex, and 22% thought the main theme was "think about the consequences"; 39% of the adolescents interpreted the song "Cuando Estomos Juntos" as saying "wait to be together" and 40% perceived the implication of postponing sex. This innovative strategy assured more airtime for the public health message than it would have been possible to buy, due to the commercial success of the songs.

In conclusion, important progress in family planning program effectiveness has been achieved over the past two decades through increasingly sophisticated utilization of mass media and interpersonal channels. In particular, the development of contraceptive social marketing approaches in the 1970s signified a landmark advance in the adoption of family planning in developing countries.

The Strategic Extension Campaigns
on Rat Control in Bangladesh
RONNY ADHIKARYA

A strategic extension campaign in Bangladesh, organized and implemented in 1983 and 1984, produced massive behavior change among
farmers in adopting methods to reduce the prevalence of and damage
caused by rats (Adhikarya & Posamentier, 1987). As in many Asian
countries, rats in Bangladesh were destroying large amounts of grain—
about 10% of the standing wheat crop yearly—and damaging physical
structures such as irrigation systems, wiring, and buildings. Farmers
had taken little action because the responsibility for such problems had
traditionally been placed in the hands of government, inexpensive
rodenticides were not easily available, and there was little cultural
precedent for village and community collaboration in controlling rats.

In the 1983 wheat farmer campaign, target behavioral outcomes
included taking action on full-moon nights (to encourage farmers to
take coordinated if not collaborative action, so that rats would not just
be driven from one farm to the next); flooding, digging, or smoking out
rats; simultaneous planting; keeping fields clean; and using a new
ready-made rat bait.

The target audience was segmented according to different levels of
knowledge, attitudes, and practices concerning rat control. The logo on
all campaign materials emphasized individual responsibility for rat
control. Positioning of the messages included religious appeal (using a
Moslem quote that killing rats is virtuous), fear arousal, awareness of
the extent of damage, guilt appeal (relating farmers' inaction to resulting food shortages and child starvation), and a ridicule appeal (posters
showing rats laughing at farmers trapped instead of rats) that served as
a discussion point.

Radio spots and posters provided general information and motivational messages. Extensive training sessions were conducted to motivate and educate the campaign workers on their specific tasks before
the campaign. Interpersonal support was provided by extension
fieldworkers, who conducted small group discussions, field demonstrations, and training sessions. Teachers, children, and agricultural
supply retailers were also used to augment the extension workers. For
example, motivational comics were distributed by teachers, and were
taken home by schoolchildren to discuss with their (farmer) parents,
most of whom are illiterate. This component was complemented by an

essay contest for schoolchildren on their parents' problems with rats, requiring family and community discussion of the topic. Posters and leaflets explaining the proper application of the rat control methods were distributed to agricultural products dealers. Over a half million motivational posters, instructional posters, comic sheets, and leaflets, numerous radio spots and television programming segments, and nearly a quarter million ready-made rat bait packets were involved in the campaign. As has been found in other health campaigns, posters were ranked by the extension workers as the most effective input (see Rice & Foote, chap. 7, this volume).

The percentage of wheat farmers who conducted rat control jumped from 10% to 32% following the 1983 campaign. Surveys showed that, compared to the farmers who did not use rat control techniques, damage was reduced by 26% for farmers who used control measures other than the ready-made bait, but 56% for those who used the ready-made bait. A total of $40,000 U.S. was spent on operational expenses and bait (with a per-farm family unit cost of $.004), while the estimated net gain from increased wheat production was more than $834,000.

The 1984 campaign attempted to solve some problems uncovered by the 1983 evaluation, such as a lower adoption by farmers with smaller plots who lived in districts that received secondary coverage, and flawed message designs in posters and other media. The new campaign was directed to farmers of all crops, and it supplemented extensive media use with interpersonal channels (such as pesticide and seed dealers, and community leaders) to encourage specific and effective rat control actions. Similarly large numbers of media, interpersonal, and bait inputs were involved as in the 1983 campaign.

After the 1984 campaign, the proportion of wheat farmers who conducted rat control rose from 32% to 40%, and the rat control practice by all kinds of farmers jumped from 49% to 67%. By providing equal campaign treatment to the districts that had received primary or secondary treatment in the 1983 campaign, the 1984 campaign achieved equal levels of adoption of rat control practices (40%) in both types of districts. Similarly, the adoption rate by large farmers rose from 47% before the campaigns to 58% after 1983, and to 72% after 1984; the figures for small farmers were 41%, 41%, and 63%, respectively. Cost-benefit results from the 1984 campaign were similar to the 1983 figures.

Several implications follow. First, the concept of conducting and systematically evaluating a multimedia campaign in developing countries is not only feasible, but effective and necessary. Second, the application of strategic planning concepts and techniques is extremely useful, especially for identifying systematic problems, formulating and targeting campaign objectives, segmenting target audiences, selecting multimedia mixes, designing messages, and developing and packaging materials. Third, the conceptual framework for strategic multimedia campaign development can be operationalized effectively if the campaign process starts with a knowledge, attitude, and practice (KAP) survey (such as focus groups and sample surveys) to identify target audiences' reasons for the nonadoption of the recommended technology.

Adhikarya and Posamentier (1987) conclude that successful campaigns (1) have well-defined problem-solving-oriented goals based upon prior problem identification; (2) have planned communication strategies; (3) use cost-effective, multimedia approaches in combination with well-trained interpersonal support; (4) use specific, action-oriented messages developed through formative evaluation; (5) are directed at large but well-understood segmented audiences; (6) have comprehensive and detailed management operation plans; (7) systematically monitor campaign implementation activities; (8) have limited time spans; (9) incorporate multimethod evaluation procedures; and (10) prepare detailed audio, visual, and written documentation of campaign processes and results to facilitate replication of the campaign methodology. The Agricultural Education and Extension Service of the United Nations Food and Agricultural Organization has translated these lessons into a series of workshops, training sessions, and campaign materials that have led to replications of this process in a wide variety of countries and problems: integrated weed management and rodent control in Malaysia, lime-sowing rice cultivation in Liberia, pest surveillance in Thailand, and land preparation, tick-borne disease control, and golden snail control in other countries.

10

Communication Campaigns to Prevent Cardiovascular Disease: The Stanford Community Studies

June A. Flora
Nathan Maccoby
John W. Farquhar

The Problem: Cardiovascular Disease

Cardiovascular diseases (CVD—fatal and nonfatal heart attacks and strokes) are the greatest cause of premature death and disability in the United States and in most Westernized industrial nations. Approximately one-half of all deaths in the United States are attributable to these disorders, with coronary heart disease (CHD) alone accounting for nearly 40% of all deaths (Eliot, 1987). CHD is a relative newcomer in the United States, rising from only 9.4% of all deaths in 1900 to an all-time high of 36% in 1967, with a decline to 30% by 1985 (U.S. Department of Health and Human Services, 1986b). These data, combined with international and other U.S. studies, led researchers to conclude that there is a significant life-style component to CHD peculiar to the twentieth century and industrialization. Life-styles that include smoking, little or no exercise, diets high in saturated fat and cholesterol, and chronic stress can lead to high blood pressure, high blood cholesterol, and obesity, all of which increase risk of CVD (Farquhar, 1987). Such behaviors are in turn influenced by individual,

Authors' Note: The research reported in this chapter was supported by U.S. Public Health Service Grant HL-07034 from the National Heart, Lung and Blood Institute to John W. Farquhar, M.D., principal investigator.

family, ethnic, cultural, and community factors (see also Wallack, chap. 16, this volume).

Fueled by concern about a disease that was reaching epidemic proportions, armed with evidence that CVD was linked to specific behaviors, and convinced that life-styles are most readily modified in the context of the community environment, Stanford University investigators initiated the Stanford Three Community Study (TCS) and, later, the Stanford Five City Project (FCP) (Farquhar, 1978; Farquhar et al., 1977, 1985). This chapter describes the research design, intervention methods, theoretical underpinnings, and final results of the TCS, as well as education-monitoring data and preliminary results of risk-factor changes from the FCP. The Stanford studies are prototypes for comprehensive programs of planned social change relevant to the prevention of many chronic disease problems and other social problems.

The Stanford Three Community Study

Given a strong rationale for the efficacy of attempting to change the life-styles of a whole population, the Stanford TCS was funded and mounted in 1971, with full field application in 1972, and extended through 1975. The primary research objective of the TCS was to investigate the influence of a large-scale intervention on the knowledge, attitudes, and risk-related behaviors of the population of two medium-sized communities relative to the change of an untreated matched control community (Farquhar et al., 1977). Specific individual behavior and risk-change objectives included the following:

(1) reductions in plasma cholesterol levels through reduced intake of saturated fat and cholesterol and increased intake of lean meats, nonfat dairy products, complex carbohydrates, and dietary fiber

(2) reductions in blood pressure levels through blood pressure checks, reduced salt intake, reduced weight, increased physical activity, and adherence to medication to control hypertension

(3) reductions in cigarette use through prevention of adoption by nonsmokers and through quitting by current smokers

(4) weight control through increased physical activity and reduced intake of fat and calories

(5) increased physical activity, primarily walking or participation in some form of aerobic activity 20 minutes per day, three or more times per week

TABLE 10.1 The Health Communication-Behavior Change Model

Communication Inputs	Communication Functions (for the Sender)	Behavior Objectives (for the Receiver)
Media messages	gain attention	become aware
	provide information	increase knowledge
Face-to-face	provide incentives	increase motivation
communication	provide models	learn and practice skills
Community events	provide training	take action, assess outcomes
	provide cues	maintain action, practice
	to action	self-management skills
	provide support,	influence social network
	self-management skills	members

Theoretical Underpinnings

TCS investigators sought to integrate theory into the fabric of design, implementation, and evaluation of the study. There was no single theoretical perspective that incorporated multiple outcomes (such as increasing knowledge, inducing behavior change, maintaining change) and multiple communication inputs and functions. Thus the TCS adopted an eclectic approach to theory development, drawing from the early work on macro-level effects of campaigns (Cartwright, 1949), individualistic behavior change approaches (Bandura, 1969), diffusion of innovations through interpersonal networks (Katz & Lazarsfeld, 1955; Rogers, 1983), individuals' hierarchies of learning (McGuire, 1969; Ray, 1973), inoculation against unhealthy messages (Lumsdaine & Janis, 1953; McGuire, 1964; Roberts & Maccoby, 1973), processes of social comparison (Festinger, 1954), and individuals' attitude change (Fishbein & Ajzen, 1975).

For practical application and long-range planning these perspectives were integrated into an overall framework that was later formulated as the Communication-Behavior Change (CBC) model (Farquhar, Maccoby, & Solomon, 1984). Table 10.1 presents the steps of the CBC model. The population behavior change objectives are listed in the right-hand column; the middle column contains the corresponding media functions required to meet those objectives; the left-hand column reminds us that media products and events must be designed, produced, and distributed, in sequence, to perform these functions.

The CBC model's consideration of knowledge gain, attitude change, and behavior change was influenced by Cartwright's (1949) identification of three psychological processes in behavior change in campaigns: (1) cognitive structures (knowledge), (2) affective structures (motivation), and (3) action structures (behavior). He points out that action structures are typically missing in mass-mediated campaigns. Cartwright concludes that media campaign messages backed up by face-to-face communication improve the likelihood of obtaining changes in behaviors, by tripping action structures, as well as in knowledge and attitudes. Cognitive response theory and studies of persuasion contributed to the ways that we conceptualized skills in the CBC. For example, Lumsdaine and Janis's (1953) research on methods of resisting persuasive messages through inoculation with two-sided arguments, supported by later work by McGuire (1964) and Roberts and Maccoby (1973), demonstrated that individuals can be inoculated against negative or health-compromising acts of persuasion. Bandura's (1969, 1977b) social learning theory increased our understanding that behavioral skills are often necessary prerequisites of the establishment of healthful habits. Skills can be acquired through social modeling and guided practice, which increases self-efficacy, provides incentives for health behavior, and gives behavioral feedback. From the point of view of the target population, this model begins with the individual's current state of knowledge, beliefs, and patterns of behavior. Communication planning depends on assessing the distance between the baseline state of affairs and outcome objectives, and determining optimal intervention points based on that information (Farquhar, Flora, Goode, & Fortmann, 1986; see also Rice & Foote, chap. 7, this volume). The health CBC model serves as a general guide to breaking down the community health promotion task into manageable pieces and pinpointing where to start with what messages.

Research Design

The TCS employed a quasi-experimental design, incorporating surveys of a randomly selected panel of participants aged 35-59 in each of three cities for each of three years. TCS tested the effects of two different types of interventions. In one intervention community (Gilroy), mass media alone were used for CHD reduction. In a comparable town (Watsonville), the media were supplemented with face-to-face skills training, incentives, and support. This media-plus treatment was directly applied to a randomly selected sample of high-risk participants (above the 75th percentile of composite CHD risk) and their spouses, drawn from the total community sample. The application of an intensive intervention to a sample of high-risk participants created three groups for analysis: Watsonville total group, Watsonville media plus intensive instruction group, and Watsonville reconstructed group (mass media-only sample obtained by eliminating intensive instructees). A third community (Tracy), comparable in size, structure, and demographics to the treatment communities, served as a control (Farquhar et al., 1977; Meyer, Nash, McAlister, Maccoby, & Farquhar, 1980).

The TCS Campaign

The TCS media campaign consisted of a planned dissemination of a variety of print and broadcast media materials (e.g., television and radio spots, newspaper columns, bus cards, cookbooks, and health booklets). The media campaign began two months after the initial baseline survey and continued for nine months in 1973, stopped during the second survey, and then continued for nine more months in 1974 at a reduced level. The study ended with a third survey a year later that was primarily a measure of maintenance of effects produced in the two preceding years. Given a sizable Spanish-speaking population, a specially tailored campaign was presented in Spanish (Maccoby, Farquhar, Wood, & Alexander, 1977).

The TCS actively incorporated formative evaluation into the campaign design process (see Atkin & Freimuth, chap. 6, this volume). Campaign design was an iterative process of audience analysis (for the baseline survey), pilot studies, product pretests, and intervention monitoring. This formative research ensured that messages were tailored to the cultural experiences, knowledge, and language of the target audience.

Results of the TCS

For most variables the media-only town (Gilroy) and the town with media plus face-to-face instruction (Watsonville) showed general improvement relative to the no-treatment community (Tracy), but the media-plus intervention had generally stronger results than the media-only intervention. The results, summarized in Table 10.2, were consistent with the Cartwright formulation, to the extent that there was considerable success when mass media were supplemented by intensive instruction (Cartwright, 1949). There were also many instances of

TABLE 10.2   Significant TCS Risk, Risk Factor, and Knowledge Changes at
the Three Surveys, Compared to the Control Community

Outcome Variable	Gilroy Media-Only (N = 363)	Watsonville Total (N = 384)	Watsonville Media Plus Instructees (N = 67)	Watsonville Reconstituted Media-Only (N = 384)
Composite CHD risk	S2, S3, S4	S2, S3, S4	S2, S3, S4	S2, S3, S4
Plasma cholesterol	S3, S4	S2, S3, S4	S2, S3, S4	S2, S3, S4
Systolic blood pressure	S2, S3, S4	S2, S3, S4	S2, S3, S4	S2, S3, S4
Smoking	S2	S2, S3, S4	S2, S3, S4	
Dietary cholesterol	S2, S3, S4	S2, S3, S4	S2, S3, S4	S2, S3, S4
Dietary saturated fat	S2, S3, S4	S2, S3, S4	S2, S3, S4	S2, S3, S4
Eggs eaten	S2, S3, S4	S2, S3, S4	S2, S3, S4	S2, S3, S4
Knowledge	S2, S3, S4	S2, S3, S4	S2, S3	S2, S3, S4

SOURCE: Adapted from Farquhar et al. (1977), Maccoby (1984), and Maccoby et al. (1978).
NOTE: S2 = survey at the end of Year 1, after the full campaign; S3 = survey at the end of Year 2, after
a reduced campaign; S4 = survey at the end of Year 3, after no campaign.

success for media alone. In the case of knowledge gain, participants in
the media-only condition showed knowledge gains similar to those of
participants in the community who received media plus supplementa-
tion. In both treatment communities, knowledge gains were significantly greater than in the no-treatment control community (Tracy).
However, when only high-risk spouses and participants (who received
additional instruction) in the media-plus community were measured,
their knowledge gains were more than twice those of the residents in
the media-only community (Farquhar et al., 1977; Maccoby, 1980;
Maccoby et al., 1977).

When the composite CHD risk score results were examined, a pattern to the knowledge gain results became evident. The composite risk
score used in these analyses incorporated age, sex, plasma cholesterol,
systolic blood pressure, and relative weight (Truett, Cornfield, & Kannel, 1967). Gilroy, the media-only town, as a whole showed a decline
similar to that of the Watsonsville participants who were not part of the
intensive instruction (Watsonville media-only reconstituted). The differences between Gilroy (media-only town) and Watsonville (media-
plus town) were greater when Gilroy was compared with the total set

of participants in Watsonville. These differences disappeared by the second year of the campaign. All treatment scores were significantly different from the control scores at Years 1 and 2 (Farquhar et al., 1977). Some changes were further extended in the third year, despite a reduced educational program (Maccoby, 1980). This was especially true in Watsonville, the community with intensive instruction under a mass media umbrella.

When the results were examined for each of the targeted health behaviors, it became evident that certain kinds of behavior associated with risk reduction can be learned through attention to the mass media alone when behavior change depends primarily on acquiring new knowledge (e.g., improved eating habits), while others (e.g., cigarette smoking cessation) required a different constellation of media events, containing a considerable amount of skills training, self-monitoring, and feedback (see McAlister, Ramirez, Galavotti, & Gallion, chap. 13, this volume). In this case, media, face-to-face communication, social support, and medications to ease physical urges (i.e., gum containing nicotine) may all be necessary for change. Media alone were not enough in this instance, although effective in producing initial behavior changes in smoking behavior.

Much of the success of the TCS campaign can be attributed to the quality of the media campaign and to the synergistic interaction of multiple educational inputs, such as interpersonal communication stimulated by media, discussions with opinion leaders, and direct face-to-face education (Maccoby et al., 1977).

The Stanford Five City Project

The Stanford Five City Multifactor Risk Reduction project (FCP) (Farquhar et al., 1985) differs from the TCS in several ways: (1) The age range of the sample of the total population chosen for surveys was increased from 35-59 in the TCS to 12-74 in the FCP, (2) program objectives include maintenance of the educational program, (3) the program includes an extensive community mobilization component, and (4) the program monitors CVD morbidity and mortality (both heart attack and stroke events) in addition to risk factors. These modifications increase the study's potential generalizability to other populations, interventions, and methods.

Research Design

The FCP was launched in 1978, after six months of planning and one year of baseline data collection. This 14-year study employs a quasi-experimental research design carried out in five northern California communities. Two communities receive the educational intervention, two serve as controls for test effects (administration of the survey and monitoring CVD instances), and one serves as a monitoring control only (Farquhar et al., 1985). The total study population is composed of approximately 325,000 individuals, with single community populations varying from 40,000 to 130,000. The four education and control communities are matched roughly as to size, employment base, and community demographics. The two education communities share a common television and radio market (newspaper markets overlap to a lesser degree), while media markets for the control communities are independent from each other and from the education communities.

A series of five cross-sectional surveys of the population combined with five surveys of a panel of individuals (cohorts) constitute the data-collection plan. As Figure 10.1 shows, the panel and the independent surveys are implemented in alternate years and conducted in only four of the target communities. The baseline survey served as both the first independent survey and as the first year of the panel. In both the panel and the cross-sectional surveys, data were collected on communication, psychological, behavioral, physical, and physiological variables (Farquhar et al., 1985).

Steps to Conducting the FCP Campaign

The results of the TCS have shown that (1) it was feasible to reach all individuals as opposed to targeting only high-risk individuals, (2) media-based strategies could be effective but were more so when supplemented with face-to-face communication, and (3) maintenance of the program required mobilization of the community as well as changing individual behavior. Once it was established that the community was the appropriate target of intervention (including sublevel targets such as organizations), planners engaged the following series of steps: (1) problem identification, (2) planning, (3) implementation, and (4) evaluation.

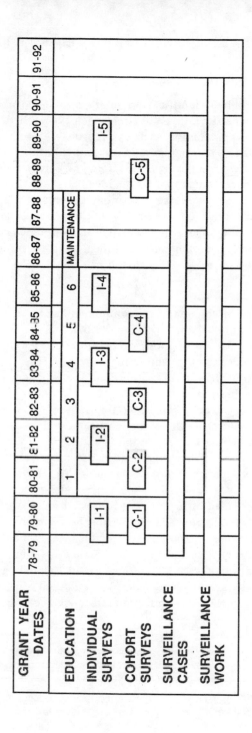

Figure 10.1. Design of the Stanford Five City Project

PROBLEM IDENTIFICATION

In general, problem identification entails a review of the scientific justification for a particular type of comprehensive public intervention. In the case of CVD prevention, there is a reasonably good international consensus that risk is determined by powerful cultural forces that may be susceptible to change through concerted and comprehensive public interventions. Other studies support the idea that planned social change based on a comprehensive linkage of medical, educational, and media resources has favorable effects on CVD. Control of blood pressure, reduction of fat and cholesterol in the diet, increased physical activity, smoking cessation, and maintenance of ideal weight were identified as change objectives for the entire population.

PLANNING

Once the CHD problem and its components were identified, planning for intervention began, involving (1) determining the theoretical orientation, (2) selecting a program planning model that translates theory into practice, and (3) conducting formative research.

. *Determining the theoretical orientation.* The FCP educational goals include achieving a significant reduction in CVD risk in the population as well as leaving behind a self-sustaining risk-reduction program. To achieve these goals, the FCP education program needed to target individuals, social networks (e.g., families and social groups), organizations (health services, restaurants, workplaces, media, and political and religious groups), and the whole community. While the CBC model (discussed above, see Table 10.1) was sufficient for individual behavior change, it provided little guidance for social-level interventions.

Community mobilization and adoption principles have been used to guide interactions with community agencies, particularly education and health groups and workplaces (see Alcalay & Taplin, chap. 5, this volume). These principles fall into three distinct models, each providing the community campaign designer with guidelines for inducing and maintaining organizational- and community-level change (Rothman, 1968):

(1) *Consensus development* emphasizes the importance of the participation of a wide array of community members throughout the campaign design and community adoption process.

(2) *Social action perspectives* call for mobilization of the masses, creation of new social structures, and activation of the political process.

(3) *Social planning* stresses the use of objective data collected through guidance of experts as the path to achieving systemwide change.

In the FCP, the model selected depended on the stage of the overall campaign (early, middle, or late) and on the objective to be achieved. For example, social action models were useful for developing environmental change strategies (such as developing advocacy and lobbying efforts for creating smoke-free environments and restricting cigarette advertising), while consensus development models were important during the process of institutionalizing programs. Social planning, with its attention to data collection and its use of direct and multiplier strategies for change, was most useful as a model of community organization to facilitate campaign planning and implementation.

Selecting program implementation models. Translating theoretical generalizations into intervention actions presented a formidable challenge for FCP campaign designers. Social marketing principles were used to bridge this gap between theory and action (Kotler, 1975; Kotler & Zaltman, 1971; also see Solomon, chap. 4, this volume). The essential aspects of social marketing used to implement the FCP included (1) developing messages, products, and services from the perspective of the consumer, allowing the campaign designer to tailor theoretic messages to audience subgroups (e.g., for teens, emphasis on the short-term consequences of smoking—bad breath, smelly clothes and hair); (2) planning campaigns as a blend of products (e.g., television public service announcements, printed materials, and curricula), prices (e.g., dollars, time, energy), places (e.g., libraries, work sites, schools), and promotions; and (3) using formative research to develop and test the elements of the campaign (Lefebvre & Flora, in press).

The process of campaign planning for the FCP included the assessment of the status quo (according to the CBC model), development of theory-based programs designed to move the target audience to a new step in the change process, and fitting those programs to individuals' social, cultural, and experiential contexts.

Conducting formative research. Health communication campaigns have usually lacked adequate formative evaluation, resulting in a common failure to meet campaign objectives (Atkin, 1981b; see Atkin & Freimuth, chap. 6, this volume). There are three general categories of formative research in the FCP: audience segmentation and needs analysis, channel analysis, and message pretesting.

Audience segmentation and needs analysis describes a set of data-collection and analysis strategies that divide the target audience into homogeneous clusters. These clusters can be classified on cognitive, behavioral, demographic, or life-style variables. The segments are then examined to determine their use of various channels of communication, their needs and interests, and thus the most effective messages to reach each group.

Channel analysis is the investigation of potential uses of media and other communication channels in interventions. Channels in a particular community can be classified by their audiences, availability for health messages, accessibility to audience members, and message characteristics (frequency, duration, and intensity). In the FCP, gatekeepers in each of the communication channels (television, newspapers, newsletters, radio) were interviewed periodically to determine channel strategies.

To illustrate our use of formative research, the next section discusses the different types of evaluation used to understand weight loss and dietary behavior, which was a subset of our overall education program.

A FORMATIVE RESEARCH CASE: WEIGHT LOSS AND DIETARY CHANGE

A series of three precampaign formative studies were conducted. The first step in planning this intervention on weight loss and diet was to analyze the basic statistics (e.g., television use, newspaper circulation, cable subscription) for each of the three primary channels of communication—television, radio, and newspaper. We next collected audience information on viewing, listening, and readership. (See Alcalay & Taplin, chap. 5, this volume, for more detailed discussion of these audience research tools.) For example, if a television PSA was aired on one local television station at 8:15 on a Tuesday night, we would know from Nielsen rating reports that approximately 11% of our intervention community would be exposed to the message. From these reports we could calculate that this 11 rating represented 4,500 households with television, 500 children ages 2-11, 1,100 teenagers (12-17 years old), 3,900 women (18+), and 2,700 men (18+) (Nielsen Media Research, 1979). We used these and similar measures to form cumulative measures such as potential "reach" (number of persons exposed) and "frequency" (average number of messages each exposed person sees) for television, radio, newspaper, and overall media exposure. This allowed us to create a media mix that included time of presentation and frequency of presentation, and maximized target audience exposure.

The final step in this channel analysis was the development of profiles of the relevant media organizations (personnel, ownership, and formats) and coordination with these organizations to determine the extent to which FCP media plans for this particular minicampaign could be realized.

The second study assessed the target audience to determine homogeneous segments and to characterize them with respect to demographics, cognitions (e.g., knowledge, intention, self-efficacy), attitudes, and health and communication behaviors, based upon the baseline population survey in the education communities. Four behavioral and demographic segments were identified: men or women up to 20% overweight and men or women more than 20% overweight. According to Metropolitan Life tables, 78% of women and 82% of men were overweight, while 43% of women and 47% of men were more than 20% overweight.

The results showed that overweight women recognized their weight problem and were highly motivated to change. They knew how many pounds they needed to lose and knew that they would feel healthier if they lost weight. Thus messages targeted to women should not focus on convincing them that they need to lose weight but instead on teaching skills for losing weight and maintaining weight loss. On the other hand, men did not realize that they needed to lose weight, underestimating their surplus pounds by 50%. In addition, men were not highly motivated to lose weight and had a poor sense of self-efficacy about losing weight and poor attitudes about maintaining weight loss. In general, men are earlier in the behavior change process, needing to improve their awareness of their body weight, increase their motivations to change, and address their poor sense of efficacy and poor attitudes. Women, too, needed to develop a stronger sense of self-efficacy and to raise their expectancy of success in behavior change (see McAlister et al., chap. 13, and Reardon, chap. 12, this volume, for discussions of self-efficacy theories).

With respect to communication patterns, women in the highest overweight category read the newspaper fewer days each week than other women and watched more television than did moderately overweight women. Men in the most overweight category watched more television and listened to the radio less.

A third study of information needs was carried out with a subset (N = 129) of individuals participating in the baseline survey. In an unstructured interview, participants responded verbally to the question "If you had the chance to talk to an expert about diet and weight loss, what would you ask?" Responses influenced the structure, content, and wording of dietary messages. For example, people wanted information that was useful to their immediate situations. Coping with situations such as trying to quit smoking and worrying about weight gain, gaining weight during pregnancy, maintaining good nutrition while trying to lose weight, and cooking balanced meals for families were all mentioned as informational needs.

In response to the audience's expressed informational needs, a series of materials were designed to be accessible over a long period of time at low or no cost so that as audience members' motivations to acquire information changed they could easily find materials (e.g., materials were promoted heavily and were available at libraries, workplaces, and clinics for several years), and to be easy to use (i.e., attractive, readable, and brief, including certificates and incentives when the program was complete).

As a result of this up-front formative research on weight and diet, FCP campaign designers created a set of change materials that included television messages targeted to men to increase awareness, correspondence courses to teach skills, self-help kits to support dietary and exercise changes, restaurant menu-labeling programs, weight-loss competitions (identified as Lighten Up) within workplaces, physical assessments to increase awareness of fitness, exercise groups run by lay leaders (identified as Heart and Sole groups) to model and support change, and exercise competitions in workplaces that emphasized walking (identified as Coming Alive). Similar formative studies were carried out on many other health habit goals, such as smoking and exercise.

Message pretesting is a final planning step prior to full implementation (see Atkin & Freimuth, chap. 6, this volume). In general, messages were developed in draft form and tested with groups from the target audience. This preimplementation effort more than pays for itself in more effective campaign messages.

IMPLEMENTATION

Decisions have to be made about the content, sequence, mixture, and duration of comprehensive community-based campaigns. These decisions are guided by the campaigns' theoretical foundations (e.g., the CBC model), other research, and earlier formative research.

As depicted in the CBC model in Table 10.1, comprehensive risk-reduction campaigns must consider multiple channels of communication, multiple objectives, and multiple targets of change (individuals, networks, organizations, and environments) (Farquhar et al., 1985).

The two treatment communities and the immediately surrounding areas received four or five education campaigns per year. Campaigns were generally carried out in both English and Spanish and were directed at some preselected segment of the total population. Campaigns in general incorporated one or more of seven types of efforts: media, face-to-face education, workplace programs, school-based efforts, food outlet programs, incentive-based contests, and health professional programs:

(1) Media programs and materials included television (PSAs, special programs), newspapers (a doctor's column in both Spanish and English papers, as well as numerous features, stories, and ads), radio (Spanish series), mass mail, and other printed materials. For the first four years of the campaign, there was a yearly multicomponent mass mailing to a randomly selected 33% or 100% of the target households; other booklets, self-help kits, and promotional brochures were disseminated in the mail, through libraries, workplaces, doctors' offices, churches, and FCP offices.

(2) More than 800 direct education sessions were conducted by project staff during the campaign years. Many of these contacts were designed to have a multiplier effect, for example, training instructors to give CVD reduction presentations and training exercisers to lead groups. This diffusion/adoption feature became more important in the last phase of the education years.

(3) Workplaces were a major focus of the second half of the education program. Most large workplaces participated by disseminating printed information, offering workshops and classes, sponsoring contests and lotteries, and assessing environmental risks (such as smoking policy and exercise facilities) (Sallis, Hill, Fortmann, & Flora, 1986).

(4) The campaign also targeted schools, students, teachers, and families. Specific curricula on resisting pressures to smoke, eating healthy foods, and increasing exercise were designed for children and adolescents as well as for parents and teachers (King et al., 1988).

(5) Restaurants, cafeterias, and grocery stores participated in specially designed healthy food programs, such as a menu-labeling program, that positively influenced customers' purchases of low-fat foods (Albright, Flora, & Fortmann, 1988). One supermarket campaign included 20 grocery stores, 400 grocery checkers, and distribution of approximately 600,000 nutrition tip sheets over 12 weeks.

(6) Health professionals participated in training programs, disseminated printed materials, received materials regularly in the mail, and implemented risk-reduction programs in their practices (Fortmann, Sallis, Magnus, & Farquhar, 1985).

(7) Contests or lotteries held in workplaces and the community at large were
used to induce changes in smoking (King, Flora, Fortmann, & Taylor,
1987), exercise, nutrition, and weight control. In each campaign,
incentives (e.g., trophies, money, and trips to Hawaii) were used to
increase participation of certain targeted subgroups, to increase
effectiveness of minimal-contact print programs, and to ensure
maintenance of change over a period of time (e.g., when a contest lasted
for three months).

EVALUATION

Each campaign used formative research to plan and test messages
(discussed above), summative evaluation to determine the effects of the
campaign at individual, organizational, and community levels, and
process evaluation to study the application of the intervention (Flora,
Jackson, & Maccoby, in press; also see Flay & Cook, chap. 8, this
volume).

Summative evaluation. Analyses of the behavioral and physiological
outcomes of the FCP after five years of campaign exposure are currently being conducted, and promising interim results have shown favorable effects in smoking, blood pressure, exercise habit, and blood
cholesterol comparable to the changes achieved in the TCS. The results
of the epidemiological surveillance will not be known until 1991, at
which time the results of an additional panel survey and a fifth cross-
sectional survey will also be available.

Process evaluation. The monitoring of campaign activities, both
successes and failures, is crucial to the understanding of effects and to
the development of future campaigns (see Rice & Foote, chap. 7, this
volume). FCP process evaluation activities concentrated on the development of a time-based intervention-monitoring system. Data were
collected on the number of messages, the outcome objectives of each
message, the risk factor addressed by the message, the potential reach
of the message, and the frequency of presentation of the message. This
information was entered into a computer system, where input variables
(described above) were combined with a set of standardized variables
(e.g., the number of individuals in the community, neighborhood, or
county) to develop a set of "constructed variables." For example,
summing the reach of all CVD messages and dividing the total figure
by the number of individuals in the community can provide an estimate
of the total number of messages sent to each member of the target
audience (Flora, Goode, MacKinnon, & Fortmann, 1985).

TABLE 10.3 Estimated Number of Educational Messages and Exposure Time Provided to Each Member of the Target Audience

Channel of Communication	Year of Campaign					
	1	2	3	4	5	All
TV/radio						
messages[a]	56.2	28.6	109.0	55.5	104.7	354.2
hours[b]	.8	1.2	2.9	2.4	1.7	9.0
Newspaper						
messages	39.3	17.0	29.2	41.8	21.5	148.7
hours	1.1	.7	.9	1.1	.9	4.7
Other print						
messages	.2	4.3	1.4	12.7	2.1	20.7
hours	.01	4.3	.8	4.9	.8	10.8
Face-to-face						
messages	.1	.1	.1	.2	2.6	3.0
hours	.08	.05	.1	.2	1.3	1.3
Total						
messages	96.0	50.0	140.0	110.0	130.8	526.6
hours	1.9	6.3	4.7	8.4	4.7	26.1

NOTE: Hours are calculated by multiplying estimated time weights by the frequency of message delivery.

a. Average number of messages sent to each member of the target audience.

b. Average amount of time spent on CVD education for each member of the target audience.

Table 10.3 displays the estimated number of messages disseminated through each channel for each year of the program. We estimated that on average each of the 80,000 community residents (aged 18-74) received over 500 risk-reduction messages over the five years of the campaign. All other things being equal, more television messages were sent than printed or face-to-face messages. Table 10.3 also presents the estimated hours of education provided to community residents. When time is considered, more time was expended on printed materials (15.5 hours) than on broadcast messages (9 hours). These two variables, quantity and time, are not directly related and are differentially important in explaining behavior change. These data, of course, do not account for differences in effectiveness of individual messages or accessibility of audience members to the messages.

Each message in the FCP education program has an assigned outcome objective (derived from the CBC model, Table 10.1). Agenda-setting was emphasized early in the campaign, while higher-level objectives were stressed later in the program. In Year 1 of the campaign, 95% of all messages were oriented toward awareness or information, while by Year 4, 50% of the messages focused on actions, skills, or behavior-change maintenance. Thus the CBC model guided both the development of individual messages and the mix of messages for the entire campaign.

Another analysis shows the proportion of individuals remembering each of the campaign components over the four surveys of the panel (Flora, Roser, Chaffee, & Farquhar, 1988). Overall exposure was high and increased over time, even though, due to limits of the survey, only 30-40% of the actual campaign messages sent to community members were measured on the survey. The proportion of television messages remembered by the education treatment rose from 35% by Cohort 2 to 66% by Cohort 3; newspaper messages, from 43% by Cohort 2 to 52% by Cohort 4; booklets and kits, from 30% by Cohort 2 to 71% by Cohort 4; and mass mail tip sheets, from 5% by Cohort 2 to 74% by Cohort 4 (see Figure 10.1 for the timetables of each cohort).

Table 10.3 and the remembered message percentages illustrate that campaign elements estimated to have occupied the largest amount of time during the campaign resulted in the greatest exposure and recall rates. Over time, the number of broadcast media messages decreased and the number of face-to-face messages increased. As noted above, as the FCP campaign progressed, more skill- and action-oriented messages were sent, while the number of CVD awareness messages was reduced. Process-evaluation data thus can serve as one illustration of the way that the FCP translated communication theory into campaign design. Comparing data similar to those presented in Table 10.2 with data similar to those in Table 10.3 and the remembered message percentages shows how the specification of the "dose" of the intervention can increase our understanding of the "response" in campaign outcomes.

Conclusion

A growing number of related community-based studies have been reported or are under way. A recent review of some 10 projects initiated between 1972 and 1982 revealed that the best-known projects are the Stanford TCS and the Finnish North Karelia Project (Puska et al., 1981). The cholesterol, blood pressure, and smoking results achieved after two and three years of education in the TCS were comparable to those achieved after the first five years of education in the North Karelia Project. Composite risk scores in each of these two studies predicted something approaching 20-25% reduction in coronary events. The Finnish study was extended over a total of 10 years in order to allow scrutiny of its impact on CVD morbidity and mortality, and favorable effects of these measures were reported in comparison not only against the adjoining county but in respect to the trends in the remaining part of Finland (Puska et al., 1985). Four other community-based studies using methods similar to the TCS and the North Karelia Project have reported their main findings. Only one of them, involving small rural South African towns, reported significant changes in cholesterol and blood pressure levels as well as in smoking (Rossouw, Jooste, Kotze, & Jordaan, 1981). Two others, in four towns in Switzerland, and a three-town study in Australia, reported a 6% and a 9% drop in smoking rates, respectively (Egger et al., 1983; Gutzwiller, Nater, & Martin, 1985). The favorable effects of these studies, combined with the early positive effects on smoking, exercise habits, and blood cholesterol of the FCP, present an encouraging and generalizable picture for community-based intervention.

Two additional ambitious and well-evaluated studies are now in progress in the United States: the Minnesota Heart Health Study, involving six communities of total population 356,000, and the Pawtucket Heart Health Study in Rhode Island, involving two cities of total population 173,000 (Blackburn, Leupker, Kline, Bracht, & Carlaw, 1984; Lasater et al., 1984). Additional comprehensive community-based demonstration projects have recently begun in some 16 different countries under the sponsorship and guidance of the World Health Organization's Interhealth program (Holland & Breeze, 1986). Later reporting of the results of these studies will add further information concerning the feasibility of carrying out such studies and will extend our understanding of behavior change methods.

An in-depth examination of the two cornerstone community studies, the TCS and the FCP, in the context of a rapid proliferation of community-based campaigns, reveals three primary principles. First, the TCS and the current FCP are characterized by unique media campaigns and supplementary activities to improve health status: Media are used in a planned fashion over a long period of time to influence multiple levels of the community (e.g., individuals, networks, and organizations), and are integrated into a variety of interventions (e.g., PSAs, contests, self-help materials). Second, the TCS and FCP use theory to guide specific campaign actions in all aspects of development, implementation, and evaluation, and social marketing principles to guide the application of theory, and rely on formative research to guide campaign design. Third, each of the studies proceeded through a sequence of problem identification, planning, implementation, and evaluation. This sequence of activities led to clear successes in the TCS and promising early results in the FCP.

11

Political Campaigns

ROBERT G. MEADOW

Overview of Political Campaigns

For the public at large, the concept of a campaign may well be defined by political campaigns. Consumers, for example, rarely see advertising campaigns as campaigns; instead, they experience an advertising campaign simply as individual advertisements. But there can be little doubt that political campaigns are communication and information activities. DeVries and Tarrance (1972) say that "the campaign process is best understood as an information and communications system" (p. 73). And as early as 1960, Stanley Kelly said that campaigning has "an informing function" for voters (p. 8).

Election and Nonelection Campaigns

Agranoff (1980) has succinctly described an election campaign as "a coordinated effort to achieve the objective of winning an election through the mobilization of human, social, material and environmental resources" (p. 47). Election campaigns may be either for candidates for political office (the focus of this chapter) or for issue referenda.

Nonelection campaigns include ideological and propaganda campaigns designed to persuade individuals and decision makers such as legislators (rather than voters) or to create a political climate in which favorable political outcomes are assured. One type of nonelection campaign is the *policy initiative* campaign. For example, in 1988 Reagan administration officials and supporters in the private sector mounted an ideological campaign to gain support by legislators and the public for the specific policy initiative of continuing aid to the Contras in Nicaragua. Another type of nonelection campaign occurs when organized interest groups such as trade associations, labor unions, or environmental activists engage in lobbying campaigns, using professional lobbyists to communicate in private sessions directly with decision makers, mobilizing their constituent members in "grass-roots" campaigns to contact decision makers. An example of such a campaign occurred in 1987, during confirmation hearings for Robert Bork to ascend to the U.S. Supreme Court; legal scholars joined civil rights groups, unions, feminist groups, and individuals mobilized through mass media advertising to oppose the nomination.

Audiences of Election Campaigns

Campaigns involve a search for the optimal mix of allocating resources from among information alternatives to reach at least four types of audiences. The primary targets of an election campaign are the ultimate decision makers—*voters* and *party members*. Although many campaigns must rely on nonpartisan appeals made to independent individual voters on the basis of issues or images of the candidates, appeals to others must simultaneously be made on the basis of pure partisan loyalties. At times, partisan and nonpartisan messages may be in conflict. In addition to voters, *news media* gatekeepers and personnel are also targets, as campaigners seek to maximize favorable campaign coverage. Thus many staged campaign events and news conferences take place without any voters present because the events are geared toward enhancing "free" campaign communication through news media coverage.

A third audience for election campaign messages may be *campaign contributors*. Those who provide the financial backing for political candidates often need to perceive themselves as campaign "insiders" with special access to the candidate and key campaign decision makers. Although some will contribute purely based on ideological preferences, major contributors also want to know the chances of a candidacy's being successful, preferring to back winners to enable postelection access. *Candidates* themselves are also the targets of some political campaigns. As campaigning becomes increasingly professionalized by managers and consultants (Sabato, 1981), candidates play smaller and smaller management and decision-making roles in their own campaigns. Yet candidates constantly need reassurance that their campaigns are running smoothly and effectively, and that campaign messages are reaching voters.

All these audiences are exposed to *authorized* campaign communications designed to persuade them either, most commonly,
through reinforcement of existing preferences or, less often, through
conversion. These communications include paid print and electronic
campaign advertising, televised debates, enhanced news coverage of
the candidates or issues, and opportunities to see and hear candidates
personally at political rallies. In addition, there are the uncontrolled,
nonpurposive, or *unauthorized* communications through interpersonal
discussions at home or work that take place outside of the organized
activities of the campaign.

Although some of the interest in campaigns can be understood by
viewing elections as rituals (Combs, 1980) as well as news media
agenda-setters (Graber, 1988; Iyengar & Kinder, 1987; Weaver, Graber,
McCombs, & Eyal, 1981), the omnipresence of campaign information
from a variety of interpersonal and mass-mediated sources makes election campaign information virtually inescapable (Graber, 1988; Patterson, 1980).

The Unique Properties
of Political Campaigns

Political campaigns, particularly election campaigns, differ from
other public communication campaigns in a variety of ways, including
timing, cyclical interest, financial uncertainty, decisiveness of outcome,
difficulty of evaluation, organizational transience, regulation, reduced
control over communication, and limits on legitimate techniques.

Political campaigns have *well-defined time periods*, both as to when
the elections are held and as to duration of campaigns. Elections are
scheduled at fixed intervals in the United States; in many parliamentary
systems, even if elections are called suddenly, the campaign period is
of short, fixed duration. Because of the fixed target date of political
campaigns, an important factor is momentum toward a climax on
election day.

Election campaigners face audiences with *cyclical interests* in
politics. On the one hand, the heightened sensitivity to politics during
specific seasonal periods may make audiences more receptive to political messages (Graber, 1988; Patterson, 1980). On the other hand,
during campaign periods voters are prepared psychologically, through
such mechanisms as selective attention, perception, and inoculation, to

defend themselves from the onslaught of political messages that or-
dinarily would be unfiltered during periods of lower political awareness (Underwood, 1978).

The fact that election campaign budgets almost always depend on
the success of fund-raising efforts introduces considerable *uncertainty*
into campaign planning. Even the most well-designed political campaign must continually readjust based on revenue shortfalls (or
surpluses), resulting in election campaigns often appearing less integrated and systematic than other campaigns.

One of the most distinctive characteristics of election campaigns is
the *decisiveness of the outcome.* Success in other public communication campaigns (higher literacy rates, lowered incidence of disease, and
so on) is often relative and measured on continuous scales. Elections
generally have clear winners and losers, although occasionally candidates run for symbolic reasons.

Most political campaign organizations, with the notable exception
of political parties, are built as *temporary organizations* designed to
suspend operations after the election. The absence of organizational
continuity prevents the development of a collective organizational
memory to assure that mistakes of the past are not repeated, and that
successes are.

Political campaigns face considerably *more regulation* than nonpolitical campaigns. In federal election campaigns, as well as in campaigns in many jurisdictions, there are laws concerning public
disclosure of campaign expenditures or limits on expenditures that in
turn limit paid campaign communications. Equal-time and fairness
doctrines of broadcast media, although now in flux, effectively have
limited access to broadcast media for many candidates for nonfederal
offices and for ballot proposition committees. Requirements for identifying the sources of paid political messages have eliminated some
campaign communication options for political campaigns that are
otherwise available to nonpolitical campaigns.

Political campaigns have considerably *less control* over campaign
communication than other campaigns. Commercial advertising campaigns, for example, are largely controlled by the communicator, who
decides the content of the message, the frequency of transmission, and
the targeted audience. In political campaigns, only paid voter communications are in the hands of the campaigner. To some extent, the
symbiotic nature of press-politician relations gives campaigners a certain ability to influence coverage through news releases and media

events. But, ultimately, journalists, particularly in national and significant statewide campaigns (because of the greater media coverage) have the final word, and may raise issues or concerns at any time. Moreover, tendencies of journalists to read one another's reports and to congregate together lead to "pack" journalism, where, once a theme is identified by one journalist, others quickly pursue that theme (Crouse, 1973; Gans, 1979; Grossman & Kumar, 1981; Tuchman, 1978; Westin, 1982).

Because there are two or more campaigns ongoing simultaneously (i.e., the opponents' campaigns), political campaigns often abandon their initial plans in order to react to issues raised by opponents and journalists. Indeed, many political battles are fought over who will control the campaign agenda (Lang & Lang, 1983). In the 1988 presidential campaigns, those outside the campaigns raised questions with which campaigners had to grapple, such as, What does Jesse (Jackson) want? Is George Bush a wimp with a long resume? Is Dan Quayle a privileged draft dodger? Does Michael Dukakis have any charisma, or is he a mere technocrat? Dukakis spent much of his effort trying to refute Bush's attacks.

There are limits to what constitutes *legitimate* campaigning. Certainly some political campaigns go beyond the norms of decency by engaging in "negative" or "hit" campaigning (such as in the 1988 presidential campaign), but candidates are, within the civic normative framework, supposed to raise issues and discuss policies rather than personalities, and to respond to the questions raised by journalists and voters. Only occasionally are there "dirty tricks" such as contacting news media with false information about opposing candidates, posing as campaign officials to cancel rallies or other events, infiltrating opposition campaigns to secure confidential information, heckling and demonstrating, tampering with sound systems, and generally creating difficulties for a political campaign.

Finally, compared to other public communication campaigns, systematic *experimental evaluation is usually absent* in political campaigns for at least three reasons. First, scarce and uncertain resources are unlikely to be expended on evaluating the effectiveness of campaigning. Second, political campaigners, unsure of exactly what "works" in a political campaign, are reluctant not to try everything, hoping that some of the many voter communications will work. Third, campaigners are reluctant to cede any possible voters, who, as control groups in field experiments, would be excluded from campaign materials and might turn to the opposing candidate.

Research on Political Campaigns

Many social science researchers have demonstrated that political knowledge increases during the course of political campaigns (see O'Keefe & Atwood, 1981). But isolating the independent contributions of each campaign information source is extraordinarily difficult. As noted above, it is nearly impossible to control access to, and content of, much campaign communication. Moreover, messages are often mutually reinforcing, further confounding the ability even of the most determined analysts to assess the independent contributions of the information sources. Recall data on the effects of a given information source must be viewed skeptically.[1]

For measuring impact on voter turnout, casual linkages are also tenuous. The decision to vote is a complicated one, affected by external, nonideological factors (convenience, time, literacy) and ideological factors (nonvoting as a protest against the system, inability to distinguish among alternatives). Although there may be indicators of success of a voting registration campaign or a campaign to have voters submit applications for absentee ballots (measured by the percentage of returned registrations or applications), it is only with considerable difficulty that researchers can determine who even voted (usually by hand checking with a registrar of voters).

In spite of the difficulty in conducting systematic evaluations of the causal factors in political campaign failure or success, since the 1940s, there has been much academic research conducted on the role of mass media in election campaigns. For the first decade of this research, the results were the same as for media effects in general: Direct effects of exposure to campaign information were limited because voters would selectively process content based on predispositions (Klapper, 1960). The findings of the "Columbia school" (Berelson, Lazarsfeld, & McPhee, 1954; Lazarsfeld, Berelson, & Gaudet, 1948) were simple: Based on socioeconomic variables and personal influence, voters made firm decisions early in campaigns, and campaigning reinforced those decisions. Mass media were shown to have little influence on changing voter intentions; if intentions were changed it was because of interpersonal communication.

Subsequent research by the "Michigan school" (Campbell, Gurin, & Miller, 1954; Campbell, Converse, Miller, & Stokes, 1960) argued that party identification and candidate characteristics determined votes, but issues were of only marginal importance, in part because of the lack of information on issues. Media influences, and certainly the influences of the campaign itself, were underemphasized.

Third-generation research of the 1960s and 1970s (see O'Keefe & Atwood, 1981) has suggested that these findings were artifacts of the times in which the studies were conducted, that issues are indeed important, and that partisanship is much more fluid than originally thought (Nie, Verba, & Petrocik, 1976). These studies also suggested that media had direct effects, and that information from mass media played a more significant role than partisanship.

Hundreds of recent mass media studies have examined topics ranging from comparative campaign news coverage to media effects on voters. These latter studies are complex, specifying many conditions enhancing or limiting effects based on voter interest, prior information, motivation, interpersonal interaction, predisposition, selectivity, socialization, partisanship, media use, race, sex, education, social status, and dozens of other variables (for thorough reviews, see Graber, 1980; Kraus & Davis, 1976; O'Keefe & Atwood, 1981; Patterson, 1980). Perhaps most important, research since 1970 has suggested that voters are not passive, but are active recipients of political campaign messages, with the success of messages dependent on uses and gratifications (Blumler & Katz, 1974; Dervin, chap. 3, this volume; Garramone, 1985; McLeod & Becker, 1981) or transactional models (Combs, 1981; Kraus & Davis, 1976).

Despite all the research on mass media and elections, research on specific election campaign techniques has been limited. There have been many studies on television advertising (Kaid, Nimmo, & Sanders, 1986), but most have measured only information gain or have been experimental laboratory studies (Meadow & Sigelman, 1982) rather than field studies. A few direct-mail firms actually try test mailings, but even then it is more often to measure the efficiency of lists than to measure the effectiveness of messages (Berrigan, 1982).

Professional campaign literature is characterized largely by "how-to-win" books (e.g., Steinberg, 1976; Woo, 1980). The remaining literature on political campaigns is derived largely from journalists' postelection accounts of a particular campaign, such as the *Making of the President* series by Theodore White (1961, 1965, 1969), campaign trail notes (Drew, 1981; Germond & Witcover, 1981, 1985), or "kiss and tell" insider reports written by campaign functionaries (Klein, 1980; Moore, 1986; Safire, 1975). Thus, despite the long research tradition, a major question remains: What specific role does campaigning play in the election process?

Theoretical Perspectives on Political Campaigning

There is no unified theory of political campaigns that would conclusively answer this question. Instead, there is a mix of psychological, rational choice, political, organizational, and systems theories that have been mapped onto politics.

Psychological theories of political campaigns are rooted in social psychology and attitude theories of political action. Essentially, campaigns are designed to reach voters at cognitive, affective, and—ultimately—behavioral levels. At the cognitive level, a candidate and his or her positions must become known to the voters. At the affective level, the candidate must be seen positively and liked, respected, or admired by the voter. At the behavioral level, the voter must want to demonstrate support for the candidate by engaging in a specific behavior—voting.

The essence of many political campaigns is to mobilize voters by awakening their ideological dispositions. In some cases, the campaigner need only reinforce existing predispositions. In other cases, undecided voters must be persuaded to support the campaigner's candidacy. In yet other cases, the voter must be converted away from supporting the opposing candidate. Some researchers have shown that campaign advertising is important in enhancing political cognition (Patterson & McClure, 1976); others have shown news media to be of primary importance. But regardless of the sources of information, enhanced cognitions are attributable to the existence of a campaign. There are, however, several limitations to the ability of campaigns to contribute to political learning. For example, Graber (1988) has shown that political learning may be enhanced (or constrained), depending on whether or not the information is processed through the schema established by each member of the campaign audience.

Traditional psychological balance theories also can explain some campaign learning (Chaffee & Miyo, 1983; Donohew & Palmgren, 1971). Campaigns that are dependent upon high voter turnout or new registration may seek first to have campaign audiences decide to vote. Then, they seek to assure that once the decision is made, the proper election choice is made.

Empirical evidence suggests that, with little campaigning, 40% of the voters in a two-candidate race will be initially supportive of one or the other of the candidates and 40% will be opposed. Hence the campaign is designed to collect, consistent with available resources, as large a share of the remaining 20% as possible. Because of these assumptions, campaigns generally will attempt either to reinforce voters (to assure that the 40% of probable supporters remains loyal) or to persuade the 20% of undecided voters. Less often, campaigns will actively try to convert the opposing 40% of voters.

Conversion is seen as a two-step process. The first step is to shake supporters of an opposing candidate from their original loyalties and move them to the undecided column. The second step is to move the newly uncertain voter into the column of supporters. This two-step process complicates campaign strategies because messages designed to convert may differ from messages designed to persuade or reinforce. For example, campaigns may extol the virtues of the candidate or appeal to the long-term partisan loyalties in their reinforcing messages. Persuasive messages might compare two candidates and offer conclusions to support the favored candidate. Converting messages might attack the opposing candidate to undermine the opponent's base of support. Yet if converting messages are widely disseminated, a campaign may be seen as "negative" by supporters, leading to a potential loss of supporters.

According to rational choice theories, campaigners operate under the assumption that voters will make a rational election choice based on systematic comparison of the alternatives and a calculation of which alternative will satisfy the voter's economic, social, or personal goals. One assumption of the rational choice model is that voters can clearly rank their preferences and weigh the relative merits of each candidate across each attribute. A second assumption is that voters will have sufficient information available about the alternatives. Thus, under this model, campaigners seek to maximize the amount of (favorable) information available. And because campaigners can never be sure of the information sources used by any single voter, under a rational choice model, they employ all possible campaign information sources and develop informational rather than emotional campaign materials.

A political approach toward campaign theory is the "permanent" campaign (Blumenthal, 1981; Hershey, 1984). Under this approach, candidates' political actions are geared not toward legislative or executive decision making, but toward reelection. Examples of permanent campaigning include issuing proclamations and sending greetings to recent graduates, newsletters to constituents, or birthday cards to octogenarians. Staff assistants routinely take unpaid leaves of absence from staff duties to run campaigns, only to return to paid staff status after the election, blurring the distinction between campaigner and official. As campaign periods have lengthened, candidates for two-year offices (congressional and many state legislative offices) find themselves running for reelection soon after taking office, making the permanent campaign a virtual necessity. Indeed, Fenno (1978) has described the legislative cycle as a continuing campaign interrupted by periods of public service.

Another perspective on political campaigns is that they are largely ritualistic exercises of political drama (Combs, 1980; Nimmo & Combs, 1983). Campaigns take the forms they do because voters expect political campaigns to conform to romantic notions of election contests. Thus candidates will find themselves ordering campaign buttons or bumper stickers not because these are likely to be persuasive campaign documents, but because a legitimate campaign must contain the popular symbols of a campaign. The prospects for innovative campaigns are limited by the need for campaign rituals such as debates, factory tours, baby kissing, and courtesy calls on respected party elders. These activities are reinforced by media definitions of campaigning as being made up largely of ritualistic and dramatic activities. Even candidates running unopposed campaign for office. Because voters witness the election as a contest with a decisive outcome, victors emerge with heroic status, which enhances their ability to govern (Combs, 1980).

There are also theories about organizational characteristics and processes of political campaigns, such as formal structure, leadership, interpersonal relations, bureaucracy, innovation and change, authority and control, and decision making (Fellow, 1988). Immediacy of mobilization is one organizational characteristic of political campaigns. Because there is no permanent structure (other than statewide or national campaigns or the permanent campaigns described above), political campaign organizations must be assembled quickly. A more important organizational constraint is the finite termination date of political campaigns, which allows for a phased planning of campaign communications; however, the uncertainty of resources in most campaigns allows only for contingency rather than certainty planning.

Another fruitful approach considers campaigns as open systems. Hershey (1984) sees campaigns as learning processes, in which communication is interactive and campaigners learn about the people, test their beliefs, and respond to voters. Campaigns are regulated through these exchanges and feedback loops, enabling campaigns to adapt and change course. New themes emerge in response to identified successes and failures of earlier messages.

Campaign Functions

Although each major campaign may differ somewhat in structure, a typical campaign is divided into five campaign functions: field operations, management, finance, research, and voter communication.

Organizational Functions

Several of these central campaign functions—such as finance and field operations—are less important than others from the perspective of one looking at political campaigns as public communication campaigns.

The campaign management function includes overall supervision and coordination among the other campaign operations. The manager strongly guides campaign planning (including selecting campaign themes, setting budget priorities, and identifying the relative importance of each voter communication effort). The finance function consists largely of coordinating fund-raising, complying with campaign disclosure laws, and assuring that funds spent do not exceed funds raised. Nonetheless, there is some communication function of fund-raising, because funds raised by mail also contain campaign messages (Craver, 1985) and major campaign fund-raising events may be reported by journalists. Field operations may include volunteer coordination, voter registration, and especially "get out the vote" efforts. Although the broad themes for the election are obvious to the field operations coordinator, unskilled volunteers may misrepresent the candidate's positions on past issue votes, undermining the systematic efforts of the voter communication program.

Research Function

Issues, opposition, and voter research are among the most important activities when political campaigns are looked at as communication campaigns. *Issues* research consists of in-depth analyses of major issues facing the constituency and detailed issue papers specifying programs and solutions. Although rarely circulated, they are important for a candidate to demonstrate competence and knowledge in symbolic settings (interviews, debates, question-and-answer sessions). *Opposition* research examines the opposing candidate, verifying personal biographical information (e.g., identifying omissions and embarrassing background information) and reviewing opposition speeches and issue statements. The information derived from opposition research may be "leaked" to journalists or saved for use in campaign literature or public debates.

Voter research includes analyses of voting trends in previous elections and public opinion survey research. Research on past election returns is used to identify the relative efforts to be placed on certain demographic or geographic groups. If candidates with similar ideological positions fared poorly in a given region, campaign efforts would be reduced in that area, but if an area has been a "swing" region in the past, greater efforts might be made there.

Public opinion survey research is at the core of most professionally run campaigns. A campaign may commission an in-depth "benchmark" survey to understand fully the issue concerns of voters, identify the characteristics sought in a candidate, and measure the image of the candidate and the opposition. Additional "tracking" surveys might be conducted during the campaign to measure campaign progress or the effectiveness of campaign messages.

Relatively few candidates will alter their positions in response to findings in public opinion surveys. However, candidates will make decisions on what issues to emphasize as a result of voter opinion surveys (Robinson & Meadow, 1982). Candidates also attempt to identify which demographic groups should be targeted with which messages. Because political campaigning is so publicly visible, candidates cannot segment their public messages, even though their survey research might suggest they should. Candidates rarely take one position before one group and the opposing position before another group, but they will *emphasize* different issues before different groups. Researchers often test campaign slogans and identify media habits so that advertising can be placed in electronic media that will reach the target audiences (see Alcalay & Taplin, chap. 5, this volume).

In addition to survey research, well-funded campaigns will often use focus group research (see Atkin & Freimuth, chap. 6, this volume) to test campaign themes. Focus groups are particularly useful in testing campaign advertising to determine if voters understand messages in the ways the producers intended, but they also have been used to test everything from campaign colors and logos to speech themes and changes in a candidate's physical appearance.

Voter Communication Function

The voter communication function includes selecting campaign messages, preparing campaign advertising, and coordinating "free" and "paid" media. Voter communication decisions are sometimes based on research on past elections or current public opinion polls, but many media consultants insist they know what "works" and have developed ritual practices that may be without empirical foundation (Meadow & Sigelman, 1982).

Early in a campaign, a candidate is introduced and name recognition and warm feelings for the candidate are enhanced. Later, the candidate makes his or her issue positions known. Finally, if a candidate is considered to be behind in the race, the opposing candidate will be criticized and attacked.

These stages, though not as formal as the steps of persuasion cited by McGuire (1985; also see chap. 2, this volume), closely parallel them. Voters first must have access to the appeal. For that reason, several media are used, including direct-mail, print, and television and radio advertising, as well as news media. Second, there must be attention to the appeal. The ritual November timing of elections themselves may simplify the problem of generating attention.[2] Some campaign materials that have little substantive value (such as billboards, bumper stickers, and signs) are designed to raise name identification, but they are also important in raising attention to the occurrence of an election itself and in bolstering support from volunteers and other campaign workers. Third, voters must comprehend the content of the message. As a result of survey and focus group research, messages generally are designed at the appropriate level of sophistication and complexity. In the absence of such research, campaigns often expect too much from voters, using arguments and appeals that are appropriate for political insiders, but that misjudge the simplicity with which voters approach elections. Fourth, McGuire also points to the steps of yielding and being convinced by the appeal. Although campaign survey researchers attempt to determine which arguments are most convincing, the point at which individual voters yield is difficult to identify. Fifth, voters are asked for retention, to hold the views until election day. Finally, they are asked to act in accordance with the persuasive appeal by voting for the candidate. Last-minute voter communications—including get-out-the-vote telephone calls to reconfirm commitment and mailings that remind voters of election day—are designed to assure a compliant response.

The voter communication program is designed to lead voters into identifying the candidate as the most appropriate choice—not through a hypodermic model of direct response, but through a program designed to appeal to the unique characteristics of each voter.

Cost-effectiveness, rather than a complex understanding of the relative efficiency of each medium, is generally the criterion for voter communication programs. Candidates for national elective office, for example, will rely almost exclusively on electronic media, which yield the lowest cost per voter. Candidates for local office, however, often will rely on direct mail, because they can target mail specifically to households in the district rather than the much wider electronic media coverage area, and even more narrowly to voting households in the district. Thus, even though the message (candidate image, for example) is more appropriate for television, mail may be used. Campaign budgets usually take precedence over theories of persuasion.

Nimmo (1976) has suggested that candidate image making may rely on both the candidate and the voter. Under the "candidate projection" approach, candidates carefully manage the impressions available to the voters, displaying the qualities and attributes a candidate would like to project. Candidates may "create" images of how they would like to be seen. Who the candidate is becomes less important than how the candidate appears. Candidates may also "reflect" their images, portraying their features in a favorable light. Under the "voter projection" approach, images of the candidates are not displayed; instead, voters see in candidates what they are predisposed to believe. Candidates—especially vague ones—may be "empty vessels" into which voters project their own aspirations, hopes, and fears. Alternatively, candidates may simply rely on their partisan identification to allow voters to make assumptions on how they stand. This theory of political campaigning proposes that party loyalties and deep-seated attitudes lead to candidate support regardless of what positions the candidate actually takes.

Many of the specific techniques of the voter communication function are derived from persuasion theory and research. In virtually all campaign media it is possible to find the classic variables of fear appeal (inflation will return if you vote for X), appeal to group norms (the only Democrat), presentation of one- or two-sided messages (side-by-side comparisons of the candidates), authority of the presenter (lists of political endorsements, celebrity appeals), amount of change advocated (candidates who will get things moving again or return to traditional values), and the use of summary and conclusions (vote for X, there is no alternative) (see Diamond & Bates, 1988; Hovland, Janis, & Kelley, 1953; Kaid et al., 1986).

Campaigns and
Multiple Information Sources

Although campaigners may not have control over all the communication aspects, they may provide communication through several information sources. The dynamics of campaign coverage by print media in visible elections are predictable, with an early introduction of the candidate, an overview of issue positions, the questioning of the claims of the candidate, reports on the horse race of the campaign (through polls or other, less empirical evidence), coverage of the campaign strategy, and ultimately the election itself. Electronic media rarely cover any but the most important regional or statewide elections, but when they do, campaign coverage is generally limited to descriptions and presentations of campaign hoopla and where the candidates have been or are going, as well as horse-race dimensions.

In national and statewide campaigns (and, with the rise of cable television, even local campaigns) televised debates between candidates are an increasingly frequent occurrence (Bishop, Meadow, & Jackson-Beeck, 1978; Kraus, 1979). In 1988, for example, there were scores of debates among the Democratic candidates, two presidential debates, and even one vice-presidential debate. On the one hand, these debates have some of the qualities of free media, such as unpaid access directly to voters and journalists posing questions. On the other hand, debates have an important characteristic of paid media in that they provide direct access to voters unfettered by editorial decisions, and the format often allows candidates to make statements directly to voters regardless of whether or not their remarks are responsive to the questions asked (Meadow, 1983).

Candidates have considerably more, but not total, control over the paid mass media. Candidates control the communications materials originating with the campaign, but not materials that come from the political party. Conventional wisdom among campaign professionals is that candidate images and increased name recognition are best developed through electronic media; print media are used for the more complicated presentation of issues and for criticism of the opposing candidate (Diamond & Bates, 1988; Sabato, 1981).

Campaigners also employ interpersonal communication, such as grass-roots campaigning through door-to-door canvassing. Supporters, precinct captains, and even candidates themselves walk precincts as much for symbolic reasons (to show concern for the common voter) as for informing voters. Although empirical evidence is limited, candidates uniformly insist that they are more successful in precincts that they have walked than in those not walked. Telephones are the primary instrument of interpersonal political campaigning, however, because of the advantages of far greater coverage and central supervision to assure a uniform canvassing script.

Direct mail lies at the junction of interpersonal and mass media. Although some campaign mailers that are not targeted to narrow constituencies differ little from print advertising, other mailers are highly targeted and individually produced, speaking directly to the concerns of the demographic group(s) of which the recipient is a member (Armstrong, 1988; Tobe, 1985).

Campaigns of the Future

A Range of New Media

Until the 1980s, candidates thought of campaign communications as involving either canvassing and telephone banks for interpersonal communication or brochures and broadcast advertising for mass media. However, along with the growth of cable television, computers, and telecommunications technologies, new political campaign applications for these technologies have emerged (Abramson, Arterton, & Orren, 1988; Meadow, 1985a, 1985b, 1986). Some candidates use cable TV to advertise to specialized audiences, but the primary impact of cable has been on other campaign media. As the share of viewers watching network television declines, campaigners are turning to other media such as direct mail to assure that voters have not been missed. Second, interactive cable systems, although not widespread, have offered voters opportunities to interact with each other as well as with candidates in ways that were not previously available (Arterton, 1987). Third, the archiving of C-SPAN and state and local government proceedings has made it possible for candidates to monitor themselves and/or opponents in order to develop campaign advertising based on publicly cablecast gaffes or grandstanding speeches.

Videocassettes are used not only to train campaign workers uniformly, but also to provide video endorsements and "personalized" messages for private campaign functions. And in more than one well-funded campaign, candidates have actually distributed videotapes by mail.

Videoconferencing increasingly is being used in statewide and national campaigns to allow campaign leaders to meet "face to face" without taxing already overburdened travel schedules. Even more important, videoconferencing allows candidates to "meet" with dozens of groups that might otherwise have been too small to warrant a personal visit. Candidates are announcing their candidacies from satellite videoconferencing facilities, enabling local news stations to carry the events "live," and allowing less sophisticated local news reporters to interview media-savvy national candidates.

Electronic mail, although not widely available to individuals, can alter the face of campaign communications as candidates seek to fill electronic mailboxes instantaneously with campaign messages or responses to other candidates' statements, at a low cost per household and with little production lead time. Graphic and text systems can essentially send electronic brochures (Garramone, Harris, & Anderson, 1986; Rice & Associates, 1984).

At present, political data bases are the new technology with the widest applications in politics. Typically, a candidate will purchase a computer list of registered voters and enhance the list through computer matching with other, rented lists of voters with special interests, such as owners of homes with high assessed values, union members, ethnic surname directories, or subscribers to certain magazines. Thus voters can receive one or more of thousands of combinations of message elements that are highly targeted, based on information derived from public opinion survey results or geodemographic analysis (Reese, 1985; Robbin, 1980). In addition, high-speed laser printers enable campaigns to produce, from the political data base, individually addressed and targeted letters at the speed of a small printing press. Laser-printed products may range from "personal" letters with the message based on variables selected from the voter file to "slate" cards and marked "sample ballots" in which the names of endorsed candidates for various offices appear in mailings only to voters residing in a given geographic area.

Personal computers and specialized campaign software (see Meadow & McMillen, 1985) allow even the smallest campaign to maintain lists of supporters and to target mail to them. Finally, new, high-tech uses of the telephone are playing roles in campaigning. Automated dialing equipment makes it possible to dial thousands of numbers daily to deliver taped campaign messages from the candidate, or allows voters punching a key on the touch-tone pad to indicate support or opposition to a candidate or policy.

Implications of New Technology for Campaigns

The evolving campaign technologies share a tendency to move toward demassification of the campaign communication environment. Virtually all of the new applications go beyond simply presenting messages to voters in the hope that there will be some penetration of the message. In a sense, the new technologies seek to turn what had been public campaign messages into personal and private campaign communications. On the one hand, it can be argued that personalized campaigns are the antidote to low voter turnout and voter alienation that observers of declining participation have noted. On the other hand, the accompanying shift from broadly cast messages that seek to celebrate and find commonalities among voters to messages that seek to exploit differences and to fragment voters can undermine the fundamental consensus upon which stable political systems rest (Rice, 1987). Single-issue politics may replace broad party politics. And in campaigns of the future, as individuals become increasingly targeted with personalized messages, voters may find themselves knowing more and more about less and less, with no place to turn to get the bigger picture (Abramson et al., 1988; Lowi, 1983). As candidates are able to bypass traditional mass media to access voters directly, candidates may no longer strive for moderation of rhetoric because they know they are in the public spotlight.

The new technologies will undoubtedly increase professionalization of political campaigning. Although the personal computer will raise the level of sophistication of the small and localized amateur campaign, high-tech experts will become more central. Television makeup artists will be less important than the creative data base manager or even the political psychological consultant who can identify psychological characteristics of voters or cues to which a voter will respond. It is important to note that even as the costs of technologies decline, the demands for increasingly sophisticated campaigns will force campaigning costs upward. New technologies may supplement instead of replace old ones.

Candidates in contested elections can never be too sure of victory, and they cannot afford to be wrong about a decision to discard an outmoded technology just because a new one has come along.

In addition, although candidates in recent decades have run as individual candidates rather than as representatives of political parties, the need for complex political data bases as a campaign tool may return control of technology to the parties, and enable parties once again to demand loyalty from their candidates in return for campaign aid.

The new technologies may make the permanent campaign even more of a reality, as targeted communications are easier, more direct, and less expensive. Still, there may be political limits to the spread of new technology; candidates who wish to maintain or develop an image as populists may seek large numbers of unskilled volunteers. Yet technology-intensive campaigns require fewer volunteers and more highly skilled equipment operators, alienating the volunteers. And candidates and public officials may be unwilling to abandon time-honored methods of political deliberation. For example, candidates subject to a "thumbs up" or "thumbs down" vote through electronic mail or interactive cable following a campaign debate may be unwilling to debate.

Conclusion

Although we can be sure that new technologies will be introduced in political campaigning, it is less clear that new theories of persuasion will be developed. There has been only a modest evolution from hypodermic thinking to more sophisticated models of persuasion that recognize the interaction between campaign messages and the voter. And despite changing technology, the basic campaign rule today is the same as it was a hundred years ago: Find your supporters and get them to the polls. But we probably can expect greater use of experiments and new methods in the evaluation of campaign effectiveness. In part, the costs of the new technologies are such that experiments may be cost-effective; for instance, before a candidate sends videotapes to everyone, he or she had better use formative evaluation to be sure they work (Atkin & Freimuth, chap. 6, this volume). Finally, as campaigns become professional, one of the limitations of political campaigns—the absence of continuity between elections, resulting in the lack of institutional memory—will disappear. Although candidates may run for office only once every two or four years, campaign professionals run elections every six months or even continuously, providing a permanent institutional base for learning about what really does "work" in political communication campaigns.

Notes

1. Proprietary survey research data I have collected for dozens of federal, state, and local campaigns suggest that survey respondents often indicate that they have seen campaign messages on television when in fact the messages were aired only on radio; or, instead of remembering a mailed campaign brochure, they recall a television ad that was never even produced. Voters will claim that they do not read "junk" campaign direct mail, but will often cite a campaign slogan that appeared only in the direct mail as a reason for supporting the candidate who mailed the brochure.

2. Data I have collected in San Diego County, though surely not representative of all areas in the United States, show radically different turnouts. In the November 1984 presidential election, for example, 72.8% of the registered voters voted. In contrast, 44.5% of the registered voters voted in June 1984. In June 1986 the turnout was 39.7%, but in November 1986 a statewide election (but nonpresidential) year, the turnout was 53.2%. In November 1987, 31.2% voted. The June 1988 primary turnout rate was 43.7%.

12

The Potential Role of Persuasion
in Adolescent AIDS Prevention

KATHLEEN K. REARDON

A key lesson from medical history is that preventing disease is usually less costly and more effective than treating and curing disease. However, as with forest fire prevention or environmental protection, most people are hesitant to commit their time, resources, and energy to crises that seem remote. With regard to health, this attitude has always been problematic. However, current high rates of drug abuse, adolescent pregnancy, alcoholism, and the threat of AIDS render such complacency a serious threat to the well-being of individuals and society.

Persuasion theory and research has much to offer a journey into the jungle of diseases for which cure is an insufficient or unachieved answer. For example, consider campaigns to combat alcoholism. What works with one age group does not necessarily work with another. The premises brought to the problem by researchers influence who must be persuaded and how. While there is consensus concerning the need to combat alcoholism, there appears to be little consensus regarding how that might be accomplished. Some researchers see alcoholism as the result of normative beliefs about alcohol use. They argue that it is necessary to identify and change the social and cultural factors influencing alcohol use. Other researchers operate on the premise that environmental factors such as availability of alcohol, laws controlling its use, and the extent to which excessive consumption of alcohol is encouraged should be the focus of research efforts. A third group of researchers proposes that alcoholism is a disease and that efforts should be focused on identifying high-risk groups and providing them with prevention interventions. Yet alcoholism is not the result of one problem either within individuals or within societies. It has a variety of precursors and a variety of variables that conspire to maintain its existence. Thus none of these premises is all right or all wrong. Each raises different questions, addresses different audiences, and requires different persuasion strategies (Tuchfield & Marcus, 1984).

The case of AIDS is similar in this regard. There is no single underlying cause for the continued spread of AIDS. Hence there is no single means of prevention. Alcoholism and AIDS require multimethod and multichannel interventions guided by prior theory and research in a variety of disciplines, of which communication is an important one. With AIDS there is an even greater urgency to discover factors that produce high-risk behavior. After all, there is no cure for AIDS at this time; there is only prevention. The answer lies in the development of persuasive interventions for use via both mass media and interpersonal communication channels.

Adolescents constitute a particularly important and challenging target for AIDS prevention interventions. Several factors increase the probability of AIDS-risky behavior by adolescents: "a sense of invulnerability, sexual exploration and experimentation, dysfunctional beliefs and attitudes towards health care services, and reliance on peer networks rather than adult sources of information" (Rotheram-Borus & Bradley, 1987, p. 2).

This persuasion challenge facing health communication experts has at least three stages: (1) identifying environmental pressures and idiosyncrasies of the target group (e.g., adolescents, intravenous drug users, prostitutes) that predispose them to risk, (2) assessing their level of media and interpersonal dependency with regard to AIDS information and the credibility they assign to each source, and (3) selecting persuasion strategies suited to the channel and target group (Reardon, 1989).

This chapter focuses on the third challenge, identifying persuasion strategies likely to be effective in encouraging adolescents to avoid high-risk behaviors associated with AIDS. It also explores the potential utility of such persuasion strategies for mass media and interpersonal channels and suggests how these strategies might be conjoined in an effective AIDS prevention intervention.

Where and When to Begin:
A Question of Values

Research on children's knowledge of the causes and cures of disease indicates that they traditionally have rarely been encouraged to take responsibility for their own health (Lewis & Lewis, 1982). With the exception of tooth decay lectures and occasional science lectures about colds and flus, young children have been led to believe that parents are responsible for the health of their children. Nothing jeopardizes or undermines attempts to prevent adolescent AIDS more than the absence of a sense of responsibility for one's own health. It is difficult for youngsters suddenly to become concerned about their health at the age of 14 or 15. Concern for health must start at a much earlier age. In particular, this early concern must be based on a set of health values derived from parents and teachers.

Adolescents who receive sex education at home and/or at school are less likely to engage in sexual intercourse (Furstenberg, Moore, & Peterson, 1985). In an international review of sex education, Dryfoos (1985) found that teacher education was a key factor in the success of such programs. Yet in most countries, teacher training in sex education is acquired through short-term workshops rather than through university courses.

The challenge remains, however, not only to educate and inform adolescents about AIDS, but to convert these gains into changed behavior and beliefs. Although the percentage of adolescents who respond accurately to questions about AIDS has risen in the past few years, still only 3% of the adolescents interviewed by Strunin and Hingson (1987) changed their behavior in response to the AIDS threat in ways that might decrease their likelihood of infection. Rotheram-Borus, Koopman, and Bradley (1988) found that while their sample of youths had a reasonably high level of AIDS knowledge, they had little personal fear of AIDS, had moderate belief in the preventability of AIDS, and were fairly confident about their ability to behave safely. These results alone indicate considerable gaps in knowledge and behaviors necessary to prevent AIDS. Their follow-up focus groups, however, showed that these same youths were in fact unable to simulate implementing safe behaviors (such as asking about a partner's sexual history, or using a condom). They also found that "perceived threat of AIDS, personal efficacy to implement safe behaviors, and knowledge of AIDS [factors] were not highly correlated" (Rotheram-Borus & Bradley, 1987, p. 9).

Parents, teachers, and youth organizations are the sources most likely to instill or fail to instill in children attitudes about responsibility with regard to sex and values that discourage behaviors that place them at risk for AIDS. Research by Schwartz and Inbar-Saban (1987) indicates that changing people's values may be one way to accomplish long-term health effects. Using Rokeach's (1987) self-confrontation approach (see also Ball-Rokeach & Rokeach in chap. 9, this volume) with obese adults, Schwartz and Inbar-Saban confronted study participants with differences in values between people who diet effectively and those who do not. Specifically, they found that effective dieters score high on the value "wisdom" and low on "happiness" as guiding principles in their lives when compared to those who fail at diets. Subjects were confronted with this information and given the opportunity to compare their own positions on these values with those of successful and unsuccessful dieters. These self-confronting subjects surpassed a discussion group and control group in the average amount of weight lost, and their weight loss persisted until the end of the study 14 months later. The researchers conclude that the value self-confrontation procedure is a "robust method which can be adapted to different settings and behaviors." The fact that weight loss due to value self-confrontation persisted for more than a year suggests that adapting strategies directed specifically at the values of subjects may prove more promising than methods that ignore variations in subjects' value orientations.

This research supports the perspective that when confronted by discrepancies between their behavior and their values, people can be persuaded to change their behaviors. Value self-confrontation encourages people to consider the relative importance of specific values in their value hierarchies.

Scant research exists on the development of values. Rokeach (1987) argues that among young children, health is low on the value hierarchy. This may be due to the previously discussed tendency to exclude children from participation in the protection of their own health. It may also be due, in part, to the fact that we have reached a point in time when most diseases are curable.

AIDS is a disease that, unlike cancer, which also frequently defies cure, is communicable. Prevention can be assured only if people place a high value on their health at an early age and throughout life. Ball-Rokeach, Rokeach, and Grube (1984) explain:

> As values and value hierarchies develop during childhood out of individual needs and coordinated societal demands, they become the standards that are applied to oneself and others. When applied to oneself, they are crucial to the formation of a self-identity, or attitude toward self, a set of beliefs around the self that becomes increasingly the most central of all components within one's belief system. When applied externally, value hierarchies guide the formation of countless favorable and unfavorable attitudes toward others encountered directly or vicariously. (p. 26)

Unlike adult groups, for which the only choice involves the difficult route of persuading them to change their value hierarchy, with children we can develop a high priority for health before they've learned to treat it with indifference. To the extent that a strong value for health can be developed in young children, they are more likely to take an interest in avoiding disease and to adopt behaviors that protect them from AIDS later.

With older children, the value for health is likely to have been low for some time. Value self-confrontation may be an effective means of encouraging them to raise the position of health in their value hierarchy. Teaching them to recognize health risks as contradictory to their values may prove an effective means of eliciting health-protective behaviors from adolescents.

Five Persuasion Approaches

The following sections explore four traditional persuasion theories and one novel approach that may be applied effectively to the problem of adolescent AIDS prevention through reinforcement and guidance in selecting behaviors consistent with emerging health values: self-efficacy, involvement, reasoning, fear, and illusion. Unfortunately, for many adolescents whose parents, teachers, and other role models have failed to instill in them strong health values, these persuasion approaches may be too little, too late.

Instilling Confidence and Motivation

It is one thing to value your health and quite another to believe that you can actually protect it. Aside from learning to value health, it is imperative that children come to believe that they have what it takes to resist pressure from peers to risk their health. Furstenberg, Moore, and Peterson's (1985) study of 15- and 16-year-olds found that sex education programs, while effective, were not as influential as peers on the level of adolescent sexual activity. The ability to resist peer pressure that encourages health risks is thus an important skill. Adolescents must believe that they can effectively resist peer pressure if they are to behave in ways consistent with strong health values.

Perceived self-efficacy is "concerned with people's judgments of how well they can organize and execute constituent cognitive, social, and behavioral skills" (Bandura, 1983, p. 467). Bandura explains that there is a marked difference between *having* skills and being able to use them well in a variety of circumstances: "In short, perceived self-efficacy is concerned not with what one has, but with judgments of what one can do with what one has" (p. 467). We may interpret this to mean that it is insufficient merely to teach children to value health and to provide them with rules. We must also help them to learn that they have the ability to apply these rules in their daily lives.

According to Bandura (1981, 1982), people acquire information about their self-efficacy in a given domain of activity from performance accomplishments, vicarious experiences, social persuasion, and inferences from physiological states. Repeated successes tend to increase self-efficacy, whereas repeated failures lower it.

Research has identified a number of factors that are related to perceptions of success and thus indirectly to perceived self-efficacy. One of these factors is *strategy training*. Research indicates that explicit training in the use of strategies fosters their acquisition and utilization and helps to develop self-efficacy (Schunk, 1985). A common form of strategy training is modeling, which involves encouraging individuals to adopt the behaviors of another, usually highly respected, person. Considerable evidence supports modeling as an effective educational practice (Rosenthal & Bandura, 1978; Rosenthal & Zimmerman, 1978). Other research suggests that merely modeling strategies for solving problems may not have much effect on children's performances if the motivation for modeling is absent (Schunk, 1984). Schunk and Gunn (1985) demonstrated that incorporating information about the importance of a strategy into cognitive modeling enhances the rate of problem solving, skill acquisition, and self-efficacy. They suggest that stressing the importance of strategies to the accomplishment of a task may enhance students' understanding of strategies, which promotes their subsequent utilization and generalization. For instance, those children initially unwilling to resist peer pressure may benefit from learning how other children found particular strategies useful in resisting pressure to engage in health risks.

Peers often have a greater impact than parents with regard to promoting or deterring health behaviors in adolescents (Gottlieb & Baker, 1986). Research indicates that peer groups are valuable resources in health interventions, especially when the focus is on teenage sexual and contraceptive behaviors, smoking, and alcohol use (Banks, Bewley, & Bland, 1981; Jessor, Donovan, & Costa, 1986; Kar & Talbot, 1981; Zelnik & Kantner, 1979). This research suggests that interpersonal communication channels such as peer counselors, informal discussion groups, and role playing with feedback might prove useful in adolescent AIDS prevention programs (see Mantell & Schinke, 1988). Role-playing activities can provide the child with low self-efficacy opportunities to experiment with resistance skill in a relatively nonthreatening environment.

Another factor related to the development of self-efficacy is *social comparison*. Research indicates that children show increasing interest in social comparison as they mature. By the fourth grade, they utilize comparative information to help form self-evaluations of competence (Ruble, Boggiano, Feldman, & Loebl, 1980; Ruble, Feldman, & Boggiano, 1976). Schunk (1983) found that providing children with comparative information indicating what average achievement levels are can enhance motivation but does not foster high self-efficacy. It may be that students benefit from reports of collective efficacy—how their school, for example, is doing in comparison to another school learning the same skills.

Another way that social comparison may prove useful for children is through observations of people they admire. If they see that most people are negligent of health standards, then they are likely to consider themselves conscientious about health if they surpass the minimal standards of others (e.g., if they engage in safe sex most of the time or avoid sharing needles most of the time). To the extent that parents and teachers are not lenient in their own health standards, children are likely to set high standards for themselves. To the extent that mass media avoid celebrating health risks, children are likely to avoid celebrating them.

Miller and Downer (1987) report that television and magazines are the primary sources of AIDS information among a sample of Seattle high school students. Research of this nature indicates the potential value of mass media for dissemination of health information, especially if variations in target audience preferences are considered. For example, given the higher risks of AIDS for blacks and Hispanics, it is important to know whether or not the media can be used effectively to introduce positive models in these communities. Williams (1986) argues that effective media messages depend upon the availability of credible role models. She points out that local media messages about AIDS are typically delivered by news reporters of nonminority status. She further argues that barriers to effective mass media campaigns are often rooted in the value systems and social structures of minorities. If these are not identified and dealt with constructively, then mass media effectiveness is likely to be limited.

A federal report on AIDS education provides some examples of mass media programs that might prove useful with minorities (Longshore, 1988). One campaign produced a videotape or telenovela called *Ojos Que No Ven* (*Eyes That Fail to See*) for AIDS education among Spanish-speaking audiences. In the videotape, a woman copes compassionately with a co-worker who has AIDS and with her own gay son. She ultimately becomes a knowledgeable AIDS educator in her community. The report explains that the telenovela format has the advantage of presenting AIDS information in a manner considered quite popular among Hispanics (see Singhal & Rogers, chap. 15, this volume).

Another option is the use of skits or what is called community *teatro*—a centuries-old tradition among Hispanics. If these skits are offered in both English and Spanish by shifting back and forth every sentence or two, everyone in the audience can benefit. A Los Angeles campaign offers this format and trains the actors to serve as AIDS educators after the performance.

Involving the Persuadee

There is an adage common in schools of education: "Children remember 20% of what you tell them and 80% of what they do." To the extent that children can be encouraged to engage in activities that clearly indicate their concern about AIDS, they are more likely to transfer that concern to their own lives.

Consistency theories of persuasion support this perspective. According to Leon Festinger's (1954) theory of cognitive dissonance, people have a basic desire for consistency among their cognitions. Moreover, the presence of inconsistency among one's relevant cognitions produces psychological discomfort—dissonance—which motivates the rearrangement of one's psychological world to restore consistency. To the extent that children value their health, they are likely to experience dissonance when they engage in or even consider engaging in health risks. (It should be noted that cognitive dissonance theory has been criticized for being unduly simplistic; see Chapanis & Chapanis, 1964; Smith, 1982.)

Counterattitudinal advocacy is one means of using cognitive dissonance in a constructive fashion. Counterattitudinal advocacy involves observing oneself engaging in behavior contrary to one's own beliefs. To avoid feeling the discomfort of inconsistency, one may develop arguments to justify the behavior and thus persuade oneself to adopt a new perspective. If children are encouraged by teachers, parents, peers, and the media to engage in healthful behaviors and are also given good reasons to do so, they may convince themselves to alter health-threatening behaviors. Counterattitudinal advocacy research suggests that this is more likely to occur if children perceive that they chose to adopt healthful behaviors and that they were not coerced or given excessive tangible rewards for changing their behavior (Cohen, 1962; Festinger & Carlsmith, 1959; Linder, Cooper, & Jones, 1967).

Other theories besides cognitive dissonance provide explanations for the effectiveness of counterattitudinal advocacy. These include (1) incentive theory, which proposes that it is the development and learning of new arguments, not inconsistency between beliefs and behaviors, that motivate people to change (Janis & Gilmore, 1965; Rosenberg, 1965); (2) self-perception theory, which assumes that the basis for attitude change after counterattitudinal advocacy is a process by which people infer their own attitudes from observing their own behavior (Bem, 1972); and (3) impression-management theory, which proposes that attitude and behavior changes following counterattitudinal advocacy are due to the individual's desire to maintain a public image of consistency (Tedeschi, Schlenker, & Bonoma, 1971).

Role playing provides children with opportunities to practice the interpersonal resistance skills and decision-making skills they learn in the classroom. Moreover, it provides opportunities for them to hear themselves publicly commit to healthful behaviors in an environment that simulates actual experiences. Role-playing activities have the added advantage of providing teachers and experimenters with opportunities for direct observation of behavior that would be difficult to capture in the natural environment (Dow, Biglan, & Glaser, 1985; Hops & Greenwood, 1981).

The Role of Reasoning

Another method of persuasion that may prove effective in AIDS prevention programs for adolescents is reasoning. For decades, persuasion research focused on methods to create imbalance or inconsistency among cognitions as a way of eliciting behavioral change. However, people are capable of rationalizing inconsistency among cognitions, or between attitudes and behaviors. For example, it is not uncommon for smokers to use the rationalization "We all have to die sometime." An effective campaign for AIDS prevention must address the issue of rationalization. What are the common rationalizations used to support avoidance of protective measures? How might children be taught to resist such rationalizations?

Reardon (1981, 1987) has developed the ACE model of reasoned behavior, which has been supported by research on how children reason about their drug use (Friedman, Lichtenstein, & Biglan, 1985; Newman, 1984). This model can be used to teach children how they reason about behavior and the types of reasoning they might expect others to use in persuading them to take health risks. According to the ACE model, people consciously and unconsciously know rules about how appropriate, consistent, or effective a behavioral option is likely to be, given the situation and relationship between communicators. *Appropriateness* refers to how the behavior in question fits with one's own value system and self-image. *Consistency* considerations respond to the question, Is the behavior something a person like me would do? *Effectiveness* pertains to the likelihood that the behavior will lead to the desired consequence or outcomes. The ACE model does not propose that people always reason about their behavior, but that when provoked to do so they use the criteria of appropriateness, consistency, and effectiveness.

The ACE model provides guidelines for teaching children the types of reasoning others are likely to use when pressuring them to take health risks. It can also be used by children to guide them in responding to such pressure. Prior research suggests that children do use these criteria both to justify bad health habits and to resist pressure to engage in them. A recent study of compliance-resisting strategies used by adolescents when pressured by peers to smoke indicates that they prefer to use appeals to consistency (e.g., I never smoke). Effectiveness strategies are their second preference (e.g., Smoking causes cancer), and appropriateness strategies (e.g., It's wrong to smoke) are the least preferred means of resisting pressure to smoke (Reardon, Sussman, & Flay, 1988). Teaching children to identify the reasoning patterns of others and reasoning patterns they might use to resist pressure from others may prove a useful path in AIDS interventions.

Both interpersonal and mass media channels may be used to this end. Interactive technologies may prove especially useful here. Videodisc programs that allow adolescents to view situations involving pressure to behave in ways that place them at risk for AIDS and then to select among a variety of possible responses, which could then be played out, is one way of utilizing modern technology for role playing. (See Williams, Rice, & Rogers, 1988, for theoretical and methodological discussions of using videodisc interaction for attitude change and role modeling.) With such technology, the adolescent could go back and select another response if the one initially chosen does not lead to a desired outcome (e.g., the persuader ceasing to exert pressure). In this way adolescents are given the opportunity to practice resistance behaviors without being observed by others.

What About Fear?

There is no doubt that AIDS is a fearful disease. Teaching children about AIDS inevitably involves some fear. The question is, How much fear is too much? A clear understanding of this element may prove useful in reducing AIDS-risk behaviors in adolescents.

The majority of studies in this area have been guided by the fear-drive model and the nonmonotonic models proposed by Janis (1967) and McGuire (1968a; also see chap. 2, this volume). This model is based on the assumption that fear serves as a drive to motivate trial-and-error behavior (Hovland, Janis, & Kelley, 1953). When fear is aroused, recipients are motivated to experiment with a variety of responses to alleviate the unpleasant state. If they are presented with reassuring recommendations for avoiding the threat, and if mental rehearsal of these recommendations is followed or accompanied by a marked reduction in fear, then the responses will be reinforced and will tend to occur under similar circumstances in the future.

Unlike the fear-drive model, nonmonotonic fear models assume that increases in fear have multiple effects, some of which facilitate persuasion and others of which interfere with persuasion. The resultant relationship between fear and acceptance is assumed to take the form of an inverted U-shaped curve. The effect of fear begins to wane when interfering effects start to increase at a faster rate than facilitating effects. In his review of fear research, Janis (1967) showed how this model could be used to reconcile conflicting findings.

McGuire (1968a) also developed a nonmonotonic model of fear-arousing communication. Reception and yielding are seen as two mediators of attitude change induced by fear. McGuire's model also predicts that a given increase in fear should increase acceptance for people with low chronic anxiety and reduce acceptance among those people with high chronic anxiety. He adds that fear level interacts with situational factors that affect the relative importance of reception and yielding in the mediating effect of fear on attitude change (e.g., if a message is simple, reception is facilitated by shifting the optimal level of fear in the direction of higher fear, since the recipient does not have to struggle with comprehension).

Sutton (1982) contends that there are a number of shortcomings in both the monotonic and the nonmonotonic fear-drive model. First, the fear-drive model is an "odd mixture" of fear arousal, which involves higher mental processes, and fear reduction and resultant behavior change, which involve low-level, animal-like processes. Second, it is unclear whether the important factor in determining the likelihood that a response will be repeated is the amount of fear reduced or the completeness of the reduction. Third, if mental rehearsal of the recommendation is successful in reducing fear, it remains unclear why this cognitive response should lead to a behavioral one. Fourth, adequate tests of the fear-drive model require continuous or near-continuous measurement of fear. Fifth, these models require elaborate factorial designs to test their predictions and they are post hoc descriptive schema that can accommodate virtually any pattern of findings. The main findings of Sutton's (1982) review are as follows:

(1) Increases in fear are consistently associated with increases in acceptance (intentions and behavior).

(2) There is no evidence that fear and acceptance are related in a nonmonotonic fashion.

(3) Increasing the efficacy of the recommended action strengthens intentions to adopt that action.

(4) Providing specific instructions about how to perform a recommended action leads to a higher rate of acting in accordance with the recommendations.

(5) Greater similarity between communicator and recipient in terms of race produces more immediate behavior change without necessarily affecting fear.

(6) There is little support for the interactions predicted by the fear-drive model.

Kirsch, Tennen, Wickless, Saccone, and Cody (1985) have offered a competing perspective on fear-related self-efficacy. Kirsch et al. conclude that phobic people generally attempt to avoid feared situations, thereby avoiding the sense of fear they expect to occur. In short, avoiding fear itself is one of the purposes of avoidance behavior. It is thus possible for people to be so afraid of being afraid, or of appearing afraid, that even perceptions of self-efficacy in terms of performing the behavior do not encourage them to do so. In other words, adolescents who are quite capable of resisting peer pressure to place their health in jeopardy may avoid doing so because compliance-resisting situations elicit in them considerable discomfort and fear of appearing afraid to take risks. Essentially, they perceive the punishment of fear as outweighing the potential benefits of protecting their health.

From research on fear, it is reasonable to include fear as one of the persuasion components in adolescent health interventions. Since there is no research evidence that fear is most effective with a particular age group, we must rely on child development research and common sense to determine when and to what extent fear should be utilized in our interventions. First, it seems unnecessary to evoke high levels of fear about AIDS or other communicable diseases in young children since they are not likely to be at high risk for AIDS and are not likely to die from most of the communicable diseases they will learn about. Second, using fear appeals with young children, before they are capable of cognitive monitoring of emotional reactions, might have a boomerang effect. Children may be compelled to deny fear messages or to respond with dysfunctionally high levels of fear, thus developing a paranoia about disease. We do not wish to create disease phobias—unreasonable fear of illness and avoidance of other children who might be ill.

Mass media may prove especially effective in visually emphasizing to adolescents the more immediate consequences of AIDS. Adolescents who perceive the threat of death as remote from their own experiences may respond to visual images of the mental problems, skin rashes and sores, and disastrous influence on a teenager's social life that accompany AIDS. Another promising approach is to emphasize the existence of these symptoms among people living in proximity to the viewer (Longshore, 1988).

Perhaps the most effective approach, however, is to combine these media images with interpersonal question-and-answer sessions. Fear research informs us not only that too much fear leads to denial, but that fear without information regarding ways to avoid the problems described or depicted in the message may also lead to denial. Adolescents lacking information and skills needed to resist pressure to engage in behavioral risks for AIDS may retreat into a state of irretrievable denial. To avoid this problem, media messages that include fear should be followed by face-to-face opportunities to discuss strategies for reducing risks for AIDS that in turn reduce fear as well as denial.

For example, Longshore (1988), in a review of AIDS intervention techniques, noted that house parties in private homes during which peers discuss AIDS or are led in discussion by people who have placed themselves at risk but changed their behaviors are alternatives that may prove useful with adolescents. Telephone hotlines offer another interpersonal opportunity for adolescents to discuss their fears. They also offer the advantage of anonymity. However, they are likely to be successful only to the degree that mass media are also effectively used to inform adolescents of their existence.

A Case for the Power of Illusion

The four methods of persuasion reviewed above—instilling confidence and motivation, involving the persuadee, reasoning, and fear—are all based on the premise that people will respond in reasonable ways when presented with messages that demonstrate that their actions are somehow out of touch with reality and thus likely to place them in considerable jeopardy. Recent research in psychology on the power of illusions suggests a fifth persuasion strategy not yet the subject of communication research: appealing to illusions rather than to reality.

Taylor and Brown (1988) argue that most people are not often in touch with reality. They propose that people operate daily on the basis of three primary illusions: unrealistically positive view of the self, illusions of control, and unrealistic optimism. They argue that most of us are actually unprepared to accept reality, since a variety of social norms and strategies of social interaction conspire to protect people from the harsher side of it. Research indicates that people are generally reluctant to give feedback to others, and that when feedback is given, it is generally positive (Blumberg, 1972; Parducci, 1968; Tesser & Rosen, 1975). Moreover, people tend to seek feedback when it is likely to be positive (Brown, 1987) and to select friends who are relatively similar to themselves (Eckland, 1968; Hill, Rubin, & Peplau, 1976). Research also indicates that negative feedback is seen as less credible, especially by people with high self-esteem (Shrauger & Rosenberg, 1970; Snyder, Shenkel, & Lowery, 1977).

Given both the tendency for people to avoid giving others negative feedback and the tendency of individuals to surround themselves with positive messages (and to deny the credibility of negative messages that do sneak through), it seems reasonable to ask why anyone should listen to, let alone be influenced by, negative information. In all likelihood, people vary in the extent to which they can cope with negative feedback. If, however, we accept that most people prefer to be told good things about themselves, it follows that persuasion strategies that focus on the positive may prove more effective. As Reardon (1989) argues:

> Even if one does not accept the premise that people are more out of- than in-touch with reality, Taylor and Brown's perspective suggests that presenting adolescents with the vivid reality of AIDS may fall on deaf ears. If children, especially those at risk, have a vested interest in maintaining a positive self image, a strong sense of control and a positive view of the future, perhaps the last thing we want to do is try to convince them that they are no different than anyone else, highly vulnerable to AIDS and thus perilously on the brink of a short, unpleasant future.

Add to this the fact that the children most at risk for AIDS are those in minority groups and among the more deprived in terms of socioeconomic status, reality training may be the last thing they need or want. How then can such children be reached? The answer may lie in our ability to identify interpersonal and mass media messages that build on rather than tear down the "illusions" held dear by children at risk for AIDS. For example, rather than bombarding them with images of their vulnerability, perhaps we should focus their attention on how protective behaviors increase their control. Rather than tear down the self-images of those who have placed themselves at risk or terrorize them with the fear that they are already the carriers of death, use positive models of young people who changed their behaviors and are free of AIDS. And rather than presenting them with bleak depictions of their futures, we might employ positive images of the healthful and happy times ahead for those who protect their health (Reardon, 1989).

Conclusion

There are no easy answers when it comes to deciding how to teach adolescents about AIDS, and persuading them to protect themselves from AIDS is an even greater challenge. Adolescents often perceive themselves to be invulnerable, and most young people perceive AIDS to be only a remote possibility. As discussed above, this perception is strengthened by the fact that they have rarely been taught to take responsibility for their health.

How does a society suddenly faced with a contagious, life-threaten-ing illness teach its young people to protect themselves? The answer lies in a massive effort on the part of families, schools, and the mass media. This chapter has explored five promising persuasion approaches, along with the likelihood of their effectiveness via inter-personal and mass media channels.

Based upon a review of AIDS studies and related interventions, Rotheram-Borus and Bradley (1987) conclude that "general knowledge of AIDS and a recognition of AIDS as a personal threat to youth is a necessary prerequisite to behavior change; however, additional skills are necessary to translate this knowledge into behavioral change" (p. 5). Skills needed include assertiveness training (e.g., to help adolescents in requesting that their sexual partners use condoms or in refusing to have sex), role playing, and rehearsal of refusal skills, identifying feelings of arousal or anxiety, and problem solving (such as evaluating the consequences of AIDS testing or risky behavior), with peers in a group setting (see also Rotheram, 1980, for a review of social skills training studies for youth). Additional important factors are the individuals' personal cost/benefit analyses of safe behaviors and access to resources (such as condoms, legal aid, or HIV testing). Each of the five persuasion approaches discussed above can contribute to provid-ing or developing these influences.

The AIDS epidemic poses a considerable challenge not only because of confusion about transmission and vulnerability, but because as a society we are unprepared to fight. Smoking and drug abuse have threatened youngsters for years. Now they face an even more insidious threat. When one consents to smoking or the use of drugs, to a large extent one consciously consents to the threats inherent in those substances. When a young person consents to unprotected sex, unless he or she perceives the sexual partner as a potential AIDS carrier, the threat is less obvious, the consent less conscious.

Communication researchers can play a vital role in assisting families, schools, and the mass media to develop effective means of convincing young people that they must take responsibility for their health. They also have much to contribute in terms of recommending the types of messages most likely to be effective with young people. AIDS is, first and foremost, a communication and persuasion challenge. There is as yet no cure for this disease; there is only prevention. Decades of research in communication can provide us with insights likely to be helpful in the fight against AIDS. It is clear that this is true for both interpersonal and mass media researchers. The war on AIDS will require a concerted effort on every front. There is no room here for the "false dichotomy" that has divided interpersonal and mass media communication research (Reardon & Rogers, 1989). As with other adolescent health issues, the fight against AIDS must be a multichannel, multimethod, multidisciplinary fight.

13

Antismoking Campaigns: Progress in the Application of Social Learning Theory

ALFRED McALISTER
AMELIE G. RAMIREZ
CHRISTINE GALAVOTTI
KIPLING J. GALLION

Cigarette smoking is a major contributor to the burden of illness in our society. Chronic, heavy smoking is a causal factor in the etiology of cardiovascular diseases, pulmonary diseases, and lung cancer (U.S. Department of Health and Human Services, 1982, 1983a, 1984a, 1986a). Along with error and negligence, smoking is also involved in thousands of accidental fires and burnings every year. Because cigarette smoking constitutes such a serious threat to public health and such a tremendous social cost, there is great interest in finding effective strategies for reducing the prevalence of smoking (Hamburg, 1979; Ockene, 1984).

There are several approaches to attempting to solve social problems, as Paisley (chap. 1, this volume) suggests. One approach is to enact laws and regulations that restrict opportunities for smoking or raise its costs. A less paternalistic solution is to conduct communication campaigns to discourage smoking. Although the vast majority of efforts have failed (Wallack, 1981), some progress is being made, particularly when media campaigns are combined with interpersonal campaigns and community programs (Danaher, Berkanovic, & Gerber, 1983; Flay, 1987b). This chapter analyzes the evolution of communication strategies designed to influence adults to quit smoking.

The research reviewed in this chapter demonstrates the importance of two general notions. The first is that communications aimed at influencing complex and persistent behaviors must perform three functions: *informing* audiences about those behaviors and their consequences, *persuading* audiences to cease or avoid those behaviors, and *training* audiences in skills necessary for the translation of intent into action. The first two functions are obvious and have been performed at least fairly well in many different communication campaigns, but the third function has usually been ignored, leading to disappointing results. As researchers have recognized this deficit and begun to study ways of including appropriate kinds of training in antismoking communications, encouraging progress has been made toward the creation of effective campaigns, mostly through applying the principle of *modeling*. Television programming in which individuals demonstrate and model specific behavioral skills and media "self-help clinics" that follow individual role models as they attempt to quit smoking have shown particular promise (Best, 1980; Danaher et al., 1983; Flay, 1987b; Puska, McAlister, Pekkola, & Koskela, 1981).

The second notion addressed in this chapter is the importance of *interpersonal support for mediated communications*. Mass communication media may effectively inform, persuade, and train their audiences, but lasting change will not be achieved in the absence of a supportive social environment. Because it is easier to distribute printed or audiovisual messages to mass audiences than it is to organize supportive interpersonal communications on a large scale (and for other political and symbolic reasons suggested by Wallack, chap. 16, this volume), campaigns have tended to rely solely on mass communication. This approach has been effective in increasing awareness, knowledge, and motivation to quit smoking, but has yielded relatively poor results otherwise. Research to date suggests that adding interpersonal support and reinforcement for behavior change through community organization can double the effects of media-only communications (Flay, 1987b), although it may not always be cost-effective to do so (see Hornik, chap. 14, this volume). Further progress toward the identification of potentially effective strategies for discouraging and reducing smoking may depend upon the creation of opportunities for interpersonal communications and social reinforcement through community-based activities and programs.

Smoking and Cessation:
Overview of Campaign Results ·

The first significant antismoking communications in recent history were the "cancer scares," news and publicity in 1951-1952 reporting a link between cigarette smoking and lung cancer (Warner, 1977, 1985). These reports led to a decline of about 10% in per capita cigarette consumption between 1952 and 1953. But this was followed by an equally sharp increase that brought per capita consumption back up until in 1962 it reached a point about 10% higher than the 1951-1952 level. The next significant event was the release of the *Surgeon General's Report on Smoking and Health* in 1963-1964. A great deal of publicity surrounded this event, and following it per capita cigarette consumption dipped a little less than 5% over two years before resuming a gradual upward climb. In 1967-1968 the Federal Communication Commission's Fairness Doctrine was interpreted in a way that required broadcasters to provide equal time for antismoking advertisements to counter the advertisements of the tobacco industry. This led to another drop in per capita cigarette consumption of about 10% over three years. In 1970 the cigarette industry voluntarily withdrew its advertising from television and the corresponding counteradvertisements were moved out of prime time. This was followed by another increase in per capita consumption of about 5%. In 1972-1973 warning labels were required on cigarette advertisements and packages and a very small dip in tobacco sales followed. Since then, per capita consumption has declined steadily, with a significant decrease in 1983 after the federal excise tax on cigarettes was raised from 8 cents to 16 cents a package.

National surveys of the prevalence of smoking show that the proportion of adult smokers has declined every year since 1965 (McGinnis, Shopland, & Brown, 1987). Among men the proportion of smokers dropped from 52% to 33% from 1965 to 1985; for women the drop was from 34% to 28%. Rates for women still remain higher than they were in 1955, when less than 25% of adult women smoked. McGinnis et al. (1987) estimated that there are currently about 37 million ex-smokers among adults in the United States. Although a majority of adult smokers have tried to quit at least once, successful cessation has tended to be concentrated among middle-aged professional men and businessmen with college educations; among younger or less affluent men, the trends have been less encouraging. Men aged 30-44 years have the highest smoking prevalence (38%), and 58% of men in this age group with less than 12 years of school are smokers, compared with 23% of men who have college degrees (National Center for Health Statistics, 1988). Women seem to have more difficulty maintaining cessation than men (Gritz, 1980; Sorenson & Pechacek, 1987). Among heavy smokers of both sexes the trends are not favorable, as the proportion of heavy smokers has risen from 24% in 1965 to 30% in 1985 (McGinnis et al., 1987). Thus the changes have been least hopeful among the heavy smokers, for whom cessation would be most beneficial.

It is very difficult to attribute favorable changes to specific antismoking campaigns. Each round of news and publicity about the dangers of smoking has been followed by a drop in tobacco consumption, but the general trend toward cessation may be motivated by a number of other social and personal factors. A number of studies have been conducted to assess the specific effects of antismoking communications. One early study by O'Keefe (1971) assessed the impact of the counteradvertising spots broadcast during 1968-1970. Interviews with smokers and nonsmokers in Florida showed that although nonsmokers tended to believe the spots were effective, smokers acknowledged little or no effect on their behavior. Later studies have confirmed these findings, suggesting that, overall, public service messages and media-only campaigns do not produce substantial behavior change (Flay, 1987b).

Several large-scale mass communication studies have examined the effects of a variety of media and community programs on smoking behavior change. Farquhar and his colleagues conducted a field experiment as part of the Stanford Three Community Study (TCS) in which two communities received a variety of media providing information and persuasion aimed to encourage smoking cessation, while another community received no special communications (Farquhar et al., 1977; see also Flora, Maccoby, & Farquhar, chap. 10, this volume). A three-year follow-up of smokers from all three communities showed no more than short-term effects of the media campaign. In one of the two media communities, a subset of high-risk subjects who received face-to-face instruction had more success in smoking cessation than did the smokers who received media and community programs only, and both groups did better than the control community (Meyer, Nash, McAlister, Maccoby, & Farquhar, 1980). However, overall smoking prevalence rates after three years were disappointing, with the intervention communities showing only slightly lower rates of smoking than the community that received no special programs.

Another large-scale media and community program was conducted in Australia in 1978, the North Coast Quit for Life program (Egger et al., 1983). This three-community study included extensive use of media in two towns (e.g., TV, radio, newspapers, as well as posters, T-shirts, and self-help quitting manuals), and additional community activities such as fun runs and skills training in one of the two communities, and no special programming in a third control community. At the end of two years, results showed that the greatest reduction in smoking prevalence among smokers had occurred in the town that was exposed to media plus community programming, the next greatest in the media-only town, and the least reduction in the control community. These results are similar to those found in the Stanford TCS.

A third study, the Quit for Life project, conducted in Sydney, Australia, used prime-time television messages to promote smoking cessation (Dwyer et al., 1986; Pierce et al., 1986). Results were evaluated by monitoring the number of calls to an advertised "quit line" and the communitywide enrollment in smoking cessation clinics, and through personal interviews. Once again, the overall reduction in smoking prevalence rates was modest (a 2.8% reduction in smoking prevalence in Sydney versus a 1.6% increase in the rest of Australia) despite a high level of exposure to the media spots and a great deal of initial activity (e.g., calls to the quit line and enrollment in smoking cessation clinics).

On the basis of these failures to demonstrate strong and specific communication effects when media-only campaigns are employed, one might conclude that the many informational and persuasive events and campaigns of the past 30 years have had only temporary or limited impact on smoking behavior. Actually, these efforts have achieved their immediate objectives quite well. People are now well informed about the health consequences of smoking. Between 1958 and 1974 the proportion of the total U.S. population believing that smoking is harmful to health went from 40% to above 80% (Gallup Opinion Index, 1974). Today nearly everyone accepts the fact that heavy smoking can have serious consequences. Results of a national survey conducted in 1985 show that 90% of U.S. adults are aware that smoking increases one's chances of heart disease (National Center for Health Statistics, 1988). Americans are also well aware of other health consequences of smoking: Over 90% know that smoking increases one's risk of emphysema and lung cancer, and 80% are aware of the increased risk of low birth weight and cancer of the esophagus.

Furthermore, most smokers are persuaded that they should stop smoking, and a majority have tried to quit at least once. In one recent study, 89% of male and 83% of female smokers reported that they had tried to stop smoking (Sorenson & Pechacek, 1987). In 1987, the American Cancer Society found that 39% of all cigarette smokers participated in the 1987 Great American Smoke-Out by not smoking or cutting down for the day. Some 11.5% quit for the day, and 7.3% reported that they were still not smoking one to three days later. But, although a majority of individuals can achieve at least short-term abstinence, most return to smoking within a relatively short period of time. The issue of how to help ex-smokers maintain their nonsmoking status over time has become the focus of much recent research (Baer & Lichtenstein, 1988; Brownell, Marlatt, Lichtenstein, & Wilson, :986; Marlatt & Gordon, 1980, 1985).

Training for Smoking Cessation

Mark Twain said that it was easy to quit smoking—he had done it "hundreds of times." That comment illustrates why merely informing and persuading smokers is not enough to induce lasting cessation. Researchers now realize that smoking behavior is part of a complex pattern influenced by psychological, environmental, and physiological factors. A substantial body of evidence pointing to the addictive nature of nicotine has led to the recent release of another report on smoking by the U.S. surgeon general that concludes that nicotine is an addictive drug and that the use of cigarettes and other forms of tobacco is addicting. Both psychological and pharmacological studies suggest that chronic nicotine use produces a definable syndrome characterized by the development of tolerance and dependence and that abstinence is accompanied by withdrawal symptoms (Henningfield, 1984; Hughes et al., 1984; U.S. Department of Health and Human Services, 1988). Further, the pharmacologic and behavioral processes that influence nicotine addiction are similar to those that determine use of other addictive drugs (Brownell et al., 1986). Hunt, Barnett, and Branch (1971) found that relapse rates for temporary abstainers from tobacco, alcohol, and heroin are essentially the same, and that 66% return to their habit within three months.

In addition to experiencing strong cravings for cigarettes and withdrawal symptoms, ex-smokers try to maintain abstinence in the face of environmental cues to smoke: high-stress situations, negative emotional states, and low expectations for success—all suspected factors in relapse (Baer & Lichtenstein, 1988; Condiotte & Lichtenstein, 1981; Marlatt & Gordon, 1985; Shiffman, 1982). To sustain abstinence the ex-smoker must learn how to cope with a variety of stresses and temptations. Adequate coping is the best predictor of successfully maintaining cessation under high-risk conditions (Shiffman, 1982, 1984; Curry & Marlatt, 1985). Furthermore, individuals who expect quitting to require active coping skills appear to be more successful at maintaining cessation. These findings clearly suggest that the individual hoping to avoid cigarettes must be *trained in skills for avoiding relapse.*

A great deal of research has been devoted to the development of effective counseling and training methods for helping adults stop smoking, but more recent research has focused on preventing relapse. There are conflicting reports as to when relapse occurs (Brownell et al., 1986; Shiffman & Jarvik, 1987; Sutton, 1979). Marlatt and Gordon (1980, 1985) have developed a model of relapse that distinguishes between a lapse and a relapse. These authors postulate that quitters are likely to experience high-risk situations where they have usually smoked before and that, depending on reactions to the situation and self-appraisals of the reactions, they may either gain greater resolve for abstaining or go quickly into full relapse. The determining factor that leads to one path or the other is based on causal attributions during the lapse episode. When attributions for a slip (smoking during a risky situation, such as a social event like a cocktail party) focus on internal, stable, and global factors (e.g., lack of willpower), emotional reactions to these attributions may contribute to relapse. The reverse is true if external, unstable, specific, and controllable causal attributions are made (Curry, Marlatt, & Gordon, 1987).

Self-efficacy is concerned with peoples' judgments of how well they can execute courses of action required to deal with prospective situations and bring about idealized expectations (Bandura, 1982). Efficacy expectations are a person's beliefs about his or her capability of performing specific behaviors in a particular situation (Schunk & Carbonari, 1984). Condiotte and Lichtenstein (1981) found that smokers with higher levels of self-efficacy showed greater abstinence for one month following treatment designed to enhance perceptions of self-efficacy.

Subjects who relapsed did so in situations for which they made the lowest efficacy judgments following treatment. McIntyre, Lichtenstein, and Mermelstein (1983) followed the same smokers for one year and found that those with initial low efficacy ratings still relapsed at six months. Thus it seems that a person's sense of efficacy affects his or her ability to change intractable behaviors for extended periods of time.

Other persons can help an individual to sustain the needed motivation to achieve and maintain a behavioral change. Social influence processes such as modeling of either the desired or undesired (e.g., smoking) behavior may affect behavior change. Social support may play an indirect role by modifying other factors that influence behavior. Support influences cessation and maintenance by helping to create a more manageable and calm interpersonal environment or by helping to alleviate daily hassles, stress, or negative emotions that overtax individuals' coping abilities and thus predispose them to relapse (Coppotelli & Orleans, 1985).

Support influences have been demonstrated to be substantial mediators of cigarette use (Cohen & Syme, 1985). Mermelstein, Cohen, Lichtenstein, Baer, and Kamarck (1986) examined three kinds of support: support from a partner directly related to quitting, perceptions of availability of general (i.e., nonsmoking) support resources, and the presence of smokers in subjects' social networks. All three factors influenced smoking behavior, but each operated at a different point in the cessation-maintenance process. Partner support and perceived availability of general support were associated with cessation and short-term maintenance (three months). Presence of smokers hindered maintenance and differentiated between relapsers and long-term abstainers (those who abstained for twelve months).

Several media-based studies have used ideas and techniques suggested by this research in developing program components that might enhance the effects of mediated communications. Explicit training in stress management has been a particularly important component, as has the training of recent ex-smokers in problem-solving skills that will help them to predict causes of relapse and to prepare for them. Individualized plans for avoiding relapse may include self-instructions designed to counter negative thoughts, diets to avoid weight gain, or idiosyncratic strategies for coping with urges to smoke (e.g., taking a walk or repeating motivational statements). Campaigns have employed role models to demonstrate specific behaviors and coping strategies, media and community organization to distribute quit-smoking materials and self-help manuals, and schoolchildren to encourage and support their parents in smoking cessation (Flay, Hansen, Johnson, & Sobel, 1983). Although, as Flay (1987b) reports in his review, media programs that combine community activities do, on average, twice as well as media-only campaigns, no well-developed theoretical basis for combining mass communication with interpersonal and community components has been elaborated.

Applying Social Learning Theory to Smoking Cessation

A notion of how to combine mass media and interpersonal communications effectively can be derived from Bandura's (1977b, 1986) social learning theory. The key concepts are *modeling* and *social reinforcement*. The first refers to the process of observational and imitative learning when the behaviors of others are copied or approximated by observers. Social models influence changes in attitudes and beliefs, decision making, and the acquisition of new patterns of behavior. Such factors as attractiveness, perceived social competence, perceived expertise, and perceived credibility determine the potency of specific models. Models who reflect socially desirable characteristics such as power, sex appeal, and courage can be particularly influential, as can models whom observers perceive as being similar to themselves. Indeed, peers are often the most influential of models in everyday social learning. For complex behaviors and skills, the most salient factor in attainment is the model's demonstration of complex sequences in a gradual, systematic manner. Modeling of difficult behavioral patterns is facilitated when persons are shown coping realistically with predictable problems. Thus models who fail occasionally are more effective than those who encounter no difficulties or setbacks in their learning process.

In social learning theory, the concept of social reinforcement can be demonstrated by considering the distinction between acquisition and performance in learning from role-model presentations. New behaviors may be *acquired* from mediated communication (e.g., from television), but they will not be *performed* unless the environment is one in which those behaviors will be reinforced. A powerful source of reinforcement is found in interpersonal communications, particularly apparent in verbal praise from significant others. From the perspective of the theory, the only necessary interpersonal components of learning are social cuing (e.g., verbal prompts) and selective evaluative statements about performances (e.g., praise for successive approximations of the desired behavior). A key psychological element in this process is the development of self-efficacy expectations. If a learner does not expect to do well, performance will be delayed. Verbal information is a powerful source of these expectations, as are direct reactions to initial efforts. Negative or critical statements can be harmful, and neutral comments are the best response to an unsatisfactory performance. For very difficult behaviors, any effort may deserve praise, and repeated reinforcement in the face of successive failures may be needed to elicit the practice and experience required for eventual success.

Social learning theory can guide the design of combined mass media and interpersonal campaigns to promote smoking cessation. Modeling concepts have obvious applications to the creation of media messages. Thus theory tells us that displays of cessation or role-model stories should be emphasized above other possible information. Research on the process of smoking cessation has identified some of the critical skills and social factors for different stages of behavior change. For example, it is helpful to identify and rehearse reasons for quitting formally in the initial stage. Table 13.1 summarizes these stages, as well as examples of each drawn from actual role models.

Although there is some overlap between stages, the preparation stage is characterized by a dissatisfaction with dependence and by decisional balance. In the action stage, the individual possesses self-efficacy regarding his or her ability to overcome the dependency. Social support and reinforcement for nonsmoking are important contributors to successful completion of this stage (Mermelstein, Cohen, & Lichtenstein, 1983). In addition, the individual goes through a process of reevaluation during which the "former" smoker attempts to reform his or her self-concept following this life-style change. This includes redefining him- or herself as a nonsmoker. In the final stage the individual attempts to maintain the life-style change by avoiding stimuli associated with smoking, acquiring new coping responses, and maintaining a general social support network. Another characteristic of the maintenance stage is an increased sense of self-efficacy regarding the ability to cope with situations that evoke the urge to smoke. These factors can form a basis for creating modeling stories to appear on television or in other mass media.

The concept of modeling can be put into practical use in a variety of ways. One approach, suitable for very brief messages, is to have actors

TABLE 13.1   Sample Quotes by Role Models for Three Stages
             of Smoking Cessation

Three States of Smoking Cessation	Examples Provided by Role Models
Preparation	
information about smoking	"I decided to quit because I was pregnant. It's okay to risk my own life, but not my unborn child."
decisional balance	"I wanted to be here [living] to see my children grown."
Taking action	
social support and reinforcement for nonsmoking	"My husband supported my decision and he joined me in the decision to stop smoking."
reevaluation of self	"I physically feel better, less fatigued, less tense; I feel better [as a nonsmoker]."
Maintenance	
increasing efficacy expectations for specific situations	"In social situations, I would review the reasons why I quit smoking."
acquisition of new coping responses	"When nervous due to not smoking, I would talk to someone."

SOURCE: McAlister et al. (1987).

display the key skills for cessation. However, the concept is more fully applied by a journalistic or documentary approach. For example, stories of persons who have quit smoking can be told and reenacted in detail to illustrate the elements of their behavior and the environment that led to success. More dramatically, persons actually making a quit attempt may be followed in a documentary fashion as they learn, on their own or with expert instruction, to stop smoking. In this case some rate of failure is inevitably presented, but, from the perspective of social learning theory, that may be considered helpful in stimulating the repetitive striving required for eventually achieving such a difficult behavioral goal as the elimination of an addictive habit.

The concepts underlying the principle of social reinforcement for the imitation of role models also have obvious applications to the organization of interpersonal communication to supplement mass media. Theoretically, if effective modeling messages are available through the mass media, the minimum necessary interpersonal contact to stimulate behavior change would consist of verbal encouragement for attention to the role models and praise for any significant efforts to imitate them. This interpersonal communication can be provided by anyone with whom the smoker has a positive relationship. It does not require professional skills, although some brief training may be helpful. The most important thing for the person providing reinforcement is to avoid responding to problems with negative comments or criticisms that decrease self-efficacy expectations and thus may deter later attempts to quit.

In a campaign to promote cessation attempts in a population of smokers, social reinforcement can be delivered in many different ways. At the most intensive level, volunteers can be trained to lead viewing groups. Health care providers can be trained to direct their clients to view and imitate televised role models. Almost all systems of interpersonal communication offer the potential for voluntary participation in an effort to encourage would-be ex-smokers to imitate media models of cessation. Thus by applying the central concepts of social learning theory, it is possible to imagine how mass and interpersonal communications can work together to provide the kinds of information that would be most helpful in stimulating the cessation of smoking. Through the use of mass media primarily to present role models and the organization of interpersonal networks to promote imitation, the unique attributes of both forms of communication can be emphasized and made to interact in the pursuit of campaign objectives. The next section provides examples of just such a combination of treatments.

Sample Studies

Pilot Study: Televised Support

McAlister (1976) combined mediated modeling and instruction with the minimum amount of organized social reinforcement and active participation required to ensure that the modeling and instruction would be learned and followed. Thus training and expert advice were communicated via television, while social reinforcement was provided by arranging for the televised messages to be received in the context of an informal self-help group under volunteer leadership. This notion was based upon the "radio forum" technique for rapidly disseminating complex innovations in developing countries (Rogers, 1983). Television was chosen as the medium of communication because it involves visual as well as aural learning modalities and thus should create a more effective learning experience than radio.

In the experiment one randomly assigned group of smokers received cessation training directly from an expert, while another watched that training over closed-circuit television. A third control group received no treatment. The training emphasized the skills and related factors corresponding to the stages of cessation. Thus the directly trained group was led through participatory experiences such as, in the later sessions, practicing responses to situations that might provoke a return to smoking. For example, participants practiced responding to offers of a cigarette or stresses and frustrations that evoke the urge to smoke in recent quitters. The television-trained group was explicitly instructed to imitate the learning experiences of the directly trained or role-model group. The viewing group was aided by an untrained volunteer with only simple print instructions. Both groups achieved promising proportions of sustained abstinence, in contrast to a control group in which no cessation was observed. In a series of later studies, videotapes of the closed-circuit presentation were shown to several more volunteer-led groups of heavy smokers, and encouraging levels of success were reported at three-month follow-ups.

This combined procedure is an example of how small-scale media may be employed creatively. The videotape instructions featured a group of smokers struggling with the task of cessation and learning to apply self-management techniques successfully, thus providing strong role models for a viewing group. The expert leader on the taped program often gave advice directly to the camera, thus explicitly cuing the viewing group to follow the same instructions that were being given to the model group. A volunteer assisting the viewing group is also directly trained and cued by what is shown on the videotape. The only responsibilities of the volunteer leader are to provide social reinforcement and to encourage participants in the viewing group to engage in discussion and to practice imitating what was seen on the videotape. In this way nearly all of the functions that require experience or expertise are provided by the televised instruction, while the volunteer leader can concentrate on the relatively simple task of providing support and encouragement.

Community Experiment: The North Karelia Project

This same notion can be put into practice in the mass media by broadcasting televised modeling and instruction to groups of smokers interested in learning how to break the habit. Puska, Koskela,

McAlister, et al. (1979) report a first test of this notion in an ambitious nationwide program in Finland. From national surveys the authors estimated that 30,000-40,000 smokers actively participated, most viewing with their families present. About 10,000 ex-smokers attributed at least one year of nonsmoking to the television series. Approximately a year after the first broadcast, the television series was again shown on Finnish television. National surveys found that about 20,000 more smokers attributed at least three months of nonsmoking to their viewing and involvement in the televised smoking cessation program. It is, of course, impossible to determine how many of these individuals would have stopped smoking spontaneously over the same time period. But it seems safe to conclude that between 2% and 4% of Finland's smokers achieved moderately sustained cessation (measured as three months or more) at least partly as a result of the television series.

The costs of producing and broadcasting the television series were extraordinarily low. Only about $10,000 was required for the original two-camera studio production, minimal editing, broadcasting, mailings, publicity, and professional involvement. For the Finnish series a cost-effectiveness of about $1 for each new ex-smoker has been estimated.

North Karelia is a county in Finland with approximately 180,000 residents. In that area, as part of a broader program to reduce cardiovascular disease, a system of interpersonal communication was established to promote attention to and imitation of the televised role models (Puska et al., 1986). The network recorded 805 volunteers from 16 municipalities who received training that included instruction on social reinforcement to be carried out in connection with the televised role-model programs. These municipal volunteers were given brief self-help booklets with content corresponding to the television broadcasts and were taught to distribute those booklets especially to smokers, to encourage people to "follow the program," and to make follow-up contacts to provide support and encouragement. Specific verbal skills were demonstrated. The volunteers were emphatically instructed to avoid negative critical responses to persons who were not interested or who tried to quit, but failed.

In a follow-up survey of the volunteers, more than half of the respondents reported influencing quit attempts and nearly that many reported that their contacts had created sustained cessation. The survey group reported a total of approximately 500 quitters. It is reasonable to estimate that 1-2% of the smokers quit in connection with this activity.

Several cross-sectional and longitudinal evaluative studies were conducted in connection with the different broadcast series between 1978 and 1982. The results consistently show higher rates of cessation in North Karelia than in the rest of the country. Although there are a number of other factors that might explain this local trend, organized social reinforcement, combined with mass media role models, was certainly an important part of the broader process of change. In 1972 and 1977, a larger proportion of residents of North Karelia reported smoking than did residents of Finland as a whole. By 1982 a comparative cross-sectional survey found less evidence of smoking in random blood samples from residents of that part of Finland.

Demonstration Program: Houston

In autumn of 1985 and again in 1986, combined role-model and community-reinforcement campaigns were conducted in Houston. The media components consisted of coproductions organized by the University of Texas Health Science Center and included the most widely viewed local television station and one of the two local newspapers. The stories were carried on television as part of early morning news, with 18 three-minute broadcasts centered on a quit day (November 21, the date of the American Cancer Society's Great American Smoke-Out) and followed three months later by a half-hour follow-up. The program followed ten role models, half from minority groups, who actually attempted to quit a few days ahead of schedule to allow for production time. The role models were videotaped in group counseling with a psychologist (C. DiClemente) and at home, work, shopping, or leisure as they enacted specific skills. The television news announcers specifically asked smoking viewers to imitate the models, among whom more than half were successful at the follow-up broadcasts. Corresponding newspaper announcements (using space donated by the Houston newspaper) featured role-model behaviors, behavioral instructions, self-tests, and motivational statements to sustain striving.

A community system to encourage role-model observation and imitation was established with minimal resources (about two people working for two to three months). One major system was that of retail drug and grocery merchants, whose employees received brief training on how to hand out encouragement along with brief viewing guides. Public schools were also involved, with teachers receiving very brief group training and distributing materials to promote role-model observation and imitation for students to take home. Large employers, unions, and fraternal organizations also received print materials and group presentations promoting the program. The consistent message was that interested smokers should be encouraged to observe and imitate the models from the television and newspapers. Approximately 250,000 pledge cards and program viewing guides were distributed in these ways, with another 1,340,000 distributed through the newspaper and 270,000 through commercial newsletters.

A follow-up survey three months after the quit date found that almost a third of smokers had seen the television programs. Among those viewers, more than 10% reported sustained cessation (three months or more) in smoking. Overall, more than 3% of all smokers in Houston reported that they gave up smoking during the campaign period (it is difficult to compare these results to the 7% quit rate from the Great American Smoke-Out, measured after only three days). The survey found a relatively high participation rate among Blacks and lower-income groups. The estimated effect in percentage terms appears small, but the absolute number of quitters was in the range of 20,000-40,000. The programs cost approximately $100,000 each year, provided by grants to the university from private sources. The yield is difficult to estimate, but benefits of cessation include on average of at least one or two years of life and medical costs averaging at least $1,000. Thus the return could be in the tens of thousands of years of life, with cost savings in the health sector of at least $5 million, with a 75% discount for inflation over twenty years.

Conclusion

The campaigns described above were explicitly designed to apply the social learning principles of modeling and reinforcement. They also illustrate three stages in action research: small-scale "laboratory" studies, community experiments, and large-scale demonstration research. The first study demonstrated that with appropriate minimal interpersonal reinforcement, a televised program can be as effective as direct behavioral counseling. The second set of studies in Finland demonstrated a national media campaign and experimentally investigated the extent to which an organized community reinforcement can enhance its effects. The third study in Houston provided case studies of how social learning concepts can be applied in the metropolitan United States and what degree of impact can be achieved.

In every case, the same basic theoretical principles were applied to create interactive mass and interpersonal communication components. The results consistently show a modest but meaningful campaign impact, demonstrating the utility of social learning theory in the development of public health communications for smoking cessation. The basic campaign approach has been employed by others, with similar degrees of success where modeling and reinforcement are appropriately employed (Flay, 1987b). Our own current research is investigating the extent to which the same approach can be employed in broadly oriented campaigns to modify other health behaviors such as alcohol and drug abuse, use of preventive services, diet and exercise, and behaviors increasing risk of AIDS or other sexually transmitted diseases (Ramirez & McAlister, in press).

14

Channel Effectiveness in Development Communication Programs

ROBERT C. HORNIK

The consensus is unmistakable: Mass media channels may be effective for creating awareness and providing knowledge, and perhaps for setting agendas; however, when it comes to persuasion to produce behavior change, face-to-face channels are essential. The derived implication is that it is foolhardy to organize a public communication program (whether to encourage seat belt use in the United States or adoption of agricultural fertilizers in Kenya) without organizing a face-to-face channel to complement mass media channels. Many of the chapters in this volume explicitly or implicitly support this proposition.

This is a deeply satisfying view for those who see debates about communication channels as a competition between human beings and machines and are quite pleased to see the value of human contact certified. However, no matter how satisfying the reaffirmation, both the consensus and the implication may be wrong, and often lead public communication program planners down mistaken paths.

This chapter examines the underlying logic and the evidence that support this communication channel hypothesis. Particular attention is paid to problems of its application in less developed countries, where organizing face-to-face channels on a large scale is often difficult. The potential for influencing behavior change through mass media alone is a special focus. Fresh illustrative evidence comes from a recent health communication program in Swaziland.

The Conventional Framework

Conventional Propositions
and Assumptions About Channel Effects

There are two major strands of research that address issues of channel competition. There is an older tradition of educational research, stimulated by the availability of technologies (such as television) with potential as teaching substitutes, that compared learning outcomes for students taught by one medium versus another. A typical early study would compare a live instructor with a televised version of the same lecture. Studies like these rarely showed significant differences and led to a recognition that little of the variance in learning is due to the technology carrying the message per se (Chu & Schramm, 1967; Schramm, 1977).

The second and dominant strand of research fits within the field of diffusion of innovations (see Rogers, 1983). Among the major elements of the diffusion framework is an assumption that adoption of an innovation occurs through a process of stages over time.

> The innovation-decision process is the process through which an individual . . . passes from first knowledge of an innovation, to forming an attitude toward the innovation, to a decision to adopt or reject, to implementation of the new idea, and to confirmation of this decision. (Rogers, 1983, p. 165)

Real-life applications, often in agriculture, have been the motivating concern for diffusion research. Thus once the stages were differentiated, a natural early question was whether or not the influence of particular channels varied with the stage in the innovation-decision process. For example, if someone were in the earlier phases, might he or she respond to information/influence from one channel, but in a later stage tend to turn to an alternative channel? A good deal of research has examined this question; again, the results are summarized by Rogers (1983):

> Mass media channels are relatively more important at the knowledge stage and interpersonal channels are relatively more important at the persuasion stage in the innovation-decision process. (p. 199)

The empirical base for this conclusion is perhaps more equivocal than suggested by this straightforward declaration. Concerns about the quality of evidence are presented in a subsequent section of this chapter. However, the commonsense logic of the conclusion has led to its ready acceptance. A list of justifications includes the following:

(1) Interpersonal channels "provide a two-way exchange of information . . . [to] secure clarification or additional information" (Rogers, 1983, p. 198).

(2) "Interpersonal contacts, the reasoning runs, are homophilic [between people who are similar] and therefore credible; consequently the messages they deliver should be credible" (Chaffee, 1982, p. 61).

(3) Changing important practices is hard, especially for an isolated individual. Adoption of an innovation will be far easier if interpersonal contacts make it clear that others around one are changing also. For most members of a community, adoption of a new practice is social behavior, reflective of reference group norms, rather than individual behavior, reflective of personal knowledge and attitude about the innovation.

(4) Interpersonal channels have the power to overcome selective exposure: It is easier to command attention to a message through face-to-face communication than through mass communication.

Authors often admit that mass media do have important roles as part of diffusion processes: Mass media reach large audiences, they can diffuse new information efficiently, well-produced messages may attract attention, and distortion of messages can be minimized. However, even while the utility of mass media is accepted, there is a nearly universal assumption that they must be complemented with organized interpersonal channels if effective diffusion is to occur.

Attitudes and actions are most influenced by mass communications when the latter are linked with, and reinforced by, agents of change in the field. . . . The performance of broadcast media in the fields of development . . . depends on . . . the extent to which these development efforts are linked with agents of change in the field. (Katz & Wedell, 1977, p. 184)

Challenges to the Conventional Framework

Most of the justifications for the predominance of interpersonal channels and the need for complementing media channels with interpersonal ones seem to be common sense. Nonetheless, a measured theoretical critique might find them wanting. Substantial concerns include the importance of homophily, the confusion of the need for social support with the need for change agents, and the legitimacy of the assumption of resistance to innovation. However, while the theoretical critique is intriguing, the most serious criticism is practical; from the point of view of cost, of feasibility, and of sustainability, organizing an effective face-to-face network is rarely possible. The following paragraphs describe the theoretical issues first and then turn to the practical critique.

Homophily. Chaffee (1982) doubts the universal equation of homophily with credibility. Perceived expertise, for example, may lend greater credibility to a mass media channel than to some interpersonal ones.

Social support. Although one may accept that social support is crucial in the adoption of some new practices, that does not necessarily translate to a requirement that outsiders organize a network of agents. Interpersonal communication networks will operate naturally, thus creating a social process around diffusion whether or not there is a paid agent to serve as interpersonal communicator. Appropriate treatment of childhood illness is a frequent topic among mothers of young children, whether or not there is a health educator there to lead the discussion.

Resistance to innovation. The assumption that individuals are typically slow to change and resistant to innovations that would substantially benefit them may also not survive close examination. If individuals already perceive and are actively trying to solve a problem, information promising a solution may be accepted regardless of the source. If information solves no perceived need, it may be rejected regardless of the source. There is good evidence from agricultural studies, for example, that farmers are often quite responsive to factors of price and risk, and that they readily adopt new technologies that provide clear benefits (see Benito, 1976; Schultz, 1964).

Effects versus effectiveness. Despite these concerns, it must be admitted that a dispute about the theoretical legitimacy of the justifications for combining interpersonal with mass communication is inevitably going to be unconvincing in the general case. A responsive, expert, hardworking, intelligent, and empathic field agent working with a potential adopter and his or her social network is surely better than any imaginable mass media-only diffusion system. The problem is that framing the dispute solely in theoretical terms is misleading. The competition between channels is largely a practical dispute, or at least, so it would seem to someone whose experience is largely in less developed countries. If there were a supply of responsive, expert, hardworking field agents who could be recruited, paid for and supported in the field, then there would be no reason to consider mass media. The problem is not whether one channel is better than the other in the abstract; the problem is to what extent one or the other can be realized in practice.

Too often, arguments about channels are framed as if reaching the entire audience with messages as frequently as would be needed are of no moment; reach and frequency (see Alcalay & Taplin, chap. 5, this volume) are assumed. It is as if the only criterion for choosing channels is an answer to the question, Which channel has greater effects alone or in combination with what other channels? But an *effects* competition between channels is different from an *effectiveness* competition between channels. The channel that has greater effects in the laboratory, when feasibility can be ignored, may not be the most effective in the field.

Planners must focus first on the practical problems of reaching the target audience as frequently as needed. That is where most programs founder, not on theoretically inappropriate choices of channels. The real questions are, What channels might be paid for with available resources? What channels can be effectively managed and implemented given available talent? What channels can be sustained over the long run? Only after hard-nosed answers are provided for these cost/feasibility questions does it become reasonable to consider relative effectiveness questions.

Organizing a field structure of interpersonal agents involves recruiting, training, supervising, paying salaries, and providing field support (office space, transportation, travel expenses). In agricultural extension some authorities would suggest 50-100 farm families per agent as an effective maximum ratio, while some successful pilot nutrition education projects have required an agent for each 100 families. There are few countries that would be able to satisfy even one-tenth of these requirements (Hornik, 1988, pp. 48-55, 118-137).

A recent review of many programs in agricultural and nutrition/health communication suggests that few countries in the developing world have been able to mount large-scale, long-term programs depending on organized face-to-face channels. The reality is that face-to-face

information distribution channels are typically weak. They may reach a small proportion of the potential audience and they carry information that is either dated or unresponsive to the needs of the audience. Agricultural extension agents are too few, have too little research and logistical support, and are too rarely rewarded for successful work with farmers. Health and nutrition education is most often a burdensome additional activity for the predominantly curative health services; ambitious outreach programs atrophy over time. (Hornik, 1988, pp. 157-158)

Evidence About Channels

If it is so difficult to mount such programs, why is the literature so confident as to the necessity for joining media and interpersonal channels for success? And why is it so adamant that media are useful only at the awareness stage, while organized interpersonal channels are crucial at the persuasion and decision stages? Three explanations are worth some attention: sentimental preference, some confusion between the role of organized field agents and that of naturally operating social networks, and too ready inferences from a large but equivocal research base.

SENTIMENTAL PREFERENCES VERSUS EMPIRICAL EVIDENCE

The first lines of this chapter referred to the great pleasure most commentators have felt in discovering the "part played by people in the flow of mass communication" (Katz & Lazarsfeld, 1955), even when the evidence is unclear. Chaffee and others have noted that the central role ascribed to personal influence by Katz and Lazarsfeld is inconsistent with much of the evidence in their landmark book. In the field study in Decatur, Illinois, respondents credited mass media at least as often as personal sources as influences on consumer purchases, motion picture choices, and fashion preferences. Winett (1986, pp. 59-82) offers a similar critique of inferences by Rogers and Kincaid (1981) that social networks played a more central role than mass media in influencing adoption of contraception among members of Korean Mothers' Clubs.

Despite the equivocal evidence, scholars accepted the underlying notion readily. The concept of opinion leadership, of a reliance by individuals on their social networks to make sense out of information received from mass media, became bedrock of the sociology of mass communication. It fit with an intuitively powerful as well as subjectively preferable notion of individuals (and social networks) as users of mass media rather than as pawns of mass media.

CONFUSION BETWEEN ROLES OF
NATURAL SOCIAL NETWORKS AND FIELD AGENT NETWORKS

While sentiment in part explains the attractiveness of the concept of the importance of social networks, there is also some evidence that supports the concept. Perhaps geographical studies provide the strongest evidence that social networks matter in adoption decisions. Lawrence Brown's book *Innovation Diffusion* (1981) shows how important geographical proximity (a surrogate measure of social proximity) is to the pattern of spread of innovations, such as urban air conditioners or tea-raising technology in Kenya. Wright (1986) summarizes other supporting evidence. However, the application of this evidence relies on a crucial distinction: Evidence that social networks matter as individuals make adoption decisions is not equivalent to evidence that people must encounter trained field agents to make those decisions. Nor is it equivalent to evidence that mass media are ineffective at the persuasion stage, nor that media are effective only if combined with an organized field agent structure.

EXTENSIVE BUT EQUIVOCAL EVIDENCE ABOUT FIELD AGENTS

The bulk of the media versus interpersonal literature fits within the diffusion research tradition. While there are hundreds of studies that led Rogers to the conclusion already cited (media for awareness, interpersonal channels for persuasion), they apparently share a common research paradigm. In general they relied on the reports of adopters recalling both the occasion and the source at each stage of the innovation-decision process. The usual result was that people recalled some use of both interpersonal and mass media sources at the earliest (awareness) stage of the innovation adoption process but then moved toward reporting heavy reliance on interpersonal sources at the persuasion and later stages. These results are consistently found, but their consistency does not guarantee that inferences about the relative potential for media and for interpersonal channels are correct.

There are two central challenges. First, self-report is only an approximate measure of actual influences on, or occurrences of, behavior. (See, for example, the extensive review of comparisons between self-report and behavioral measures of the same phenomena by Bernard, Killworth, Kronenfeld, & Sailer, 1984.) Surely such reports are a reflection not only of what the innovation-decision process was like but of the demands associated with the research context. Respondents are not used to reproducing an influence history that requires them to recognize discrete stages in a process and articulate often single sources of influence at each stage. If the influence of mass media took a subtle form it might not be reported readily. Perhaps a particularly credible media spokesman provided the first awareness of a new seed variety, but at the same time led the farmer to be quite favorably disposed to the variety—nonetheless, the media might be reported as the source of awareness without being clearly perceived as persuasive as well. Similarly, if multiple sources were all around an individual, the tendency to report a single source might bias results toward a conventional persuasive source (e.g., an extension agent, the nurse in the clinic, a neighbor) rather than an unconventional source like radio.

A second challenge is that many of these studies investigate mass media as sources of information without first establishing that a medium could have been a source. Nonreliance on mass media may simply reflect a lack of exposure to any media or a lack of adoption-relevant persuasive content on mass media, not an intrinsic channel failing (see Flora, Maccoby, & Farquhar, chap. 10, and Rice & Foote, chap. 7, this volume). Studies reviewed elsewhere suggest that neither most agriculture nor most health broadcasting provides content consistently useful for the intended audiences (Hornik, 1988). In many countries there is little development broadcasting altogether. Where there is broadcasting it often is done without detailed knowledge of the problems audiences are trying to solve, and it may incorporate only generalized "good" messages rather than messages meant to persuade listeners to adopt specific behaviors, such as using fertilizer versus using this particular fertilizer on that crop in this amount on that schedule, or choosing to have children you are able to clothe and feed versus going to the local clinic on Wednesday to obtain an IUD.

If the persuasive content simply is not available through the mass media (and thus the respondents may report that media are not influential), that would not justify any blanket rejection of mass media as a persuasive mechanism. The question would still remain: If the organizational failings that lead to irrelevant content were remedied, might not mass media be persuasive without the necessity for incorporating field agents?

However, suggesting that existing evidence does not justify the conventional wisdom is not the same as saying it justifies the reverse conclusion. An inference that mass media alone can affect behavior awaits positive evidence. What would constitute positive evidence?

Formally, any evidence that a campaign using mass media exclusively achieved some behavior change would be sufficient. Yet, as a practical matter, one would want stronger, comparative evidence. While commentators have declared that mass media alone cannot achieve behavior change, few really mean it in an absolute sense, one supposes. The argument is about *comparative* power—the real hypothesis is that media alone would be much less effective than an interpersonal channel in achieving change. Then persuasive evidence would be comparative and would consider issues of reach as well as effects; ideally, it would show relative power to achieve effects, relative ability (given available resources) to reach a mass audience, and relative effort and costs to conduct either type of campaign.

Evidence would need to be drawn from communication programs that attempt to use both mass media *and* interpersonal channels. The programs would have to use channels well by providing useful and actionable messages understandably and frequently. The programs should operate under realistic and large-scale conditions, allowing some estimate of the operational reach of alternative channels. Ideally, channels would be experimentally assigned in an elegant two-factor design; in practice, if some members of the audience were exclusively exposed to each channel and others to both channels, it might be sufficient.

Alternative Views of Channel Effects

The prior discussion has emphasized the centrality of feasibility issues in considering channel choices. That is the appropriate focus of new attention, and will be the major question for the study to be reported below. Nonetheless, the framework of considering the effects issue also merits some additional development. It appears that there are at least five viable alternative hypotheses about these relationships between mass media and interpersonal channels. The first two hypotheses fall within the conventional wisdom: They do not admit to any effect of mass media in the absence of a complementary field agent. The other three are challenges to the conventional wisdom in that they allow such an effect. These five alternative formulations are presented in the following paragraphs and in Figure 14.1. The independent variables are exposure to messages advocating the adoption of a new behavior, either through mass media or through a field agent.

The extreme view of the conventional wisdom hypothesis (some might claim it is a straw man) says that if an agent is present there will tend to be an effect, but that the presence or absence of mass media would be irrelevant (agent effects only hypothesis; see Figure 14.1A). An alternative version of this conventional wisdom would allow mass media to have an effect, but only when there is an active field agent (agent necessary for media effects hypothesis; see Figure 14.1B).

A separate formulation hypothesizes that both mass media and field agents realize change but there is no interaction between them (additive hypothesis; Figure 14.1C). The fourth formulation assumes that both channels have effects but are functional substitutes for each other. A member of the audience will change maximally in the presence of either one channel or the other (substitution hypothesis; Figure 14.1D). Finally, it is possible that both channels have independent effects, but if both are present there is a positive interaction (reinforcement hypothesis; Figure 14.1E).

Some skepticism is justified, then, about the consensus concerning the relative roles of mass media and interpersonal communication in the persuasion stages of the adoption process, and about the resulting inference that field agents must complement mass media if the latter are to be useful. The essential points are these:

(1) Adoption may indeed be a social process, but that is not equivalent to requiring that outsiders organize a field agent system to stimulate that process.

(2) Field agents, if there were enough of them and they practiced as textbooks say they should, would likely be an excellent communication channel; however, there are few countries and few development sectors within countries that can organize and pay for such an agent network on a large scale and over the long term. Channel choice criteria include relative costs, feasibility, and sustainability as well as relative effects.

(3) Evidence that people rely on mass media only in the awareness stage and are not affected in later stages of the adoption process is open to challenge, both on methodological grounds (studies depend on respondent recall) and on substantive grounds (persuasive content is often unavailable on mass media).

(4) There are five alternative hypotheses that relate mass media and interpersonal channels to behavioral outcomes. Additive, substitution, and reinforcement effects hypotheses challenge the two hypotheses that fit within the conventional framework, namely, the agent effects only and agent necessary for mass media effects hypotheses.

The next section summarizes portions of a recent study from Swaziland. The study permits an examination of many of the issues raised in this chapter, including reach of channels, relative effects of channels in producing practice change, and the fit of observed data to alternative effects models. The cost/feasibility argument, which is the centerpiece of the challenge to the conventional wisdom, is addressed through combining the answers to the relative reach and relative effects analyses.

Channel Effects in the
Swaziland Health Communication Program

In the African nation of Swaziland, the government implemented an intense public health communication campaign directed toward the treatment of diarrheal disease in children, beginning in September 1984 and continuing through March 1985.[1] Oral rehydration therapy (ORT) holds the promise of substantially ameliorating one of the chief causes of infant mortality in the developing world—dehydration from diarrheal disease. Many current deaths from this disease are avoidable, but realization of this goal faces substantial obstacles. While some of these obstacles are technical or economic, there is also a substantial educational component: Among other things, parents must learn when and how to use rehydration solutions (see Rice & Foote, chap. 7, this volume).

Beginning in April 1984, campaign staff prepared radio programming for broadcast on established development programs on the national radio system, printed materials (including a flyer with mixing instructions and posters for display at health clinics and other points), and conducted workshops to train much of the country's health staff (as well as other extension personnel and local volunteers) in the treatment of diarrheal disease. Local volunteers and other information-distribution personnel were given yellow flags to display outside of their homes to indicate that they could help with diarrheal disease treatment.

By the start of the campaign, a radio workshop had produced 20 radio programs (15 minutes long), 46 radio inserts (5 minutes long), and 22 spot announcements. Throughout the campaign, 5 or 6 programs were broadcast each week on the national radio station in addition to several daily spot announcements. A total of 18 training workshops had been held for health personnel, covering about one-third of the profes-

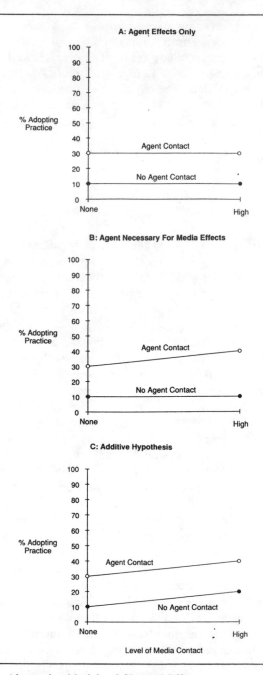

Figure 14.1. Alternative Models of Channel Effects

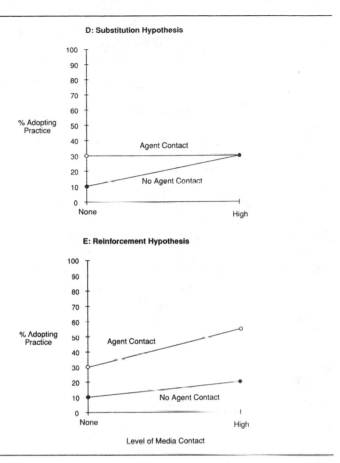

Figure 14.1. Continued

sional staff of public health facilities. Secondary training activities reached additional outreach workers. Also, 260,000 flyers and 7,500 posters were printed and distributed.

The campaign focused on a number of objectives, but for this chapter the most interesting is the acceptance of the use of home-mixed water-sugar-salt solution (SSS) as an ORT treatment for diarrheal disease. The overall evaluation of the program relied on data from a number of sources; here the relevant data are derived from interviews with randomly selected national samples of about 430 caretakers (largely mothers) of children less than 5 years old. Surveys were done both before and after the campaign, but the data reported here are almost entirely from the post-campaign survey.

Channel Exposure Variables

This was a short campaign: six months from initiation of the technical assistance to the first campaign broadcast, and then seven months of information-diffusion activity. Nonetheless, it reached a large proportion of the Swazi nation; nearly 85% of all homesteads were substantially exposed to at least one of the campaign's channels.

Radio listening. This 0-5-point scale (called LISTEN) represented likely exposure to diarrheal disease messages over the radio. An individual received one point for each of the following conditions: (1) Her family owned a working radio, (2) she reported listening to the radio, (3) she reported listening to at least two of the three programs on which the messages were inserted, (4) she reported listening to at least two of the three programs in the previous week, and (5) she reported remembering the content of the broadcast for at least two of the programs. About 20% of the sample achieved scores of 4 or 5 (intense exposure), another 40% were substantially exposed (3), 12% were somewhat exposed (2), and the rest were either minimally exposed (1) or not exposed at all (0).

This scale does not depend on self-reported exposure to the campaign (i.e., "Did you hear any messages about ORT?") but on self-reported exposure to the channels on which the messages were known to have been broadcast. The indirectness of this measure avoided major problems in making inferences about causal direction. Typically, when the outcome is a behavior and the measure of exposure is recall of messages about the behavior, one is never sure whether an observed correlation between exposure and behavior reflects the effects of exposure on behavior or the effects of behavior on the tendency to recall exposure. The present approach does, however, risk producing a lower-than-true estimate of the effects of exposure, since it is only an indirect measure of message exposure.

Interpersonal channels. Three interpersonal sources were expected to be carriers of diarrheal disease control messages: (1) health care professionals at the clinics and hospitals, (2) rural health motivators and other health extension agents who were likely to visit individual homesteads, and (3) individuals in communities who were given some SSS training and who displayed yellow flags to indicate that they could provide assistance. This last group may sometimes overlap with the second group.

Estimating exposure to such personal sources of information is, like exposure to radio, largely a matter of seeing what opportunities individuals have had for such exposures. The most common opportunity was at the clinic, when caretakers brought their children under 5 years old for treatment of diarrhea. Caretakers are said to have had exposure if their clinic visit included all of the following elements: (1) contact with a clinic nurse, (2) during the previous six months, (3) for the treatment of the last case of diarrheal disease for a child under 5, and (4) treatment with rehydration solution for this case. Using that criterion, about 22% of the sample had high probability of contact with a nurse about campaign messages (called CLINIC).

In addition, 42% of the sample reported home visits either by the rural health motivator or by another health worker. However, diarrheal treatment was reported only rarely, by 16% of the visited homesteads and 7% of the entire sample, as the topic of such visits, so only the 7% were assumed to be exposed to diarrheal disease messages through this channel. The last personal source checked was the one explicitly developed by the campaign: the yellow flag volunteer. Productive educational contact with these people was not common. While half the sample reported knowing that a yellow flag volunteer had something to do with health, and one-third reported that someone "around here" had such a flag, only one respondent in eight reported personal contact with a volunteer. Virtually all of those people who had personal contact with a volunteer said that they learned about SSS from them. There was some overlap between the two types of outreach contact (health extension workers and yellow flag volunteers), thus a total of 16% of the sample reported out-of-clinic contact (called OUTREACH).

In total, 35% of the sample appeared to have had some sort of face-to-face contact about campaign messages (CLINIC or OUTREACH). In contrast, more than 60% of the sample was substantially exposed to the messages over radio (LISTEN).

Water-sugar-salt use. For this analysis, the dependent variable combines self-reported prior use of a rehydration solution with evidence about knowledge of how to mix it. Caretakers were asked, "Have you ever used water-sugar-salt to treat your child's diarrhea?" Separately they were asked (if they claimed that they knew) to describe the formula for mixing the solution. The correct answer was 8 bottle caps of sugar, ½ bottle cap of salt, and 1 liter of water. If they said they had

TABLE 14.1 Results from Regressing Dependent Variable of Knowledgeable Use of SSS, on Control and Channel Variables (N = 431)

Predictors	Mean	S.D.	Cumulative R^2 (%)	Coefficients B	Beta
Control variables					
interviewer	nr	nr	2.2	nr	nr
education	nr	nr	2.7	.118	.069
Channel variables			7.9		
interpersonal					
OUTREACH	.17	.37		.201	.149
CLINIC	.22	.41		.181	.150
mass media					
LISTEN	2.49	1.51		.034	.102
Constant				.298	

NOTE: nr = not relevant.

ever used the solution and knew the correct amounts of two of the three ingredients, they were considered knowledgeable ever-users and were coded 1; otherwise they were coded as 0. About 42% of the sample satisfied this criterion after the campaign (called KNOWLEDGEABLE USE). This can be compared with only 15% who did so before the campaign, clear evidence of the campaign's overall power.[2]

Control variables. In addition, the analysis makes use of two sets of control variables. The first are dummy variables representing interviewers (called INTERVIEWER). There are statistically significant differences among interviewers in the responses they obtained about diarrheal disease treatment. Also, to lessen some of the differences in treatment associated with socioeconomic status that also might be associated with access to channels, respondent's education (coded in years, called EDUC) was also controlled.

Estimation of Channel Effects

The relationships of control variables and channel variables to rehydration therapy use are summarized in a regression equation, shown in Table 14.1. The control variables account for 2.7% of the variance; the channel variables account for an additional 5.2%. These are relatively small amounts of variance accounted for, but the picture of effects of channels takes on a different and more impressive view when we focus elsewhere.

For the issues of this chapter the most interesting results are the unstandardized coefficients (Bs) of the three channel variables.[3] A convenient interpretation of the unstandardized coefficients is that they represent the number of units of change on the dependent variable associated with each unit of change on the particular independent variable. Respondents who were one unit apart on the OUTREACH variable would be, on the average, .2 units apart on the KNOWL-EDGEABLE USE variable. Concretely, those who had contact with an outreach worker were about 20% more likely than those who had no contact to have ever used the solution and to use at least two ingredients correctly.

Contact with a clinic nurse (CLINIC) has a coefficient of similar magnitude: Those with contact were about 18% more likely to have used the solution than those without contact. At first glance, radio use (LISTEN) appears to be less related (its unstandardized coefficient is .034). However, while both OUTREACH and CLINIC are 0-1 variables, LISTEN varies from 0 to 5. For each point respondents report higher on the LISTEN scale they are likely to go up 3.4% in KNOWL-EDGEABLE USE. Thus, contrasting respondents at the lowest and highest level of the LISTEN scale, the expected difference in KNOWL-EDGEABLE USE is 5 × 3.4, or 17%. Again, this is of a similar magnitude to the effects of each of the face to face channels.

Taken at face value, this would suggest that exposure to any of three channels more or less equally affected the probability of use of the SSS. This result needs to be combined with the earlier information about relative exposure to each of the channels: 16% were exposed to a yellow flag volunteer and 22% to a clinic nurse, but more than 60% were substantially exposed to radio. Considering the comparable effects among channels but great disparity in reach, it appears that radio is the channel of the greatest power. This result stands in sharp contradiction to the conventional wisdom. The combined measure of reach (exposure) and effects (change in behavior and knowledge) can be considered a measure of channel effectiveness.

Table 14.2 presents the combined measure of effectiveness more clearly, where the proportion exposed to a channel (its reach) is multiplied by the unstandardized coefficient (its estimated effectiveness, per unit of exposure) and the number of exposure units difference between those counted as unexposed and those considered exposed. The result-

TABLE 14.2 Combined Effects of Reach and Effectiveness of Each Channel
           on Knowledgeable Use of SSS

Channel	Percentage Exposed	Beta Coefficient	Points Shifted	Channel Effectiveness
CLINIC	22	.181	1.0	4.0
OUTREACH	16	.201	1.0	3.2
LISTEN	60	.034	4.0[a]	8.2

a. Point shift between nonlisteners and the average score of those considered substantially exposed.

ing product is labeled *channel effectiveness*. In this analysis, the radio channel (LISTEN) effectiveness score is about double the scores of the alternative channels (CLINIC and OUTREACH). The channel effectiveness score may be interpreted as the average percentage change in SSS use for the sample as a whole related to each channel, given different levels of exposure or access by the target audience. The incremental effect associated with either clinic or outreach exposure was about 4% and that associated with radio exposure about 8%.[4]

Interestingly, the effects of one channel are largely independent of the effects of the other channels: There are no significant interactions among the channels. The hypothesis that best fits the data is the additive hypothesis pictured in Figure 14.1C.

Of course, given that this is only one project in one country, there is nothing conclusive to be said about the general dominance of one or another of the hypotheses. Nonetheless, these results may well reflect more generally the contrasting reach to be achieved by a mass medium versus interpersonal channels. Swaziland, with only 800,000 people, great ethnic homogeneity, and a relatively small land mass, may have found it easier to rely on interpersonal channels than would many other countries with larger populations and greater diversity.

Some Other Criteria for Choosing Channels

This study dealt with two elements appropriate to any discussion of channel choice: reach of a channel and effects of the channel. Together they are called channel effectiveness. But there are two other elements discussed earlier that are not considered here: cost, and managerial feasibility and sustainability.

The combined outcome measure might be a reasonable approximation of effectiveness, but effectiveness measures not associated with relative cost measures may be of limited use. For example, even if radio were twice as effective as an outreach channel, if its cost (such as training, salaries, and transportation) were four times as large it would not be cost-effective and not viewed with enthusiasm. Absolute cost data for each channel in this campaign are unavailable, so this analysis has to be viewed as incomplete. (See Jamison, Klees, & Wells, 1978, for a general methodology for determining cost-effectiveness and cost-benefits in education and development campaigns and for some useful case studies.)

The second missing element is managerial feasibility and sustainability. In part, the feasibility of implementing interpersonal and mass-mediated channels is captured in their relative reach. If one channel reaches the audience as intended and the other does not, that is prima facie evidence that they are differentially feasible. However, reach is also affected by other factors, including how much attention each channel was actually given. Thus judgment about managerial feasibility may require looking more carefully at the actual administrative obstacles that operate in a particular context. Such an analysis may lead one to different choices than either effectiveness or cost-effectiveness analyses would lead.

Surely, working with a centralized national radio station has to be less complex than trying to arrange for the employment, training, deployment, and supervision of a large force of change agents. However, if that management has to be done by a substantive government bureaucracy (a ministry of health or of agriculture, for example) accustomed to operating through field agents and not to managing mass communication channels, the trade-off may not be so easily judged. Using mass media in a serious way may be outside of the standard operating procedure of a particular bureaucracy, and may be rejected or may produce great strain despite its apparent cost-effectiveness.

Closely linked to managerial feasibility is the issue of sustainability. Sometimes this is framed as an issue of recurring costs. Even if financial support can be found for the first six months of operation (the Swaziland program was funded predominantly by the U.S. Agency for International Development), how are continuing operations to be funded? Will sustainability be different for different channels? Recurring costs are a large problem for programs expecting to create and maintain a large corps of field agents. They may also be a problem for programs intending to use mass media. While the per audience member cost of producing and broadcasting radio messages may be low, the absolute cost to a ministry budget may be viewed as excessive. This is the case, in particular, where a ministry is unaccustomed to using part of its hard-won funds to buy media time from commercial networks.

Just as one can think about recurring costs, one can think about the recurring management demands associated with operating a given channel. Even if enthusiasm for a program's objectives produce early effects, will it be possible to continue to operate a given channel over time? Programs that depend on volunteer field agents, for example, may do fine in the first blush of excitement, but inevitably face attrition and then a constant demand for recruiting and training. Similarly, paid field agents may trek out to visit their assigned homesteads in the first six months with great determination. However, they may find few incentives to continue when their supervisors rarely are seen, and their promotions are closely tied to the care with which in-office paperwork is completed rather than to the practice changes stimulated among clients. (For example, continued training of field agents under conditions of high turnover was a problem in the projects discussed by Rice & Foote, chap. 7, this volume.)

Mass media channels, in the abstract, face fewer logical managerial obstacles to sustainability. However, just as transplanted organs in the human body are increasingly subject to rejection, communication entities in an alien bureaucracy may find themselves always struggling for survival, with their call on national budgets always under challenge.

Thus any analysis of channel competition must not stop with measures of simple relative effects. Judgment should also reflect costs, managerial feasibility, and sustainability. A debate that focuses on effects, alone, is unproductive and even misleading for communication program planners.

Conclusion

This chapter questioned the conventional wisdom that organized field agent networks are superior to or must complement mass media broadcasts if a substantial effect on behavior is the target. It pointed to some doubts about the real-life feasibility of organizing a field agent network as well as about the conceptual underpinnings and the empirical support for that proposition; then a study whose results directly challenge the assumption was presented. As part of the process there was an explicit statement of five alternative formulations of media competition hypotheses. Both data and complementary arguments suggest that the allocation of resources among channels should reflect not only relative effects but also reach, cost, managerial feasibility, and sustainability. In many contexts those considerations will lead away from an emphasis on interpersonal channels and toward increasing reliance on mass media channels.

Most of the conceptual doubts and methodological questions have appeared elsewhere (see Chaffee, 1972, 1982; Schramm, 1977). However, the empirical study is fresh and addresses the research question more directly than much prior work. Nonetheless, it is but one study in what will need to be a longer sequence if its conclusions are to be applied more broadly.

So long as the truism—media for awareness, field agents for practice change—is accepted, and so long as communication program planners fail to admit the difficulty of organizing and sustaining such agent networks, communication programs are unlikely to succeed as motivators of behavior change. Under this logic, broadcasters set themselves the limited tasks of improving awareness and emphasizing production values, and leave the responsibility for changing practice to field agents (what Flay & Cook, chap. 8, this volume, call the "advertising paradigm").

In fact, it appears that mass media channels, without field agents, can affect behavior. However, they must be used by producers with detailed knowledge of audiences, with objectives reflecting the material possibilities for change among audiences, with enough resources to reach audiences frequently and clearly, and with the ability to coordinate with the actions of other institutions, as many of the chapters in this volume argue.

A reader ought not leave this chapter with the sense that all public communication programs operate, in fact, under the awareness only from mass media assumption, even though the literature so often declares it to be truth. Perhaps it is time that the explicit models of change both reflect what we do and admit to the possibility that it might work, and figure out just how to realize the potential. If field agent structures can be organized and are cost-effective in a particular context, that is well and good. Otherwise, the limits of what can be done through mass media alone are worth exploring.

Notes

1. The Public Health Unit and other components of the Ministry of Health carried out the campaign with technical assistance from the Academy for Educational Development under contract with the U.S. Agency for International Development. Significant financial support for the implementation came through the Combatting Childhood Communicable Disease program of the Centers for Disease Control, also under USAID funding. These implementing groups asked the Annenberg School of Communications at the University of Pennsylvania to design and supervise the implementation of a small-scale evaluation of the campaign. The full evaluation is reported by Hornik et al. (1986).

2. This choice for a dependent variable is appropriate for the points to be made in this chapter about channel effects. Without further discussion it should not be considered an appropriate criterion for project success, since someone who was considered successful under this criterion could make inappropriate use of the solution if the third ingredient was incorrect, or if the quantity used was too small.

3. All of the exposure variable coefficients represent statistically significant ($p < .01$) relationships with the dependent variable. However, while the unstandardized coefficients are unbiased when a dichotomous dependent variable is used in ordinary least squares regression (OLS), tests of their statistical significance tend to be conservative. Their sampling error tends to be larger than it ought to be (Aldrich & Nelson, 1984). Since the magnitude of the channel coefficients are of major interest, since they are all significantly different from zero even with the inflated sampling error, and since readers may be more accustomed to reading the results of ordinary least squares regression rather than technically appropriate logistic regression, the results are reported in OLS format.

4. One must be careful about making causal statements from such cross-sectional data, of course. Other unincluded variables may explain the observed covariation between any of the exposure variables and the outcome measure and call into doubt any inference about effects. Nonetheless, it is helpful to present these data, albeit tentatively, since they are so suggestive concerning the alternative channel hypotheses.

15

Prosocial Television
for Development in India

ARVIND SINGHAL
EVERETT M. ROGERS

> *Hum Log* is entertaining, socially relevant, and highly educative. It brings
> us face to face with the social realities of present-day India. (from one of
> the 400,000 *Hum Log* viewers who wrote to the Indian television system)

For 18 months in 1984-1985, the Indian television network broadcast *Hum Log* (*We People*), a soap opera designed to promote such
socially desirable behaviors as a more equal status for women and
smaller family size. The *Hum Log* television series displayed certain
qualities typical of communication campaigns. A *communication campaign* (1) intends to generate specific outcomes or effects, (2) in a
relatively large number of individuals, (3) within a specified period of
time, and (4) through an organized set of communication activities
(Rogers & Storey, 1987, p. 821; see also the Preface to this volume).
Each of the messages in a campaign should ideally be interrelated and
should contribute toward the campaign objectives. *Hum Log* (1) was
intended to generate such specific effects as a more equal status for
women, (2) among its approximately 60 million viewers, (3) during,
and after, the 18 months of its television broadcast, and (4) through an
organized set of communication messages transmitted by Doordarshan,
the Indian government television system.

Our research on *Hum Log* provided a unique opportunity for a better
understanding of such human communication theories as social learn-

Authors' Note: Our research in India was funded by the Rockefeller Foundation. The
present chapter draws upon Singhal and Rogers (1988a, 1988b) and Singhal, Doshi,
Rogers, and Rahman (1988).

ing (Bandura, 1977b) and parasocial interaction (Horton & Wohl, 1956). Our study is also unique in that the main component of the communication campaign was a television soap opera, one of the most popular genres of television programming in the United States, Latin America, and many other nations (Rogers & Antola, 1985; Whetmore & Kielwasser, 1983).

Our research on *Hum Log* centered on seven research questions:

(1) To what extent did the television series reach a large audience of viewers?

(2) To what extent did the content of the television series actually feature socially desirable norms?

(3) To what extent did viewers identify with prosocial models of behavior from the soap opera?

(4) To what extent did viewers' letters provide useful feedback about the television series?

(5) To what extent did parasocial interaction take place between the viewers and the characters in the soap opera?

(6) To what extent were the intended effects of *Hum Log* achieved, such as increased awareness and change in attitudes and behaviors about the status of women, and promotion of smaller family size norms?

(7) What are some of the indirect impacts of *Hum Log*?

We also compare our findings from the study of *Hum Log* to parallel experiences with entertainment-education messages in the United States and in Spanish-speaking Latin America, where in 1986 a rock music song was utilized to promote sexual abstinence among teenagers.

Entertainment Versus Educational Television

The U.S. mass media generally separate entertainment messages from educational messages. The commercial television networks broadcast predominantly entertainment programs because this content achieves higher audience ratings, in order to maximize advertising incomes.

On a few occasions, U.S. television networks broadcast programs to raise public consciousness and to inform the audience about a social issue, usually a liberal cause (Breed & DeFoe, 1982; Cantor, 1979; McGhee, 1980; Montgomery, 1981, 1989). For example, the highly viewed 1977 ABC miniseries *Roots*, and its sequel *Roots: The Next Generation*, focused on Black people's struggle for freedom from slavery and for equality with whites. Norman Lear's popular CBS television program in the 1970s, *All in the Family*, called attention to ethnic prejudice through a highly bigoted character, Archie Bunker. Lear, by mixing humor with bigotry, intended to parody ethnic prejudice. Presumably, to the extent that viewers recognized the ridiculous nature of Archie's prejudices, they realized their own prejudices, and changed them due to the uncomfortable self-confrontation. However, the prosocial objectives of *Roots* and *All in the Family* were by-products of television shows primarily designed to attract large audiences. Studies of the audience effects of *Roots* and *Roots: The Next Generation* as well as *All in the Family* showed that these American television programs increased audience awareness of racial and ethnic issues (Ball-Rokeach, Grube, & Rokeach, 1981; Tate & Surlin, 1976; Vidmar & Rokeach, 1974; Wander, 1977). Some already-prejudiced viewers, however, were reinforced in their prejudice (Vidmar & Rokeach, 1974).

Certain mass media organizations in Third World countries recently have questioned the division of entertainment versus educational content, and have utilized television soap operas to promote development goals. (The development of Third World countries consists of activities, mainly by governments, to advance the socioeconomic well-being of a nation's people.) In the 1980s, television systems expanded tremendously in such Third World nations as China, India, Mexico, and Indonesia. The Third World countries' share of the world population of TV sets has increased steadily, from 5% in 1965, to 10% in 1975, to 20% in 1984, to 35% in 1987.[1] During the eight-year period from 1980 to 1987, the number of television sets in China increased 15 times; in India, the number increased 10 times.[2] Television now reaches an audience of at least 550 million of China's population (50%), about 80 million in India (10%), and about 70 million in Mexico (87%). These millions of new television viewers provide a tremendous potential for development communication.

However, neither private-commercial nor government television has been utilized effectively to promote literacy, improve nutrition, limit family size, or increase productivity, because television content in the Third World is dominated by entertainment programs, including imported reruns from the United States, such as *I Love Lucy*, *Kojak*, and *Dallas*. These entertainment programs contribute little toward the development goals of Third World nations in Latin America, Africa, and

Asia. Much television content is potentially antidevelopment, such as advertising and entertainment programs that encourage consumerism, thus creating frustration among poor and disadvantaged viewers in reaching material goals (Singhal & Rogers, 1988a; Wallack, chap. 16, this volume). Also, television advertisements and entertainment programs generally depict urban life as attractive and desirable, thus inadvertently promoting rural-urban migration to Third World cities that cannot cope with their rate of growth. Even government-operated educational television systems do not contribute effectively toward national development goals, because their programs are perceived as dull and attract only very small audiences.

Prodevelopment Soap Operas: The Example of *Hum Log*

Prodevelopment Soap Operas

Prodevelopment soap operas are an exception to the division of contemporary television programming into entertainment versus education. A *prodevelopment soap opera* is a melodramatic television serial that is broadcast in order to entertain and to convey subtly an educational or development theme (Singhal & Rogers, 1988b).

An early large-scale example of such prodevelopment programs was a series of Mexican soap operas (called *telenovelas*) that capitalized on a lesson learned accidentally from a 1969 Peruvian soap opera, *Simplemente María*. This television series told the rags-to-riches story of a migrant girl, María, and addressed educational-development themes such as the liberation of women, class conflict, and intermarriage between the urban rich and the migrant poor. María achieved socioeconomic success through her proficiency with a Singer sewing machine. *Simplemente María* achieved very high television ratings in Peru and throughout Latin America (when it was exported in the early 1970s). The sales of Singer sewing machines increased sharply wherever the series was broadcast in Latin America, as did the number of young women who began to sew.

Inspired by lessons drawn from the audience effects of *Simplemente María*, Miguel Sabido of Televisa (the private Mexican television network) designed six prodevelopment soap operas that were broadcast in Mexico from 1975 to 1981. *Ven Conmigo (Come with Me)*, in 1975-76, promoted adult literacy by motivating audience members to enroll in adult literacy classes, and achieved average audience ratings of 33 (much higher than the ratings for other soap operas on Televisa). *Ven Conmigo* was one influence leading to the enrollment of about a million illiterates in adult education classes, an increase of 63% over the previous year (Berrueta, 1986). Another prodevelopment soap opera, *Acompáñame* (*Come Along with Me*), designed to promote family planning, was broadcast in Mexico during 1977-78 (Rogers & Antola, 1985). This highly rated series helped convince half a million Mexicans to visit government family planning health clinics in order to adopt contraceptives, an increase of 32% over the previous year (Televisa's Institute of Communication Research, 1981).[3] Other prodevelopment soap operas in Mexico dealt with child rearing, female equality, and national history.

A somewhat similar approach to the Mexican soap operas, that of combining educational and entertainment objectives, has occurred in Jamaica, where Elaine Perkins has produced several radio soap operas, including *Naseberry Street,* which has promoted family planning since 1985. This program reaches an audience of about 40% of Jamaica's population (approximately a million people), and audience surveys indicate the soap opera is affecting family planning adoption (Hazzard & Cambridge, 1988).

Hum Log

The Indian soap opera *Hum Log* represented an extension of the hybrid combination of education and entertainment-style content inspired by the Mexican experience with prodevelopment soap operas.

The Center for Population Communications-International, headquartered in New York City, played a key role in the diffusion of the Mexican soap opera experience to India in the form of *Hum Log*. The series was broadcast by Doordarshan, the government television system in India, for 17 months in 1984-85. The 156 episodes were broadcast in Hindi; each lasted 22 minutes. This television series was an attempt to blend Doordarshan's stated objective of providing entertainment to its audience with promotion of such socially desirable behaviors as a more equal status for women, family harmony, and smaller family size.

At the close of each episode, a famous actor in Hindi films, Ashok Kumar, briefly summarized the main concepts, providing viewers with appropriate guides to action.[4] Each epilogue of approximately 30 to 50 seconds was a concentrated educational message, drawing out the key lessons for behavior change. The epilogues were very attractive to viewers, and our survey respondents indicated that most of them stayed tuned. The idea of explicitly stating the educational lessons from entertainment episodes originated in the Mexican soap operas in the late 1970s.

Such summarization, as well as the dramatic depictions in the soap operas, is consistent with Bandura's (1977b) social learning theory, which provided one basis for designing the educational soap operas in Mexico and in India. Bandura developed a social psychological theory about the ways in which humans learn social behaviors from models through the process of observational learning. He claims real-life and television models do not differ in influencing the learning of new behaviors. Models presented in televised forms are so effective in holding attention that viewers easily learn the models' behaviors (Bandura, Grusec, & Menlove, 1966). Bandura's theory explains how television viewers can learn to imitate certain behaviors by observing positive and negative models depicted in a soap opera (Bandura, 1986).

Methods and Hypothesized Effects

Our conclusions about the effects of *Hum Log* are based upon (1) a content analysis of 149 episodes of *Hum Log* (we could not obtain 7 *Hum Log* scripts) conducted to identify the prodevelopment themes that were portrayed and to evaluate the prosocial versus antisocial behavior of the ten main *Hum Log* characters, (2) an audience survey of 1,170 adult respondents who were mainly viewers (83% of the respondents had watched at least one episode of *Hum Log*) residing in and around Delhi (a Hindi-speaking area in North India), in and around Pune (a Marathi-speaking area in western India near Bombay), and in and around Madras (a Tamil-speaking area in South India),[5] and (3) a content analysis of a random sample of 500 viewers' letters and a mailed questionnaire returned by 287 of 321 letter writers for whom adequate addresses were available (a response rate of 90%).[6] Mass media communication is usually one-way, from one source to many audience individuals, but *Hum Log* was unusual in that audience feedback via viewers' letters was used in writing and rewriting the story line, suggesting new twists to the plot and new characterizations. For example, the series' scriptwriter, Manohar Shyam Joshi, received numerous viewers' letters pleading that Grandmother be cured of cancer (she dies in the final episode of the series anyway, but at least Joshi delayed her death).

Results

The Audience

Question 1 asked: To what extent did *Hum Log* reach a large audience of viewers? *Hum Log* achieved audience ratings from 65% to 90% in North India (a predominantly Hindi-speaking area), and between 20% and 45% in the main cities of South India, where Hindi-language programs cannot be understood by most television viewers. An audience of 50 million people watched the average *Hum Log* broadcast. At the time (1984-85), this audience was the largest for a television program in India.[7]

Results from our 1987 survey of 1,170 Indian adults showed that 96% of our respondents who had seen at least one episode of *Hum Log* liked it.[8] Some 94% thought it was entertaining, 83% said it was educational, and 91% said that it addressed social problems. In Madras, a South India Tamil-speaking area, only 48% of our respondents had seen at least one episode of *Hum Log* (not only was *Hum Log* broadcast in the North Indian language of Hindi, but it also mainly displayed North Indian culture, which is very different from South Indian culture). However, the individuals who did view *Hum Log* in Madras liked the program (93%) about as much as did the Hindi-speaking viewers in North India. Many Madras viewers had some degree of Hindi fluency from having lived in North India or from having studied Hindi.

Why was *Hum Log* so popular with Indian viewers? Timing and audience involvement appear to be the primary factors. *Hum Log* was broadcast at a time when Doordarshan, the government national television network, was experiencing an unparalleled expansion. Black-and-white television had previously changed to color, and the launch of the Indian National Satellite (INSAT-1B) in 1983 resulted in a large-scale expansion of television access in rural, remote areas of India. The television viewing audience increased in India from 30 million in 1983, to 60 million in 1985, to 80 million in 1987.

For many Indian viewers, *Hum Log* seemed to blur the line between image and reality, allowing for increased audience involvement. The series centered on three generations of a lower-middle-class family who lived together in one house. These characters seemed true to life, and millions of Indian viewers identified with them. *Hum Log* emphasized the family relationships between parent and child, husband and wife, brother and sister, grandparents and grandchildren, and mother-in-law and daughter-in-law, and many viewers became vicariously involved in the family's daily affairs (see the results for question 5, below).

Prosocial Themes

Question 2 asked: To what extent did the content of *Hum Log* actually feature socially desirable norms? Our content analysis of 149 episodes indicates that the television series addressed many of the important social issues confronting Indian society: family disharmony, unequal status of women, lack of national integration, unsuccessful family planning and health programs, problems of urban life, and the lack of national welfare programs (Table 15.1). So the stated objectives of *Hum Log* seem to have been carried out in the content that was broadcast.

Hum Log began as primarily a family planning soap opera. Pressures from audiences, sponsors, and debates in the Indian Parliament resulted in toning down the family planning theme (only 6% of the total series content emphasized family planning). After the first 13 episodes, scriptwriter Joshi emphasized such closely related themes as the status of women, family harmony, and family welfare, and decreased the prior "hard sell" approach to family planning.

Television Characters as Models

Question 3 asked: To what extent did viewers identify with prosocial models of behavior from the soap opera? Our 1987 survey of 1,170 adults showed that 37% of the respondents believed Grandfather (intended by the designers of *Hum Log* to be a positive role model in that he is hardworking, highly moral, and a strict disciplinarian) was the best exemplar to copy in real life, while 18% of our respondents chose to emulate Bhagwanti (a stereotype of the traditional Indian wife/mother and hence a negative role model for gender equality). Some 11% believed Badki (a positive role model for female equality in that she is self-sufficient and, although rather plain, marries a handsome medical doctor) to be the best exemplar, and 5% chose Chutki (a career-oriented young girl). Only 1% of our respondents believed Majhli (a negative female role model with loose morals and a warped

TABLE 15.1 Extent to Which Socially Desirable Themes Were Emphasized on *Hum Log*

Theme (Example)	Percentage of Subthemes in 149 Episodes
	(N = 10, 668)
Family harmony (family is close-knit despite individual differences among family members)	38
Status of women (Badki's efforts to fight for the status of women at a women's welfare organization)	26
Character and moral development (Grandfather's commentary on behaviors that are right and wrong)	12
National integration (marriage of a North Indian girl to a South Indian boy)	7
Family planning (Rajjo's determination to undergo tubectomy after giving birth to her fourth daughter)	6
Health (ill effects of alcohol on Basesar Ram's health)	5
Problems of urbanization (Lalloo's retreat to his village in order to cope with the high cost of urban life)	4
National welfare programs (eye-donation drive for Inspector Samdar)	2
Total	100

NOTE: Each percentage here is the portion of the total number of subthemes (10,668) identified in 149 episodes of *Hum Log*. The subthemes identified in each episode could fall under any of the eight mutually exclusive thematic categories. An average *Hum Log* episode had about 70 subthemes that we identified. The intercoder reliability coefficient is .78.

sense of modernity) to be the best exemplar, and 4% chose to emulate Basesar Ram (a negative male role model depicted as a drunken, chauvinistic father). The remaining 24% of our respondents chose generally neutral characters (that is, neutral in terms of the stated purpose of the educational soap opera) such as Nanhe, Grandmother, Lalloo, and others as best models. So our respondents believed in copying the positive role models in the TV program (53% in total) more than in imitating the negative role models (a total of 23%).

When *Hum Log* was planned, Bhagwanti was conceived as a negative (in the sense of the educational purpose of the soap opera) role model for female equality. She quietly let her husband and mother-in-law berate her for her inadequate family lineage, her lack of culinary skills, and so forth. However, some viewers sympathized with Bhagwanti's character and perceived her as a positive role model of tolerance, compromise, and patience. One 75-year-old woman wrote: "Bhagwanti is an epitome of tolerance. She suffers, but quietly. Young

Indian women should learn a lesson in patience from Bhagwanti."
Results from our 1987 survey show that 80% of viewers who chose
Bhagwanti as a positive role model were women; 76% of housewives
compared to 7% of the employed women chose to emulate Bhagwanti.
This differential identification with Bhagwanti's role suggests that
Hum Log's modeling effects were mediated by the viewers' prior atti-
tudes and experiences. As in the previously cited study by Vidmar and
Rokeach (1974) of Archie Bunker's viewers, televised behavior that is
ironic or satirical can reinforce negative behavior by viewers.

Viewers' Letters

Question 4 asked: To what extent did viewers' letters provide useful
feedback about the television series? The Doordarshan television network received an average of 400 letters a day from viewers during the
17 months of *Hum Log*'s broadcast, a total of about 200,000 letters (an
additional 200,000 letters were sent by viewers to the series actors and
actresses). Such an outpouring from viewers is unprecedented in the
history of worldwide television (for example, the 150,000 letters
received by NBC when *Star Trek* was canceled was thought to be the
previous record in the United States). The viewers' letters stressed the
importance of family harmony and family solidarity, and voiced concern about such social ills as dowry and alcoholism. Many letters
pleaded for more women's welfare organizations, encouraged eye
donations, and demanded improved treatment for cancer patients (an
eye transplant operation and a death due to cancer were part of the *Hum
Log* story). So most viewers' letters suggested that the planned objectives of the television series were being fulfilled. A content analysis of
our sample of 500 letters written to Doordarshan showed that 76%
expressed an opinion about the behavior of a program character, 66%
showed identification with one of the characters, 39% expressed an
opinion about a social issue raised by the soap opera, and 36%
responded to one of Ashok Kumar's epilogues.

Parasocial Interaction

Question 5 asked: To what extent did parasocial interaction take
place between the viewers and the characters in the soap opera?
Parasocial interaction refers to the seemingly face-to-face inter-

TABLE 15.2 Degree of Parasocial Interaction in Letters from *Hum Log*
            Viewers

Indicators of *Parasocial Interaction*	*Percentage of Letters That* *Indicate Parasocial Interaction*
Viewer indicates a strong involvement with *Hum Log* characters.	93
Viewer likes and respects Ashok Kumar, who delivers the epilogue at the end of each episode.	83
Viewer compares his or her ideas with those of *Hum Log* characters.	65
Viewer perceives a character as a down-to-earth, good person.	43
Viewer talks to his or her favorite character while watching the program.	39
Viewer feels that Ashok Kumar helps him or her to make various decisions, and looks to him for guidance.	39
Viewer adjusts his or her schedule to watch *Hum Log* so as to have a regular relationship with a television character.	30

personal relationships between a television viewer and a television performer (Horton & Wohl, 1956). Viewers can perceive their relationship with a television character as real, as if it were a face-to-face encounter. Many *Hum Log* viewers felt that they knew the television characters, even though they never actually met them. For example, many young women wrote to Badki to tell her that she should resolve her indecision about marrying her boyfriend Ashwini. The day that Badki and Ashwini got married on television, some shops and bazaars in North India closed early for the celebration. Doordarshan received many telegrams and handmade cards wishing the couple a happy married life (Jain, 1985). To many viewers Badki was not just a television character played by an actress, but a real person.

Past research has suggested that television viewers can exhibit parasocial interaction in at least seven ways (Guthrie, 1987; Horton & Wohl, 1956; Levy, 1979; Nordlund, 1978; Perse & Rubin, 1987). Table 15.2 shows the degree of parasocial interaction, in the form of these seven indicators, exhibited by our sample of 500 letter writers. It should be remembered that only .5% of all *Hum Log* viewers wrote letters to Doordarshan. The letter writers are highly untypical of the total viewing audience, and thus represent extreme responses to parasocial interaction. Nevertheless, their uniqueness also informs us in certain ways about the impacts of *Hum Log*.

Intended Effects

Question 6 asked: To what extent were the intended effects of *Hum Log* achieved, such as increasing awareness and changing attitudes and behaviors about the status of women, and promoting smaller family size norms? A substantial number of our 1,170 survey respondents said they learned prosocial attitudes and behaviors from *Hum Log*, including that women should have equal opportunities (70%), women should have the freedom to make their personal decisions in life (68%), family size should be limited (71%), family harmony should be promoted (75%), cultural diversity should be respected (68%), and women's welfare programs should be encouraged (64%).

Of our 500 viewers' letters, 92% show that *Hum Log* influenced the letter writer in a prosocial direction. Some 47% of the letters indicated that the program affected the letter writer's awareness of social issues, 33% showed that it influenced the letter writer's attitudes regarding these social issues, and 7% showed that it resulted in behavioral change on the letter writer's part. For example, a member of a Delhi youth club wrote to Ashok Kumar to say: "Inspired by *Hum Log*, our club has enrolled 892 people for eye donations. We hope to enroll 5,000 people by next month." Such behavior, while very uncharacteristic of the average viewer, suggests that the program achieved certain effects on overt behavior. Behavior change is the bottom line in the hierarchy of media effects (see chap. 2), and one would expect it to occur only rarely as the result of a television soap opera.

Unintended Impacts

Question 7 asked: What were some of the unintended impacts of *Hum Log*? Several unintended impacts occurred. *Hum Log* launched the era of commercially sponsored programs on Doordarshan. A sponsored television program is one in which an advertiser pays the production costs of the program, in return for several minutes of spot advertisements, just before, during, or immediately following broadcast of the program. Maggi 2 Minute Noodles, a product marketed by a Nestle subsidiary in India called Food Specialties Limited, were heavily advertised on *Hum Log*. Noodles were previously unknown in India (they were perceived as Chinese), as was the more general idea of quick-preparation foods. So Maggi 2 Minute Noodles was a radical consumer innovation in India. The successful experience of Food

Specialties Limited in advertising this new product on *Hum Log* convinced many other advertisers in India that television program sponsorship was a promising investment. Before long, advertisers were lined up at Doordarshan, eager to buy advertising. So *Hum Log* was the key turning point in the commercialization of Doordarshan.[9]

Hum Log's commercial success led to a proliferation of domestically produced television serials on Doordarshan. When *Hum Log* went on the air in 1984, it was the first long-running indigenous television serial broadcast on national television. Three years later, in 1987, over 40 such domestically produced series were being broadcast on Doordarshan: soap operas, detective serials, situation comedies, educational serials, quiz shows, and biographies of Indian leaders. These Indian-produced television programs are consistently more popular than are foreign (imported) serials, which is the main reason Doordarshan broadcasts so much less imported programming than most Third World countries (Rogers & Antola, 1985). Our 1987 survey showed that 88% of the respondents said they liked Hindi television serials, and 55% of our respondents said they did not like imported, foreign serials. One reason for this strong preference for Indian-made television programs is the audience's favorable initial experience with *Hum Log*. This TV series demonstrated that domestically produced TV shows could be very attractive to the Indian audience, even more attractive than *I Love Lucy* and *Diff'rent Strokes*.

The proliferation of domestically produced programs on Doordarshan happened thanks to important inputs from the Bombay film industry (which produces more feature films annually than any other nation except the Soviet Union). Bombay film moguls, once apprehensive about sponsored television serials like *Hum Log*, soon rushed to Delhi to get their programs approved or their story lines cleared by Doordarshan authorities. Television's expansion created a need for the film industry's equipment, studio facilities, and creative talent. Harish Khanna, former director-general of Doordarshan, said, "It is a marriage of convenience between Bombay and Delhi." In India in the 1980s, as in the United States in the 1950s, the film industry at first fought the rise of television, and then joined it with enthusiasm. Following the commercial success of *Hum Log*, most Indian television production moved from Delhi (which remains the headquarters for Doordarshan) to Bombay, where film production facilities and talent were converted to television production.

Conclusion

Our seven questions have been answered as follows:

(1) *Hum Log* was highly popular among Hindi-speaking viewers in North India, and it was relatively less popular in South India.

(2) The themes emphasized in the soap opera series were family harmony, more equal status for women, and proper character and morals. Family planning, national integration, health, problems of urbanization, and national welfare themes were also emphasized, but less heavily.

(3) Viewers reported copying the positive role models in the television soap opera more than they imitated the negative role models.

(4) Viewers' letters expressed like/dislike for the television series, suggested new plots, responded to issues raised by Ashok Kumar in his epilogues, and expressed opinions about the behavior of the show's characters.

(5) Viewers indicated strong involvement with the characters: They perceived the program's characters as down-to-earth, good people, they adjusted their schedules to watch *Hum Log*, they talked to their favorite characters, and they compared their ideas with those of the series' characters.

(6) Most viewers reported learning positive attitudes and behaviors about family harmony, equal status for women, and smaller family size norms.

(7) *Hum Log* helped commercialize Indian television, led to a proliferation of domestically produced television programs, and encouraged the Bombay film industry to become heavily involved in television.

A three-year gap occurred after the sixth prodevelopment soap opera in Mexico and the first adaptation of this concept in India. During this hiatus, David Poindexter and other individuals were promoting the idea of prodevelopment soap operas to various nations, but the typical reaction was: "Okay, Mexico did it, but they have a genius in Miguel Sabido. Without Sabido, we cannot produce a successful family planning soap opera." The *Hum Log* experience in India in 1984-85 showed that another nation could successfully follow Mexico's lead, even without the unique talents of Miguel Sabido. *Hum Log* has been off the air since late 1985, but its effects continue.[10]

Hum Log demonstrated that India could effectively adapt the Mexican strategy of prodevelopment soap operas to India's specific sociocultural conditions. This successful experience persuaded several other Third World countries to launch television programs patterned after *Hum Log*. Kenya went on the air with its first family planning television soap opera, *Tushauriani* (*Let's Discuss*), in 1987. *Tushauriani* is broadcast in Swahili, the lingua franca of Kenya, and is scheduled to run for 197 episodes. It has received very high television ratings in Kenya. Nigeria has a prodevelopment soap opera on the drawing board. Mexico's Televisa is producing another family planning soap opera, to be broadcast in seven Latin American nations. The epilogue at the end of each episode will be delivered by a well-known national figure in each country, an individual equivalent to Ashok Kumar. J.R.D. Tata, a leading Indian industrialist, pledged financial support for a successor to *Hum Log*, which is being produced in Bombay. Several other Third World nations plan to produce television soap operas for family planning in the near future.

Hum Log ushered in a new era on Indian television, which was aided by the simultaneous expansion of the television audience in India via satellite transmission. *Hum Log* was a success with both its audience and its advertisers, but was somewhat of a mixed success in achieving its educational-development goals. Table 15.3 presents the pros and cons of the *Hum Log* experience in India, suggesting some of the main lessons learned. The effects of *Hum Log* were mediated by its language (and culture) of broadcast and by the preexisting attitudes and experiences of its viewers (as is illustrated by viewers who interpreted Bhagwanti's character as a positive role model).

While *Hum Log* was not manifestly designed as a communication campaign, it displayed several qualities that are typical of communication campaigns (such as that it was intended to achieve specific effects). *Hum Log* displayed one additional quality that is not typical of communication campaigns, in that it centered on an entertainment format: the television soap opera. However, the television soap opera is only one of several mass media entertainment formats used in Third World countries to deliver educational-development messages, as the following section illustrates.

Rock Music for Teenage Sexual Abstinence in Latin America

Early pregnancy is a major social problem in many Third World nations, and especially in Latin America. The main targets for contraceptive messages—preteens and teenagers—are especially difficult to reach through conventional development communication channels. In 1986, a unique communication project was launched in Spanish-speaking Latin American countries: a rock song and video that

TABLE 15.3 Pros and Cons of *Hum Log*

Pros	Cons
Full government support (initially)	Some government support lost over time
Intended to promote development	Intentions not fully carried out (e.g., the family planning content was considerably deemphasized after the first 13 episodes)
Highly popular in Northern India, as it used the rustic language spoken by an average North Indian	Less popular in South India because of language and culture differences
High audience involvement, illustrated by the 400,000 letters written by viewers	Little follow-up by Doordarshan with viewers' letters; many were not opened
Family drama based on an understanding of the Indian ethos	Major cops-and-robbers underworld subplot with little educational relevance
Very effective television scriptwriting	Written under great time pressure, with writer trying to serve two masters (Doordarshan and the commercial sponsors)
Major commercial success	Content influenced by advertising sponsors; promoted consumerism
Tripartite arrangement among Doordarshan, the advertising sponsor, and the scriptwriter	Constant struggle over control of episodes
First Indian TV soap opera	Mistakes made were not attended to as useful lessons for the benefit of later TV series in India
Low-cost production	Relatively poor production quality due to the lack of adequate prior experience and television production equipment
Liked by middle and lower-middle class	Less well-liked by skeptical urban elites

promoted sexual abstinence, titled "Cuando Estemos Juntos" ("When We Are Together"). This song was number one on the pop music charts within six weeks of its release in Mexico, and soon was also the top-rated song in 11 other Latin American countries. The success of this music video resulted from the joint efforts of communication researchers, funding from the U.S. Agency for International Development, and the assistance of entertainment industry executives and rock musicians.

Patrick Coleman, director of Population Communication Services at Johns Hopkins University, provided the impetus for this entertainment-education project. His organization conducted formative evaluation research that indicated that the common denominator for young people throughout Latin America is music. Coleman contacted organizations that work with young people to develop a message that could be communicated by a rock music video, but that would be acceptable to the government and to the religious institutions of Latin American countries. Coleman conducted focus groups with a sample of teenagers to determine message content acceptable to them. Having refined the message, Coleman involved the EMI Capitol recording company, who hired Tatiana, a 16-year-old singer from Mexico, and Johnny, a 17-year-old Puerto Rican singer. A competition among 20 professional composers created the music and lyrics for the song. The lyrics argued for sexual abstinence: "You will see that I'm right when I say no, even though my heart is burning." Finally, Coleman contracted for marketing the song through a commercial marketing firm in Mexico City. (See Alcalay & Taplin, chap. 5, and Atkin & Freimuth, chap. 6, this volume, for more detailed discussions of formative evaluation and media planning, and Solomon, chap. 4, this volume, for a discussion of social marketing.)

The song was launched on *Siempre de Domingo*, the most popular television show in Latin America, which reached a viewing audience of 130 million people. The music video was advertised through public service announcements on television and radio, and in newspapers. Broadcasting stations could play the song without paying a broadcast fee if they agreed to accompany the music with an announcement about where teenagers could visit a local family planning clinic for contraceptive services. Once the audio and video versions of the song became popular, both Tatiana and Johnny made numerous media and personal appearances to promote their song, the issue of teenage sexual abstinence, and contraception. Further, ads promoting abstinence and contraception were widely disseminated that utilized the song as background music in order to attract attention. An estimated one million hours of free radio and television time were provided by broadcasting stations in Latin America for playing and discussing the song (Coleman, 1988).

In Mexico alone, Tatiana's album featuring "Cuando Estemos Juntos" sold over 500,000 copies. Evaluation research in Mexico by the Institute for Communication Research (1987) showed that the song did more than sell videos and audiotapes and records. It encouraged teenagers to talk more freely about teenage sex, reinforced teenagers who already had decided to use restraint, sensitized younger viewers to the importance of the topic, and disseminated information about contraception.

For a second rock song about sexual abstinence in 1988, data were gathered from a sample of Latin American teenagers coming to family planning clinics for the first time. Such point-of-referral monitoring, which provides relatively hard data about behavior change (the bottom line in the hierarchy of effects), could not be gathered for "Cuando Estemos Juntos" or for *Hum Log* in India, because communication research on the messages' effects could not be conducted until after the broadcasts had ended—six months later in the case of the first rock song in Latin America, and more than a year for the Indian soap opera.[11]

For the second teenage music video in Latin America on sexual abstinence, a second family planning soap opera in India, and the next Mexican family planning soap opera (all three of which are now in production), the investigation of effects will be launched prior to the first broadcast, thus resulting in a more rigorous research design.

Two key lessons have been learned from the recent experiences with the entertainment-education mass communication strategy utilized by the creators of *Hum Log* and "Cuando Estemos Juntos." First, the mixture of entertainment and educational content represented by the Indian soap opera and the Latin American music video attracted large audiences and earned high profits from advertising or sales. The entertainment component of such messages helps break down audience barriers and resistances to the educational content (such as the perception that educational messages are usually dull), and moves the messages farther along the hierarchy of effects. The large audiences achieved by entertainment-educational messages make them popular with commercial advertisers. While educational efforts are usually a budget expense to a government treasury, entertainment-education communication is often very profitable. So the entertainment-education strategy represents a win-win situation.

Second, entertainment-education communication cannot make the educational content too blatant or hard sell, because a mass audience will not be attracted to such messages. An example of this point is the first 13 episodes of *Hum Log* that were broadcast in India in 1984; these episodes attracted low audience ratings because they hammered on the family planning issue, which was unpopular with the Indian television audience. Formative evaluation, facilitated by the exceptional audience feedback in the form of letter writing, helped identify the nature of this problem. When the family planning theme was less heavily emphasized, and such other issues as female equality and family harmony were stressed, television ratings of *Hum Log* jumped to record levels.

Notes

1. Third World countries include all Middle Eastern countries, all African countries except South Africa, all Asian countries except Japan, and all of the countries in Latin America.

2. Data on the worldwide diffusion of TV sets are compiled from the BBC's *World Radio and Television Receivers* (1987).

3. Televisa created as well as evaluated its prodevelopment soap operas in Mexico, and thus its claims of very strong effects might be questioned by some critics. Our evaluation of *Hum Log* was conducted by researchers outside of Indian television.

4. Ashok Kumar is the doyen of the Indian film industry, with an image somewhat akin to that of Burt Lancaster in Hollywood.

5. Marathi is a close derivative of Hindi, with many cognates between the two languages. Tamil is a Dravidian language, quite different from Hindi, with a completely different script and grammar. We selected Delhi, Pune, and Madras as sample areas for our audience survey in order to determine the effects of language differences on our respondents' viewing behavior.

6. These letters were sampled from a nonrandom sample of the estimated 400,000 letters written to Doordarshan and to the actors and actresses in response to *Hum Log*.

7. It should be noted that *Hum Log*'s average audience of 50 million individuals, while representing a rating of 65 (that is, 65% of the 80 million television viewers in India), is only 6% of the total population of 800 million. Further, only one television channel can be received in most areas in India, so a rating of 65, which would be unbelievably high in the United States, must be viewed in context.

8. Viewers' liking of the soap opera was measured by asking them "To what extent did you like the *Hum Log* television series?" Responses were measured on a three-point scale—not at all, somewhat, and a lot. Positive scale values of "somewhat" and "a lot" were collapsed to measure liking.

9. McQuail (1986) provides a detailed discussion of positive and negative consequences of the commercialization of broadcast media. He argues that advertising can help move products and services, and that this can contribute to economic growth. In Third World countries, however, commercialization can upset the balance between the sociocultural goals of the mass media and the mass consumer goals of the national economy. *Hum Log*'s impact in promoting sales of Maggi noodles could be viewed as an indirect prodevelopment outcome if one accepts the argument that individual-level adoption of Maggi noodles freed Indian women from the stove.

10. Given that *Hum Log* was so successful, why did it go off the air after 18 months? Unlike soap operas in the United States, which often continue for many years, in most other nations (including Mexico, whose soap operas directly influenced *Hum Log*) a soap opera ends after one, or at most two, years. Further, the producer, Ms. Shobha Doctor, claimed that she was losing money during the final episodes because costs, such as the actors' salaries, had risen, but she was locked into a fixed contract with Doordarshan for the series. So the program was brought to a climax (Grandmother's death due to cancer), and ended. A more detailed discussion on why *Hum Log* ended is provided in Singhal and Rogers (1988a).

11. Such point-of-referral monitoring was successfully conducted for a family planning variety show on television, *In a Lighter Mood*, broadcast in Enugu, Nigeria, in 1986-1987 (Winnard, Rimon, & Convisser, 1987). The point-of-referral data were

gathered at the only family planning clinic in Enugu. A 147% increase occurred in the number of adopters of family planning over the 14 months since the broadcasts began, and 60% of all adopters reported the television program as their source of referral to the clinic.

Part IV

Epilogue

In the closing chapter, Lawrence Wallack presents a critical perspective on the strengths and weaknesses of the mass media's role in health promotion. He argues that the media are an excellent vehicle for transmitting information to mass audiences, but are relatively powerless in stimulating significant behavioral and structural change. Wallack debunks the "mass media fantasy" conception that health problems can be addressed successfully if only the "magic formula" can be discovered and implemented, citing faulty assumptions and unrealistic expectations that ignore fundamental social and economic obstacles. He believes that health problems are quite complex and that health status is often beyond the control of the individual who is the target of media messages, and that the commercial media provide a hostile environment, filled with advertising and entertainment that undermines public health and reinforces the dominant socioeconomic system, where corporate needs prevail over the good of the general citizenry.

16

Mass Communication and Health Promotion: A Critical Perspective

LAWRENCE WALLACK

The great potential of mass media for promoting social good has long been a source of both hope and frustration for Americans. Over the past 150 years, from telegraph lines to communication satellites, each technological advance in communication carried an implicit promise of a better society through increased availability of and access to information. Yet this promise has never been realized to the extent anticipated. As technologies mature and are implemented, the needs of a corporate economy prevail over those of the general citizenry. Media become a means for reinforcing existing social and economic arrangements, and for providing entertainment rather than stimulating change.

Public health practitioners in particular have an extensive history of using available mass media to communicate health information to the general population. As Paisley (chap. 1, this volume) summarizes, historically in America there has been a strong belief in the ability of media to communicate information, transform public opinion, and potentially change individual health behavior. These efforts, sometimes quite well conceived and extensive in scope, have not been without effect. Yet most contemporary campaigns appear to have little demonstrable lasting effect on personal behavior or societal disease rates.

The central argument of this chapter is that the role of mass media is often overemphasized and inappropriately suggested as a solution to serious public health issues. This chapter will address two key issues in attempting to develop an enhanced understanding of the media and health issues. The first issue is the "mass media fantasy": Why are mass media so attractive to those seeking to address public health problems? The second issue is the nature of public health problems: The solution to such problems is incompatible with the sole or primary use of mass media.

The Mass Media Fantasy

The mass media fantasy is, in brief, that almost any given social or health problem can be adequately addressed if the right message could be communicated to the right people in just the right way at the right time. The magic formula for media efficacy, according to this perspective, will be based not on a new understanding of the place of media in society but on acquiring better knowledge of the audience, developing better message strategies, assuring better message placement and media mix, and finding better ways of monitoring audience response.

However, the media fantasy and much of the research that has provided us with hope in this area is based on a set of assumptions that are inappropriate for the public health problems that we seek to address. By refining the prevailing fantasy based on questionable assumptions (critiqued in this section—see also Dervin, chap. 3, this volume), we may reinforce attention to variables with limited potential per se and deflect attention from key variables that must be addressed to stimulate change.

There are at least three sets of reasons for the media's attractiveness as an outlet to society for addressing social and health problems. First, use of the media is consistent with a basic understanding of problems as *inherently individual* in nature and thus responsive to information and education approaches. Second, it is a *conservative* approach that ignores or avoids the factors external to the individual that might be more politically charged. Third, the *reach* of the mass media, particularly television, is so great that it would be foolish to ignore even the slightest chance of success.

The Individual Focus:
"To the Victim Belong the Flaws" (Galanter, 1977)

As Blum (1980) notes, "There is little doubt that how a society views major problems . . . will be critical to how it acts on the problems" (p. 49). If we alter the definition of problems, then the response also changes (Powles, 1979). However, this process of definition, although critical, seldom receives sufficient thought or attention.

The tendency in American society is to attempt to develop clear and concise definitions of problems to facilitate concrete, commonsense-type solutions. Often, however, problems of health and social well-being are difficult to define, much less solve, and increasing levels of the complexity of a problem are highly correlated with rising disagreement on the definition of a problem. One of the techniques commonly used in science and practice to get a firm handle on complex problems is to reduce them to more basic, smaller problems that appear more manageable. Society's drug problem, an enormously complex issue that involves every level of society, is reduced to an inability of the individual to "just say no." This reinforces the notion of information as a "magic bullet" shot at audiences by the media—this time in the form of a clear-cut, forceful slogan.

Once the problem is broken into smaller parts, attention is turned to solving each of the smaller problems. In the case of drugs, one focus would be on making sure that each individual has the right information about the consequences of, and alternatives to, drug use. If we can solve the "information deficit" problem of each individual, each of these "solutions" is then summed and presumed to add to a solution of the societal drug problem. Typical of this process, health problems are commonly reduced to individual-level single factors such as "foolish" behaviors (Will, 1987), bad habits (Knowles, 1977), or unhealthy life-styles (U.S. Department of Health, Education and Welfare, 1979).

A key question is, Why do we typically break problems down into smaller parts rather than define them as part of a larger, more complex whole? The answer is, in part, that we as a society share a common view about the concept of individualism. As Bellah, Madsen, Sullivan, Swidler, and Tipton (1985) note in their seminal work on American life, "Individualism lies at the very core of American culture" (p. 142). Concepts of individualism and self-determination carrying almost a religious mystique are central to the economic and social structure of American society; they are a key part of America's classical liberal heritage (Ladd, 1981). Neubauer and Pratt (1981) suggest that

> the concept of individualism carries great weight. . . . Americans have customarily believed that if each person independently applies his or her own talent to his or her own interest, the best possible, in this case the healthiest—society will result. (pp. 214-215)

Yet this fundamental belief in individualism leads to the notions that individuals determine the choices in a "free market" economy, victims thus bear the blame of negative consequences of these choices, and public health and public policy are best managed through market mechanisms.

Though many would argue that there is a great deal of corporate control over many aspects of life in the United States, there is also a strong image of the consumer being in control. The concept of a marketplace democracy where each consumer votes his or her preference and the sum of the aggregated choices carries the decision, which organizations then attempt to fulfill, lies at the base of the consumer society and derives its legitimacy from basic notions of individualism (Galbraith, 1973). Marketplace decisions affecting the well-being of millions are seen as the aggregation of individual preferences rather than corporate decisions motivated by profit.

Cigarette smoking—the greatest cause of preventable morbidity and mortality in the United States—is linked not to large corporations that deftly market and promote a dangerous product but primarily to those who "choose" to smoke and implicitly accept the consequences. This approach keeps the focus on the individual and results in programs (e.g., public communication campaigns, such as those described by McAlister, Ramirez, Galavotti, & Gallion, chap. 13, this volume) designed to help the consumer make a better-informed, more knowledgeable choice but does little to address the important contributory causes that are external to the individual. Thus one implication of the consumer-driven image of the economic system is an orientation toward "blaming the victim" (Ryan, 1976). Hence, with choice and responsibility at the individual level, there is little need to focus on the broader social and political environment; the solution is to provide the individual with information to make the right choices.

Comfortable Bedfellows:
Mass Media and Public Health Problems

Participation in health promotion campaigns is attractive for the mass media as well as for local agencies and organizations. It is estimated that each of the three major networks donates the equivalent of $200 million annually in time for public service announcements. A 1987 National Association of Broadcasters survey found health-related issues to be the priority topic for local stations (Mandese, 1987). Les Brown, longtime media watcher, has commented on a "new wisdom" in the industry regarding local involvement. In discussing Wishnow's (1983) concept of "activist public service," he notes, "Alert broadcasters have found that profits flow fastest to stations that are super-citizens of the community. . . . Word is out in the industry that com-munity involvement is good business" (Brown, 1987, p. 26).

Media gatekeepers, through participation in health-related cam-paigns, can be responsive to community needs regarding outlets for disseminating information and can play a role in addressing local-level problems. These activities help satisfy radio and television stations' public service obligations. At the same time, media outlets can cul-tivate substantial goodwill at the community level, promote entertain-ment and news personalities through appearances at public service functions, and gain an edge over competitors entering the media market.

The service ethic of many media outlets clearly provides a sig-nificant community resource. Local organizations and agencies that work well with the media can reap considerable benefits. Receiving good airplay and support for a message can provide increased visibility and enhanced legitimacy of campaign goals (see Alcalay & Taplin, chap. 5, this volume). Public service campaign support from a station (e.g., providing time, involving personalities at local functions, and cosponsoring events) can spill over into news coverage of campaign-related activities and development of supportive editorial positions. An ongoing partnership with media outlets can be an extremely valuable resource for an agency with strong commitment to public education about health issues but with a weak budget.

There are a few barriers to participation by media outlets in "legiti-mate" causes. The demand for media time will always exceed available resources, and media outlets will not be able to address all health concerns of the community (see Mandese, 1987; Sloan, 1987). In addition, the increasingly political nature of the decision-making pro-cess for airing PSAs makes media participation a much more compli-cated issue, as groups, community concerns, and sometimes competing agendas must be balanced. The need to avoid controversy is a key factor in media participation. An individualized view of public health problems usually will ensure that no powerful commercial or moral interests are alienated.

AIDS education in the media provides an interesting example of the necessary balance between addressing a controversial topic and serving the public interest. Prime-time programming commonly discusses (directly or indirectly) topics such as condoms and information about AIDS transmission and prevention (Baker, 1987), yet television sta-tions rarely carry condom advertising despite the urging of the surgeon general (Werner, 1987) and considerable public support for these ads (Belkin, 1987). When such ads are shown, they tend to be somewhat obscure regarding use and other relevant factors. The somewhat sanitized definition of the problem that facilitated initial mass media responsiveness was as follows: (1) AIDS is a heterosexual problem (thus avoiding focusing on homosexuals and IV drug users, two socially marginal populations); (2) AIDS can be reduced to individual behavior, such as condom use, but only by ignoring other safer but more controversial sex practices; and (3) the prevention of AIDS is seen as an individual behavior and responsibility (hence deflecting attention from the highly political and cultural issues regarding homosexuality, civil rights, and drug use).

The Reach of Media: "I Like to Watch"

There is no question that contemporary mass media possess an unprecedented ability to reach great portions of the population instantaneously and repeatedly. In 1986 there were 1,285 television stations in the United States, over 10,000 radio stations, and almost 1,700 daily newspapers with an average circulation of 63 million per day. Yet for all the print media and radio stations, television is America's primary medium. For adults, 60% of overall media time (television, radio, newspapers, magazines) is spent with television (Television Information Office, 1987). Americans, like Jerszy Kozinski's (1970) media-spawned hero of *Being There*, Chauncey Gardner, "like to watch."

Watching television is indeed the national pastime. In the 1985-86 season, household usage reached a new high of 7 hours and 10 minutes per day and on any given evening, about 100 million people were staring at the television screen (Nielsen Media Research, 1987).

People are not only exposed to massive doses of television, but they learn from it as well. Television is well established as a major source of observational learning (Comstock, 1976; Hamburg & Pierce, 1982), as a cultivator of beliefs and values about the world (Gerbner, Gross, Morgan, & Signorielli, 1986; Gerbner, Morgan, & Signorielli, 1982), as a mechanism for maintaining dominant ideology (Gitlin, 1987), and as a major agent of socialization outside of traditional institutions such as the family (Meyrowitz, 1985). While there is controversy over what people learn, how they learn, and the implications of learning from television, it is clear that they learn about a wide range of topics, including health (National Institute of Mental Health, 1982; Pearl, Bouthilet, & Lazar, 1982).

It is often said that media, particularly television, may not tell people *what* to think, but certainly tell them what to think *about*. In addition, by increasing visibility of a topic and lending legitimacy to it, mass media may well "defuse" potentially embarrassing topics—such as incest or AIDS—and facilitate interpersonal as well as public discussion (see, for example, Greenberg & Gantz, in chap. 9, this volume).

Television is generally regarded as the most credible medium and primary source of news (Television Information Office, 1987). On the local level, 42% of Americans report getting their health/fitness information from television, compared to 21% for magazines and 17% for newspapers. Yankelovich, Skelly and White, Inc. (1979) found that after "doctors and dentists," "television programs" were listed as the main source of health information. Respondents who were poorly informed were more likely to rely on "television programs" as a main source for health information. Freimuth, Greenberg, DeWitt, and Romano (1984) reported that more than 80% of respondents in a national survey conducted for the American Cancer Society said that they had heard about cancer on television. About 65% of the respondents cited newspapers as a main source of cancer information, compared to 61% citing magazines and 42% mentioning radio.

In sum, mass media represent an extremely attractive delivery system for health promotion messages. Television in particular, with its broad reach and ability to provide repeated exposures, presents great potential. Also, for the general public, television "may well be the single most pervasive source of health information" (Gerbner, cited in Waters, 1982), though the credibility of the information seems somewhat questionable.

The Reality of Public Health Problems

The reasons just described for using mass media to promote health seem compelling. Yet the promise is, in large part, illusory, partly because it is based on a limited understanding both of health and of the more general role of mass media in society. Four assumptions form the basis for this perceived promise. First, public health issues are reduced to neat, well-structured individual problems and the related "information-deficit" understanding of health and disease. Second, health messages in mass media are assumed to be limited to PSAs and other public service time, and any negative health messages (e.g., in advertising, programs, or articles) are either irrelevant or can be offset by "good"

public service spots. Third, the negative influence of advertiser support
of program and news content (such as inhibiting health promotion
messages) is assumed to be negligible. Fourth, mass media in this
society are assumed to be effective agents in the development of
improved health status for the general population.

Public Health and Complexity

Public health problems are complex. They pose serious dilemmas
for planners and are not easily reducible to smaller, more manageable
problems. Indeed, they are inextricably linked to a broader social and
political context in which the nature of the problems and the best
approaches for solution are hotly debated and contested. One of the
ways to ignore the debate and take what appears to be meaningful
action is to talk about life-style factors as being significant influences
on health status. This is a basic marketplace concept that suggests that
health problems are "purchased" as a by-product of goods consumed.

The life-style argument has several serious flaws. First, there are
doubts that even when significant life-style changes are made (and this
is fairly seldom) there is a subsequent change in health status (Lorig &
Laurin, 1985). Further, the long-term maintenance of these changes is
likely to be limited (as McAlister et al., chap. 13, this volume, note in
their discussion of smoking cessation campaigns). Second, it assumes
that all people have a reasonably equal opportunity to participate. Yet
substantial segments of the population, particularly those in greatest
need, have limited social and economic resources to facilitate the
change process. Third, and perhaps most important, major determinants of health thought to reside within the individual in life-style
theory are in fact known to be external factors (e.g., Crawford, 1977;
Czitrom, 1982; Waitzkin, 1983).

There is broad consensus in the public health field that health status
is largely dependent on factors external to the individual over which he
or she exercises little or no control (Mechanic, 1982). One of the most
resistant and predictive major factors of morbidity and mortality experience is income—persons in lower socioeconomic classes have higher
rates of almost every disease (Syme & Berkman, 1981). In addition, the
value of social ties and support in health promotion is supported by an
impressive body of evidence (Cassel, 1976; Lindheim & Syme, 1983;
Mechanic, 1982; Minkler, 1986).

Introducing broad sociopolitical issues such as racism, poverty, and
unemployment to health promotion campaigns would certainly create a

great deal of complexity. The message, rather than being simple and clear-cut, would be quite complicated and provide little direction for individual action. Yet these conditions have a major impact on health status in our society.

In sum, the very nature of public health problems is ill suited to the type of information that mainstream mass media typically provide. The nature of these problems is complex and controversial because causes are external to the individual—rooted in causes generated by a consumption-oriented society that trades off health for goods. The apparent promise of mass media to contribute to significant improvements in health status by marketing health information is in fact illusory. Information is necessary but not sufficient to alter the determinants of health. Regulatory strategies that contribute to a generally more healthy society are also necessary. Public policies that address the basic inequalities in society that detract from health status are also part of a comprehensive health promotion approach. Yet the role of the media in this area is seriously underdeveloped.

Television: The Health Message in the Medium

Public service campaigns are often viewed as one of the main sources of mass media health messages. In reality, no matter how extensive, they are likely to account for only a small proportion of health related content in the mass media. Audiences are exposed to a constant stream of information about health through talk shows, call-in programs, news, prime-time entertainment programming, special columns, and feature articles.

Because of this extensive provision of health-related messages in regular mass media content, public service campaigns to promote health take place in a relatively hostile environment. Smoking, drinking, risky driving, and poor eating habits are examples of life-styles and behaviors strongly linked to health status. Yet these behaviors are also a product of extensive marketing strategies, in which advertising through the media plays a key role. The consumption ideology is not only promoted through advertising but reinforced in entertainment programming, as Gerbner (1987) explains:

> Ideologically, the messages [in entertainment programming] tend to cultivate, and advertising to confirm and reinforce, dominant notions about styles and functions of drinking, smoking and drug-taking, not to mention other habits, while supporting the industries that cater to them. (p. 124)

Gerbner's research suggests that heavy television viewing may in fact be a *risk factor* for poor health. Heavier viewing, for example, was found to be associated with increased complacency about diet and nutrition, increased likelihood of being a smoker, and decreased likelihood of deriving satisfaction from one's health (Gerbner, Morgan, & Signorielli, 1982). Overall, Gerbner and his colleagues report that television presentations of nutrition, obesity, automobile driving, smoking, and drinking are in serious conflict with realistic guidelines for health.

Television content provides information about health in several ways. First, general program content reflects frequent and generally unrealistic alcohol use (e.g., Breed & DeFoe, 1981; Greenberg, Fernandez-Collado, Graef, Korzenny, & Atkin, 1979; Lowry, 1981; Wallack, Breed, & Cruz, 1987), poor nutrition (e.g., Kaufman, 1980), unsafe driving behavior (Greenberg & Atkin, 1983), potential positive role models for smoking (Cruz & Wallack, 1986), and inferences concerning unprotected sexual intercourse (Fernandez-Collado, Greenberg, Korzenny, & Atkin, 1978). In general, health issues are seldom addressed in depth and, even when they are, the information conveyed to the audience is of questionable value (Greenberg, 1981). Rather, television content could be a *barrier* to health promotion efforts, as it presents disinformation about health issues and causes confusion about what is important.

Second, a good deal of information is conveyed through television about the medical profession and its role in health and disease. TV doctors symbolize a great deal of power and authority and ability to affect positively the lives of those with whom they come in contact (McLaughlin, 1975). On television, the primary methods for treating illness and disease tend to be machines and drugs, with a heavily biomedical emphasis (Turow & Coe, 1985). Medical care and the diseases it treats are portrayed as apolitical and independent of economic and social issues central to contemporary debates about the role of medicine in the health care system (Turow & Coe, 1985). This reinforces the notion that health and disease are ultimately matters best understood at the individual level. If the person gets sick, it is a function of life-style or the "randomness" of disease. Gerbner, Gross, Morgan, and Signorielli (1981) note that heavier television viewers tend to have an unrealistic belief in the "magic of medicine" and high confidence in the medical profession. Television may help to reinforce viewer malaise about the value of health-promoting activities and "justify 'live-for-today' attitudes (and sales) and lack of interest in prevention; if any problem arises, the doctor will surely provide the cure" (p. 904).

A third way television provides specific information about health is through made-for-television movies. Sometimes referred to as "disease-of-the-week" movies, recent programs have focused on AIDS, bulimia, alcoholism, drug addiction, Alzheimer's disease, incest, teenage pregnancy, and drunk driving. *Shattered Spirits* (seen by 24 million viewers) addressed the effects of alcoholism on the family. This movie followed a fairly standard formula for disease-of-the-week movies in what it did and did not do. It showed a problem that has some social stigma happening to an intact, white, middle-class family. The family either denies the existence of a problem or tries to deal with it by relying on internal resources. After a period, a crisis arises, usually as a consequence of an adverse interaction with the police, friends, or a social welfare agency. The family is formally forced to seek help (e.g., by the court) or reluctantly realizes that the problem is too big for them to handle alone. Help often consists of professional counseling or medical intervention. Despite the seriousness of the disease, some positive resolution is reached. In the case of *Shattered Spirits*, after an attempt at treatment for the family and the alcoholic, the family is on the way to recovery and the alcoholic father is making slow, but promising, steps to recovery.

The message of such programs is usually that awareness of the problem is essential and that the key to recovery is knowledge about the disease and self, or, with fatal diseases, acceptance and family unity. The problem is presented as a property of the individual, with adverse effects on the family. The causes and cures exist at the family level—reinforcing the role of the family and at the same time minimizing the importance of factors external to the individual and the family. According to a network executive quoted by Gitlin (1983), "The networks are always mistaking real social issues for little human condition stories" (p. 179). Alcoholism, AIDS, mental illness, and homelessness are consequences of public policies as well as of individual behavior, but this is seldom discussed. This genre of movie generally fails to question the social arrangements that contribute to the problem, and ignores crucial facts such as the relationship between poverty and disease in society. True to the needs of the sponsors, television movies may make us sad and weepy, but they seldom make us angry or uncomfortable (Taylor, 1987).

Advertising

Health promotion campaigns generally provide messages of thoughtfulness, caution, moderation, and restraint in life-style. Advertising, on the other hand, promotes higher levels of consumption of a range of potentially health-compromising products through life-style appeals. Health campaigns urging people to "just say no" to drugs, sex, alcohol, or an extra dessert are surrounded by commercial ads with attractive role models suggesting the appropriateness of no restraint. After even a brief review of print and electronic advertising, one might well think the national slogan is "Go for It."

Advertising is ubiquitous in our society. For example, over the course of a year, the average child watching television will see over 22,000 commercials promoting consumption (Gerbner, Morgan, & Signorielli, 1982), including 11,000 "low nutrition-junk food" ads (Jeffrey, McLellarn, & Fox, 1982). Another 5,000 ads are network beer commercials, often viewed by adolescents (Atkin, Neuendorf, & McDermott, 1983). Both Jeffrey et al. and Atkin et al. have linked exposure to advertisements with poor health habits.

The effects of advertising on inhibiting health promotion messages can be seen in two areas. The first is that cigarette, alcohol, food, and automobile advertising often relies on appeals that systematically ignore or minimize health concerns, promote products through irrelevant appeals such as peer acceptance, sexual attractiveness, or success, or do both (Neubauer & Pratt, 1981).

The second area of concern is that advertising cannot be separated from the entertainment (Barnouw, 1978; Gitlin, 1983) or news functions (Bagdikian, 1983; Goldstein, 1985; Parenti, 1986; Sperber, 1985) of the media. As well as purveying the consumption-at-any-cost message, advertising colors the way that entertainment and news programming conveys information and ideas that are often important to the way we understand and respond to health issues as individuals and as a society.

"Network executives," Gitlin (1983) explains, "internalize the desires of advertisers as a whole" (p. 253). This results in the avoidance of controversy or any topic that might contaminate the fertile environment in which corporations seek to advertise their products. Advertisers accept the theme of disease as an individual flaw, thus reinforcing the view that the problem is in the person and not because of the product, and even allows advertisers simultaneously to turn their skills to helping some of those who abuse the product (overeat, overdrink, drive too fast) by developing public service announcements.

The role that advertising plays in subtle censorship, often self-cen-
sorship, is difficult to elaborate fully. The clearest example of the
influence of advertisers over editorial content related to health is the
cigarette issue (e.g., Bagdikian, 1983; Warner, 1986; Minkler, Wallack,
& Madden, 1987; Whelan, Sheridan, Meister, & Mosher, 1981). The
diversification of tobacco companies into the areas of food, beer, and
other beverages presents cause for concern regarding the potential of
major conglomerates to affect reporting of health risks associated with
their products.

Mass Media as Change Agents

Much of our use of mass media is based on the assumption that the
media are able to act as a positive force for planned change in the health
arena. There is little evidence to support this, whether we consider
change in individual terms as the effect of directed media (e.g., public
service campaigns or other special programming) or look at it as
indicated by the way we as a society think about or respond to health
issues on a broader level (Wallack, 1981).

Public health problems are rooted in basic social structures that
contribute to inequality and differential access to opportunities for
health and well-being. It is fairly typical for people to see the mass
media as an able agent in the effort to facilitate a more equal and just
society through the ability to impart information to large numbers of
people. Yet mass media health promotion efforts focus on symptoms,
not causes; emphasize the most obvious (and politically) safest point of
intervention, the individual; and ignore the social roots of disease.

Health promotion, if it is to focus on the conditions that give rise to
and sustain health problems, will be extremely political and controversial. Beauchamp (1976) notes two key factors about our most intractable public problems: "First, they occur to a relative minority of our
population (even though that minority may number in the millions of
people). Second, they result in significant part from arrangements that
are providing substantial benefits or advantages to a majority or powerful minority of citizens" (p. 3).

The mass media are part of a broader mass communication system
that is growing increasingly concentrated. Bagdikian (1985) estimates
that approximately 40 corporations control over half of all mass media
output. This level of control results in a relatively narrow range of ideas
that generally support the existing sociopolitical relationships in
society, in spite of the large number of media outlets (see pp. 358-359,

364). Ideologically, it can be argued that the mass media reproduce the culture rather than change the culture, and serve the interests of a broader corporate community rather than those of the general population. Because corporations have the greatest stake in the social and economic arrangements that buttress their power, the media that they control will be hesitant to challenge those existing arrangements (Schiller, 1973).

A popular assumption is that mass media, television in particular, have the ability to forge significant *changes* in what people know, believe, and do about personal and social problems. The ubiquity of mass media and the fascination with the perceived success of advertising form the basis for this assumption. But, as I have argued, it is more likely the case that mass media, because of their integral role in the social and economic system, serve as *barriers* to change by promoting a consumption ethic and by assessing the relevance of content based on how well it fits with the needs of the sponsors. For the most part, television reinforces existing unequal power relationships, negative stereotypes, and an unrealistic view of the health and medical world (Gerbner et al., 1981; Gerbner, Morgan, & Signorielli, 1982).

Conclusion

There is a saying that when you have a hammer, everything looks like a nail. The mass media become a simple and convenient approach to problems. They are an excellent vehicle for transmitting information to a large audience. For reasons outlined above, we tend to define fundamental problems as a basic lack of information and then to rely on the mass media to provide the right information in the right way to the right people at the right time. This overemphasis on the value of information per se and on the role of the media deflects attention away from more realistic, long-term approaches to addressing the serious social and health problems that detract from the quality of life in contemporary society.

Overall, it can hardly be expected that the mass media will seriously question the values of the economic interests from which they derive sustenance. The reliance on theories of disease causality and health promotion derived from the needs of a mass-production oriented society will continue to guide the way the media conveys information about health. These theories lead us to question the motives and psychology of the individual who "abuses" a product, but not the ethic of consumption that is so skillfully promoted by marketers. The "manufacturers of illness" (McKinlay, 1979) are not singled out for attention in the media to the same extent as are the casualties of the system who fail to adapt to a hazardous environment. The mass media, being an integral part of the larger society and increasingly owned by the corporate captains of that society, can hardly be expected to stimulate the type of critical thinking that questions the ethic of consumption that trades off public health for private profit.

The role of mass media in generating the type of social change that may well be the key to health promotion and disease prevention remains largely unexplored. The notion that mass media can be used to develop critical thinking about health issues and motivate social and economic change to contribute to a more democratic and just society may be as unrealistic as the notion that mass communication campaigns are an adequate response to health promotion issues. Nonetheless, it is time we start to increase our attention to alternative roles the media can play in the public health arena.

Appendix:
Annotated Bibliography
of Campaign-Related Books

There is a growing number of books available on public communication campaigns, nonprofit advertising, and public relations, all indicating the importance of this field of research, practice, and policy. This appendix presents a list of some works that have not already been noted especially in the chapters of this volume.

Bogart, L. (1984). *Strategy in advertising: Matching media and messages to markets and motivations.* Chicago: Crain.

This is an advanced but still practical guide to selection of media channels and message strategies for various target audiences. The book stresses the process of communication and examines measurement of exposure and effects of campaigns.

Brawley, E. (1983). *Mass media and human services.* Beverly Hills, CA: Sage.

This guidebook provides practical suggestions for communicating effectively through the media in promoting public sector programs, particularly in the social work field. It emphasizes applied techniques and illustrations rather than a theoretical approach to education and persuasion of mass audiences.

Fine, S. (1981). *The marketing of ideas and social issues.* New York: Praeger.

This book treats noncommercial ideas as products to be promoted via social marketing techniques to achieve social change. It covers communication models and channels, consumer research, and segmentation, and features a detailed case study.

Frederiksen, L., Solomon, L., & Brehony, K. (1984). *Marketing health behavior: Principles, techniques, and applications.* New York: Plenum.

This book combines behavioral medicine and social marketing approaches to changing health-related behaviors, with four principle/technique chapters and four applications to specific settings and projects (hypertension, Stanford Heart, corporation, hospital).

Green, L., & Lewis, F. (1986). *Measurement and evaluation in health education and health promotion.* Palo Alto, CA: Mayfield.

This is an advanced text focusing on the role of evaluation research in health promotion, adapting standard social/education research methods to the substantive field (measurement theory, reliability, validity, and instrumentation, plus qualitative and quantitative design, sampling, and analysis techniques).

Grunig, J., & Hunt, T. (1984). *Managing public relations.* New York: Holt, Rinehart & Winston.

This is the most theoretically sophisticated of the current public relations texts, covering the standard material comprehensively. There is a chapter devoted to public communications campaigns, along with chapters on evaluation research and message creation.

Hastings House. (1977). *Controversy advertising: How advertisers present points of view in public affairs*. New York: Author.

This book was prepared by the International Advertising Association and explores the subject of public service and advocacy advertising campaigns by corporations and interest groups, covering strategies, audiences, and management, with plenty of case studies from the United States, Europe, and the Third World.

Kotler, P. (1987). *Marketing for health care organizations*. Englewood Cliffs, NJ: Prentice-Hall.

Kotler, P. (1982). *Marketing for non-profit organizations* (2nd ed.). Englewood Cliffs, NJ: Prentice-Hall.

These are part of a series of books by Kotler dealing with social marketing principles in various contexts. The first is a recent application of marketing ideas to hospitals and clinics, while the second provides a broader theoretical perspective. Communication campaigns play a small but important role in the overall mix of research and conceptual approaches derived from the general marketing field.

Leathar, D., Hastings, G., & Davies, J. (Eds.). (1981). *Health education and the media*. Oxford: Pergamon.

This book presents proceedings of an international conference featuring theoretical papers by several U.S. researchers (Mendelsohn, McAlister-Maccoby, Beck) and Europeans (Dorn, Albert, Budd-McCron), plus major sections on developing media materials and evaluation of the effectiveness of smoking, cancer, and hygiene campaigns.

Leathar, D., Hastings, G., O'Reilly, K., & Davies, J. (Eds.). (1986). *Health education and the media II*. Oxford: Pergamon.

This volume presents proceedings of the second international conference, featuring brief reports (averaging 5-6 pages) from dozens of researchers and health professionals, including several from the United States (Mendelsohn, Beck, Romano, Flay), although most are from Europe, primarily Great Britain. The content is similar to that in the volume above, with more emphasis on new technologies but narrower theoretical treatments.

Manoff, R. K. (1985). *Social marketing: New imperative for public health*. New York: Praeger.

The author, a pioneer in applying communication campaign strategies and marketing techniques to health education, describes the development of the field, specific how-to procedures (research, media planning, message design), case histories, and barriers to effectiveness. The book is a well-integrated combination of applied theory and real-world experiences with family planning, nutrition, and other public health campaigns, primarily in Third World settings.

Meyer, M. (Ed.). (1981). *Health education by television and radio.* Munich: K.G. Saur Verlag KG. (Reprinted in German and French versions in 1982 and 1983)

This volume presents proceedings of an international conference featuring theoretical papers by several researchers from the United States (Atkin, Kline, Maccoby-Solomon, Flay) and Europe (McCron-Budd, Puska, Lohr), along with descriptions of specific programs designed to educate audiences about health topics.

Paletz, D. (1977). *Politics in public service advertising on television.* New York: Praeger.

In this book, the role of TV PSA campaigns mounted by the Advertising Council and government/nonprofit agencies is approached from a critical political science perspective. The limitations of access are highlighted, and the values behind acceptable material are discussed. A content analysis and description of persuasive techniques is included.

Rogers, E. M. (1983). *Diffusion of innovations* (3rd ed.). New York: Free Press.

In presenting a broad range of generalizations and principles pertaining to the nature of the adoption of new ideas and practices, a modest emphasis is accorded to the role of communication campaigns in creating awareness and contributing to acceptance. The book stresses stages of individual response and social structural variables rather than campaign strategies. There are examples of campaigns, primarily in Third World settings.

Rothman, J., Teresa, J., Kay, T., & Morningstar, G. (1983). *Marketing human service innovations.* Beverly Hills, CA: Sage.

This book reports on an evaluation of two different social marketing approaches (low-intensity mass mailings with different appeals sent to different organizational entry points and high-intensity workshops offered to personnel at different levels of internal or external organizational membership) for specific human service innovations.

Salmon, C. (Ed.). (1989). *Information campaigns: Managing the process of social change.* Newbury Park, CA: Sage.

This volume presents ten chapters examining interpersonal and mediated information campaign processes from a theoretical framework emphasizing management of social change. The opening section on conceptual frameworks discusses campaign philosophies, comparative perspectives in different political systems, and ethical implications of campaigns. The core of the book presents theories and research in four domains: commercial product advertising, political electioneering, promotion of family planning and safe sexual practices, and sociopolitical movements to achieve fundamental change. The final topics include community-based campaign planning, devising channel and message strategies, and developing audience typologies.

Schultz, D. (1984). *Strategic advertising campaigns.* Chicago: Crain.
    This book presents communication principles relevant to advertising
strategy, and reviews planning, objectives, budgeting, creative strategy, formative and summative evaluation, and promotion in campaigns for commercial
products. It includes case studies. This is the leading campaign-oriented undergraduate text.

Selnow, G., & Crano, W. (1987). *Planning, implementing, and evaluating
    targeted communication programs: A manual for business communicators.*
    New York: Quorum.
    This book provides very detailed and readable coverage of a general model
of targeted commercial communication, the fundamentals of persuasion
theories and results, characteristics of mass media, the importance of interpersonal components, techniques for improving feedback, a tutorial on survey
techniques and research designs, and a very comprehensive discussion of program strategy. A final section includes contributed sections on public opinion
about business, corporate audits, and advocacies for the use of radio, television,
magazine, and newspaper advertising.

Windsor, R., Baranowski, T., Clark, N., & Cutter, G. (1984). *Evaluation of
    health promotion and education programs.* Palo Alto, CA: Mayfield.
    This book covers approaches to conducting evaluations, program planning,
research designs for evaluating effectiveness, and applied techniques of data
collection and analysis. It pays minor attention to mass media message design
and testing due to a broadly comprehensive overview of total evaluation process.

Winnett, R. (1986). *Information and behavior: Systems of influence.* Hillsdale,
    NJ: Erlbaum.
    This book presents a "behavioral systems framework" for understanding
behavior change, access to communication systems, and equity in the use of
social information. The framework attempts to integrate principles from social
learning, communication, behavior analysis, and social marketing. Separate
chapters are devoted to prosocial television, diffusion of innovations, social
marketing, new media, health behavior, and consumer behavior.

Winston, W. (Ed.). (1986). *Advertising handbook for health care services.* New
    York: Haworth.
    This handbook applies marketing and advertising strategies to promotion of
commercial health services such as HMOs, walk-in clinics, and hospitals. It
focuses on case studies and features examples of successful advertisements.

    Finally, we note that communication campaign research stems, in part, from
early concerns and research about the use of the mass media for propaganda.
The following journal section reviews 13 recent books about propaganda:

Various. (1987). Propaganda and persuasion: The re-emergence of a research
    tradition. *Journal of Communication, 37*(1), 97-114.

References

Abramson, J., Arterton, F., & Orren, G. (1988). *The electronic commonwealth: The impact of new media technologies on democratic politics.* New York: Basic Books.

Academy for Educational Development. (1981). *Honduras implementation plan.* Washington, DC: Author.

Adhikarya, R., & Posamentier, H. (1987). *Motivating farmers for action: How strategic multi-media campaigns can help.* Eschborn, FRG: Deutsche Gesellschaft fur Technische Zusammenarbeit (GTZ).

Adorno, T., Frenkel-Brunswick, E., Levinson, D., & Sanford, R. (1950). *The authoritarian personality.* New York: Harper.

Agranoff, R. (1980). Campaign management: Benefits of the professional approach. *Campaigns & Elections, 1,* 46-60.

AHF Marketing Research. (1976). *Forest fire prevention: An awareness and attitudes study.* New York: Author.

Aird, J. (1978). Fertility decline and birth control in the People's Republic of China. *Population and Development Review, 4*(2), 225-254.

Ajzen, I., & Fishbein, M. (1980). *Understanding attitudes and predicting social behavior.* Englewood Cliffs, NJ: Prentice-Hall.

Albert, W. (1981). General models of persuasive influence for health education. In D. Leather, G. Hastings, & J. Davies (Eds.), *Health education and the media.* Oxford: Pergamon.

Albright, C., Flora, J., & Fortmann, S. (1988). *Restaurant menu labeling: An environmental strategy for encouraging dietary changes.* Manuscript submitted for publication.

Aldrich, J., & Nelson, F. (1984). *Linear probability, logit, and probit models.* Beverly Hills, CA: Sage.

Applied Communication Technology. (1985). *The mass media and health practices evaluations in Honduras and The Gambia: Summary report of the major findings.* Menlo Park, CA: Author.

Archarya, L., & Fellow, A. (1988, May). *Ethnic differences in response to AIDS information.* Paper presented to the Health Division at the annual meeting of the International Communication Association, New Orleans.

Armstrong, R. (1988). *The next hurrah: The communications revolution in the American political process.* New York: William Morrow.

Arterton, F. (1987). *Teledemocracy: Can technology protect democracy?* Newbury Park, CA: Sage.

Asch, S., & Zukier, H. (1984). Thinking about persons. *Journal of Personality and Social Psychology, 46,* 1230-1240.

Ashworth, A., & Feachem, R. (1985). Interventions for the control of diarrhoeal diseases among young children: Weaning education. *Bulletin of the World Health Organization, 63*(6), 1115-1127.

Atkin, C. K. (1979). Research evidence on mass mediated health communication campaigns. In D. Nimmo (Ed.), *Communication yearbook 3* (pp. 655-669). New Brunswick, NJ: Transaction.

Atkin, C. K. (1981a). Mass communication research principles for health education. In M. Meyer (Ed.), *Health education by television and radio* (pp. 41-55). Munich: Saur.

Atkin, C. K. (1981b). Mass media information campaign effectiveness. In R. E. Rice & W. J. Paisley (Eds.), *Public communication campaigns* (pp. 265-280). Beverly Hills, CA: Sage.

Atkin, C. K., Garramone, G., & Anderson, R. (1986, May). *Formative evaluation research in health campaign planning: The case of drunk driving prevention.* Paper presented at the annual meeting of the International Communication Association, Chicago.

Atkin, C. K., & Greenberg, B. (1980). *The portrayal of driving on prime time commercial television* (Tech. Rep. for the National Highway Traffic Safety Administration). Washington, DC: U.S. Department of Transportation.

Atkin, C. K., Nuendorf, K., & McDermott, S. (1983). The role of alcohol advertising in excessive and hazardous drinking. *Journal of Drug Education, 13*(4), 313-325.

Atwood, R., Allen, R., Bardgett, R., Proudlove, S., & Rich, R. (1982). Children's realities in television viewing: Exploring situational information seeking. In M. Burgoon (Ed.), *Communication yearbook 6.* Beverly Hills, CA: Sage.

Atwood, R., & Dervin, B. (1981). Challenges to socio-cultural predictors of information seeking: A test of race vs. situation movement state. In M. Burgoon (Ed.), *Communication yearbook 5.* New Brunswick, NJ: Transaction.

Baer, J., & Lichtenstein, E. (1988). Classification and prediction of smoking relapse episodes: An exploration of individual differences. *Journal of Consulting and Clinical Psychology, 56*(1), 104-110.

Bagdikian, B. (1983). *The media monopoly.* Boston: Beacon.

Bagdikian, B. (1985, Summer). The U.S. media: Supermarket or assembly line? *Journal of Communication,* pp. 97-109.

Baggaley, J. (1988). Perceived effectiveness of international AIDS campaigns. *Health Education Research, 3*(1), 7-17.

Bagozzi, R. (1982). A field investigation of causal relations among cognitions, affect, intentions, and behavior. *Journal of Marketing Research, 19*, 562-584.

Baker, K. (1987, October 21). Dealing with AIDS. *San Francisco Examiner,* p. E-7.

Ball, S. (1976). Methodological problems in assessing the impact of television programs. *Journal of Social Issues, 32*, 8-17.

Ball-Rokeach, S. J. (1974). *The information perspective.* Paper presented at the annual meetings of the American Sociological Association, Montreal.

Ball-Rokeach, S. J. (1985). The origins of individual media system dependency: A sociological framework. *Communication Research, 12*, 485-510.

Ball-Rokeach, S. J., & DeFleur, M. (1976). A dependency model of mass media effects. *Communication Research, 3*, 3-21.

Ball-Rokeach, S. J., Grube, J., & Rokeach, M. (1981). *Roots: The Next Generation:* Who watched and with what effect. *Public Opinion Quarterly, 45*, 58-68.

Ball-Rokeach, S. J., Rokeach, M., & Grube, J. (1984). *The Great American Values Test: Influencing behavior and belief through television.* New York: Free Press.

Bandura, A. (1969). *Principles of behavior modification.* New York: Holt, Rinehart & Winston.

Bandura, A. (1977a). Self-efficacy: Toward a unifying theory of behavioral change. *Psychological Review, 84*(2), 191-215.

Bandura, A. (1977b). *Social learning theory.* Englewood Cliffs, NJ: Prentice-Hall.

Bandura, A. (1981). Self-referent thought: A developmental analysis of self-efficacy. In J.H. Flavell & L. Ross (Eds.), *Social cognitive development: Frontiers and possible futures.* Cambridge: Cambridge University Press.

Bandura, A. (1982). Self-efficacy mechanism in human agency. *American Psychologist,* *37*(2), 122-147.

Bandura, A. (1983). Self-efficacy determinants of anticipated fears and calamities. *Journal of Personality and Social Psychology, 45,* 464-469.

Bandura, A. (1986). *Social foundations of thought and action: A social cognitive theory.* Englewood Cliffs, NJ: Prentice-Hall.

Bandura, A., Grusec, J., & Menlove, F. L. (1966). Observational learning as a function of symbolization and incentive set. *Child Development, 37,* 499-506.

Banks, M., Bewley, B., & Bland, J. (1981). Adolescent attitudes to smoking: Their influence on behavior. *International Journal of Health Education, 24,* 39.

Barban, A., et al. (1981). *Advertising media sourcebook and workbook* (2nd ed.). Columbus, OH: Grid.

Barnouw, E. (1978). *The sponsor.* New York: Oxford University Press.

Baudrillard, J. (1983). *In the shadow of the silent majorities. . . Or the end of the social and other essays.* New York: Semiotext(e).

Bauer, R. (1964). The obstinate audience: The influence process from the point of view of social communication. *American Psychologist, 19,* 319-328.

Baume, C. (1988). *Healthcom: Preliminary report on the results from the 1987 resurvey in Honduras.* Menlo Park, CA: Applied Communication Technology.

Beauchamp, D. (1976). Public health as social justice. *Inquiry, 12,* 3-14.

Belkin, L. (1987, March 21). TV contraceptive ads backed in poll. *New York Times.*

Bell, P. (1987, October 18). Central American presidents show real grit in quest for peace. *Los Angeles Times,* V-1.

Bellah, R., Madsen, R., Sullivan, W., Swidler, A., & Tipton, S. (1985). *Habits of the heart.* Berkeley: University of California Press.

Belville, H. M., Jr. (1988). *Audience ratings: Radio, television, cable* (2nd ed.). Hillsdale, NJ: Erlbaum.

Bem, D. (1970). *Beliefs, attitudes and human affairs.* Belmont, CA: Brooks/Cole.

Bem, D. (1972). Self perception theory. In L. Berkowitz (Ed.), *Advances in experimental social psychology* (Vol. 6., pp. 2-63). New York: Academic Press.

Benfari, R. C., Eaker, E., & Stoll, J. G. (1981). Behavioral interventions and compliance to treatment regimens. *Annual Review of Public Health, 2,* 431-471.

Benito, A. (1976). Peasant's response to modernization projects in minifundia economics. *American Journal of Agricultural Economics, 58*(2), 143-151.

Bennett, W., & Edelman, M. (1985). Toward a new political narrative. *Journal of Communication, 35,* 156-171.

Berelson, B., Lazarsfeld, P., & McPhee, W. (1954). *Voting.* Chicago: University of Chicago Press.

Berkowitz, L., & Walker, N. (1967). Laws and moral judgments. *Sociometry, 30,* 410-422.

Berlyne, D. (1967). Arousal and reinforcement. In D. Levine (Ed.), *Nebraska Symposium on Motivation.* Lincoln: University of Nebraska Press.

Bernard, H., Killworth, P., Kronenfeld, D., & Sailer, L. (1984). The problem of informant accuracy: The validity of retrospective data. *Annual Review of Anthropology, 13,* 495-517.

Berrien, F. (1968). *General and social systems.* New Brunswick, NJ: Rutgers University Press.

Berrigan, J. (1982). The cost effectiveness of grass-roots campaign activities. *Campaigns & Elections, 3,* 25-33.

Berrueta, M. (1986). *The soap opera as a reinforcer of social values.* Unpublished master's thesis, IberoAmericano University, Mexico City.

Berscheid, E., & Walster, E. (1978). *Interpersonal attraction* (2nd ed.). Reading, MA: Addison-Wesley.

Bertalanffy, L. von. (1968). *General systems theory.* New York: Braziller.

Bertrand, J. T. (1978). *Communications pretesting.* Chicago: University of Chicago, Community and Family Study Center.

Bertrand, J., Pineda, M., & Soto, F. E. (1978). *Communicating family planning to rural Guatemala.* Chicago: University of Chicago, Community and Family Study Center.

Best, J. (1980). Mass media, self management, and smoking modification. In P. O. Davidson (Ed.), *Behavioral medicine: Changing health lifestyles.* New York: Brunner/Mazel.

Birkby, R. (1969). The Supreme Court and the Bible belt: Tennessee reaction to the "Schempp" decision. In T. Becker & M. Feeley (Eds.), *The impact of Supreme Court decisions.* New York: Oxford University Press.

Bishop, G., Meadow, R., & Jackson-Beeck, M. (Eds.). (1978). *The presidential debates: Media, policy and electoral perspectives.* New York: Praeger.

Blackburn H., Leupker, R., Kline, F., Bracht, N., & Carlaw, R. (1984). The Minnesota Heart Health Program: A research and demonstration project in cardiovascular disease prevention. In J. Matarazzo, S. Weiss, J. Herd, & N. Miller (Eds.), *Behavioral health: A handbook of health enhancement and disease prevention* (pp. 1171-1178). New York: John Wiley.

Blane, H., & Hewitt, L. (1980). Alcohol, public education, and mass media: An overview. *Alcohol Health and Research World, 5*(1), 2-16.

Bloom, P., & Novelli, W. (1981). Problems and challenges in social marketing. *Journal of Marketing, 45,* 79-88.

Blum, H. (1980). Social perspective on risk reduction. *Family and Community Health, 3,* 41-61.

Blumberg, H. (1972). Communication of interpersonal evaluations. *Journal of Personality and Social Psychology, 23,* 157-162.

Blumenthal, S. (1981). *The permanent campaign.* New York: Simon & Schuster.

Blumler, J., & Katz, E. (Eds.). (1974). *The uses of mass communications: Current perspectives on gratifications research.* Beverly Hills, CA: Sage.

Boone, M., Farley, J., & Samuel, S. (1985). A cross-country study of commercial contraceptive sales programs: Factors that lead to success. *Studies in Family Planning, 16*(1), 30-38.

Boorstin, D. (1965). *The Americans: The national experience.* New York: Vintage.

 Bratic, E., Greenberg, R., & Peterson, P. (1980). HMTS: Improving the quality of public service announcements through standardized pretesting. *Journal of the Academy of Marketing Science, 9*(1), 40-51.

Breed, W., & DeFoe, J. (1981). The portrayal of the drinking process on prime-time television. *Journal of Communication, 31*(1), 58-67.

Breed, W., & DeFoe, J. (1982). Effecting media change: The role of cooperative consultation on alcohol types. *Journal of Communication, 32,* 88-99.

Britain, G. M. (1981). Contextual evaluation: An ethnographic approach to program assessment. In R. F. Conner (Ed.), *Methodological advances in evaluation research.* New York: Russell Sage.

British Broadcasting Corporation, International Broadcasting and Audience Research Library. (1987). *World radio and television receivers.* London: Author.

Brown, J. (1987). *Evaluating one's abilities: The self-assessment versus self-enhancement debate revisited.* Manuscript submitted for publication.

Brown, L. (1981). *Innovation diffusion: A new perspective.* London: Methuen.

Brown, L. (1987). Hype in a good cause. *Channels, 7*(7), 26.

Brown, R. (1984). Community organization influence on local public health care policy: A general research model and comparative case study. *Health Education Quarterly, 10,* 205-233.

Brownell, K., Marlatt, G., Lichtenstein, E., & Wilson, G. T. (1986). Understanding and preventing relapse. *American Psychologist, 4*(7), 765-782.

Buckley, W. (Ed.). (1968). *Modern systems research for the behavioral scientist.* Chicago: Aldine.

Calder, B., Insko, C., & Yandell, B. (1974). The relation of cognitive and memorial processes to persuasion in a simulated jury level. *Journal of Applied Social Psychology, 4,* 62-93.

Campbell, A., Converse, P., Miller, W., & Stokes, D. (1960). *The American voter.* New York: John Wiley.

Campbell, A., Gurin, G., & Miller, W. (1954). *The voter decides.* Evanston, IL: Row Peterson.

Campbell, D., & Stanley, J. (1966). Experimental and quasi-experimental designs for research. Skokie, IL: Rand McNally.

Campbell, D., Steenbarger, B., Smith, T., & Stucky, R. (1982). An ecological systems approach to evaluation: Cruising in Topeka. *Evaluation Review, 6*(5), 625-648.

Cantor, M. G. (1979). The politics of popular drama. *Communication Research, 6.* 387-406.

Carter, R. (1973). *Communication as behavior.* Paper presented at the annual meeting of the Association for Education in Journalism, Fort Collins, CO.

Carter, R. (1974). *Toward more unity in science.* Seattle: University of Washington.

Carter, R. (1980). *Discontinuity and communication.* Paper presented at the East-West Center Conference on Communication Theory East and West, Honolulu.

Carter, R. (1982). *Button, button. . . .* Paper presented at the annual meeting of the Association for Education in Journalism.

Carter, R., Ruggels, W., Jackson, K., & Heffner, M. (1972). Application of signaled stopping technique to communication research. In P. Clarke (Ed.). *New models for communication research.* Beverly Hills, CA: Sage.

Cartwright, D. (1949). Some principles of mass persuasion. *Human Relations, 2,* 253-267.

Cassel, J. (1976). The contribution of the social environment to host resistance. *American Journal of Epidemiology, 104*(2), 107-123.

Cell, C. (1977). *Revolution at work.* New York: Academic Press.

Chaffee, S. (1972). The interpersonal context of mass communication. In F. G. Kline & P. J. Tichenor (Eds.), *Current perspectives in mass communication research.* Beverly Hills, CA: Sage.

Chaffee, S. (1982). Mass media and interpersonal channels: Competitive, convergent or complementary? In G. Gumpert & R. Cathcart (Eds.), *Inter/media: Interpersonal communication in a media world.* New York: Oxford University Press.

Chaffee, S., & Miyo, Y. (1983). Selective exposure and the reinforcement hypothesis: An intergenerational panel study of the 1980 presidential campaign. *Communication Research, 10,* 3-36.

Chaiken, S., & Eagly, A. (1976). Communication modality as a determinant of message persuasiveness and message comprehensibility. *Journal of Personality and Social Psychology, 34,* 605-614.

Chapanis, N., & Chapanis, A. (1964). Cognitive dissonance: Five years later. *Psychological Bulletin, 61,* 1-22.

Chu, G., & Schramm, W. (1967). *Learning from television: What the research says.* Washington, DC: National Association of Educational Broadcasters.

Cialdini, R., & Petty, R. (1981). Anticipatory opinion effects. In R. Petty, T. Ostrom, & T. Brock (Eds.), *Cognitive responses in persuasion* (pp. 217-235). Hillsdale, NJ: Erlbaum.

CIBA Foundation. (1976). *Symposium 42: Acute diarrhea in childhood.* Amsterdam: Elsevier-Excerpta Medica, North-Holland.

Cochran, N. (1978). Grandma Moses and the "corruption" of data. *Evaluation Quarterly, 3,* 363-373.

Cohen, A. (1962). An experiment on small rewards for discrepant compliance and attitude change. In J. Brehm & A. Cohen (Eds.), *Explorations in cognitive dissonance* (pp. 73-78). New York: John Wiley.

Cohen, S., & Syme, S. (1985). Issues in the study and application of social support. In S. Cohen & S. Syme (Eds.), *Social support and health.* New York: Academic Press.

Coleman, J., Katz, E., & Menzel, J. (1966). *Medical innovation: A diffusion study.* New York: Bobbs-Merrill.

Coleman, P. (1988). Enter-educate: New word from Johns Hopkins. *JOICEP Review,* pp. 28-51.

Colletti, G., & Brownell, K. D. (1982). The physical and emotional benefits of social support: Application to obesity, smoking, and alcoholism. *Progress in Behavior Modification, 3,* 109-178.

Combs, J. (1980). *The dimensions of political drama.* Santa Monica, CA: Goodyear.

Combs, J. (1981). A process approach. In D. Nimmo & K. Sanders (Eds.), *Handbook of political communication.* Beverly Hills, CA: Sage.

Comstock, G. (1976). The impact of television on American institutions. *Journal of Communication, 28,* 12-28.

Condiotte, M., & Lichtenstein, E. (1981). Self-efficacy and relapse in smoking cessation programs. *Journal of Consulting and Clinical Psychology, 49,* 648-658.

Conrad, C. (1985). *Strategic organizational communication: Cultures, situations, and adaptation.* New York: Holt, Rinehart & Winston.

Contractor, N., Singhal, A., & Rogers, E. M. (1988). Meta-theoretical perspectives on satellite television and development in India. *Journal of Broadcasting and Electronic Media, 32,* 129-148.

Cook, T. D. (1985). Postpositivist critical multiplism. In L. Shotland & M. M. Mark (Eds.), *Social science and social policy* (pp. 21-62). Beverly Hills, CA: Sage.

Cook, T. D., & Campbell, D. (1979). *Quasi-experimentation: Design and analysis issues for field settings.* Skokie, IL: Rand McNally.

Cook, T. D., Gruder, C., Hennigan, K., & Flay, B. (1979). History of the sleeper effect: Some logical pitfalls in accepting the null hypothesis. *Psychological Bulletin, 86,* 662-679.

Cook, T. D., & Leviton, L. (1980). Reviewing the literature: A comparison of traditional methods with meta-analysis. *Journal of Personality, 48,* 449-472.

Cook, T. D., Leviton, L., & Shadish, W., Jr. (1985). Program evaluation. In G. Lindzey & E. Aronson (Eds.), *Handbook of social psychology* (3rd ed., pp. 699-777). New York: Random House.

Cooke, T., & Romweber, S. (1977a). *Mass media nutrition education: Vol. 2. Nicaragua* (draft final report for USAID Office of Nutrition). New York: Manoff International.

Cooke, T., & Romweber, S. (1977b). *Radio, advertising techniques and nutrition education: A summary of a field experiment in the Philippines and Nicaragua* (final report for USAID Office of Nutrition). New York: Manoff International.

Cooke, T., & Romweber, S. (1977c). *Radio nutrition education: A test of the advertising technique: Philippines and Nicaragua.* Unpublished report, Manoff International, Washington, DC.

Cooper, H. (1984). *The integrative research review.* Beverly Hills, CA: Sage.

Coppotelli, H., & Orleans, C. (1985). Partner support and other determinants of smoking cessation maintenance among women. *Journal of Consulting and Clinical Psychology, 53,* 455-460.

Cox, F. (1979). Alternative conceptions of community: Implications for community organization practice. In F. Cox, J. Erlich, J. Rothman, & J. Tropman (Eds.), *Strategies of community organization* (2nd ed., pp. 224-234). Itasca, IL: Peacock.

Craver, R. (1985). Direct mail and fund raising with new technologies. In R. Meadow (Ed.), *New communication technologies in politics.* Washington, DC: Washington Program of the Annenberg Schools.

Crawford, R. (1977). You are dangerous to your health: The ideology and politics of victim blaming. *International Journal of Health Services, 7*(4), 663-680.

Cronbach, L. (1982). *Designing evaluations of educational and social programs.* San Francisco: Jossey-Bass.

Cronbach, L., Ambron, S., Dornbusch, S., Hess, R., Hornik, R., Walker, D., & Weiner, S. (1980). *Toward reform of program evaluation.* San Francisco: Jossey-Bass.

Crouse, T. (1973). *The boys on the bus.* New York: Random House.

Cruz, J., & Wallack, L. (1986). Trends in tobacco use on television. *American Journal of Public Health, 76*(6), 698-699.

Curry, S., & Marlatt, G. (1985). Unaided quitters' strategies for coping with temptations to smoke. In S. Shiffman & T. Wills (Eds.), *Coping and substance use* (pp. 243-265). New York: Academic.

Curry, S., Marlatt, G., & Gordon, J. R. (1987). Abstinence violation effect: Validation of an attributional construct with smoking cessation. *Journal of Consulting and Clinical Psychology, 55*(2), 145-149.

Czitrom, D. (1982). *Media and the American mind.* Chapel Hill: University of North Carolina Press.

Danaher, B., Berkanovic, E., & Gerber, B. (1983). Smoking and television: Review of the extant literature. *Addictive Behaviors, 8,* 173-182.

DeMartini, J., & Whitbeck, L. (1986). Knowledge use as knowledge creation: Reexamining the contribution of the social sciences to decision making. *Knowledge: Creation. Diffusion, Utilization, 7,* 383-396.

Dervin, B. (1976). Strategies for dealing with human information needs: Information or communication? *Journal of Broadcasting, 20,* 324-333.

Dervin, B. (1980). Communication gaps and inequities: Moving toward a reconceptualization. In B. Dervin & M. Voigt (Eds.), *Progress in communication sciences* (Vol. 2). Norwood, NJ: Ablex.

Dervin, B. (1983, May). *An overview of sense-making research: Concepts, methods, and results to date.* Paper presented at the annual meeting of the International Communication Association, Dallas.

Dervin, B., & Clark, K. (1987). *ASQ: Asking significant questions. Alternative tools for information needs and accountability assessments by librarians.* Sacramento: California State Libraries.

Dervin, B., & Dewdney, P. (1986, Summer). Neutral questioning: A new approach to the reference interview. *RQ,* pp. 506-513.

Dervin, B., & Harlock, S. (1976, May). *Health communication research: The state of the art.* Paper presented at the annual meeting of the International Communication Association, Portland, OR.

Dervin, B., Harlock, S., Atwood, R., & Garzona, C. (1980). The human side of information: An exploration in a health communication context. In D. Nimmo (Ed.), *Communication yearbook 4.* New Brunswick, NJ: Transaction.

Dervin, B., Jacobson, T., & Nilan, M. (1982). Measuring information seeking: A test of a quantitative-qualitative methodology. In M. Burgoon (Ed.), *Communication yearbook 6.* New Brunswick, NJ: Transaction.

Dervin, B., & Nilan, M. (1986). Information needs and uses: A conceptual and methodological review. *Annual review of information science and technology* (Vol. 21, pp. 3-33). White Plains, NY: Knowledge Industries.

Dervin, B., Nilan, M., & Jacobson, T. (1981). Improving predictions of information use: A comparison of predictor types in a health communication setting. In M. Burgoon (Ed.), *Communication yearbook 5.* New Brunswick, NJ: Transaction.

De Tocqueville, A. (1961). *Democracy in America.* New York: Schocken. (Original work published 1835)

Deutsch, M., & Gerard, H. (1955). A study of normative and informational social influences upon individual social judgment. *Journal of Abnormal and Social Psychology, 51,* 629-636.

DeVries, W., & Tarrance, V., Jr. (1972). *The ticket-splitter.* Grand Rapids, MI: Eerdman's.

Dewdney, P. (1986). *The effects of training reference librarians in interview skills: A field experiment.* Unpublished doctoral dissertation, University of Western Ontario.

Dewey, J. (1922). *Human nature and conduct.* New York: Modern Library.

Dewey, J. (1938). *Logic: The theory of inquiry.* New York: Holt, Rinehart & Winston.

Diamond, E., & Bates, S. (1988). *The spot: The rise of political advertising on television.* Cambridge: MIT Press.

DiClemente, C., & Prochaska, J. (1982). Self-change and therapy change of smoking behavior: A comparison of processes of change in cessation and maintenance. *Addictive Behaviors, 7,* 133-142.

Djukanovic, V., & Mach, E. (1975). *Alternative approaches to meeting basic health needs in developing countries.* Geneva: World Health Organization.

Donohew, L., & Palmgren, P. (1971). A reappraisal of dissonance and the selective exposure hypothesis. *Journalism Quarterly, 48,* 412-420.

Doordarshan, Audience Research Group. (1986). *Television in India.* New Delhi: Author.

Dow, M., Biglan, A., & Glaser, S. (1985). Multimethod assessment of socially anxious and socially nonanxious women. *Behavioral Assessment, 7,* 273-282.

Drew, E. (1981). *Portrait of an election.* New York: Simon & Schuster.

Dryfoos, J. (1985). What the United States can learn about prevention of teenage pregnancy from other developed countries. *SIECUS Report, 14,* 1-7.

Dupuy, J. (1980). Myths of the information society. In K. Woodward (Ed.), *The myths of information: Technology and post-industrial culture.* Madison, WI: Code.

Dworkin, M. (1986). *Making sense with television news: Situation, context, and psychology of the audience experience.* Unpublished doctoral dissertation, University of Washington, Seattle.

Dwyer, J. (1983). *Statistical methods for the social and behavioral sciences.* New York: Oxford University Press.

Dwyer, T., Pierce, J., Hannam, C., Burke, N., & Quit for Life Steering Committee. (1986). Evaluation of Sydney quit for life: Part 2. Changes of smoking prevalence. *Medical Journal of Australia, 144,* 344-347.

Eagly, A. (1981). Recipient characteristics as determinants of responses to persuasion. In R. Petty, T. Ostrom, & T. Brock (Eds.), *Cognitive responses in persuasion.* Hillsdale, NJ: Erlbaum.

Eagly, A. (1983). Gender and social influence: A social psychological analysis. *American Psychologist, 38,* 971-981.

Eagly, A., & Chaiken, S. (1984). Cognitive theories of persuasion. In L. Berkowitz (Ed.), *Advances in experimental social psychology* (Vol. 17, pp. 267-359). Orlando, FL: Academic Press.

Eckland, B. (1968). Theories of mate selection. *Eugenics Quarterly, 15,* 71-84.

Egger, G., Fitzgerald, N., Frape, G., Monaem, A., Rubinstein, P., Tyler, C., & McKay, B. (1983). Result of a large scale media anti-smoking campaign in Australia: North Coast "Quit for Life" Programme. *British Medical Journal, 286,* 1123-1128.

Ehrenreich, B., & English, D. (1979). *For her own good: 150 years of the experts' advice to women.* Garden City, NY: Anchor.

Eliot, R. (1987). Coronary artery disease: biobehavioral factors. *Circulation, 76*(Suppl. 1), I110-I112.

Esrey, S., Feachem, R., & Hughes, J. (1985). Interventions for the control of diarrhoeal diseases among young children: Improving water supplied and excreta disposal facilities. *Bulletin of the World Health Organization, 63*(4), 757-772.

Evans, R., Rozelle, R., Lasater, F., Dembroski, T., & Allen, B. (1970). Fear arousal, persuasion, and actual versus implied behavioral change: New perspectives utilizing a real-life dental hygiene program. *Journal of Personality and Social Psychology, 16,* 220-227.

Farquhar, J. (1978). The community-based model of lifestyle intervention trials. *American Journal of Epidemiology, 108,* 103-111.

Farquhar, J. (1987). *The American way of life need not be hazardous to your health* (rev. ed.). Reading, MA: Addison-Wesley.

Farquhar, J., Flora, J., Goode, L., & Fortmann, S. (1986). *Comprehensive integrated health promotion programs.* Manuscript prepared for the Henry J. Kaiser Family Foundation.

Farquhar, J., Fortmann, S., Maccoby, N., Haskell, W., Williams, P., Flora, J., Taylor, C., Brown, B., Jr., Solomon, D., & Hulley, S. (1985). The Stanford Five City Project: Design and methods. *American Journal of Epidemiology, 122*(2), 323-334.

Farquhar, J., Maccoby, N., & Solomon, D. (1984). Community applications of behavioral medicine. In E. Gentry (Ed.), *Handbook of behavioral medicine* (pp. 437-478). New York: Guilford.

Farquhar, J., Maccoby, N., & Wood, P. (1985). Education and community studies. In W. Holland, R. Detels, & G. Knox (Eds.), *Oxford textbook of public health* (pp. 207-221). Oxford: Oxford University Press.

Farquhar, J., Maccoby, N., Wood, P., Alexander, J., Breitrose, H., Brown, B., Haskell, W., McAlister, A., Meyer, A., Nash, J., & Stern, M. (1977). Community education for cardiovascular health. *Lancet*, 1192-1195.

Feachem, R. (1986). Preventing diarrhoea: What are the policy options? *Health Policy and Planning, 1*(2), 109-117.

Feachem, R., Hogan, R., & Merson, M. (1983). Diarrhoeal disease control: Reviews of potential interventions. *Bulletin of the World Health Organization, 61*(4), 637-640.

Federal Register. (1984). *Federal motor vehicle safety standards: Occupant crash protection* (Final Rule 48, no. 138). Washington, DC: U.S. Department of Transportation.

Fellow, T. (1988). *Computers and politics: Predictors of innovation in political campaign organizations.* Unpublished doctoral dissertation, University of Southern California, Annenberg School of Communications.

Fenno, R., Jr. (1978). *Home style: House members in their districts.* Boston: Little, Brown.

Ferguson, K. (1984). *The feminist case against bureaucracy.* Philadelphia: Temple University Press.

Fernandez-Collado, C., Greenberg, B., Korzenny, F., & Atkin, C. (1978, Summer). Sexual intimacy and drug use in TV series. *Journal of Communication*, pp. 30-37.

Festinger, L. (1954). A theory of social comparison processes. *Human Relations, 7*, 117-140.

Festinger, L. A. (1957). *A theory of cognitive dissonance.* Evanston, IL: Row Peterson.

Festinger, L., & Carlsmith, J. (1959). Cognitive consequences of forced compliance. *Journal of Abnormal and Social Psychology, 58*, 203-210.

Fine, S. (1984). The health product: A social marketing perspective. *Hospitals*, pp. 66, 68.

Fishbein, M., & Ajzen, I. (1975). *Belief, attitude, intention and behavior.* Reading, MA: Addison-Wesley.

Flay, B. R. (1981). On improving the chances of mass media health promotion programs causing meaningful changes in behavior. In M. Meyer (Ed.), *Health education by television and radio* (pp. 56-91). Munich: Saur.

Flay, B. R. (1985). Psychosocial approaches to smoking prevention: A review of the findings. *Health Psychology, 4*(5), 449-488.

Flay, B. R. (1986). Efficacy and effectiveness trials (and other phases of research) in the development of health promotion programs. *Preventive Medicine, 15*, 451-474.

Flay, B. R. (1987a). Evaluation of the development, dissemination and effectiveness of mass media health programming. *Health Education Research, 2*(2), 123-130.

Flay, B. R. (1987b). *Selling the smokeless society* (APHA Public Health Practice Series). Washington, DC: American Public Health Association.

Flay, B. R., & Best, J. (1982). Overcoming design problems in evaluating health behavior programs. *Evaluation and the Health Professions, 5*(1), 43-69.

Flay, B. R., Hansen, W., Johnson, C., & Sobel, J. (1983). *Involvement of children in motivating smoking parents to quit smoking with a television program.* Paper presented at the World Conference on Smoking and Health, Winnipeg, Manitoba.

Flexner, E. (1975). *Century of struggle: The women's rights movement in the United States.* Cambridge, MA: Harvard University Press.

Flora, J., Good, L., MacKinnon, J., & Fortmann, S. (1985, November). *A prototype educational monitoring system for community-based health promotion programs.*

Paper presented at the annual meeting of the American Public Health Association, Washington, DC.

Flora, J., Jackson, C., & Maccoby, N. (in press). Indicators of societal action to promote physical health. In S. Kar (Ed.), *Individual and societal actions for health promotion: Strategies and indicators.* Beverly Hills, CA: Springer.

Flora, J., Roser, C., Chaffee, S., & Farquhar, J. (1988, July). *Information campaign effects of different media: Results from the Stanford Five City Project.* Paper presented at the annual meeting of the Association for Education in Journalism and Mass Communication, Portland, OR.

Fortmann, S., Sallis, J., Magnus, P., & Farquhar, J. (1985). Attitudes and practices of physicians regarding hypertension and smoking: The Stanford Five City Project. *Preventive Medicine, 14*, 70-80.

Foucault, M. (1980). *Power/knowledge: Selected interviews and other writings.* New York: Pantheon.

Frank, R., Massy, W., & Wind, Y. (1972). *Market segmentation.* Englewood Cliffs, NJ: Prentice-Hall.

Frankel, S. (1986, Summer). To the left of Madison Avenue. *Mother Jones.*

Frederiksen, L., Solomon, L., & Brehony, K. (Eds.). (1984). *Marketing health behavior: Principle, techniques, and applications.* New York: Plenum.

Freimuth, V. S. (1985). Developing the public service advertisement for nonprofit marketing. In R. Belk (Ed.), *Advances in nonprofit marketing* (Vol. 1, pp. 55-95). Greenwich, CT: JAI.

Freimuth, V. S., Greenberg, R., DeWitt, J., & Romano, R. (1984). Covering cancer: Newspapers and the public interest. *Journal of Communication, 34*(1), 62-73.

Freimuth, V. S., & Van Nevel, P. (1981). Reaching the public: An analysis of the asbestos awareness campaign. *Journal of Communication, 31*, 155-167.

Freire, P. (1983). *Education for critical consciousness.* New York: Continuum.

Friedman, L., Lichtenstein, E., & Biglan, A. (1985). Smoking onset among teens: An empirical analysis of initial situations. *Addictive Behaviors, 10*, 1-13.

Furstenberg, F., Moore, K., & Peterson, J. (1985). Sex education and sexual experience among adolescents. *American Journal of Public Health, 75*, 1331-1332.

Galanter, R. (1977). To the victim belong the flaws. *American Journal of Public Health, 67*(11), 1025-1026.

Galbraith, J. K. (1973). *Economics and the public purpose.* New York: Mentor.

Gallup Opinion Index. (1974, June 20-21). *Report 108.*

Gambrill, E. (1977). *Behavior modification: Handbook of assessment, intervention, and evaluation.* San Francisco: Jossey-Bass.

Gandy, O. (1987). The political economy of communication competence. In V. Mosco & J. Wasko (Eds.), *The political economy of information.* Madison: University of Wisconsin Press.

Gans, H. (1979). *Deciding what's news: A study of the CBS Evening News, NBC Nightly News, Newsweek and Time.* New York: Pantheon.

Gantz, W. (1975). *The movement of taboos: A message-oriented approach.* Unpublished manuscript.

Garramone, G. (1985). Motivation and political information processing: Extending the gratifications approach. In S. Kraus & R. Perloff (Eds.), *Mass media and political thought.* Beverly Hills, CA: Sage.

Garramone, G., Harris, A., & Anderson, R. (1986). Uses of political computer bulletin boards. *Journal of Broadcasting and Electronic Media, 30*, 325-339.

Geen, R., & Quanty, M. (1977). The catharsis of aggression. In L. Berkowitz (Ed.), *Advances in experimental social psychology* (Vol. 10, pp. 1-37). New York: Academic Press.

Geller, E. S. (1985). *Community safety belt programs.* Blacksburg: Virginia Polytechnic Institute and State University.

Gerbner, G. (1987). *Stories that hurt: Tobacco, alcohol and other drugs in the mass media.* Philadelphia: University of Pennsylvania, Annenberg School of Communications.

Gerbner, G., & Gross, L. (1976). Living with television: The violence profile. *Journal of Communication, 26*(2), 173-199.

Gerbner, G., Gross, L., Morgan, M., & Signorielli, N. (1981). Special report: Health and medicine on television. *New England Journal of Medicine, 305*(15), 901-904.

Gerbner, G., Gross, L., Morgan, M., & Signorielli, N. (1982). Charting the mainstream: Television's contributions to political orientations. *Journal of Communication, 32,* 100-127.

Gerbner, G., Gross, L., Morgan, M., & Signorielli, N. (1986). Living with television: The dynamics of the cultivation process. In J. Bryant & D. Zillman (Eds.), *Perspectives on media effects* (pp. 16-40). Hillsdale, NJ: Erlbaum.

Gerbner, G., Morgan, M., & Signorielli, N. (1982). Programming health portrayals: What viewers see, say and do. In D. Pearl, L. Bouthilet, & J. Lazar (Eds.), *Television and behavior: Ten years of scientific progress and implications for the eighties* (Vol. 2, pp. 291-307) (DHHS Publication No. ADM 82-1196). Washington, DC: Government Printing Office.

Germond, J., & Witcover, J. (1981). *Blue smoke & mirrors.* New York: Viking.

Germond, J., & Witcover, J. (1985). *Wake us when it's over.* New York: Macmillan.

Giddens, A. (1989). The orthodox consensus and emerging synthesis. In B. Dervin, L. Grossberg, B. O'Keefe, & E. Wartella (Eds.), *Rethinking communication: Vol. 1. Paradigm issues.* Newbury Park, CA: Sage.

Gitlin, T. (1980). *The whole world is watching: Mass media in the making and unmaking of the new left.* Berkeley: University of California Press.

Gitlin, T. (1983). *Inside prime time.* New York: Pantheon.

Gitlin, T. (Ed.). (1987). *Watching television.* New York: Simon & Schuster.

Glass, G., & Ellet, S., Jr. (1981). Evaluation research. In M. Rosenzweig & L. Porter (Eds.), *Annual review of psychology* (Vol. 32). Palo Alto, CA: Annual Reviews.

Glass, G. V., McGaw, B., & Smith, M. (1981). *Meta-analysis in social research.* Beverly Hills, CA: Sage.

Goldsmith, A., Pillsbury, B., & Nicholas, D. (1985). *Community organization.* Bethesda, MD: PRICOR.

Goldstein, T. (1985). *The news at any cost.* New York: Simon & Schuster.

Gottlieb, N., & Baker, J. (1986). The relative influence of health beliefs, parental and peer behaviors and exercise program participation on smoking, alcohol use and physical activity. *Social Science and Medicine, 22,* 915-927.

Graber, D. (1980). *Mass media and American politics.* Washington, DC: Congressional Quarterly Press.

Graber, D. (1988). *Processing the news.* New York: Longman.

Green, E. (1986). Diarrhea and the social marketing of oral rehydration salts in Bangladesh. *Social Science Medicine, 23*(4), 357-366.

Greenberg, B. (1981). Television: Health issues on commercial television series. In M. Trudeau & M. Angle (Eds.), *Health promotion and the mass media* (Institute of Medicine, Conference Summary). Washington, DC: National Academy Press.

Greenberg, B., & Atkin, C. (1983). The portrayal of driving on television, 1975-1980. *Journal of Communication, 33*, 44-55.

Greenberg, B., Fernandez-Collado, C., Graef, D., Korzenny, F., & Atkin, C. (1979). Trends in use of alcohol and other substances on television. *Journal of Drug Education, 9*, 243-253.

Greenberg, D. (1986, March). Whatever happened to the war on cancer? *Discover*, pp. 47-56.

Greenwald, A., Brock, T., & Ostrom, T. (Eds.). (1968). *Psychological foundations of attitudes*. New York: Academic Press.

Griffiths, M., Zeitlin, M., Manoff, R., & Cook, T. (1983). *Kader evaluation: Nutrition communication and behavior change component, Indonesia nutrition development program*. New York: Manoff International.

Gritz, E. (1980). Problems related to the use of tobacco by women. In O. Kalant (Ed.), *Research advances in alcohol and drug abuse* (Vol. 5, pp. 487-543). New York: John Wiley.

Grossman, M., & Kumar, 1. (1981). *Portraying the president: The White House and the news media*. Baltimore: Johns Hopkins University Press.

Grunig, J. (1983). Communication behaviors and attitudes of environmental publics: Two studies. *Journalism Monographs, 81*, 1-47.

Guthrie, K. (1987). *Para-social interaction among viewers of home shopping programs*. Unpublished paper, University of Southern California, Annenberg School of Communications.

Gutzwiller, F., Nater, B., & Martin, J. (1985). Community-based primary prevention of cardiovascular disease in Switzerland: Methods and results of the National Research Program (NRP 1A). *Preventive Medicine, 14*, 482-491.

Habermas, J. (1984). *The theory of communicative language: Vol. 1. Reason and the rationalization of society*. Boston: Beacon.

Hall, B., & Dodds, T. (1977). Voice for development: The Tanzanian national radio study campaigns. In P. Spain, D. Jamison, & E. McAnany (Eds.), *Radio for education and development: Case studies*. Washington, DC: World Bank.

Hamburg, B., & Pierce, C. (1982). Introductory comments. In D. Pearl, L. Bouthilet, & J. Lazar (Eds.), *Television and social behavior: Ten years of scientific progress and implications for the eighties* (Vol. 2). Rockville, MD: National Institute of Mental Health.

Hamburg, D. (1979). Disease prevention: Challenge of the future. *American Journal of Public Health, 69*, 1026-1034.

Hardin, G., & Baden, J. (Eds.). (1977). *Managing the commons*. San Francisco: Freeman.

Harvey, P. (1984). Advertising family planning in the press: Direct response results from Bangladesh. *Studies in Family Planning, 15*(1), 40-42.

Haskins, J. (1970). Evaluative research on the effects of mass communication safety campaigns: A methodological critique. *Journal of Safety Research. 2*, 86-96.

Hazzard, M., & Cambridge, V. (1988). *Socio-drama as an applied technique for development communication in the Caribbean: Specialized content and narrative structure in the radio dramas of Elaine Perkins in Jamaica*. Paper presented at the Caribbean and Latin American Studies Conference, Guadeloupe, French West Indies.

HealthCom. (1984-1985). *Communication and health literacy evaluation of the Peru program.* Philadelphia: University of Pennsylvania, Annenberg School of Communications.

Heath, L., Kendzierski, D., & Borgida, E. (1982). Evaluation of social programs: A multidimensional approach combining a delayed treatment true experiment and multiple time series. *Evaluation Review, 6*(2), 233-246.

Hedges, L., & Olkin, I. (1985). *Statistical methods for meta-analysis.* Orlando, FL: Academic Press.

Hennigan, K., Flay, B. R., & Haag, R. A. (1979). Clarification of concepts and terms commonly used in evaluative research. In R. Kleine, M. Read, H. Riecken, J. Brown, A. Peradalli, & C. Daza (Eds.), *Evaluating the impact of nutrition and health programs* (pp. 387-432). New York: Plenum.

Henninger, M., & Wyer, R. (1976). The recognition and elimination of inconsistencies among syllogistically related beliefs: Some new light on the "Socratic effect." *Journal of Personality and Social Psychology, 34,* 680-693.

Henningfield, J. (1984). Pharmacologic basis and treatment of cigarette smoking. *Journal of Clinical Psychology, 45,* 24-34.

Hershey, M. (1984). *Running for office: The political education of campaigners.* Chatham, NJ: Chatham House.

Higginbothan, J., & Cox, K. (1979). *Focus group interviews: A reader.* Chicago: American Marketing Association.

Hilgard, E. (1971). Hypnotic phenomena: The struggle for scientific acceptance. *American Scientist, 59,* 567-577.

Hill, C., Rubin, Z., & Peplau, L. (1976). Breakups before marriage: The end of 103 affairs. *Journal of Social Issues, 32,* 147-168.

Holland, W., & Breeze, E. (1986). Good life-styles for good health. *World Health Forum, 7*(4), 380-386.

Hops, H., & Greenwood, C. R. (1981). Social skills: Current research practices and future directions. *Behavior Therapy, 14,* 3-18.

Hops, H., Weissman, W., Biglan, A., Thompson, R., Faller, C., & Severson, H. (1986). A taped situation test of cigarette refusal skill among adolescents. *Behavioral Assessment, 8,* 145-154.

Hornik, R. (1985). *Nutrition education: A state of the art review.* Washington, DC: World Bank.

Hornik, R. (1988). *Development communication.* New York: Longman.

Hornik, R., Sankar, P., Huntington, D., Matsebula, G., Mndzebele, A., & Magongo, B. (1986). *Communication for diarrheal disease control: Evaluation of the Swaziland program.* Washington, DC: Academy for Educational Development.

Horton, D., & Wohl, R. (1956, August). Mass communication and para-social interaction: Observation on intimacy at a distance. *Psychiatry,* pp. 215-229.

Hovland, C., Janis, I., & Kelley, H. (1953). *Communication and persuasion.* New Haven, CT: Yale University Press.

Hovland, C., Lumsdaine, A., & Sheffield, F. (1949). *Experiments on mass communication.* Princeton, NJ: Princeton University Press.

Hughes, J., Hatsukami, D., Pickens, R., Krahn, D., Malin, S., & Luknic, A. (1984). Effect of nicotine on the tobacco withdrawal syndrome. *Psychopharmacology, 83,* 82-87.

Hunt, W., Barnett, L., & Branch, L. G. (1971). Relapse rates in addiction programs. *Journal of Clinical Psychology, 27,* 455-456.

Hyman, H., & Sheatsley, P. (1947). Some reasons why information campaigns fail. *Public Opinion Quarterly, 11*, 412-423.

Injury in America: A continuing public health problem. (1985). Washington, DC: National Academy Press.

Institute for Communication Research and Johns Hopkins University/Population Communication Services. (1987). *Evaluation of Communication for Young People Project* (PCS Project No. LA-MEX-02). Baltimore: Author.

Irle, M., & Katz, L. (Eds.). (1982). *Studies in decision making: Social psychological and socio-economic analyses.* Berlin: Walter de Gruyter.

Iyengar, S., & Kinder, D. (1987). *News that matters: TV and American opinion.* Chicago: University of Chicago Press.

Jain, M. (1985, April 14-20). Be Indian, see Indian. *Sunday*, pp. 24-26.

Jamison, D., et al. (Eds.). (1975). Evaluation of instructional technology [Special issue]. *Instructional Science, 4*, 189-406.

Jamison, D., Klees, S., & Wells, S. (1978). *The costs of educational media.* Beverly Hills, CA: Sage.

Janis, I. (1967). Effects of fear arousal on attitude change: Recent developments in theory and experimental research. In L. Berkowitz (Ed.), *Advances in experimental social psychology* (Vol. 3). New York: Academic Press.

Janis, I., & Gilmore, J. (1965). The influence of incentive conditions on the success of role playing in modifying attitudes. *Journal of Personality and Social Psychology, 1*, 17-27.

Janis, I., Kaye, D., & Kirschner, P. (1965). Facilitating effects of "eating-while-reading" on responsiveness to persuasive communications. *Journal of Personality and Social Psychology, 1*, 181-186.

Jeffrey, D., McLellarn, R., & Fox, D. (1982). The development of children's eating habits: The role of television commercials. *Health Education Quarterly, 9*(2-3), 78-93.

Jensen, K. (1987). Qualitative audience research: Toward an integrative approach to reception. *Critical Studies in Mass Communication, 4*, 21-36.

Jessor, R., Donovan, J., & Costa, F. (1986). Psychosocial correlates of marijuana use in adolescence and young adulthood: The past as prologue. *Alcohol, Drugs, and Driving, 2*, 31-49.

Jessor, R., & Jessor, S.L. (1977). *Problem behavior and psychosocial development: A longitudinal study of youth.* New York: Academic Press.

Johnston, J., & Ettema, J. (1982). *Positive images: Breaking stereotypes with children's television.* Beverly Hills, CA: Sage.

Johnston, J., Ettema, J., & Davidson, T. (1980). *An evaluation of Freestyle: A television series to reduce sex-role stereotypes.* Ann Arbor, MI: Institute for Social Research.

Johnston, L., O'Malley, P., & Bachman, J. (1987). *National trends in drug use and related factors among American high school students and young adults, 1975-1986* (DHHS Publication No. ADM 87-1535). Washington, DC: Government Printing Office.

Kaid, L., Nimmo, D., & Sanders, K. (Eds.). (1986). *New perspectives on political advertising.* Carbondale: Southern Illinois University Press.

Kar, S., & Talbot, J. (1981). *Impact of peer counseling on teen contraception in Los Angeles.* Paper presented at the annual meeting of the American Public Health Association.

Katz, D. (1960). The functional approach to the study of attitudes. *Public Opinion Quarterly, 24*, 163-204.

Katz, E. (1980). On conceptualizing media effects. *Studies in Communication, 1,* 119-141.

Katz, E., & Lazarsfeld, P. (1955). *Personal influence.* New York: Free Press.

Katz, E., & Wedell, G. (1977). *Broadcasting in the Third World: Promise and performance.* Cambridge, MA: Harvard University Press.

Kaufman, L. (1980). Prime time nutrition. *Journal of Communication, 32,* 37-46.

Kelly, S. (1960). *Political campaigning: Problems in creating an informed electorate.* Washington, DC: Brookings Institution.

King, A., Flora, J., Fortmann, S., & Taylor, C. (1987). Smokers' challenge: Immediate and long term findings of a community smoking cessation contest. *American Journal of Public Health, 77,* 1340-1341.

King, A., Saylor, K., Foster, S., Killen, J., Telch, M., Farquhar, J., & Flora, J. (1988). Promoting dietary change in adolescents: A school-based approach for modifying and maintaining healthful behavior. *American Journal of Preventive Medicine, 4,* 68-74.

Kinkead, G. (1987, November 9). America's best-run charities. *Fortune,* pp. 145-150.

Kirsch, I. (1982). Efficacy expectations or response predictions: The meaning of efficacy ratings as a function of task characteristics. *Journal of Personality and Social Psychology, 42,* 132-136.

Kirsch, I., Tennen, H., Wickless, C., Saccone, A., & Cody, S. (1985). The role of expectancy in fear reduction. *Behavior Therapy, 14,* 520-533.

Klapper J. (1960). *The effects of mass communication.* Glencoe, IL: Free Press.

Klein, H. (1980). *Making it perfectly clear.* Garden City, NY: Doubleday.

Kleinot, M., & Rogers, R. (1982). Identifying effective components of alcohol misuse prevention programs. *Journal of Studies on Alcohol, 43*(7), 802-811.

Knowles, J. (1977). Doing better and feeling worse: Health in the United States. *Daedalus, 106,* 1-7.

Kotler, P. (1972). A generic concept of marketing. *Journal of Marketing, 36,* 46-54.

Kotler, P. (1975). *Marketing for nonprofit organizations.* Englewood Cliffs, NJ: Prentice-Hall.

Kotler, P., & Zaltman, G. (1971). Social marketing: An approach to planned social change. *Journal of Marketing, 35,* 3-12.

Kozinsky, J. (1970). *Being there.* New York: Harcourt Brace Jovanovich.

Kraus, S. (Ed.). (1979). *The great debates: Carter vs. Ford, 1976.* Bloomington: Indiana University Press.

Kraus, S., & Davis, D. (1976). *The effects of mass communication on political behavior.* State College: Pennsylvania State University Press.

Krauss, R., Freedman, J., & Whitcup, M. (1978). Field and laboratory studies of littering. *Journal of Experimental Social Psychology, 14,* 109-122.

Krugman, H. (1965). The impact of television advertising: Learning without involvement. *Public Opinion Quarterly, 29,* 349-356.

Krugman, H. (1977). Memory without recall, exposure without perception. *Journal of Advertising Research, 17*(4), 7-12.

Kumar, V., Monga, O., & Jain, N. (1981). The introduction of oral rehydration in a rural community in India. *World Health Forum, 2*(3), 364-366.

LaBarbera, P. (1980, July 25). Time compressed tapes increase learning efficiency of students. *Marketing News, 1,* p. 7.

Ladd, E. (1981, June/July). 205 and going strong. *Public Opinion,* pp. 7-12.

Lamb, C. (1987). Public sector marketing is different. *Business Horizons,* pp. 56-60.

Lang, G., & Lang, K. (1983). *The battle for public opinion: The president, the press and the polls during Watergate.* New York: Columbia University Press.

LaRose, R. (1980). Formative evaluation of children's television as mass communication research. In B. Dervin & M. Voigt (Eds.), *Progress in communication sciences* (Vol. 2, pp. 275-297). Norwood, NJ: Ablex.

Lasater, T., Abrams D., Artz, L., Beaudin, P., Cabrera, L., Elder, J., Ferreira, A., Knisky, P., Peterson, G., & Rodrigues, A. (1984). Lay volunteer delivery of a community-based cardiovascular risk factor change program: The Pawtucket experiment. In J. Matarazzo, S. Weiss, J. Herd, & N. Miller (Eds.), *Behavioral health: A handbook of health enhancement and disease prevention* (pp. 1166-1170). New York: John Wiley.

Lasswell, H. (1948). The structure and function of communication in society. In L. Bryson (Ed.), *Communication of ideas.* New York: Harper.

Lazarsfeld, P., Berelson, B., & Gaudet, H. (1948). *The people's choice.* New York: Columbia University Press.

Lazarus, R. (1980). The stress and coping paradigms. In C. Eisdorfer, D. Cohen, A. Klienmen & P. Maxim (Eds.), *Theoretical bases for psychopathology* (pp. 177-214). New York: Spectrum.

Lazarus, R. (1984). On the primacy of cognition. *American Psychologist, 39,* 124-129.

Lazarus, R., & Monat, A. (Eds.). (1977). *Stress and coping.* New York: Columbia University Press.

Lefebvre, C., & Flora, J. (in press). Social marketing and public health intervention. *Health Education Quarterly.*

Lesser, G. (1974). *Children and television: Lessons from Sesame Street.* New York: Random House.

Leventhal, H., Meyer, D., & Nerenz, D. (1980). The common sense representation of illness danger. In S. Rachman (Ed.), *Medical psychology.* New York: Pergamon.

Leventhal, H., Shafer, M., & Panagis, D. (1983). The impact of communications on the self-regulation of health beliefs, decision, and behavior. *Health Education Quarterly, 10,* 3-29.

Levinson, D. (1978). *Seasons of a man's life.* New York: Knopf.

Levitt, T. (1960). Marketing myopia. *Harvard Business Review, 38,* 45-56.

Levy, M. (1979). Watching TV news as para-social interaction. *Journal of Broadcasting, 23,* 69-80.

Lewis, C., & Lewis, M. (1982). Children's health-related decision making. *Health Education Quarterly, 9,* 129-141.

Ley, P. (1982). Satisfaction, compliance and communication. *British Journal of Clinical Psychology, 21,* 241-254.

Lichtenstein, E. (1982). The smoking problem: A behavioral perspective. *Journal of Consulting and Clinical Psychology, 50,* 804-819.

Liebes, T. (1988). On the convergence of theories of mass communication and literature regarding the role of the reader. In B. Dervin & M. Voigt (Eds.), *Progress in communication sciences* (Vol. 9). Norwood, NJ: Ablex.

Linder, D., Cooper, J., & Jones, E. (1967). Decision freedom as a determinant of the role of incentive magnitude in attitude change. *Journal of Personality and Social Psychology, 6,* 39-45.

Lindheim, R., & Syme, L. (1983). Environments, people, and health. *Annual Review of Public Health, 4,* 335-359.

Liu, A.P.L. (1981). Mass campaigns in the People's Republic of China. In R. E. Rice & W. Paisley (Eds.), *Public communication campaigns* (pp. 199-223). Beverly Hills, CA: Sage.

Longshore. D. L. (1988). *AIDS education for higher-risk populations.* Washington, DC: U.S General Accounting Office.

Lorig, K., & Laurin, J. (1985). Some notions about assumptions underlying health education. *Health Education Quarterly, 12*(3), 231-243.

Lovelock, C., & Weinberg, C. (1978). *Readings in public and nonprofit marketing.* Palo Alto, CA: Scientific Press.

Lowi, T. (1983). The political impact of information technology. In T. Forester (Ed.), *The microelectronics revolution: The complete guide to the new technology and its impact.* Cambridge: MIT Press.

Lowry, D. (1981). Alcohol consumption patterns and consequences on prime time network TV. *Journalism Quarterly, 37,* 3-8.

Lumsdaine, A., & Janis, I. (1953). Resistance to counterpropaganda produced by one-sided and two-sided communication. *Public Opinion Quarterly, 17,* 311-318.

Maccoby, N. (1980). Promoting positive health behaviors in adults. In L. Bond & J. Rosen (Eds.), *Competence and coping during adulthood* (pp. 218-243). Hanover, NH: University Press.

Maccoby, N., Farquhar, J., Wood, P., & Alexander, J. (1977). Reducing the risk of cardiovascular disease: Effects of a community-based campaign on knowledge and behavior. *Journal of Community Health, 3,* 100-114.

Maccoby, N., & Roberts, D. (1985). Effects of mass communication. In G. Lindzey & E. Aronson (Eds.), *Handbook of social psychology* (Vol. 2, 3rd ed.). New York: Random House.

Mahai, B., et al. (1975). *The second follow-up formative evaluation report of the "Food Is Life" campaign.* Dar es Salaam, Tanzania: Institute of Adult Education.

Maiman, L., & Becker, M. (1974). The health belief model: Origins and correlates in psychological theory. In M. Becker (Ed.), *The health belief model and personal health behavior* (pp. 9-26). Thorofare, NJ: Charles B. Slack.

Mandese, J. (1987, May 18). PSAs: Too many issues, not enough time. *Adweek,* pp. 52, 56.

Manoff, R. (1985). *Social marketing: New imperative for public health.* New York: Praeger.

Mantell, J., & Schinke, S. (1988). The crisis of AIDS for adolescents: The need for preventive risk-reduction interventions. In A. Roberts (Ed.), *Crisis intervention handbook.* New York: Springer.

Marascuilo, L., & Zwick, R. (1983). Comment on Barnard: Another look at strength and direction of attitude using contrasts. *Psychological Bulletin, 94,* 534-539.

Marlatt, G., & Gordon, J. (1980). Determinants of relapse: Implications for the maintenance of behavioral change. In P. Davidson & S. Davidson (Eds.), *Behavioral medicine: Changing health lifestyles.* New York: Brunner/Mazel.

Marlatt, G., & Gordon, J. (Eds.). (1985). *Relapse prevention: Maintenance strategies in the treatment of addictive behaviors.* New York: Guilford.

Marx, K. (1913). *A contribution to the critique of the political economy.* Chicago: Kerr. (Original work published 1859)

McAlister, A. (1976, May). *"Mini-experiments" to mass media: Developing communications for behavior change.* Paper presented at the annual meeting of the International Communication Association, Portland. OR.

McAlister, A., Ramirez, A., Stern, M., & Amezcua, C. (1987). *To your health: Media and community program A Su Salud* (Tech. Rep.). Bethesda, MD: National Cancer Institute.

McClelland, D. (1975). *Power: The inner experience*. New York: Halsted.

McCollum/Spielman & Company, Inc. (1980, August). Starpower. *Topline, 2*(3).

McCombs, M., & Shaw, D. (1972-1973). The agenda setting function of mass media. *Public Opinion Quarterly, 36,* 176-187.

McDivitt, J., & Myers, C. (1987). *HealthCom: Preliminary results from the follow-up survey in The Gambia.* Menlo Park, CA: Applied Communication Technology.

McGhee, P. (1980). Toward the integration of entertainment and educational functions of television: The role of humor. In P. Tannenbaum (Ed.), *The entertainment functions of television* (pp. 183-208). Hillsdale, NJ: Erlbaum.

McGinnis, J., Shopland, D., & Brown, C. (1987). Tobacco and health: Trends in smoking and smokeless tobacco consumption in the United States. *Annual Review of Public Health, 8,* 441-467.

McGuire, W. J. (1960). A syllogistic analysis of cognitive relationships. In C. Hovland & M. Rosenberg (Eds.), *Attitude organization and change* (pp. 65-111). New Haven, CT: Yale University Press.

McGuire, W. J. (1964). Inducing resistance to persuasion. In L. Berkowitz (Ed.), *Advances in experimental social psychology* (Vol. 1, pp. 191-229). New York: Academic Press.

McGuire, W. J. (1966). The current status of cognitive consistency theories. In S. Feldman (Ed.), *Cognitive consistency* (pp. 1-46). New York: Academic Press.

McGuire, W. J. (1968a). Personality and attitude change: An information-processing theory. In A. Greenwald, T. Brock, & T. Ostrom (Eds.), *Psychological foundations of attitudes.* New York: Academic Press.

McGuire, W. J. (1968b). Personality and social influence. In E. Borgatta & W. Lambert (Eds.), *Handbook of personality theory and research* (pp. 1130-1187). Chicago: Rand McNally.

McGuire, W. J. (1969). Attitude and attitude change. In G. Lindzey & E. Aronson (Eds.), *Handbook of social psychology* (2nd ed., pp. 136-314). Reading, MA: Addison-Wesley,

McGuire, W. J. (1974). Psychological motives and communication gratification. In J. Blumler & E. Katz (Eds.), *The uses of mass communications: Current perspectives on gratifications research* (pp. 167-196). Beverly Hills, CA: Sage.

McGuire, W. J. (1980). Behavioral medicine, public health, and communication theories. *National Forum, 60,* 18-24.

McGuire, W. J. (1981). The probabilogical model of cognitive structure and attitude change. In R. Petty, T. Ostrom, & Brock, T. (Eds.), *Cognitive responses in persuasion.* Hillsdale, NJ: Erlbaum.

McGuire, W. J. (1983). A contextualist theory of knowledge: Its implications for innovations and reform in psychology research. In L. Berkowitz (Ed.), *Advances in experimental social psychology* (Vol. 16, pp. 1-47). New York: Academic Press.

McGuire, W. J. (1984). Public communication as a strategy for inducing health promoting behavioral change. *Preventive Medicine, 13,* 299-319.

McGuire, W. J. (1985). Attitudes and attitude change. In G. Lindzey & E. Aronson (Eds.), *Handbook of social psychology* (3rd ed.). New York: Random House.

McGuire, W. J. (1986). A perspectivist looks at contextualism and the future of behavioral science. In R. Rosnow & M. Georgordi (Eds.), *Contextualism and understanding in behavioral science: Implications for research and theory* (pp. 271-301). New York: Praeger.

McGuire, W. J. (1989). The structure of individual attitudes and attitude systems. In A. Pratkanis, S. Breckler, & A. Greenwald (Eds.), *Attitude structure and function* (pp. 37-69). Hillsdale, NJ: Erlbaum.

McGuire, W. J., & Millman, S. (1965). Anticipatory belief lowering following forewarning of a persuasive attack. *Journal of Personality and Social Psychology, 2,* 471-479.

McIntyre, D., Lichtenstein, E., & Mermelstein, R. (1983). Self-efficacy and relapse in smoking cessation: A replication and extension. *Journal of Consulting and Clinical Psychology, 51,* 632-633.

McKinlay, J. (1979). A case for refocussing upstream: The political economy of illness. In E. Jaco (Ed.), *Patients, physicians and illness.* New York: Free Press.

McLaughlin, J. (1975). The doctor shows. *Journal of Communication, 25*(3), 182-184.

McLeod, J., & Becker, L. (1981). The uses and gratifications approach. In D. Nimmo & K. Sanders (Eds.), *Handbook of political communication.* Beverly Hills, CA: Sage.

McMillan, M. (Ed.). (1973). *Using commercial resources in family planning programs: The international experience.* Honolulu: University Press of Hawaii.

McNamara, E., Kurth, T., & Hansen, D. (1981). Communication efforts to prevent wildfires. In R. E. Rice & W. J. Paisley (Eds.), *Public communication campaigns* (pp. 143-160). Beverly Hills, CA: Sage.

McQuail, D. (1986). Commercialization. In D. McQuail & K. Siune (Eds.), *New media politics* (pp. 152-178). London: Sage.

Meadow, R. G. (1983). Televised campaign debates as whistle stop speeches. In W. Adams (Ed.), *Media coverage of the 1980 election.* Norwood, NJ: Ablex.

Meadow, R. G. (1985a). Political campaigns, new technology and political communication research. In D. Nimmo, K. Sanders, & L. Kaid (Eds.), *Political communication yearbook, 1984.* Carbondale: Southern Illinois University Press.

Meadow, R. G. (1985b). Political campaigns, new technology and political competition. In R. G. Meadow (Ed.), *New communication technologies in politics.* Washington, DC: Washington Program of the Annenberg Schools.

Meadow, R. G. (1986). The electronic machine: New technologies in political campaigns. *Election Politics, 3,* 26-31.

Meadow, R. G., & McMillen, W. (1985). The architecture of campaign software: Microcomputers in political campaigns. In R. G. Meadow (Ed.), *New communication technologies in politics.* Washington, DC: Washington Program of the Annenberg Schools.

Meadow, R. G., & Sigelman, L. (1982). Some effects and non-effects of campaign commercials: An experimental study. *Political Behavior, 4,* 163-175.

Mechanic, D. (1982). Disease, mortality, and the promotion of health. *Health Affairs, 1*(3), 28-32.

Mendelsohn, H. (1973). Some reasons why information campaigns can succeed. *Public Opinion Quarterly, 37,* 50-61.

Mermelstein, R., Cohen, S., & Lichtenstein, E. (1983). *Psychosocial stress, social support and smoking cessation and maintenance.* Paper presented at the annual meeting of the American Psychological Association, Anaheim, CA.

Mermelstein, R., Cohen, S., Lichtenstein, E., Baer, J. S., & Kamarck, T. (1986). Social support and smoking cessation and maintenance. *Journal of Consulting and Clinical Psychology, 51*(4), 447-453.

Meyer, A., Maccoby, N., & Farquhar, J. (1977). The role of opinion leadership in a cardiovascular health education campaign. In D. Rubin (Ed.), *Communication yearbook 1.* New Brunswick, NJ: Transaction.

Meyer, A., Nash, J., McAlister, A., Maccoby, N., & Farquhar, J. (1980). Skills training in a cardiovascular health education campaign. *Journal of Consulting and Clinical Psychology, 48*(2), 129-142.

Meyrowitz, J. (1985). *No sense of place.* New York: Oxford University Press.

Mielke, K., & Chen, M. (1983). Formative research for *3-2-1 Contact:* Methods and insights. In M. Howe (Ed.), *Learning from television* (pp. 31-55). London: Academic Press.

Mielke, K., & Swinehart, J. (1976). *Evaluation of the* Feeling Good *television series.* New York: Children's Television Workshop.

Milla, A. (Ed.). (1985). *Annotated bibliography on oral rehydration therapy.* Dhaka, Bangladesh: International Centre for Diarrhoeal Disease Research.

Miller, G., Galanter, E., & Pribrum, K. (1960). *Plans and the structures of behavior.* New York: Holt.

Miller, L., & Downer, A. (1987). *Knowledge and attitude changes in adolescents following one hour of AIDS instruction.* Paper presented at the International Conference on AIDS, Washington, DC.

Miller, N., & Dollard, J. (1941). *Social learning and imitation.* New Haven, CT: Yale University Press.

Miller, N., Maruyama, G., Beaber, R., & Valone, K. (1976). Speed of speech and persuasion. *Journal of Personality and Social Psychology, 34,* 615-624.

Ministerio de Salud Publica y Asistencia Social. (1972). *Encuesta demografico nacional de Honduras.* Honduras: Author.

Ministerio de Salud Publica y Asistencia Social. (1977). *Plan nacional de desarrollo: Plan nacional de salud 1979-1983.* Honduras: Author.

Ministerio de Salud Publica y Asistencia Social. (1978). *Memoria anual.* Honduras: Author.

Minkler, M. (1986, Fall). The social component of health. *American Journal of Health Promotion,* 33-38.

Minkler, M., Wallack, L., & Madden, P. (1987). Alcohol and cigarette advertising in *Ms.* magazine. *Journal of Public Health Policy, 8*(2), 164-179.

Montgomery, K. (1981). Gay activists and the networks. *Journal of Communication, 31,* 49-57.

Montgomery, K. (1989). *Target prime time: Advocacy groups and entertainment TV.* New York: Oxford University Press.

Moore, J. (Ed.). (1986). *Campaign for president: The managers look at '84.* Dover, MA: Auburn House.

Morrison, E. (1976). *Guardian of the forest: A history of the Smokey Bear program.* New York: Vantage.

Moss, R. (1980, February). The cancer establishment: Whose side are they on? *Progressive,* pp. 14-18.

Muir, W., Jr. (1967). *Prayer in the public schools: Law and attitude change.* Chicago: University of Chicago Press.

Murdock, G. (1989). Critical inquiry and audience activity. In B. Dervin, L. Grossberg, B. O'Keefe, & E. Wartella (Eds.), *Rethinking communication: Vol. 1. Paradigm issues.* Newbury Park, CA: Sage.

Murphy, P. (1984). Analyzing markets. In L. Frederiksen, L. Solomon, & K. Brehony (Eds.), *Marketing health behavior.* New York: Plenum.

National Cancer Institute. (1982). *Pretesting in health communications* (NIH Publication No. 83 1493, rev.). Washington, DC: Government Printing Office.

National Cancer Institute. Office of Cancer Communications. (1975a). *NCI information and communications activity: A position paper.* Bethesda, MD: U.S. Public Health Service, NCI-OCC.

National Cancer Institute, Office of Cancer Communications. (1975b). *The Office of Cancer Communications: Where we are and where we are going.* Bethesda, MD: U.S. Public Health Service, NCI-OCC.

National Cancer Institute, Office of Cancer Communications. (1980). *Progress against breast cancer: Report on evaluation of a public educational program on breast cancer.* Bethesda, MD: U.S. Public Health Service, NCI-OCC.

National Cancer Institute, Office of Cancer Communications. (1984). *Pretesting in health communications: Methods, examples, and resources for improving health messages and materials.* Bethesda, MD: U.S. Public Health Service, NCI-OCC.

National Cancer Institute, Office of Cancer Communications. (1986). *Partners in prevention: Case studies of cancer prevention in the community.* Bethesda, MD: U.S. Public Health Service, NCI-OCC.

National Center for Health Statistics. (1988). *Health promotion and disease prevention: United States, 1985* (Vital and Health Statistics, Series 10, No. 163, DHHS Publication No. PHS 88-1591). Washington, DC: Government Printing Office.

National Institute of Mental Health. (1982). *Television and behavior: Ten years of scientific progress and implications for the eighties* (DHHS Publication No. ADM 82-1195). Washington, DC: Government Printing Office.

Neubauer, D., & Pratt, R. (1981). The second public health revolution: A critical appraisal. *Journal of Health Politics, Policy and Law, 6,* 205-228.

Newman, I. (1984). Capturing the energy of peer pressure: Insights from a longitudinal study of adolescent cigarette smoking. *Journal of School Health, 54,* 146-148.

Newsom, D., & Scott, A. (1985). *This is P.R.: The realities of public relations* (3rd ed.). Belmont, CA: Wadsworth.

Nie, N., Verba, S., & Petrocik, J. (1976). *The changing American voter.* Cambridge, MA: Harvard University Press.

Nielsen Media Research. (1979). *Viewers in profile: July, 1979, Monterey/Salinas, CA.* Chicago: A. C. Neilsen Co.

Nielsen Media Research. (1987). *1987 Nielsen report on television.* Northbrook, IL: A. C. Nielsen Co.

Nilan, M. (1985). *Structural constraints and situational information seeking: A test of two predictors in a sense-making context.* Unpublished doctoral dissertation, University of Washington, Seattle.

Nimmo, D. (1976). Political image makers and the mass media. *Annals of the American Academy of Political and Social Science, 427,* 33-44.

Nimmo, D., & Combs, J. (1983). *Mediated political realities.* New York: Longman.

Noelle-Neumann, E. (1974). The spiral of silence. *Journal of Communication, 24*(2), 43-51.

Nordlund, J. (1978). Media interaction. *Communication Research, 5,* 150-175.

Novelli, W. (1982). You can produce effective PSAs. *Public Relations Journal, 16.* 30-32.

Obetsebi-Lamptey, J. (1973). Development of the Ghana advertising campaign. In
    M. McMillan (Ed.), *Using commercial resources in family planning communication
    programs: The international experience.* Honolulu: University Press of Hawaii.
Ockene, J. (1984) Toward a smoke-free society. *American Journal of Public Health,*
    77(11), 1198-1200.
Ogilvy, D., & Raphaelson, J. (1982). Research on advertising techniques that work—and
    don't work. *Harvard Business Review, 18,* 14-15.
O'Keefe, G. J. (1985). "Taking a bite out of crime": The impact of a public information
    campaign. *Communication Research, 12*(2), 147-178.
O'Keefe, G. J. (1986). The "McGruff" national media campaign: Its public impact and
    future implications. In D. Rosenbaum (Ed.), *Community crime prevention: Does it
    work?* Beverly Hills, CA: Sage.
O'Keefe, G. J., & Atwood, L. (1981). Communication and election campaigns. In
    D. Nimmo & K. Sanders (Eds.), *Handbook of political communication.* Beverly Hills,
    CA: Sage.
O'Keefe, G. J., & Reid, K. (in press). *Promoting crime prevention competence among the
    elderly.* Washington, DC: National Institute of Justice.
O'Keefe, M. T. (1971). The anti-smoking commercials: A study of television's impact on
    behavior. *Public Opinion Quarterly, 35,* 242-248.
O'Malley, M., & Thistlethwaite, D. (1980). Inference in inconsistency reduction: New
    evidence on the "Socratic effect." *Journal of Personality and Social Psychology, 39,*
    1064-1071.
Palmer, E. (1981). Shaping persuasive messages with formative research. In R. E. Rice
    & W. J. Paisley (Eds.), *Public communication campaigns.* Beverly Hills. CA: Sage.
Parducci, A. (1968). The relativism of absolute judgments. *Scientific American, 219,*
    518-528.
Parenti, M. (1986). *Inventing reality.* New York: St. Martin's.
Patterson, T. (1980). *The mass media election.* New York: Praeger.
Patterson, T., & McClure, R. (1976). *The unseeing eye.* New York: Putnam's.
Pear, R. (1988, August 6). Chinese who shun 1-child plan get asylum. *New York Times.*
Pearl, D., Bouthilet, L., & Lazar, J. (Eds.). (1982). *Television and social behavior: Ten
    years of scientific progress and implications for the eighties* (Vol. 2). Rockville, MD:
    National Institute of Mental Health.
Pendleton, D. (1985). Towards more effective medical practice. *Journal of Applied
    Communication Research, 13,* 96-102.
Perse, E., & Rubin, A. (1987). *Television program satisfaction: Testing a uses and effects
    model.* Paper presented at the annual meeting of the Broadcasting Education
    Association, Dallas.
Petty, R., & Cacioppo, J. (1981). *Attitudes and persuasion: Classic and contemporary
    approaches.* Dubuque, IA: Wm. C. Brown.
Petty, R., & Cacioppo, J. (1986). *Communication and persuasion: Central and peripheral
    routes to attitude change.* New York: Springer-Verlag.
Petty, R., Ostrom, T., & Brock, T. (Eds.). (1981). *Cognitive responses in persuasion.*
    Hillsdale, NJ: Erlbaum.
Pierce, J., Dwyer, T., Frape, G., Chapman, S., Chamberlain, A., Burke, N., & Quit for
    Life Steering Committee. (1986). Evaluation of the Sydney quit for life anti-smoking
    campaign: Part I. Achievement of intermediate goals. *Medical Journal of Australia,
    144,* 341-347.

Population Information Program, Johns Hopkins University. (1977). *Media communications in population/family planning programs: A review* (Population Reports, Series J, No. 16). Baltimore: Author.

Population Information Program, Johns Hopkins University. (1980). *Community-based and commercial contraceptive distribution: An inventory and appraisal* (Population Reports, Series J, No. 19). Baltimore: Author.

Population Information Program, Johns Hopkins University. (1984). *Social marketing: Does it work?* (Population Reports, Series J, No. 21). Baltimore: Author.

Population Information Program, Johns Hopkins University. (1985). *Contraceptive social marketing: Lessons from experience* (Population Reports, Series J, No. 30). Baltimore: Author.

Powers, W. (1978). Quantitative analysis of purposive systems: Some spadework at the foundations of scientific psychology. *Psychological Review, 85*, 417-435.

Powles, J. (1979). On the limitations of modern medicine. In D. Sobel (Ed.), *Ways of health: Holistic approaches to ancient and contemporary medicine*. New York: Harcourt Brace Jovanovich.

Prochaska, J., & DiClemente, C. (1983). Self change processes, self-efficacy and decisional balance across five stages of smoking cessation. In A. R. Liss (Ed.), *Advances in cancer control: Epidemiology and research*. New York: Alan R. Liss.

Puska, P., Koskela, K., McAlister, A., Mayranen, H., Smolander, A., Moisio, S., Viri, L., Korpelainen, V., & Rogers, E. M. (1986). Use of lay opinion leaders to promote diffusion of health innovations in a community programme: Lessons learned from the North Karelia project. *Bulletin of the World Health Organization, 64*(3), 347-446.

Puska, P., Koskela, K., McAlister, A., et al. (1979). A comprehensive television smoking cessation program in Finland. *International Journal of Health Education, 22*(Suppl.), 1-26.

Puska, P., McAlister, A., Pekkola, J., & Koskela, K. (1981). Television in health promotion: Evaluation of a national programme in Finland. *International Journal of Health Education, 24*(4), 2-14.

Puska, P., Nissinen, A., Tuomilehto, J., Salonen, J., Koskela, K., McAlister, A., Kottke, T., Maccoby, N., & Farquhar, J. (1985). The community-based strategy to prevent coronary heart disease: Conclusions from the ten years of the North Karelia Project. *Annual Review of Public Health, 6*, 147-193.

Puska, P., Tuomilehto, J., Salonen J., Nissinen, A., Virtamo, J., Bjorkqvist, S., Koskela, K., Neitaanmaki, L., Takalo, T., Kottke, T., Maki, J., Sipila, P., & Varvikko, P. (1981). *The North Karelia Project: Evaluation of a comprehensive community programme for control of cardiovascular diseases in 1972-1977 in North Karelia, Finland* (Public Health in Europe, WHO/EURO Monograph Series). Copenhagen: World Health Organization.

Putnam, L. (1982). Procedural messages and small group work climates: A lag sequential analysis. In M. Burgoon (Ed.), *Communication yearbook 5*. New Brunswick, NJ: Transaction.

Rakow, L. (1989). Information and power: Toward a critical theory of information campaigns. In C. Salmon (Ed.), *Information campaigns: Managing the process of social change*. Newbury Park, CA: Sage.

Ramirez, A., & McAlister, A. (in press). Mass media campaign: A Su Salud. *Preventive Medicine*.

Ray, M. (1973). Marketing communication and the hierarchy of effects. In P. Clarke (Ed.), *New models for mass communication research* (pp. 147-176). Beverly Hills, CA: Sage.

Reardon, K. K. (1981). *Persuasion: Theory and context.* Beverly Hills, CA: Sage.

Reardon, K. K. (1987). *Interpersonal communication: Where minds meet.* Belmont, CA: Wadsworth.

Reardon, K. K. (1989). A sequel to the "false dichotomy perspective": Applications to the challenge of teaching children about AIDS. In B. Ruben & L. Lievrouw (Eds.), *Information and behavior* (Vol. 3). New Brunswick, NJ: Transaction.

Reardon, K., & Rogers, E. (1989). Interpersonal versus mass communication: A false dichotomy. *Human Communication Research, 15,* 284-307.

Reardon, K. K., Sussman, S., & Flay, B. (1988, May). *Can adolescents "Just say 'no' " to smoking?* Paper presented at the annual meeting of the International Communication Association, New Orleans.

Reed, J., & Baxter, P. (1983). *Library use: A handbook for psychology.* Washington, DC: American Psychological Association.

Reese, M. (1985). From telephone to telelobby. In R. G. Meadow (Ed.), *New communication technologies in politics.* Washington, DC: Washington Program of the Annenberg Schools.

Resnik, H. (1972, October 14). Putting VD on public TV. *Saturday Review*, pp. 33-38.

Rice, R. E. (1980). The impacts of computer organizational and interpersonal communication. In M. Williams (Ed.), *Annual review of information science and technology* (Vol. 15, pp. 221-249). White Plains, NY: Knowledge Industries.

Rice, R. E. (1987). Communication technologies, human communication networks and social structure in the information society. In J. Schement & L. Lievrouw (Eds.), *Competing visions, complex realities: Social aspects of the information society* (pp. 107-120). Norwood, NJ: Ablex.

Rice, R. E., & Associates. (1984). *The new media: Communication, research and technology.* Beverly Hills, CA: Sage.

Riche, M. (1982, March). VALS: Values + attitudes + lifestyles. *American Demographics*, pp. 38-39.

Ries, A., & Trout, J. (1980). *Positioning: The battle for your mind.* New York: McGraw-Hill.

Ries, A., & Trout, J. (1986). *Marketing warfare.* New York: McGraw-Hill.

Robbin, J. (1980). Geodemographics: The new magic. *Campaigns & Elections, 1,* 25-45.

Roberts, D., & Maccoby, N. (1973). Information processing and persuasion: Counterarguing behavior. In P. Clarke (Ed.), *New models for mass communication research* (pp. 269-307). Beverly Hills, CA: Sage.

Robertson, L. (1976). The great seat belt campaign flop. *Journal of Communication, 26,* 41-46.

Robertson, L. (1983). *Injuries: Causes, control strategies, and public policy.* Lexington, MA: Lexington.

Robertson, L., Kelley, A., O'Neill, B., Wixom, C., Eisworth, R., & Haddon, W., Jr. (1974). A controlled study of the effect of television messages on safety belt use. *American Journal of Public Health, 64,* 1071-1080.

Robin, D. (1974). Success in social marketing. *Journal of Business Research, 2,* 303-310.

Robinson, J., & Meadow, R. G. (1982). *Polls apart: Divergences and convergences in foreign policy surveys.* Cabin John, MD: Seven Locks.

Rodgers, H., Jr., & Bullock, C., III. (1972). *Law and social change: Civil rights laws and their consequences.* New York: McGraw-Hill.

Rogers, E. M. (1972). *Taboo communication and social change: Family planning in Asia, and some suggested modifications in the classical diffusion model.* Paper presented to the Department of Human Communication, Rutgers University, New Brunswick, NJ.

Rogers, E. M. (1973). *Communication strategies for family planning.* New York: Free Press.

Rogers, E. M. (1983). *Diffusion of innovations* (3rd ed.). New York: Free Press.

Rogers, E. M., & Antola, L. (1985). Telenovelas in Latin America: A success story. *Journal of Communication, 35,* 24-35.

Rogers, E. M., & Kincaid, D. L. (1981). *Communication networks: Toward a new paradigm for research.* New York: Free Press.

Rogers, E. M., & Storey, D. (1987). Communication campaigns. In C. Berger & S. Chaffee (Eds.), *Handbook of communication science* (pp. 817-846). Newbury Park, CA: Sage.

Rogers, R. W. (1975). A protection motivation theory of fear appeals and attitude change. *Journal of Psychology, 91,* 93-114.

Rohde, J., & Northrup, R. (1986). Diarrhea is a nutritional disease. In *Second International Conference on Oral Rehydration Therapy* (pp. 30-41). Washington, DC: USAID.

Rokeach, M. (1973). *The nature of human values.* New York: Free Press.

Rokeach, M. (1979). Value theory and communication research: Review and commentary. In D. Nimmo (Ed.), *Communication yearbook 3* (pp. 1-28). New Brunswick, NJ: Transaction.

Rokeach, M. (1987). *Health values.* Presentation to the Institute for Health Promotion and Disease Prevention, Pasadena, CA.

Rosenberg, M. (1965). When dissonance fails: On eliminating evaluation apprehension from attitude measurement. *Journal of Personality and Social Psychology, 1,* 28-42.

Rosenthal, R. (1984). *Meta-analytic procedures for social research.* Beverly Hills, CA: Sage.

Rosenthal, T., & Bandura, A. (1978). Psychological modeling: Theory and practice. In S. Garfield & A. Bergin (Eds.), *Handbook of psychotherapy and behavior change: An empirical analysis* (2nd ed., pp. 621-658). New York: John Wiley.

Rosenthal, T., & Zimmerman, B. (1978). *Social learning and cognition.* New York: Academic Press.

Rossouw, J., Jooste, P., Kotze, J., & Jordaan, P. (1981). The control of hypertension in two communities: An interim evaluation. *South African Medical Journal, 60,* 208.

Rotheram, M. (1980). Social skills training programs in elementary and high school classrooms. In D. Rathjen & J. Foreyt (Eds.), *Social competence: Intervention for children and adults* (pp. 69-112). New York: Pergamon.

Rotheram-Borus, M., & Bradley, J. (1987, September). *Prevention of HIV infection among adolescents.* Paper prepared for Women and Aids Conference, National Institute of Mental Health, Washington, DC.

Rotheram-Borus, M., Koopman, C., & Bradley J. (1988). Barriers to successful AIDS prevention programs with runaway youth. In J. Garrison & A. Eichler (Eds.), *AIDS prevention with emotionally disturbed youth.* Washington, DC: Janis.

Rothman, D. J., & Rothman, S. M. (Eds.). (1975). *Sources of the American social tradition* (Vol. 1). New York: Basic Books.

Rothman, J. (1968). Three models of community organization practice, their mixing and phasing. In F. Cox, J. Erlich, J. Rothman, & J. Tropman (Eds.), *Strategies of community organization* (pp. 22-36). Itasca, IL: Peacock.

Ruble, D., Boggiano, A., Feldman, N., & Loebl, J. (1980). Developmental analysis of the role of social comparison in self-evaluation. *Developmental Psychology, 16*, 105-115.

Ruble, D., Feldman, N., & Boggiano, A. (1976). Social comparison between young children in achievement situations. *Developmental Psychology, 12*, 191-197.

Ryan, W. (1976). *Blaming the victim* (rev. ed.). New York: Vintage.

Sabato, L. (1981). *The rise of political consultants.* New York: Basic Books.

Safire, W. (1975). *Before the fall.* Garden City, NY: Doubleday.

Sallis, J., Hill, R., Fortmann, S., & Flora, J. (1986). Health behavior change at the worksite: Cardiovascular risk reduction. *Progress in Behavior Modification, 20*, 161-167.

Salomon, G. (1979). *Interaction of media, cognition and learning.* San Francisco: Jossey-Bass.

Sandman, P. (1987). Getting to maybe: Some communication aspects of hazardous waste facility siting. In R. Lake (Ed.), *Resolving locational conflict.* New Brunswick, NJ: Rutgers University, Center for Urban Policy Research.

Sandman, P., Weinstein, N., & Klotz, M. (1987, Summer). Public response to the risk from geological radon. *Journal of Communication*, pp. 93-108.

Sawyer, A. (1981). Repetition, cognitive response, and persuasion. In R. Petty, T. Ostrom, & T. Brock (Eds.), *Cognitive responses in persuasion.* Hillsdale, NJ: Erlbaum.

Schellstede, W., & Ciszewski, R. (1984). Social marketing of contraceptives in Bangladesh. *Studies in Family Planning, 15*(1), 30-39.

Schiller, H. (1973). *The mind managers.* Boston: Beacon.

Schneider, A. (1982). Studying policy implementation: A conceptual framework. *Evaluation Review, 6*(6), 715-730.

Schramm, W. (1977). *Big media, little media.* Beverly Hills, CA: Sage.

Schultz, T. (1964). *Transforming traditional agriculture.* New Haven, CT: Yale University Press.

Schunk, D. (1983). Developing children's self-efficacy and skills: The roles of social comparative information and goal setting. *Contemporary Educational Psychology, 8*, 76-86.

Schunk, D., 91984). Enhancing self-efficacy and achievement through rewards and goals: Motivational and information effects. *Journal of Educational Research, 78*, 29-34.

Schunk, D. (1985). Self-efficacy and classroom learning. *Psychology in the Schools, 22*, 208-222.

Schunk, D., & Carbonari, J. (1984). Self-efficacy models. In J. Matarazzo, S. Weiss, J. Herd, & N. Miller (Eds.), *Behavioral health: A handbook of health enhancement and disease prevention.* New York: John Wiley.

Schwartz, S., & Inbar-Saban, N. (1987). *Value self-confrontation as a method to aid in weight loss.* Unpublished manuscript, Hebrew University of Jerusalem.

Sherif, M., & Hovland, C. (1961). *Social judgment: Assimilation and contrast effects in communication and attitude change.* New Haven, CT: Yale University Press.

Shiffman, S. (1982). Relapse following smoking cessation: A situational analysis. *Journal of Consulting and Clinical Psychology, 50*, 71-86.

Shiffman, S. (1984). Cognitive antecedents and sequelae of smoking relapse crises. *Journal of Applied Social Psychology, 14*(3), 296-309.

Shiffman, S., & Jarvik, M. (1987). Situational determinants of coping in smoking relapse crises. *Journal of Applied Social Psychology, 17*(1), 3-15.

Shilts, R. (1987). *And the band played on.* New York: St. Martin's.

Shrauger, J., & Rosenberg, J. (1970). Self-esteem and the effects of success and failure feedback on performance. *Journal of Personality, 38*, 404-417.

Simmons Market Research Bureau, Inc. (1985). *Simmons 1985 study of media and markets.* New York: Author.

Singhal, A., Doshi, J., Rogers, E. M., & Rahman, A. (1988, May). *The diffusion of television in India.* Paper presented at the annual meeting of the International Communication Association, New Orleans.

Singhal, A., & Rogers, E. M. (1988a). *India's information revolution.* New Delhi: Sage.

Singhal, A., & Rogers, E. M. (1988b). Television soap operas for development in India. *Gazette, 41*, 109-126.

Sinha, T. (1973). The Ghana case: Introduction. In M. McMillan (Ed.), *Using commercial resources in family planning communication programs: The international experience.* Honolulu: University Press of Hawaii.

Slack, J. (1984). Surveying the impacts of communication technologies. In B. Dervin & M. Voigt (Eds.), *Progress in communication sciences* (Vol. 5). Norwood, NJ: Ablex.

Sleet, D. (1987). Motor vehicle trauma and safety belt use in the context of public health priorities. *Journal of Trauma, 27*, 695-702.

Sloan, P. (1987, June 8). Too much? Media swamped with anti-drug ads. *Advertising Age.*

Smith, M. (1982). *Persuasion and human action.* Belmont, CA: Wadsworth.

Snyder, C., Shenkel, R., & Lowery, C. (1977). Acceptance of personality interpretations: The "Barnum effect" and beyond. *Journal of Consulting and Clinical Psychology, 44*, 564-572.

Snyder, L. (1987). *Learning and acting in a health communication campaign: Teaching rural women to prevent infant dehydration through diarrheal disease control in The Gambia, West Africa.* Unpublished doctoral dissertation, Stanford University.

Solomon, D. S. (1984). Social marketing and community health promotion: The Stanford heart disease prevention program. In L. Frederiksen, L. Solomon, & K. Brehony (Eds.), *Marketing health behavior* (pp. 115-135). New York: Plenum.

Sorenson, G., & Pechacek, T. (1987) Attitudes toward smoking cessation among men and women. *Journal of Behavioral Medicine, 10*(2), 129-136.

Sperber, A. (1986). *Murrow: His life and times.* New York: Freundlich.

Staats, A. (1975). *Social behaviorism.* Homewood, IL: Dorsey.

Star, S., & Hughes, H. (1950). Report on an education campaign: The Cincinnati plan for the United Nations. *American Journal of Sociology, 55*, 389-400.

Staub, E. (1978). *Positive social behavior and morality* (Vol. 1). New York: Academic Press.

Staub, E. (1979). *Positive social behavior and morality* (Vol. 2). New York: Academic Press.

Steinberg, A. (1976). *The political campaign handbook: Media, scheduling and advance.* Lexington, MA: D. C. Heath.

Stewart, J. (1964). *Repetitive advertising in newspapers.* Cambridge, MA: Harvard University Press.

Strunin, L., & Hingson, R. (1987). Acquired immunodeficiency syndrome and adolescents: Knowledge, beliefs, attitudes and behaviors. *Pediatrics, 79*, 825-828.

Suchman, E. (1967). *Evaluative research.* New York: Russell Sage Foundation.

Suls, J., & Miller, R. (Eds.). (1977). *Social comparison processes.* New York: John Wiley.

Surmanek, J. (1986). *Media planning: A practical guide.* Chicago: Crain.

Sutton, S. (1979). Interpreting relapse curves. *Journal of Consulting and Clinical Psychology, 47,* 96-98.

Sutton, S. (1982). Fear-arousing communications: A critical examination of theory and research. In J. R. Eiser (Ed.), *Social psychology and behavioral medicine.* New York: John Wiley.

Sweeney, P., & Gruber, K. (1984). Selective exposure: Voter information preferences and the Watergate affair. *Journal of Personality and Social Psychology, 46,* 1208-1221.

Syme, L., & Berkman, L. (1981). Social class, susceptibility, and sickness. In P. Conrad & R. Kern (Eds.), *Sociology of health and illness* (pp. 35-44). New York: St. Martin's.

Taplin, S. (1981). Family planning communication campaigns. In R. E. Rice & W. Paisley (Eds.), *Public communication campaigns* (pp. 127-142). Beverly Hills, CA: Sage.

Tate, E., & Surlin, S. (1976, Summer). Agreement with opinionated TV characters across cultures. *Journalism Quarterly,* pp. 199-203.

Taylor, E. (1987, August 16). TV dramas: Sweet agreement, little grit. *New York Times.*

Taylor, S., & Brown, J. (1988). Illusion and well-being: A social psychological perspective on mental health. *Psychological Bulletin, 103,* 193-210.

Tedeschi, J., Schlenker, B., & Bonoma, T. (1971). Cognitive dissonance: Private ratiocination or public spectacle? *American Psychologist, 26,* 685-695.

Televisa's Institute for Communication Research. (1981). *Toward the social use of commercial television: Mexico's experience with the reinforcement of social values through TV soap operas.* Paper presented at the meeting of the International Institute of Communication, Strasbourg, France.

Televisa's Institute for Communication Research. (1987). *Evaluation of communication for young people project* (Report to Johns Hopkins University/Population Communication Services). Mexico City: Author.

Television Information Office. (1987). *Roper report.* New York: Roper.

Tesser, A. (1978). Self-generated attitude change. In L. Berkowitz (Ed.), *Advances in experimental social psychology* (Vol. 11, pp. 289-338). New York: Academic Press.

Tesser, A., & Rosen, S. (1975). The reluctance to transmit bad news. In L. Berkowitz (Ed.), *Advances in experimental psychology* (Vol. 8, pp. 193-232). New York: Academic Press.

Tichenor, P., Donohue, G., & Olien, C. (1971). Mass media flow and differential growth in knowledge. *Public Opinion Quarterly, 34,* 159-170.

Tobe, F. (1985). New techniques in computerized voter contact. In R. G. Meadow (Ed.), *New communication technologies in politics.* Washington, DC: Washington Program of the Annenberg Schools.

Top events ran gamut—AIDS to Lady Liberty. (1986, December 29). *Advertising Age,* pp. 2, 29-30.

Towers, I., Goodman, L., & Zeisel, H. (1962). A method of measuring the effects of television through controlled field experiments. *Studies in Public Communication, 4,* 87-110.

Truett, J., Cornfield, J., & Kannel, F. (1967). Multivariate analysis of the risk of coronary heart disease in Framingham. *Journal of Chronic Disease, 20,* 511-524.

Tuchfield, B., & Marcus, S. (1984). Social models of prevention in alcoholism. In J. Matarazzo, S. Weiss, J. Herd, & N. Miller (Eds.), *Behavioral health: A handbook of health enhancement and disease prevention* (pp. 1041-1046). New York: John Wiley.

Tuchman, G. (1978). *Making news: A study in the construction of reality.* New York: Free Press.

Turow, J., & Coe, L. (1985). Curing television's ills: The portrayal of health care. *Journal of Communication, 35,* 36-51.

TV Bureau of Advertising, Inc., Research Department. (1986). *Trends in viewing.* New York: Author.

Underwood, G. (Ed.). (1978). *Strategies of information processing.* London: Academic Press.

U.S. Department of Health and Human Services. (1982). *The health consequences of smoking. Cancer: A report of the surgeon general.* Rockville, MD: Office on Smoking and Health.

U.S. Department of Health and Human Services. (1983a). *The health consequences of smoking. Cardiovascular disease: A report of the surgeon general.* Rockville, MD: Office on Smoking and Health.

U.S. Department of Health and Human Services. (1983b). *Making PSAs work: A handbook for health communication professionals.* Bethesda, MD: Government Printing Office.

U.S. Department of Health and Human Services. (1984a). *The health consequences of smoking. Chronic obstructive lung disease: A report of the surgeon general.* Rockville, MD: Office on Smoking and Health.

U.S. Department of Health and Human Services. (1984b). *Pretesting in health communications* (NIH Publication No. 84-1493). Bethesda, MD: National Cancer Institute.

U.S. Department of Health and Human Services. (1986a). *The health consequences of smoking: A report of the surgeon general.* Rockville, MD: Office on Smoking and Health.

U.S. Department of Health and Human Services. (1986b). *The 1900 health objectives for the nation: A midcourse review.* Washington DC: Office of Disease Prevention and Health Promotion.

U.S. Department of Health and Human Services. (1988). *The health consequences of smoking. Nicotine addiction: A report of the surgeon general.* Rockville, MD: Office on Smoking and Health.

U.S. Department of Health, Education and Welfare. (1979). *Healthy people: The surgeon general's report on health promotion and disease prevention.* Washington, DC: Government Printing Office.

U.S. Department of Transportation. (1985). *Drunk driving public information program strategies and planning guide* (Publication No. DOT HS 806 680). Washington, DC: Government Printing Office.

Vidmar, N., & Rokeach, M. (1974). Archie Bunker's bigotry: A study in selective perception and exposure. *Journal of Communication, 24,* 36-47.

Waitzkin, H. (1983). *The second sickness.* New York: Free Press.

Walker, N., & Argyle, M. (1964). Does the law affect moral judgments? *British Journal of Criminology, 4,* 570-581.

Wallack, L. (1981). Mass media campaigns: The odds against finding behavior change. *Health Education Quarterly, 8*(3), 209-260.

Wallack, L., Breed, W., & Cruz, J. (1987). Alcohol on prime time television. *Journal of Studies on Alcohol, 48*(1), 33-38.

Wander, P. (1977). On the meaning of "Roots." *Journal of Communication, 27,* 64-69.

Ward, S., & Reed, L. (Eds.). (1983). *Knowledge structure and use: Implications for synthesis and interpretation.* Philadelphia: Temple University Press.

Warner, K. (1977). The effects of the anti-smoking campaign on cigarette consumption. *American Journal of Public Health, 67,* 645-650.

Warner, K. (1981). Cigarette smoking in the 1970s: The impact of the anti-smoking campaigns on consumption. *Science, 211,* 729-731.

Warner, K. (1985). Cigarette advertising and media coverage of smoking and health. *New England Journal of Medicine, 312*(6), 384-388.

Warner, K. (1986). *Selling smoke: Cigarette advertising and public health.* Washington, DC: American Public Health Association.

Waters, H. (1982, December 6). Life according to TV. *Newsweek.*

Watts, W., & McGuire, W. J. (1964). Persistence of induced opinion change and retention of inducing message contents. *Journal of Abnormal and Social Psychology, 68,* 233-241.

Weaver, D., Graber, D., McCombs, M., & Eyal, C. (1981). *Media agenda-setting in a presidential election.* New York: Praeger.

Weber, M. (1930). *The Protestant ethic and the spirit of capitalism.* New York: Scribners. (Original work published 1903)

Webster, F. (1975). Social marketing: What makes it different? *Management Decision, 13*(1), 70-77.

Weiner, B. (1974). *Achievement motivation and attribution theory.* Morristown, NJ: General Learning Press.

Weiss, C. (Ed.). (1977). *Using social research in public policy making.* Lexington, MA: D. C. Heath.

Wells, W. (1975). Psychographics: A critical review. *Journal of Marketing Research, 12,* 196-213.

Werner, L. (1987, February 11). Surgeon general urges ads on TV for condoms in combating AIDS. *New York Times,* p. 1.

Westin, A. (1982). *Newswatch: How TV decides the news.* New York: Simon & Schuster.

Whelan, E., Sheridan, M., Meister, K., & Mosher, B. (1981). Analysis of coverage of tobacco hazards in women's magazines. *Journal of Public Health Policy, 2,* 28-35.

Whetmore, E. J., & Kielwasser, A. P. (1983). Soap opera audience speaks: A preliminary report. *Journal of American Culture, 6,* 110-115.

White, T. (1961). *The making of the president 1960.* New York: Athenium.

White, T. (1965). *The making of the president 1964.* New York: Athenium.

White, T. (1969). *The making of the president 1968.* New York: Athenium.

Wholey, J. (1979). *Evaluation: Promise and performance.* Washington, DC: Urban Institute.

Whyte, M., & Gu, S. (1987). Popular response to China's fertility transition. *Population and Development Review, 13*(3), 471-493.

Wicklund, R. (1974). *Freedom and reactance.* New York: John Wiley.

Wicklund, R., & Brehm, J. (1976). *Perspectives on cognitive dissonance.* Hillsdale, NJ: Erlbaum.

Wiebe, G. (1952). Merchandising commodities and citizenship on television. *Public Opinion Quarterly, 15,* 679-691.

Will, G. (1987, June 7). AIDS: The real danger. . . . *Washington Post.*

Williams, F., LaRose, R., & Frost, F. (1981). *Children, television and sex-role stereotyping.* New York: Praeger.

Williams, F., Rice, R. E., & Rogers, E. M. (1988). *Research methods and the new media.* New York: Free Press.

Williams, L. (1986, Winter). AIDS risk reduction: A community health education intervention for minority high risk group members. *Health Education Quarterly,* pp. 407-421.

Wimmer, R., & Dominick, J. (1987). *Mass media research: An introduction* (2nd ed.). Belmont, CA: Wadsworth.

Winett, R. (1986). *Information and behavior: Systems of influence.* Hillsdale, NJ: Erlbaum.

Winnard, K., Rimon, J., & Convisser, J. (1987). *The impact of television on the family planning attitudes of an urban Nigerian audience: The NTA/Enugu experience.* Paper presented at the annual meeting of the American Public Health Association.

Wirt, F. (1970). *Politics of southern equality: Law and social change in a Mississippi county.* Chicago: Aldine.

Wishnow, J. (1983). *The activist.* New York: National Broadcast Association for Community Affairs.

Woelfel, J., Cody, M., Gillham, J., & Holmes, R. (1980). Basic premises of multi-dimensional attitude change theory: An experimental analysis. *Human Communication Research, 6,* 153-167.

Woo, L. (1980). *The campaign organizer's manual.* Chapel Hill, NC: Carolina Academic Press.

World Health Organization. (1978). *Declaration of Alma-Ata: Primary health care report of the International Conference on Primary Health Care, Alma-Ata, USSR, September 6-12.* Geneva: Author.

World Health Organization, Programme for Diarrhoea Control. (1983). *Third Programme report, 1981-1982.* Geneva: Author.

Wright, C. (1986). *Mass communication: A sociological perspective.* New York: Random House.

Yankelovich, Skelly & White, Inc. (1979). *The General Mills American family report 1978-79: Family ties in an era of stress.* Minneapolis: General Mills.

Zajonc, R. (1980). Feeling and thinking: Preferences need no inferences. *American Psychologist, 35,* 151-175.

Zajonc, R. (1984). On the primacy of affect. *American Psychologist, 39,* 117-123.

Zanna, M., & Fazio, R. (1983). The attitude-behavior relation: Moving toward a third generation of research. In M. Zanna, E. Higgins, & C. Herman (Eds.), *Consistency in social behavior: The Ontario Symposium* (Vol. 2). Hillsdale, NJ: Erlbaum.

Zanna, M., Olson, J., & Herman, C. (Eds.). (1987). *Social influence: The Ontario Symposium* (Vol. 5). Hillsdale, NJ: Erlbaum.

Zelnik, M., & Kantner, J. (1979). Reasons for nonuse of contraception by sexually active women aged 15-19. *Family Planning Perspectives, 11,* 269-296.

Ziegler, S., & Howard, H. (1978). *Broadcast advertising: A comprehensive working textbook.* Columbus, OH: Grid.

Zuckerman, M. (1974). The sensation seeking motives. In B. Maher (Ed.), *Progress in experimental personality research.* New York: Academic Press.

Index

About the Authors

Ronny Adhikarya (Ph.D., Stanford University) currently works for the Agricultural Extension Service, Food and Agriculture Organization, United Nations, in Rome, Italy.

Rina Alcalay (Ph.D., Stanford University) is Assistant Professor at the School of Public Health, University of California, Los Angeles. She conducts research and designs community health campaigns primarily in the areas of smoking prevention and cessation, perinatal care, family planning, and AIDS. She has served as consultant for the National Institute of Health, the National Cancer Institute, and the Pan American Health Organization.

Charles K. Atkin (Ph.D., University of Wisconsin) is a Professor in the Departments of Communication and Telecommunication at Michigan State University, where he specializes in mass media effects. He has held visiting positions at Stanford University and the University of Southern California. His current research focuses on health campaigns, particularly prevention of alcohol misuse and risky driving. He has also written extensively about political communication, television violence, commercial advertising, and information seeking.

Sandra Ball-Rokeach is Professor at the Annenberg School of Communications and the Department of Sociology, University of Southern California.

Robert B. Cialdini is Regents Professor of Psychology at Arizona State University, where he has been on the faculty since 1971. His interests include the social influence process and strategies of self-presentation.

Thomas D. Cook (Ph.D., Stanford University) is currently Professor of Psychology, Education, and Policy Studies at Northwestern University. He has made extensive contributions to the methodological literatures in social psychology, communications research, and evaluation, including the coauthored book *Quasi-Experimentation: Design and Analysis Issues for Field Settings* (1979). He recently completed a term as a Russell Sage Foundation scholar.

Brenda Dervin (Ph.D., Michigan State University) is Professor and former Chair of the Department of Communication at Ohio State University. She is coauthor, with Bradley Greenberg, of *Uses of the Mass Media by the Urban Poor*, and is Editor of the Ablex Communication and Information Science series. She is a Fellow and Past President of the International Communication Association, and a member of the International Council of the International Association of Mass Communication Researchers.

John W. Farquhar (M.D., University of California, San Francisco), a cardiologist, joined the Stanford medical faculty in 1961. He is founder and Director of the Center for Research in Disease Prevention. He is also active in the World Health Organization of the United Nations and is a member of the Institute of Medicine of the National Academy of Sciences.

Brian R. Flay is Associate Professor and Director, Prevention Research Center, School of Public Health, University of Illinois at Chicago. Until 1987, he was Deputy Director of the Institute for Health Promotion and Disease Prevention Research at the University of Southern California. His recent book is *Selling the Smokeless Society: Fifty-six Evaluated Mass Media Programs and Campaigns Worldwide* (1987).

June A. Flora (Ph.D., Arizona State University) is currently an Assistant Professor in the Institute for Communication Research and Associate Director of the Stanford Center for Research in Disease Prevention. Since 1983, she has directed the education program of the Stanford Five City Project.

Dennis Foote (Ph.D., Stanford University) has concentrated on evaluating the impact of social programs, both in the United States and abroad. He began the work reported in this volume while a Professor at Stanford's Institute for Communication Research, and completed it as President of Applied Communication Technology (Menlo Park, CA).

Vicki Freimuth (Ph.D., Florida State University) is Associate Professor in the Department of Communication Arts and Theater at the University of Maryland, where she is Director of the Health Communication Program. Her interests include message pretesting, campaign design, and the content and effects of media health messages.

Christine Galavotti (Ph.D., University of Texas, Austin) is Senior Research Associate, University of Texas Health Science Center, Houston. Her research interests include community psychology and public health.

Kipling J. Gallion (M.A., Stanford University) conducts research in public health and media-based community interventions. He is currently a doctoral student at the University of Texas at Austin, and is a media producer at the University of Texas Health Science Center, Houston.

Walter Gantz (Ph.D., Michigan State University) is Professor and Director of Graduate Studies in the Department of Telecommunication at Indiana University.

E. Scott Geller, Ph.D., is Professor of Psychology at Virginia Polytechnic Institute and State University, in Blacksburg. His primary writings and research have focused on the application of behavioral science toward solving problems in corporate and community settings. He is a Fellow of the American Psychological Association, Editor of the *Journal of Applied Behavior Analysis* (through 1992), and an Associate Editor of *Environment and Behavior*.

Bradley Greenberg (Ph.D., University of Wisconsin) is Professor and Chairman of the Department of Telecommunications at Michigan State University. He has investigated the content and effects of televised portrayals of sex, violence, social roles, and substance use, and is currently examining patterns of audience selection and processing of television messages. He is coauthor, with Brenda Dervin, of *Uses of the Mass Media by the Urban Poor*.

Robert C. Hornik is Professor of Communications at the Annenberg School of Communications at the University of Pennsylvania. His current research focuses on development communication, and he directs two major programs of evaluation of health communication projects in Third World countries. He is author of *Development Communication* and coauthor of *Toward Reform of Program Evaluation and Television and Educational Reform: The El Salvador Experience*.

Robert LaRose (Ph.D., University of Southern California) is Associate Professor, Department of Telecommunications, Michigan State University. He participated on the *Freestyle* evaluation team.

Nathan Maccoby (Ph.D., University of Michigan) was a communication psychologist with the U.S. Army during World War II, and was the Chairman of the Department of Psychology and of the Division of Research of the School of Public Communication at Boston University. In 1972, he was named Director of the Institute for Communication Research at Stanford University, and he is currently Professor Emeritus and Associate Director of the Stanford Center for Research in Disease Prevention.

Alfred McAlister (Ph.D., Stanford University) is Associate Director and Associate Professor, Center for Health Promotion Research and Development, University of Texas Health Science Center, Houston. He was formerly at the Harvard School of Public Health. He is particularly interested in media and community applications of social learning theory.

William J. McGuire (Ph.D., Yale University) is Chairman of the Department of Psychology at Yale University. He served in the army, and studied on a Fulbright in Belgium. He is widely known for his publications, largely in the area of persuasion, and has served on many editorial boards and received many awards, including a Guggenheim at the London School of Economics.

Robert G. Meadow (Ph.D., University of Pennsylvania) is President of Decision Research, a California-based political consulting and survey research company. He is also Adjunct Professor at the University of Southern California, and was the founding Director of the University of Kentucky Survey Research Center. Books he has authored or edited include *Politics as Communication*; *The Presidential Debates: Media, Policy and Electoral Perspectives*; *Polls Apart*; and *New Technologies in Political Campaigns*.

Hendrika W.J. Meischke is a doctoral student in the Department of Communication at Michigan State University. A native of the Netherlands, she received an M.P.H. degree from the University of Michigan. She is currently studying family planning campaigns and effects of media sexual portrayals.

Garrett J. O'Keefe (Ph.D., University of Wisconsin) is Professor of Agricultural Journalism at the University of Wisconsin—Madison. He has written extensively on the uses and effects of public information campaigns, as well as on political communication and socialization.

William Paisley (Ph.D., Stanford University) taught in the Stanford Communication Department from 1965 to 1985. His research interests include public knowledge, human information processing, information systems and programs, and communication technology. He is currently Executive Vice President of Knowledge Access Inc., an electronic publishing company.

Amelie G. Ramirez (M.P.H., University of Texas, Houston) is Faculty Associate and Director of Media Development and Production, University of Texas Health Science Center, Houston. Her research interests include Hispanic health promotion research, using both media and community interventions.

Kathleen K. Reardon (Ph.D., University of Massachusetts) is Associate Professor of Business Communication at the University of Southern California and author of *Persuasion: Theory and Context*; *Gift-Giving Around the World*; and *Interpersonal Communication: Where Minds Meet*. Her current research focuses on persuasion and its application to health, particularly cancer and AIDS.

Kathaleen Reid (Ph.D., University of Denver) is Assistant Professor of Language Arts at Lee College. She has worked extensively on the uses and effects of information campaigns, particularly involving crime and the elderly, and on rhetorical analysis and criticism.

Ronald E. Rice (Ph.D., Stanford University) is Associate Professor, Rutgers University School of Communication, Information and Library Studies. His research interests include the social impacts of telecommunications, implementation of information systems, diffusion of innovations, network analysis, and public communication campaigns. He is coauthor or coeditor of *Public Communication Campaigns*; *The New Media: Communication, Technology, and Research*; *Managing Organizational Innovation*; and *Research Methods and New Media*.

Everett M. Rogers (Ph.D., Iowa State University) is Professor of Communications at the Annenberg School of Communications at the University of Southern California. His research interests include the diffusion of innovations, development communication, and social impacts of new media technologies. His many books include *Diffusion of Innovations, Communication Networks, Communication Technology*, and *Research Methods and New Media*.

Milton Rokeach was Professor at the Annenberg School of Communications and the Department of Psychology, University of Southern California, at the time of his death in late 1988.

Arvind Singhal (Ph.D., University of Southern California) conducts research on development communication, international communication, and social impacts of new media technologies. He is coauthor of *India's Information Revolution*.

Douglas S. Solomon (Ph.D., Stanford University) is Manager of Market Intelligence at Apple Computer, responsible for market research and competitive analysis. His publications focus on the application of marketing concepts to public sector programs, especially health communication. He is a husband and father of three, and lives in Palo Alto, California.

Shahnaz Taplin (M.A., Stanford University) has been working in the field of communication for over 15 years, from creating pilot educational television programs in India to working with a large advertising firm in San Francisco. For 10 years, she was Director of Public Information and Public Affairs at Planned Parenthood Alameda/San Francisco. She is currently an independent communication consultant.

Lawrence Wallack, Doctor of Public Health, is Associate Professor in the School of Public Health, University of California, Berkeley; Senior Research Fellow, Prevention Research Center, Berkeley; and an Adjunct Investigator, Kaiser Foundation Research Institute, Oakland, CA. He has published extensively on the prevention of public health problems, emphasizing mass media's role and alcohol-related issues.